THE NONPROFIT SECTOR IN
INTERNATIONAL PERSPECTIVE

YALE STUDIES ON NONPROFIT ORGANIZATIONS

Program on Non-Profit Organizations
Institution for Social and Policy Studies
Yale University

JOHN G. SIMON, CHAIRMAN
PAUL DIMAGGIO, DIRECTOR

The Nonprofit Sector in International Perspective

Studies in Comparative Culture and Policy

Edited by
ESTELLE JAMES

New York · Oxford
OXFORD UNIVERSITY PRESS
1989

Oxford University Press

Oxford   New York   Toronto
Delhi   Bombay   Calcutta   Madras   Karachi
Petaling Jaya   Singapore   Hong Kong   Tokyo
Nairobi   Dar es Salaam   Cape Town
Melbourne   Auckland

and associated companies in
Berlin   Ibadan

Published by Oxford University Press, Inc.,
200 Madison Avenue, New York, New York 10016

Oxford is a registered trademark of Oxford University Press

Library of Congress Cataloging-in-Publication Data

The Nonprofit sector in international perspective : studies in
comparative culture and policy / [edited by] Estelle James.
   p. cm.—(Yale studies on nonprofit organizations)
   Bibliography: p.
   Includes index.
   ISBN 0-19-505629-9
   1. Corporations, Nonprofit.   I. James, Estelle.   II. Series.
HD2769.15.N66   1989
338.7′4—dc19   88-1120   CIP

Printing (last digit): 9 8 7 6 5 4 3 2 1

Printed in the United States of America
on acid-free paper

Series Foreword

This volume and its siblings, composing the Yale Studies on Non-profit Organizations, were produced by an interdisciplinary research enterprise, the Program on Non-Profit Organizations, located within Yale University's Institution for Social and Policy Studies.[1] The Program had its origins in a series of discussions initiated by the present author in the mid-1970s while serving as president of Yale. These discussions began with a number of Yale colleagues, especially Professor Charles E. Lindblom, Director of the Institution, and Professor John G. Simon of the Law School faculty. We later enlisted a number of other helpful counselors in and out of academic life.

These conversations reflected widespread agreement that there was a serious and somewhat surprising gap in American scholarship. The United States relies more heavily than any other country on the voluntary nonprofit sector to conduct the nation's social, cultural, and economic business—to bring us into the world, to educate and entertain us, even to bury us. Indeed, the United States can be distinguished from all other societies by virtue of the work load it assigns to its "third sector," as compared to business firms or government agencies. Yet this nonprofit universe had been the least well studied, the least well understood aspect of our national life. And the nonprofit institutions themselves were lacking any connective theory of their governance and function. As just one result, public and private bodies were forced to make policy and management decisions, large and small, affecting the nonprofit sector from a position of relative ignorance.

To redress this startling imbalance, and with the initial assistance of the late John D. Rockefeller III (soon joined by a few foundation donors), the Program on Non-Profit Organizations was launched in 1977. It seeks to achieve three principal goals:

1. to build a substantial body of information, analysis, and theory relating to nonprofit organizations;

---

[1] The sharp-eyed editors at Oxford University Press requested that we explain the presence of an intrusive hyphen in the word "Non-Profit" in the Program's title, and suggested that the explanation might be of interest to this volume's readers. The explanation is simple: At the Program's inception, it adopted the convention, in wider currency than it is today but even at that time incorrect, of hyphenating *non-profit*. Since then the Program has mended its ways wherever the term *nonprofit* is not used as part of the Program's title. But in the Program's title, for reasons both sentimental and pragmatic, the hyphen remains, as a kind of trademark.

2. to enlist the energies and enthusiasms of the scholarly community in research
   and teaching related to the world of nonprofit organizations; and
3. to assist decision makers, in and out of the voluntary sector, to address major
   policy and management dilemmas confronting the sector.

Toward the first and second of these goals the Program has employed a range of strategies: research grants to senior and junior scholars at Yale and at forty-one other institutions; provision of space and amenities to visiting scholars pursuing their research in the Program's offices; supervision of graduate and professional students working on topics germane to the Program's mission; and a summer graduate fellowship program for students from universities around the country.

The Program's participants represent a wide spectrum of academic disciplines—the social sciences, the humanities, law, medicine, and management. Moreover, they have used a variety of research strategies, ranging from theoretical economic modeling to field studies in African villages. These efforts, supported by fifty foundation, corporate, government, and individual donors to the Program, have gradually generated a mountain of research on virtually every nonprofit species—for example, day-care centers and private foundations, symphony orchestras and wildlife advocacy groups—and on voluntary institutions in twenty other countries. At this writing the Program has published 100 working papers and has sponsored, in whole or in part, research resulting in no fewer than 175 journal articles and book chapters. Thirty-two books have been either published or accepted for publication. Moreover, as the work has progressed and as Program-affiliated scholars (of whom, by now, there have been approximately 150) establish links to one another and to students of the nonprofit sector not associated with the Program, previously isolated researchers are forging themselves into an impressive and lively international network.

The Program has approached the third goal, that of assisting those who confront policy and management dilemmas, in many ways. Researchers have tried to design their projects in a way that would bring these dilemmas to the fore. Program participants have met with literally hundreds of nonprofit organizations, either individually or at conferences, to present and discuss the implications of research being conducted by the Program. Data and analyses have been presented to federal, state, and local legislative and executive branch officials and to journalists from print and electronic media throughout the United States to assist them in their efforts to learn more about the third sector and the problems it faces.

Crucial to the accomplishment of all three goals is the wide sharing of the program's intellectual output not only with academicians but also with nonprofit practitioners and policymakers. This dissemination task has been an increasing preoccupation of the Program in recent years. More vigorous promotion of its working paper series, cooperation with a variety of non-academic organizations, the forthcoming publication of a handbook of re-search on nonprofit organizations, and the establishment of a newsletter (published with increasing regularity for a broad and predominantly non-academic list of subscribers) have all helped to disseminate the Program's research results.

These efforts, however, needed supplementation. Thus, the program's working papers, although circulated relatively widely, have been for the most part drafts rather than finished papers, produced in a humble format that renders them unsuitable for the relative immortality of library shelves. Moreover, many of the publications resulting from the Program's work have never found their way into working paper form. Indeed, the multi-disciplinary products of Program-sponsored research have displayed a dis-concerting tendency upon publication to fly off to separate disciplinary corners of the scholarly globe, unlikely to be reassembled by any but the most dogged, diligent denizens of the most comprehensive of university libraries.

Sensitive to these problems, the Lilly Endowment made a generous grant to the Program to enable it to overcome this tendency toward centrifugal-ity. The Yale Studies on Nonprofit Organizations represent a particularly important part of this endeavor. Each book features the work of scholars from several disciplines. Each contains a variety of papers, many unpub-lished, others available only in small-circulation specialized periodicals, on a theme of general interest to readers in many regions of the nonprofit universe. Most of these papers are products of program-sponsored re-search, although each volume contains a few other contributions selected in the interest of thematic consistency and breadth.

Thus, the present volume, edited by Estelle James, professor of econom-ics at the State University of New York at Stony Brook, deals with non-profit sectors outside the United States, in both the industrialized and the less developed countries. The papers assembled here reflect growing inter-national interest among scholars and policy makers in the potential con-tribution of nonprofit organizations to the solution of thorny social and economic dilemmas. Together, they examine and explain the varying con-tours and roles of nonprofit sectors throughout the modern world.

As the reader will already have observed, I do not write this foreword as a stranger. I am very much a member of the family, someone who was present at the creation of the Program of Non-Profit Organizations and continues to chair its Advisory Committee, and who also serves Oxford as Master of University College. What this extended family is doing to ad-vance knowledge about the third sector is a source of considerable satis-faction. From its birth at a luncheon chat more than a decade ago, the Program on Non-Profit Organizations has occupied an increasingly impor-tant role as the leading academic center for research on voluntary institu-tions both in America and abroad. And now the publication by Oxford University Press of this volume and the other Yale Studies on Non-profit

Organizations enlarges the reach of the Yale Program by making its research more widely available within the scholarly community and to the larger world beyond.

London   Kingman Brewster

Preface

This book draws together papers written by scholars of many different nationalities and disciplines, depicting the operations of the nonprofit sector in a variety of industries and countries. Despite this diversity, I believe that a general pattern of nonprofit behavior does indeed emerge, as described in the Introduction to the book.

Research on nonprofit organizations in the United States has proliferated over the past decade, as documented by the other volumes in this series emanating from the Program on Non-Profit Organizations at Yale University. It is less well known but nonetheless true that this has been a burgeoning area of research in other countries as well. Upon further thought, this confluence of interests is not surprising since it reflects a common set of forces that we all face: increasing social wants, scarce public resources, and a perception that government bureaucracies do not always provide the best solutions to pressing societal problems. In this context, nonprofit organizations are seen, both by researchers and policymakers, as an alternative institutional form that may work in situations where government and for-profit firms have failed.

Researchers and policymakers then, have similar motivations to explore the operations of the nonprofit sector. However, with most publications focusing on the American scene, they have had no single source to which to turn in order to find out about the nonprofit sector in other countries. Such international comparisons are invaluable as a source of ideas about alternative options and as a laboratory for investigating how well real world experiments have worked. But in fact, researchers in diverse countries often carry out their studies in isolation, not knowing of related work being done a few hundred miles away. The present volume is intended to break down this isolation and thereby facilitate the sharing of ideas.

All of us who have studied the nonprofit sector over the last few years owe a great debt to Yale's Program on Non-Profit Organizations (PONPO), directed first by John Simon and then by Paul Dimaggio. By providing seed money and a "home" for scholarly interaction, PONPO has stimulated work in this area both at Yale and at many other universities. I particularly appreciate the encouragement, advice, and support PONPO ha given my work on the economics of nonprofit organizations and private education. I also wish to thank the Lilly Endowment Incorporated for its financial support of this volume and the series in which it is included.

I began assembling this volume while I was a fellow at the Netherlands

Institute of Advanced Study, for whose support I am grateful, and I completed it while a guest scholar at the Brookings Institution. I appreciate the typing and editorial assistance provided by Linda Josephs and Susanne Lane, at the final stage. My hope is that this volume will prove interesting enough to stimulate further work on the nonprofit sector from a comparative international perspective. Much remains to be discovered and analyzed.

Washington, D.C.   E.J.
May 1988

Contents

Contributors

Helmut K. Anheier is Assistant Professor of Sociology at Rutgers University. He holds a Ph.D. from Yale, where he was also associated with the Yale Program on Non-Profit Organizations. His research interests focus on the nonprofit sector in European and African countries. He is currently coediting a volume on nonprofit organizations in comparative perspective and writing a book on nongovernment organizations in Africa.

Christoph Badelt is Associate Professor, University of Economics, Vienna, Austria, and was previously Visiting Associate Professor, University of Wisconsin, Madison. He has worked broadly in the areas of social policy, public finance, and the economics of nonprofit organizations. His major publications include *The Economics of Volunteer Labor and Market Incentives in the Public Sector.*

Hugo Fruhling is a Professor at the Programa de Derechos Humanos of the Academia de Humanismo Cristiano and researcher at the Inter-American Institute of Human Rights. He has edited *Represion Politica y Defensa de los Derechos Humanes* and is the author of numerous articles about human rights in Chile.

John Hills is Codirector of the Welfare State Programs at the London School of Economics, where his current research is concerned with housing finance. He has previously undertaken research at the Institute for Fiscal Studies, London, on the U.K. taxation system and has worked as an economic adviser on housing and taxation issues to the governments of Botswana, the United Kingdom, and Zimbabwe. One of his major publications was *Savings and Fiscal Privilege,* and he has published numerous papers on housing finance.

Ellen Jane Hollingsworth is Research Scientist, University of Wisconsin, Madison. She has written many articles and books about social policy and her recent work focuses on health policy.

Rogers Hollingsworth is Professor of History and Sociology and Chairperson of the Program in Comparative History at the University of Wisconsin, Madison. He has written numerous articles and books in the area of social policy.

Estelle James is Professor of Economics at the State University of New York, Stony Brook. She was previously Chairperson of the Economics Department and Provost of Social and Behavioral Sciences at Stony Brook. She has coauthored three books: *Hoffa and the Teamsters: A Study in Union Power; The Nonprofit Enterprise in Market Economies;* and *Public Policy and Private Education in Japan.* She has also written numerous articles on the economics of education, the economics of nonprofit organizations, and other topics in applied welfare theory.

Ken Judge is currently Director of the King's Fund Institute for Health Policy Analysis. Previously he was lecturer at Bristol University and Deputy Director of the Personal Social Services Research Unit at the University of Kent. His publications include *Rationing Social Services* and *Charging for Social Care.* He is Chairperson of the Camden and Islington Family Practitioner Committee.

Martin Knapp is a Reader in the Economics of Social Policy and Deputy Director of the Personal Social Services Research Unit, University of Kent at Canterbury. He has written books on *The Economics of Social Care; Care in the Community;* and *Old People's Homes and the Production of Welfare.* He is currently coediting *Pluralism in Practice: Yearbook of Voluntary Action Research 1989* and writing a book on the role of the government sector in supporting nonprofit services in Britain.

Ralph Kramer is a Professor in the School of Social Welfare at the University of California, Berkeley. He is the author of numerous articles on citizen participation, social planning and the voluntary sector. His books include *Voluntary Agencies in the Welfare State; Participation of the Poor;* and *Community Development in Israel and the Netherlands.*

Daniel C. Levy holds a joint appointment in Educational Administration and Policy Studies and Latin American studies at the State University of New York, Albany. He is the author of *Higher Education and the State in Latin America: Private Challenges to Public Dominance,* as well as two books on Mexico (one coauthored). He has long been affiliated with PONPO and edited a book *(Private Education)* in Oxford's nonprofit series. Most of his scholarly articles also deal with politics and education.

J. Mark Davidson Schuster is Associate Professor of Urban Studies and Planning at the Massachusetts Institute of Technology. He was a postdoctoral fellow in the Research Division of the French Ministry of Culture. His research interests focus on government policy vis-à-vis culture and environmental design. His publications include *Patrons Despite Themselves: Taxpayers and Arts Policy* and *Supporting the Arts: An International Comparative Study.*

Wolfgang Seibel is Assistant Professor of Administrative Science at the Department of Economics at the University of Kassel, Federal Republic of Germany. He received his Master's Degree in Administrative Science at the Hochschule fur Verwaltungswissenschafter Speyer, FRG, and his Doctor's Degree in Economics and Social Science at the University of Kassel. He is author of three books and numerous articles on organizational problems in the nonprofit sector and technology policy in public administration. His current research includes an analysis of the third sector in comparative perspective (France and Germany) and a history of German public administration during the Nazi period.

Brian H. Smith holds the Charles and Joan Van Zoeren Chair in Religion, Ethics and Values at Ripon College, Ripon, Wisconsin. He formerly taught Political Science at the Massachusetts Institute of Technology. His research interests include religion and political development in the Third World and the role of nonprofit institutions in North–South relations. His books include *The Church and Politics in Chile* and *The Politics of International Charities*.

Jillian Smith is Head of Information Technology at Save the Children Fund. Previously, she was Research Associate at the Personal Social Services Unit, University of Kent at Canterbury, and Research Officer at the London School of Economics.

THE NONPROFIT SECTOR IN
INTERNATIONAL PERSPECTIVE

Introduction

ESTELLE JAMES

The essays in this book are about the nonprofit sector in a diverse set of countries and industries, written by scholars from a variety of disciplinary backgrounds. Originally they were written as independent pieces, not as part of an integrated volume. What can we learn from this diversity? Do we find a random assortment of observations or does a meaningful pattern emerge? And if it does, what light does this throw on the theory of non-profit organizations (NPOs) and on public policies that exist, or should exist, toward the nonprofit sector?

I believe that these essays do indeed provide us with a coherent picture of the nonprofit sector and with insights into the causes and consequences of institutional choice. Much nonprofit theory and discussions of related public policies have been developed by American scholars with the American situation in mind, as set forth in earlier volumes of this series. These theories are then presented as a generic model of nonprofit origins and behavior. But the American situation may be very special, rather than generic, in certain respects.

Nonprofit organizations (i.e., organizations that are constrained from distributing a monetary profit to their members) do indeed exist in most societies, although they are called by many different names—nongovernmental organizations, private voluntary organizations, community associations, and so on.[1] However, their characteristics in other countries may be quite different from those in the United States. By drawing on the experience of a large set of countries we can avoid the trap of formulating a "general theory" that only fits a particular case. At the same time, the elements of a truly general theory begins to emerge, inductively.

INTERNATIONAL RESEARCH, NONPROFIT THEORY, AND PUBLIC POLICY ISSUES

Imperfect Information and Trustworthiness

For example, an important line of economic theories about NPOs views for-profit enterprises as the major institutional competitor to nonprofits and attempts to draw the boundary line between the two.[2] These theories stress that NPOs will be found in situations where consumers do not have enough information to evaluate the quality of a product and therefore must place their trust in the enterprise that is producing it. Consumers may be more willing to trust nonprofit organizations, where, because of the non-distribution constraint, managers do not have the same monetary incentive to downgrade quality that profit-making managers would have. For similar reasons, potential donors (of money or volunteer labor) are more willing to donate to nonprofit organizations, which are deemed more likely to use donations for the intended purpose. Therefore, such organizations develop where trustworthiness is important because of asymmetrical information between consumers and producers or because of monitoring problems faced by donors. Examples are frequently given from the fields of education, health, and culture.

Some Unanswered Questions

Although this kind of theory may help explain the American situation, where private funding from fees and philanthropy are a major source of nonprofit revenues and therefore for-profit organizations would seem to be the major institutional competitor, they do not address some of the major questions that arise when we look at other countries. Four such questions are particularly important.

First, we observe that NPOs in many countries are in competition with services provided by government, particularly local government, not with for-profit firms. Therefore, we need to draw the boundary line between the private nonprofit and public sectors even more than that between NPOs and for-profit organizations; we must explain why NPOs produce the same goods as local governments and why government production is used in some cases, nonprofit production in others.

Second, we observe that, although government is a substitute for NPOs in production, it is usually a complement in financing. Indeed, from a worldwide point of view private philanthropy is insignificant whereas government subsidies are a crucial source of funds to nonprofit organizations—and this is particularly the case in countries where the nonprofit sector is large. Therefore, we need to explain why governments contribute substantial resources to NPOs and explore some of the problems that this creates.

Third, we observe that, almost universally, the major founders of NPOs are organized religions or other ideological groups rather than individual entrepreneurs. Surely this curious empirical fact must be incorporated into a general theory of nonprofit origins.

Finally, we observe that the size of the nonprofit sector varies widely from one country to another and even from one region to another within a given country. It seems unlikely that informational asymmetry and monitoring problems vary so widely across geographical areas; some other explanation is therefore needed for the existence and distribution of NPOs.

I believe that these simple empirical observations and the questions they raise, all of which are well illustrated by the essays in this volume, can help us to develop an alternative theoretical paradigm, and suggest policy implications for this paradigm. In this alternative general theory, the growth of the nonprofit sector depends on consumer demand and government demand for its services and on the supply of nonprofit-motivated entrepreneurship. Each of these elements will be discussed in turn.

Consumer Demand: Excess and Differentiated Demand

Our analysis of consumer demand starts with the observation that many of the services provided by NPOs are quasi-public goods; that is, goods that yield both private and social benefits and therefore can be funded either by the private or public sectors. Government services, when available, typically have a competitive (price) advantage in the marketplace because they are tax-financed. The demand for private services can then be viewed as a market response to situations where the government does not produce as much service or the precise kind of service that people want; people are then willing to pay for the desired service and fees are a feasible financing method. These elements—of excess demand and differentiated demand—were first mentioned by Weisbrod[3] and have been developed further in my work on the growth of private education (see the chapters on Sweden, Holland, and Japan in this volume).[4] Therefore the private nonprofit sector would be expected to be larger in cases where government production is limited (e.g., this explains private schools in developing countries) or where tastes are differentiated, sometimes along quality lines but more commonly stemming from deep-seated cultural (religious, linguistic) heterogeneity (e.g., this explains private schools in modern countries). Chapters in this volume by James, Levy, Hollingsworth and Hollingsworth, Badelt, and Anheier all present confirming evidence about the importance of excess and differentiated demand from consumers in explaining the growth of the nonprofit sector.

Thus, NPOs can be thought of as organizations tied to interest-based communities that are an alternative institutional form to geographical-based communities for providing quasi-public services.[5] In particular, a social choice is often made between the nonprofit sector and local governments as the chief producer of education, health, and social services. Local governments provide variety and choice regarding bundles of quasi-public goods, all tied to the consumers' place of residence, but NPOs provide this choice for each good separately, without requiring movement to another geographic area. Chapters by James, Hollingsworth and Hollingsworth, Judge and Smith, Hills, and Badelt all depict this social choice between the local government and private nonprofit institutional form for delivering services.

Entrepreneurship: Religion and Ideology

My analysis of "nonprofit entrepreneurship" starts with the observation that many NPOs are founded by religious and other ideological organizations, groups that are supplying services to meet (or to create) the heterogeneous demand just discussed. These organizations use the nonprofit form because their objective is to maximize faith or adherents rather than monetary profits. They consequently choose to enter those industries (such as education or health) that foster taste formation, socialization, and group identification. (These services, by their very nature, are also quasi-public goods, allocated to individuals but of concern to the group as a whole.) Because the religious "parents" can subsidize their nonprofit "offspring" with venture capital and volunteer labor, they have a cost advantage over for-profit firms and can even compete effectively with government production. We would therefore expect NPOs to be concentrated in geographic areas with strong independent religious groups (e.g., missionaries, caste societies, dissenting churches) competing for clients, currently or in the recent past. The important role of religious competition (and to a lesser extent the role of other ideological groups such as political parties) in determining the supply of nonprofit entrepreneurs is documented in the chapters by James, Levy, Judge and Smith, Badelt, Smith, Anheier, and Fruhling.

Government Demand

Our explanation of "government demand" starts with the observation that, once nonprofit organizations have been started, funding for their activities comes heavily from the government, in the form of grants, purchase of service, or implicit tax subsidies. Although philanthropy and fee financing play a key role on the American nonprofit scene, government subsidies are the major source of revenue in most countries, especially in advanced industrial states. (Even in the United States the government contributes over one-quarter of nonprofit revenues and more if implicit tax subsidies are taken into account.[6]) Funding responsibility is often vested in the government, even when production responsibility has been delegated to NPOs. We would then expect the nonprofit sector to be larger where government subsidies are larger and granted more widely. Chapters by James, Judge and Smith, Badelt, Seibel, Knapp, Kramer, Hills, and Smith all stress the importance of government funding.

This leads immediately to the key policy questions: in what situations will the government delegate production responsibility for quasi-public goods? When does it choose nonprofit rather than for-profit organizations? And what difference does this delegation make? This is different from the usual question in the area of public finance, which investigates the types of goods government funds for political reasons or should fund for efficiency reasons. Here we ask, given the decision to fund, under what conditions are NPOs used to deliver the service?

One common argument for delegating production to private organizations is that they operate at lower cost than government agencies, may charge fees for service, and (if NPOs) benefit from donations, thereby imposing a lower burden on the public treasury than would full public production. Ironically, private organizations may be used to bypass the bureaucracy, red tape, and civil service rules that government has imposed on itself, which have the effect of raising costs and possibly reducing quality of service. However, the cost-reducing rationale, although plausible in the short run, may be more questionable in the long run, as fees and donations fall, professional staff members replace volunteer labor, and government standards are imposed as subsidies grow. For a fuller discussion of relative costs and how they may be affected by subsidies see the chapters by James, Levy, Hollingsworth and Hollingsworth, Knapp, Hills, Badelt, and Smith.

Another rationale is simply that policymakers sometimes face political pressure to provide services differentiated by religion or language, and delegation of responsibilities to the private sector is a convenient way to satisfy these pressures. Since the pressures for differentiation and delegation typically come from politically powerful religious organizations, it is not surprising that the subsidies are restricted to nonprofit organizations in these cases. (See the chapters by James, Badelt, and Kramer).

More generally, once the decision is made to use the private sector, nonprofit organizations rather than profit-making organizations are often chosen in situations where the final product is difficult to define and measure, many small enterprises are involved (e.g., schools or nursing homes), and monitoring each separately would be a costly endeavor. Requiring nonprofit status is an easier alternative, affording some assurance that the subsidy will indeed be spent on the intended purpose; the danger of political scandal due to misappropriation of funds may be less when the distribution of monetary profits is ruled out. In this sense, asymmetric information and trustworthiness may enter into the choice of nonprofit organizations after all—but as a result of government behavior rather than the behavior of many small consumers and donors.

A number of chapters in this volume suggest that private nonprofit production is combined with public funding for "political" rather than purely economic motives. Thus, the English Conservative ideology in favor of private enterprise and voluntary action leads to favorable tax treatment of donations (see the chapter by Schuster) and the Labor ideology leads to less contracting out of social services (in the chapter by Judge and Smith);[7]

the political battle between the central government (Conservative) and local governments (many of them Labor) leads to growing reliance on housing associations (as analyzed in the chapter by Hills); the Senegal government uses NPOs to bypass a powerful opposing group of marabouts (in the paper by Anheier) whereas the Austrian government fosters market sharing among NPOs with different political affiliations (in the chapter by Badelt); the nonprofit sector is used in Germany to create the illusion of doing something about new social problems that are basically insoluble (according to the chapter by Seibel); and European NPOs become conduits of development aid to avoid the appearance of foreign encroachment or to maintain communication with "opposition" groups (in the chapter by Smith). In all these cases, consumers and their preferences are relegated to the background. Instead, the government is seen to be engaged in a delicate balancing act in which it wishes to strengthen its friends and weaken its enemies, to act unofficially and maintain "deniability" and it can do so more subtly by funneling its resources through supposedly neutral organizations that turn out to be not completely neutral, upon closer examination.

Finally, NPOs serve quite another political function—as informational and advocacy groups aiding the government (see the James chapter on Sweden) or as opposition groups defending human rights against authoritarian regimes (see the Fruhling chapter on Chile). These are public goods that by definition must be provided by nongovernment "communities of interest," such as the nonprofit sector.

Accountability and Regulation

In a democratic system there may be a conflict between public funding and private management. How does the government manage to hold NPOs accountable for the funds they receive? What strings, if any, go with these funds? Do the regulations imposed seriously alter the nature of nonprofit services? Whereas consumer demand, government demand, and the supply of religious entrepreneurship are hypothesized to determine the size of the nonprofit sector across countries and industries, the nature of government regulations determines how distinctive it remains or whether, as it grows larger and more heavily subsidized, it also becomes more like the public sector. The accountability and regulatory issues are discussed at length by James, Kramer, Hills, Seibel, Smith, and Anheier.[8]

Needed: A Theory of State Action

This discussion strongly suggests that a comprehensive theory of nonprofit organizations first requires a theory of the state. The state, with its powers of compulsory taxation, can unilaterally determine the quantity and variety of goods it will supply at low price and therefore the consumer demand that will remain for a private supplement or substitute. The state also determines the subsidies it will pay the nonprofit sector, the services it will contract out and the regulations to which nonprofit enterprises are subsequently subject. In the extreme, the state can proscribe NPOs, nationalize them, or prohibit consumers from using their services.

How *does* the state make these decisions in a positive sense? And, from a normative point of view, how *should* the state make these decisions, which influence institutional choice? The economic (class) interests of the ruling group, the political power of religious organizations, and the nature of the electoral system play an important role here; but these elements have yet to be merged into a single generally accepted theory of state behavior. These chapters show, however, that, in a nontotalitarian society, for every state action there is a private reaction and these private reactions in turn alter the consequences of the initial state action (see the chapters by James, Seibel, Hills, and Anheier). Thus, while the nonprofit sector flourishes at the will of the government, its existence also limits the power of the state, in democratic societies.

SUMMARY OF THE CHAPTERS

With these general themes in mind we move to a more detailed summary of the chapters in this volume. Broadly speaking, Part I deals with the nonprofit sector as a market response; that is, with consumer demand and private supply. Part II deals with the causes and consequences of government demand; that is, issues associated with public funding and accountability. Part III deals with the special problems of economic development and human rights. It is perhaps not surprising that the market response examples are drawn from the fields of education and health, where the private rate of return to consumers is often high, whereas the government demand examples are drawn from the social services, which are explicitly aimed at those who are unable to pay. However, the reader will quickly notice a great deal of overlap among the chapters in these three parts; these themes cannot in fact be neatly separated.

Nonprofit Organizations in Sweden and Holland: Differentiated Demand

The paper by Estelle James on the nonprofit sector in Sweden, as compared to that in Holland, illustrates many of the points in the theory just presented. Differentiated consumer tastes about quasi-public services, availability of nonprofit entrepreneurship, and government subsidies all play an important role—albeit in a negative sense. Sweden is one of the most homogeneous and egalitarian countries in the world, with an established church that faces little competition from other religions, and Swedish NPOs receive few government grants or tax privileges for producing services. Therefore we would expect—and indeed we find—that Sweden has only a small nonprofit sector; geographically based communities (local governments) have won out over interest-based communities (NPOs) as the mechanism for delivering quasi-public services. In contrast, strong religious cleavages in Holland have led to a system in which the government finances but the (religious) NPOs produce most education, health, and social services.

Besides investigating the conditions that determine whether the nonprofit sector is large or small, James investigates the behavior of Swedish NPOs in those areas where they do (or did) exist: private secondary schools for girls prior to 1927 (when girls were admitted to state secondary schools); the few private schools found today; and adult education provided by nonprofit associations during the 1960s and 1970s. She finds that the private sector does indeed respond to a demand that is not satisfied by government production; that in these cases minority religions play an important entrepreneurial role, but in Sweden this is supplemented by other ideological organizations (labor unions and political parties); and that currently NPO production flourishes only in those areas—sports, culture, and adult education—where it is sanctioned by government policy and supported by subsidies.

Those NPOs without subsidies survive by keeping expenses low, primarily by choosing a low cost product mix and by using low-wage or volunteer labor; but once government subsidies are instituted wages and other costs rise rapidly. Some of these observations are supported by other studies in this volume (Levy, Hollingsworth and Hollingsworth, Knapp, and Hills), which bear on the issue of whether NPOs are more cost-effective than government agencies. To the extent that their cost advantage comes from the use of volunteers, it may not be maintained in the long run if nonprofits financed by government subsidies become the accepted way of delivering public services.

Provision of services by NPOs often leads to social segmentation along cultural or ideological lines, given their source of demand and entrepreneurship. However, it need not stratify along economic (class) lines. Indeed, in Holland and Sweden NPOs and government agencies serve much the same socioeconomic mix; contrary to the American situation, private schools and other services do not "cream" and are not "elite." The factors that systematically determine relative quality and prestige will be discussed in several other chapters in this volume (see the James chapter on Japan, Levy, Hollingsworth and Hollingsworth, and Hills).

A final word is needed about the political function of NPOs in Sweden. As "interest groups" they play an important informational and advocacy role, representing their constituencies (immigrants, the handicapped, pensioners, youth) on government boards that study issues, formulate legislation, and administer the resulting laws. And their administrative staff is subsidized for doing so. In this way they influence the provision of public services even if they do not produce much themselves. This institutionalized role of NPOs within the Swedish government is a sharp contrast to their opposition role in Chile (see the Fruhling chapter), but in both cases they are a democratizing instrument.

Private Education in Japan: Excess Demand

Whereas the chapter on Sweden and Holland focuses on the role of differentiated demand in stimulating nonprofit production, the chapter by James on Japan depicts excess demand as the driving force behind the private sector. A theoretical model is presented in which excess demand for education and other quasi-public goods exists when the quantity supplied by the public sector does not satisfy the full demand. The "leftover" consumers try to purchase the service in the private market. Supply-side (religious) variables then explain how large the private sector grows to meet this demand and why it often takes the nonprofit form.

Although excess demand in education is usually characteristic of developing rather than developed countries, James argues that it applies also to Japan, where public academic secondary schools and universities do not provide a place for everyone. She demonstrates statistically that the private educational sector is highest in prefectures (states) with the greatest excess demand and supply of nonprofit entrepreneurs; that is, in prefectures with a high per capita income, a low supply of public school places, and early Christian missionary activity in starting private schools. The quantity–quality trade-off is also important: prefectures that spend more on quality have less money to spend on quantity, hence have a smaller public and a larger private sector.

Much of this result hinges on the fact that rich and poor prefectures have similar resources to spend on public goods, because of the method of financing these goods in Japan. Although local taxes based on local income are higher in rich prefectures, they get less "shared tax," which is paid by the central government to poor prefectures as a redistributive device. The poor prefectures, which tend to be rural, have disproportionate political power, which enables them to get the resources to provide education and other quasi-public goods at little cost to themselves; and they support the conservative ruling party, the LDP, in return. As an ironic consequence, those prefectures that are the most conservative have a small private educational sector and a large public sector. Also benefiting from this system and supporting the LDP are the upper classes in rich prefectures, who do not have to pay the higher local taxes that would support a larger public system. Therefore, Japan has the essential components of a theory of collective action, in which the size and nature of the public sector reflects the interests of the ruling group, while the private sector develops to accommodate those who are left out or who want a very different kind of service.

Private Higher Education in Latin America: Causes and Comparisons

Daniel Levy outlines the growth of higher education in Latin America, where private universities now enroll one-third of the total student body. He sees three sequential waves of private university growth, most of which occurred in the period after 1930.

First came the wave of religious (Catholic) universities, created by the church when it found that it could not control the public ones, after the colonial era ended. Second came the elite private universities, which developed in those countries (e.g., Venezuela and Ecuador) where the public sector became increasingly large and nonselective. Since entering students are a major input into the educational production function, diminishing selectivity decreased the final academic output as well as the prestige of public institutions, leaving a gap for the private sector to fill.

The third wave was a response to excess demand, particularly in those countries (such as Brazil) where the public sector remained small and selective. Excess-demand–driven private sectors are the largest but also the least prestigious; they add to the human capital of the country at low cost to the public treasury but often with low quality as well.

This illustrates the point that the private sector is not always the elite sector, as we in the United States tend to think; but neither is the public–private pecking order a random one. In situations where public education remains limited, competitive, and selective, it also remains elite (as in the earlier chapter on Japan) and a private sector develops to accommodate the leftovers; while the opposite is true in situations where the public sector becomes more open and egalitarian. In most Latin American countries, except for Brazil, public education has apparently emphasized quantity over quality during the last quarter century, so the private sector has become increasingly the elite one.

Levy contrasts public and private universities with respect to fields of study and source of finance. Private universities are largely financed by fees, with only Catholic universities receiving significant state subsidies and only a few prestigious universities benefiting substantially from domestic or international donations. Consistent with this financing picture, private universities are mainly teaching institutions, with little research activity, and concentrate on subjects such as social science and business administration rather than natural science, engineering, or medicine. One possible inference is that they have a limited conception of their role, leaving public universities with a broader set of social responsibilities. An alternative explanation is that they are compelled (by their financial sources) to concentrate on subjects whose production costs will be covered by fees paid by students on a voluntary basis; this usually means low-cost, low-capital subjects with a high rate of return in the labor market. Those private universities that receive government subsidies or private donations are more likely to undertake prestigious but loss-making activities such as research and laboratory sciences; their set of outputs looks more like that of public universities.

The complex issue of socioeconomic distribution of the student body is also discussed by Levy. In this analysis it becomes clear that enrollment by the lower classes can be limited by academic or price barriers. The former are found in all selective universities, whether public or private; the latter are found mainly in private universities. Therefore, the public sector will not necessarily draw from a broader economic base than the private sector; indeed, the opposite may be the case where the public sector is small and selective, as in Brazil. In that situation, the upper classes enjoy the dual benefits of prestigious higher education, financed by the public treasury. On the other hand, the most income-biased institutions are likely to be those where academic and price barriers to admission coexist—as in the elite private universities in other Latin American countries.[9]

Public versus Private Hospitals in England and Wales

Shifting now to the health industry, J. Rogers Hollingsworth and Ellen Jane Hollingsworth trace the historical development of public and voluntary (nonprofit) hospitals in England and Wales prior to the National Health Service. Consistent with the framework set forth earlier in this Introduction, voluntary hospitals played a major role in the nineteenth and early twentieth centuries, financed largely by donations of money and time, before a consensus developed on the need for a broad-based, publicly funded hospital system. When the decision was taken after World War I, to increase public expenditures and, after World War II, to institute social insurance, this could have taken the form of grants and insured fees for service paid to private hospitals, many of which already existed, as in the United States and Holland, but instead there was a shift to public production under local government administration. The Hollingsworths do not fully analyze the reasons for this social choice, but it parallels the decision about primary and secondary education made much earlier in England. Presumably, the central government preferred direct hierarchical control of the health system and felt it could get this through local government administration, whereas its control over voluntary hospitals, particularly over such questions as location, size, and target population was deemed more indirect and tenuous. We shall return to this question when we discuss the Hills paper, since the central government in the United Kingdom now seems to be making the opposite choice in some service areas.

When public and voluntary hospitals coexisted, as in the 1930s, what were the differences between them? The Hollingsworths show that voluntary hospitals tended to be smaller; had more nurses, doctors, technical staff, and specialists per bed than public hospitals; yet operated at a very similar cost per patient week. Their greater cost effectiveness stemmed in part from their access to volunteer or low-salaried workers, characteristic of many NPOs; whether this cost advantage could have been retained in an enlarged government funded but privately managed hospital system is dubious but will never be known. (For further elaboration of cost effectiveness, see the chapter by Knapp.)

The two sectors also served a very different patient mix, the public hospitals treating more of the poor, the chronically ill, and the aged. This difference in patient mix helps explain why nurses and doctors were willing to work for lower pay in the voluntary sector (just as teachers work for lower pay in private schools that have a preferred student body) and throws further doubt on whether the lower pay would remain in an enlarged system. It also greatly complicates the task of comparing outcomes in the two sectors.

However, to the degree that inputs per bed are a measure of quality, it appears that the public sector chose to produce quantity, leaving quality to the private sector. Clearly in England voluntary hospitals were the elite ones, serving the middle and upper classes, just as private universities do in many Latin American countries but in contrast to public–private rankings in countries such as Japan and Brazil. I would suggest that these divergent choices about public sector quantity versus quality should be analyzed as indicators of the distribution of political and economic power in these societies (see the James chapter on Sweden and the Levy chapter on Latin America).

Contracting Out of Social Services in England

Part II of this volume focuses on issues arising from government funding of the nonprofit sector. The first three chapters discuss the "political" reasons for using NPOs to deliver quasi-public services (consumer preferences play only a minor role here). The following chapters discuss some of the consequences for costs, quality, and accountability.

In contrast to the Hollingsworths' paper, Ken Judge and Jillian Smith examine a situation where the British government has chosen to purchase social services from voluntary agencies rather than provide them directly. Practitioners often explain this by pointing to the traditional existence of voluntary organizations serving religious denominations, the access these organizations have to donations and volunteer labor, and the flexibility and variety provided through the nonprofit sector.

However, in their econometric analysis of differences across British localities, Judge and Smith found these variables to be relatively unimportant. Instead, Labour party control of the local authority has the most consistent (and negative) effect on "contracting out." This is consistent with the point just made that different methods of service provision benefit different groups, and therefore the policy choice depends on the interests of the group having dominant political power.

Judge and Smith also measured the "Catholic" effect as an index of religious heterogeneity and found it to be positive although statistically weak. This contrasts with results I obtained elsewhere, which demonstrate that religious heterogeneity and the presence of a large Catholic minority go far toward explaining the geographic distribution of NPOs in education in many countries.[10] The divergent results obtained here illustrate the inherent difficulty in modeling and quantifying the complex religious heterogeneity variable.

Nonprofit Organizations in Austria: Cost Saving?

The nonprofit sector in Austria is small but of growing interest to politicians. According to Christoph Badelt, much of the recent rhetoric has the hidden agenda of shifting costs from the public to the private sectors, by drawing on fees and volunteer labor. Nonprofit enterprises, it is believed, have access to a different technology (more personalized, with greater commitment) than do government agencies, perhaps because they are not subject to the bureaucratic rules that government has imposed on itself; and this technology lowers their costs and raises their quality. The chapter by Knapp provides some evidence that public and private agencies do indeed use different technologies (also see the chapters by Levy and the Hollingsworths). But it appears that the savings in costs may be short run and limited. In the long run NPOs can be relied on for the large-scale delivery of social services only if they are heavily subsidized by government; and then they are likely to be subject to the same procedures and costs as government agencies (see Knapp on England and James on Sweden and Holland).

Badelt's description of the amount and distribution of volunteer labor supports this hypothesis. He finds volunteers to be heavily concentrated in the social services, where they exceed the paid labor force, and largely "informal" (i.e., engaged in helping relations among households, outside formal organizational structures). Such arrangements, which arise spontaneously in a community, may be quite efficient, with low opportunity and transactions costs. Formal nonprofit organizations, it seems, depend mainly on wage labor (albeit sometimes on low-paid, part-time labor). And one would expect them to depend on wage labor, paid at market rates, even more if their government-sanctioned responsibilities and related subsidies increased. Informal activities, on the other hand, may be difficult to coordinate and expand unless professional leadership is provided, and this in turn will raise their costs. These empirical findings underscore the limits on cost savings than can be achieved through shifts of responsibility to the nonprofit sector.

Mellow Weakness in the German Third Sector

Wolfgang Seibel draws an illustration from the German situation to argue provocatively that nonprofit organizations are used by politicians "not to do things better but to disguise better how poorly things are done." In developing this argument Seibel presents three case studies: of the "autonomous women's houses" (homes for battered women and their children); of the semipublic system of hospital funding that has tried, unsuccessfully, to place a lid on rapidly rising costs; and of the "workshops for handicapped persons" that attempt to reintegrate such persons into the labor market. In each case he documents their multiple goals and the conflict between their ideology of autonomy, informality, and egalitarianism and their need for government funding, accountability, and continuity.

Although NPOs are sometimes criticized for their absence of formal hierarchical structures (as in government) and clearcut measurable goals (as in profit-maximizing firms), Seibel sees these very ambiguities as their raison d'être, as characteristics that allow them to serve a broader social purpose even if they are dysfunctional to the individual organization. This "organizational slack" enables NPOs to blur the issue of whether something has really been accomplished and, if not, who is to blame. It creates an illusion of problem solving, thereby helping to stabilize a political system where real solutions to serious problems often do not exist. By shifting the responsibility to NPOs, politicians escape the onus of their failure to solve problems that are basically insoluble. Therefore, the "mellow weakness" of NPOs is their special strength, allowing them to garner public funds and consequently to survive, despite their lack of professionalization and control.

Upon reflection, many of the organizations that Seibel is describing (e.g., the homes for battered women and workshops for handicapped persons) are similar to one of Badelt's categories: self-help and grassroots organizations that were set up to deal with "new" social problems. These are problems that are beyond the capability of individuals and their families to solve, but there is also no consensus that the government should provide the resources necessary to solve them. (Indeed, there may be no consensus on how they could be solved, even with resources.) This is the "excess demand" phase of nonprofit activity, when small groups or enterprises arise to fill the gap. Since social services are often aimed at low-income clients with limited capacity to pay, costs are covered by donations, volunteer or low-paid labor, and partial subsidy, in the hope that this will cause the problem to go away. These organizations display the characteristics of amateurism, altruism, solidarity, personal trust, and informality that provide the smokescreen about whether something is really going on, as described by Seibel.

In contrast are the formal organizations in Badelt's other categories, which deal with problems that are considered soluble and where a consensus exists for substantial funding by the government. These organizations have simply been delegated the task of delivering such services, often as a response to differentiated demand and lobbying by religious or political nonprofit suppliers. They are not the organizations with which Seibel is primarily concerned. They have become professionalized, bureaucratic, hierarchical, and accountable according to government prescription (see the chapters by James, Kramer, and Hills). In fact, they may resemble government agencies more than they do some of the fledgling groups in their own sector.

Thus, we find extreme diversity in organizational form within the nonprofit sector. Together with the different sources of demand and funding for nonprofit services go different organizational characteristics, which may be functional given the nature of the problems faced at different stages. At least, this would be an interesting hypothesis to explore in future research.

Comparative Efficiency and Cost Effectiveness: Child Care in England

Because the political argument for supporting nonprofit organizations often rests on the assumption that they have access to different technologies and are more cost effective than government agencies, it is important to test this empirically. But, as discussed earlier, such tests are complicated by the different clientele of each sector, so that observed cost differentials may be due to these disparities in patient inputs or student inputs rather than to organizational behavior. The task for the analyst is to disentangle these two forces, a task requiring detailed data on client characteristics that often are not available.

Martin Knapp tackles the difficult issue of assessing relative efficiency in the public, nonprofit, and for-profit sectors, with particular reference to residential child care in England and Wales. Using a rich data set, Knapp estimates the cost function for children's homes run by local authorities and the fee function for homes run by for-profit enterprises, including child characteristics as explanatory variables. Both cost and fee functions are estimated for nonprofit homes; the difference between the two, the mark up, is usually negative, covered by philanthropic donations.

Knapp indeed finds that different production technologies operate in the three sectors, as indicated by the fact that somewhat different variables explain their costs (or fees). There is little evidence of economies or diseconomies of scale in the public or for-profit sectors, except at the extremes. But in nonprofit homes average costs rise monotonically with the size of the home. Apparently, smaller homes benefit from volunteer or low-paid labor, whereas the professionalism that comes with larger homes raises their expenses and reduces their cost advantage vis-à-vis the other sectors. This is similar to the results Knapp obtained earlier for day-care services for the elderly and to the observation in other countries that production by NPOs is cheaper chiefly because of the lower wages they pay. Once the lower wages and volunteers are eliminated, the cost disparity is greatly narrowed (see the James chapter on Sweden). Unfortunately, the absence of direct output measures makes it impossible to ascertain whether the wage–cost differential also implies a quality differential.

Although some patient characteristics always enter into cost and fee functions, the characteristics that matter differ across the three sectors. Specifically, in the two private sectors factors related to "difficult cases" raise costs whereas they do not raise costs in public homes. Is this evidence of organizational slack in the public sector, or is it an indication that local authorities do not provide enough resources to handle difficult cases and simply downgrade quality instead? In the absence of direct output measures, once again we do not have the answer to that crucial question.

Overall, for-profit homes are cheaper than nonprofit ones, and nonprofit homes (many of them associated with religious denominations) are cheaper than public homes. How much of this difference is due to differing technologies, and how much is due to differing child and home characteristics? Knapp separates out these factors by estimating what nonprofit costs would be, given their own technology (cost function), if they had the average characteristics of children and homes in the public sector. Conversely, he estimates what public costs would be, given their own technology, if they had average nonprofit sector characteristics. Significantly, standardizing for child and home characteristics does not narrow the disparity between the public and private sectors; the technology used by the private sector continues to produce cheaper services. It does, however, narrow the disparity between the nonprofit and for-profit sectors, suggesting that the latter have kept costs low partially by their selection of easy clients and cases.

On the basis of the evidence, contracting out residential child care in England, as an alternative to direct public production, currently does save the taxpayer money. However, Knapp questions whether this cost effectiveness will continue in the long run as the proportion of "difficult" children rises and the supply of motivated volunteers or quasi-volunteers (i.e., low-paid staff) correspondingly declines.

Autonomy, Regulation, and Accountability in Four Welfare States

Ralph Kramer analyzes some of the consequences for voluntary nonprofit social service agencies of their increasing dependence on government funds in four countries: the United States, England, Israel, and the Netherlands. In Holland, as discussed in the chapter by James, social services are usually delivered by voluntary organizations but with most costs covered by subsidies or social insurance; direct government production is relatively small. Together with the great expansion of the government budget over the past three decades has come an expansion of service, an even greater increase in costs, and a shift from volunteer to professional labor. In contrast, in England public production is the preferred mode of social service delivery (as we saw in the Hollingsworths' chapter), with partially subsidized NPOs filling in the gaps. The situation is similar in Israel except that contributions (often from abroad) play a larger role. In the United States philanthropy is much more important and there is considerable purchase of services by government from both nonprofit and for-profit organizations.

Does reliance on government funds decrease the autonomy of voluntary social service agencies? Kramer argues that it does not, a finding that seems to conflict with other chapters in this volume (e.g., see the chapters by James and Smith). This apparent conflict is partially resolved when we realize that most of the regulations found by James apply to inputs rather than outputs (whereas Kramer is looking at outputs) and that much of the government influence found by Smith operates via its selection of organi-

zations to support rather than via direct controls over the supported organizations.

On the first point, when large subsidies are involved, government is more
likely to require the staff to have specified credentials, to receive the same
wages and working conditions as civil servants, and so on. These input-
related requirements may be imposed because inputs are more readily observed than outputs, hence they are used as a proxy for quality; or they
may prevail because workers have more powerful protectors (unions) than
consumers have.

On the second point, when government is the major source of funding,
those organizations flourish that are doing things the government wants
done. Even if government does not directly control a given organization,
it does select among different organizations and in so doing indirectly shapes
the configuration of the nonprofit sector. This selectivity would not show
up as "interference" in a sample survey, but it is influential nonetheless.
Of course, the same is true when private donors are the major source of
funds: they indirectly shape the configuration of the sector via the causes
they select. Then, the resulting shape may be different depending on who
provides the funds and selects the recipients. Perhaps the key question here,
as Kramer suggests, concerns the number of donors from which NPOs
may choose: the greater the variety, the greater the discretion left to NPOs.
In most cases I would expect to find more donor variety, therefore more
organizational autonomy, when the government is not the only or even the
dominant source of funds.

The other side of the coin from autonomy is accountability: how does
the government monitor the use of its funds? Monitoring the actions of
many small agencies is a difficult and expensive job and therefore not always done very carefully—another explanation for Kramer's finding that
subsidy does not impair institutional autonomy. At the same time, reporting requirements proliferate, imposing a heavy administrative burden on
small voluntary agencies. This detracts from the resources available to provide services—yet it is a necessary condition for some degree of majoritarian control over organizations receiving public funds. The accountability
dilemma is discussed further in the chapters by Hills and Seibel.

Housing Associations in England: Provision by NPOs versus Local Government

Most of the examples of NPOs we have discussed until now are in the
education, health, or social service industries. The paper by John Hills
deals with housing, an industry in which nonprofit organizations have begun to play an important role in recent years in countries such as Great
Britain and Germany.

In housing, as in other industries covered in this volume, NPOs have
developed as an alternative to local government production rather than to
for-profit production. Public policies first made private enterprise nonvia-

ble in the rental market, then turned the responsibility over to local governments, and finally subsidized production and management by nonprofit enterprises. In other words, politicians, rather than individual consumers, found NPOs more "trustworthy" than for-profit enterprises. (Also see the Badelt chapter on the politicians' distrust of for-profit organizations.)

More specifically, in the early twentieth century rent controls effectively choked off the private for-profit supply of rental units, which accounted for 90 percent of all housing stock in 1914, and less than 10 percent today. But the demand for rental housing was not eliminated. To meet this demand, the central government undertook the task of subsidizing and local governments undertook the task of building and managing rental housing stock—just as they took over the responsibility for hospitals and secondary schools at about the same time (see the Hollingsworth and Hollingsworth chapter).

A combination of monopoly power and limited resources led to a litany of familiar complaints against public housing: poor design, low maintenance, bureaucratic management. With the private for-profit landlord still distrusted, nonprofit housing associations were the logical alternative to local government production. They were seen as more efficient, flexible, and responsive than local government, less interested in personal monetary returns than for-profit landlords, hence a desirable avenue through which to funnel public subsidies. A sequence of market failure induced by public policy, followed by planning failure, then, has left housing associations the most rapidly growing alternative in the housing market.

Although many associations were started by religious or political groups and benefit from the time and enthusiasm of volunteer labor, their growth is closely tied to their access to public funds—as is the case for other nonprofit industries we have examined. Hills discusses in some detail the operations of the subsidy system, under which capital costs are covered by central government grants. Since the associations must turn over to the government a high proportion of their current account "profit," this greatly reduces their incentive to keep costs under control—a generic problem with cost-related subsidies, and one which proposed changes in the system are now intended to remove. As a substitute for market forces, the building associations are subject to extensive government regulations: building costs must fall within specified guidelines, fair rents must be charged, voluntary management committees must conform to government models, and financial accounts are regularly scrutinized by the Public Housing Corporation, which also has the power to make detailed recommendations and appoint people to the management committee. But day-to-day efficiency, responsiveness to tenants and criteria for allocating scarce space remain discretionary and difficult to monitor, raising the common problem of accountability when private organizations use public funds.

This case study makes it clear, however, that production by local governments also does not ensure accountability—to tenants, taxpayers, or the central government. Indeed, housing associations seem to be preferred by many tenants and by a central government that is currently at odds with many local authorities (who come from an opposing political party). In this political battle the central government has now proposed to introduce greater competition, giving public housing tenants the right to opt out of local authority management and choose management by housing associations instead. (Along similar lines, the government has proposed that parents in public schools be permitted to opt out of local authority management.) Will large numbers of housing estates opt out of local management? Will the system become more efficient? Or will it become more segmented, with the housing associations "creaming" the better council estates? Will housing associations tend to allocate scarce space on a less egalitarian basis than local authorities would? How will the public sector respond? The next few years in Great Britain should be watched carefully to see how the competition between local government and nonprofit provision of quasi-public services plays itself out.

Indirect Tax Subsidies: The British Deed of Covenant

In most countries nonprofit organizations benefit from some form of tax relief, which can be thought of as an indirect government subsidy. Because it is indirect, this kind of subsidy usually entails fewer government controls than do more direct grants. The paper by J. Mark Schuster describes the British deed of covenant, a system for granting tax deductions for charitable contributions, and contrasts it with the American system.

Under the pure deed of covenant system, in effect until 1980, individuals making charitable contributions could not deduct them from their taxable income, but the charity could reclaim this tax from the government providing certain conditions were met (e.g., the contribution had to represent a long-term, not simply a 1-year, commitment). Thus, this system made it clear that the government was foregoing revenue as a result of the special tax incentive.

This system also made it difficult for donors to earmark the use of the funds accruing from the tax rebate, thereby giving NPOs greater discretionary authority. Moreover, until 1980 the charity could only reclaim taxes at the basic rate, even if taxpayers actually paid a higher rate, unlike the American system where high-income donors get greater tax relief than low-income donors. In this sense, the deed of covenant system might be considered more equitable than ours. But it also disadvantages high-income donors and the activities they prefer (e.g., high culture and education), presumably discouraging giving by these groups.

It is probably not surprising that when the Thatcher government, with its emphasis on private enterprise and voluntarism, came to power in 1979, one of its first acts was to change the tax system, lowering rates, allowing tax deductibility for short-term contributions and giving full tax relief for high-income donors—thereby making the British system more like the American one. Thus, the deed of covenant may be doomed; nevertheless, it is worth study because it embodies certain principles that we would do well to consider in designing tax policy toward charitable contributions.

NPOs and Economic Development: Sri Lanka

Part III explores the special role of the nonprofit sector in furthering economic development and human rights. Estelle James depicts the nonprofit sector in Sri Lanka as consisting of two subsets: large multipurpose organizations that are financed mainly by Western donors and much smaller health and welfare organizations funded mainly by domestic governments. As in other countries, many NPOs in Sri Lanka have a religious affiliation and carry out social service activities, although a few of the largest are engaged in social overhead capital formation—a nonprofit function that is probably unique to developing countries.

One of the most important issues explored by James concerns the causes and consequences of the flow of foreign donations to developing countries through the nonprofit sector, an issue that is further analyzed in the chapters by Smith, Anheier, and Fruhling. Presumably individual donors donate because they care about the welfare of people in other countries, particularly people with much lower incomes but with whom they share some strong (religious, ethnic) "community of interest."

Western governments contribute in order to support worthwhile projects and sympathetic groups abroad. NPOs (rather than profit-maximizing organizations or governments) are used as a conduit for this aid because they provide trustworthy information and low-cost administration and can often operate in politically sensitive areas where governments would be suspect. These points are elaborated upon in the chapter by Smith. That Western donors have made this institutional choice is, in fact, a rationale for the growth of the nonprofit legal form in developing countries: they are permitted to operate because they bring with them scarce foreign exchange that might not come otherwise. Of course, this means that foreign donors are also in a position to determine which development projects get undertaken and under whose management. The ambivalence of the Sri Lankan government toward this situation is demonstrated by the fact that it encourages NPOs via grants and tax privileges but also scrutinizes and regulates their activities, particularly their access to foreign funds. These points are also emphasized in Anheier's chapter on African NPOs.

Although data on volunteer labor, which does not pass through the market nexus, is always difficult to obtain, James estimates that donations of time far exceed domestic monetary contributions in Sri Lanka. This may be an economically efficient way to mobilize and train labor in a developing country, where jobs are scarce, needs are plentiful, and market imperfections prevent wages from falling to market-clearing levels. Will volunteer labor decline as unemployment falls in the process of economic development? The paper by Badelt suggests it remains, but it is largely confined to informal household-to-household helping activities. The ability of more formal NPOs to replace their volunteers with a professional labor force, which requires a large growth in donor contributions or government subsidies, will determine the long-run viability of the nonprofit sector as development proceeds.

The Ambiguous Political Role of European International Charities

Although most of the papers in this volume maintain that NPOs receive public funding because they help their governments carry out desired policies, Brian Smith asks a perplexing question: why are international charitable agencies heavily supported even when they openly oppose official aid and trade policies toward developing countries? He answers this question by providing extensive evidence of the ways in which nonprofit aid organizations are valuable to their governments, even while opposing official policies. They are a reliable and cost effective conduit for reaching the poor in developing countries; they help keep open channels of communication with foreign groups with whom domestic governments wish to maintain contact but cannot do so formally; and they serve an important information and advocacy role. (See the James chapter on Sweden for evidence of this role relative to domestic rather than foreign policy.)

When the opposition politics of the international charities becomes too active and outweighs their benefits, European governments can place restrictions on their use of funds, diminish their subsidies, revoke their tax-exempt status, or threaten other legal sanctions. Thus, nonprofit organizations that strongly disagree with their governments face a trade-off between autonomy and funds; they may have to modify their actions in order to maintain their flow of resources. Most choose funds but a few (with strong preferences and alternative sources of finance) choose autonomy and forego public subsidies. As discussed earlier, this same trade-off is faced by domestic NPOs when extensive regulations accompany access to public funds, and most make the same choice in favor of funds.

One of the most interesting points in Smith's paper concerns the reliance of international NPOs on multiple sources of private donations, from donors whose varying objectives range from humanitarian emergency relief to long-run radical political change. The NPOs adapt by channeling different information about their activities to different donor groups and by concealing their true political orientation from those donors who probably would not be sympathetic. Occasionally this strategy backfires, during periodic exposés when donors learn they have been misled.

This empirical observation has important implications for nonprofit theory. A major theoretical rationale for nonprofit enterprises is that they will have less incentive than for-profit enterprises to "cheat" and misinform consumers and donors. Yet Smith provides contrary evidence, suggesting that nonprofit organizations depend on secrecy and often mislead donors—albeit for "altruistic" political rather than personal pecuniary motives. This underscores the point that pursuit of profits is not the only objective that will lead organizations to "cheat"; nonprofit groups may do so to further their own ideological goals.[11] Ironically, if their "altruistic" commitment is strong they may be no more trustworthy than their "selfish" profit-maximizing counterpart.

The Diverse Role of Voluntary Organizations in Africa

Helmut Anheier examines the other side of the coin from Smith. He asks, why are NPOs allowed to operate in developing countries even when they are highly critical of these regimes and are committed to basic economic and political reforms? And, to what extent is it desirable for NPOs to set the development agenda in these countries?

Anheier argues that the answer varies across countries, depending on their scarcity of economic resources (which determines the urgency of their need for nonprofit funding) and the political power structure (which determines whether NPOs are useful allies in the struggle against political opponents). The NPO sector is important in Togo for the first reason and in Senegal for the second reason, while in Nigeria it is small but reflects fundamental religious and regional cleavages within the country.

Anheier analyzes in some detail the role of religious organizations in founding and funding African NPOs. In Togo religious (particularly Christian) NPOs dominate, their development work closely tied to their religious proselytizing objectives. In contrast, in Islamic Senegal, where historical competition from Christian missionaries was small, most NPOs are secular and are used by the government to bypass rural power structures that are tied to Islamic tradition. In Nigeria a vigorous competition between Islam and the various Christian churches has played itself out in the NPO sector, both historically and currently. In a detailed analysis of organizations for the handicapped, Anheier ties the regional distribution of public and private agencies, secular and religious NPOs, to religious heterogeneity and political competition.

In all three countries domestic NPOs are heavily dependent on foreign funds from international NPOs (see the chapters by James and Smith). However, the dependency of the countries on NPO resources, and therefore the public policies toward the nonprofit sector, vary greatly. In Senegal and even more so, Togo, NPOs are a major source of foreign exchange for the country as a whole, whereas in Nigeria private investment and direct government aid play a much more important role. Thus, Nigeria can ignore NPOs in its development plan (and indeed, "nationalized" many NPO projects during the oil boom of the 1970s), while Togo and Senegal cannot afford to do so. The differential attitude toward these three countries by Western donors who fund the NPOs is not very clear: both the supply of and demand for funds determine the final outcome but only the demand side is discussed in this chapter. In any event, in all three cases, as in other Third World countries, NPOs must walk a delicate line between independence, on the one hand, and acknowledgement of state supremacy in development planning, on the other, between establishing their own priorities, which may appeal to donors, and following the priorities of the African governments, which have their own political agenda.

Indeed, in Anheier's view all other variables are mediated through political forces, the role of the state and its attitude toward nonprofit organizations. This brings us back to one of the main points mentioned at the beginning of this Introduction: we can explain and predict the role of the nonprofit sector as a response to exogenous government action, but the much more difficult task is to make the government action itself endogenous, a function of more basic variables.

Human Rights Organizations in Chile

The final chapter in this volume, by Hugo Fruhling, presents a fascinating and extreme account of how NPOs can act contrary to the policies of an existing government, even an authoritarian government, and still survive. Despite the militaristic rule and repression of dissidents that prevail in Chile, a group of human rights organizations has developed, most of them associated with the Catholic Church and other religious institutions, to denounce civil liberties violations, deliver social services to the poor, and reinforce the political opposition. Their affiliation to an international network gives the NPOs foreign visibility and financial support and enables them to provide a protective umbrella to all these antigovernment activities in Chile. However, they were less successful in protecting human rights in Argentina, where the church was more ambivalent on these issues, the opposition was reluctant to unify along nonprofit, nonpartisan lines, and the government was more repressive and less sensitive to public opinion abroad.

Fruhling's story begins in 1973 when leaders of all the major religious groups assembled to establish a human rights NPO, COPACHI, in Santiago. Crucial international contacts were immediately established with their religious counterparts abroad. With the eyes of the world on Chile, which remained sensitive to international pressure, COPACHI was permitted to collect information on human rights violations and aid thousands of people in need of legal aid and material support. COPACHI was eventually disbanded but it paved the way for numerous separate organizations representing a variety of religious and secular groups—all forging links with similar foreign institutions as well as their own domestic communities. Although they have not succeeded in eliminating authoritarian rule in Chile, Fruhling believes they have limited some of the worst excesses of that regime and provided an environment where dissidents are able to meet and interact, thereby keeping the opposition alive.

Apparently NPOs, as an "international community of interest" concerned about human rights, have the ability to constrain the actions of authoritarian regimes with total police power within their own states. In this sense they function as an informal international watchdog in the absence of a formal international government. This lends credence to the argument that the nonprofit sector should be fostered for political as well as economic reasons—as an instrument of pluralism, democracy, and freedom.

We move on now, to let the papers speak for themselves.

NOTES

1. In the United States, NPOs are often defined in terms of their eligibility for tax exemptions and tax-deductible contributions (i.e., they are the 501 CC (3) organization). Tax laws differ in other countries, so this definition cannot be used in an international context. The nonprofit distribution constraint gives us a more general structural definition of NPOs, which is independent of tax laws. This volume and this introductory essay deal only with service-production NPOs and not with organizations such as trade associations, labor unions, or political parties, per se.

2. See Henry Hansmann, "The Role of Nonprofit Enterprise," *Yale Law Journal* 89 (1980): 835–98; David Easley and Maureen O'Hara, "The Economic Role of the Nonprofit Firm," *Bell Journal of Economics* 14 (1983): 531–38.

3. Burton Weisbrod, "Toward a Theory of the Voluntary Nonprofit Sector in a Three-Sector Economy," in *Altruism, Morality and Economic Theory,* ed. E. Phelps, (New York: Russell Sage Foundation, 1975), pp. 171–91; and *The Voluntary Nonprofit Sector* (Lexington, Mass.: Lexington Books, 1977).

4. Also see Estelle James, "Benefits and Costs of Privatized Public Services: Lessons from the Dutch Educational System," *Comparative Education Review* (1984); "The Public/Private Division of Responsibility for Education: An International Comparison," *Economics of Education Review* (1987); 1–14; "Institutional Choice in the Education Industry," Paper delivered to the International Workshop on Institutional Choice, Vienna, 1987.

5. They are analytically very similar to "clubs," which have been extensively analyzed in the economics literature. For a survey of this literature see Richard Cornes and Todd Sandler, *The Theory of Externalities, Public Goods and Club Goods* (Cambridge: Cambridge University Press, 1986).

6. See Estelle James and Susan Rose-Ackerman, *The Nonprofit Enterprise in Market Economies,* a monograph in the Fundamentals of Pure and Applied Economics, eds. J. Lesourne and H. Sonnerschein (London: Harwood Academic Publishers, 1986).

7. However, it would be misleading to place too much credence on "ideology" as a determinant of policy. For example, the conservative government took over private schools in Sweden in the early twentieth century, when this was in the interests of its supporters. Similarly, the largest public sectors are found in some of the most conservative states in Japan and Austria, when the dominant political groups benefitted from them (see the chapters by James and Badelt).

8. Many books and papers have been written on this perplexing topic. See, for example, B. L. R. Smith and D. C. Hague, eds., *The Dilemma of Accountability in Modern Government: Independence versus Control* (New York: St. Martin's Press, 1971). Other references are given in the relevant chapters.

9. For further discussion of this issue see Estelle James and Gail Benjamin, "Educational Distribution and Redistribution through Education in Japan," *Journal of Human Resources* (1987).

10. See Estelle James, "The Public/Private Division of Responsibility for Education"; and "Institutional Choice in the Education Industry."

11. Along similar lines, nonprofit organizations may divert donated funds through cross-subsidization, in order to carry out activities they consider socially desirable but that society is not willing to finance more directly. See Estelle James, "How Nonprofits Grow: A Model," *Journal of Policy Analysis and Management* (1983): 350–65.

REFERENCES

Cornes, Richard, and Todd Sandler. *The Theory of Externalities, Public Goods and Club Goods.* Cambridge: Cambridge University Press, 1986.

Easley, David, and Maureen O'Hara. "The Economic Role of the Nonprofit Firm." *Bell Journal of Economics* 14 (1983): 531–38.

Hansmann, Henry. "The Role of Nonprofit Enterprise." *Yale Law Journal* 89 (1980): 835–98.

James, Estelle. "Benefits and Costs of Privatized Public Services: Lessons from the Dutch Educational System." *Comparative Education Review* (1984); an expanded version was reprinted in *Private Education: Studies in Choice and Public Policy,* ed. D. Levy. New York: Oxford University Press, 1986.

———. "How Nonprofits Grow: A Model." *Journal of Policy Analysis and Management* (1983): 350–65; reprinted in S. Rose-Ackerman, ed., *The Economics of Nonprofit Institutions: Studies in Structures and Policy.* New York: Oxford University Press, 1986.

———. "Institutional Choice in the Education Industry." Paper delivered at the International Workshop on Institutional Choice, Vienna, 1987.

———. "The Public/Private Division of Responsibility for Education: An International Comparison." *Economics of Education Review* (1987): 1–14; reprinted in *Comparing Public and Private Schools: Institutions and Organizations,* vol. 1, ed. T. James and H. Levin. London: Falmer Press, 1988.

James, Estelle, and Gail Benjamin. "Educational Distribution and Redistribution through Education in Japan." *Journal of Human Resources* (1987): 469–489.

James, Estelle, and Susan Rose-Ackerman. *The Nonprofit Enterprise in Market Economies,* a monograph in the Fundamentals of Pure and Applied Economics series. London: Harwood Academic Publishers, 1986.

Smith, Bruce L. R., and D. C. Hague, eds. *The Dilemma of Accountability in Modern Government: Independence versus Control.* New York: St. Martin's Press, 1971.

Weisbrod, Burton. "Toward a Theory of the Voluntary Nonprofit Sector in a Three-sector Economy." In E. Phelps, ed., *Altruism, Morality and Economic Theory,* pp. 171–91. New York: Russell Sage Foundation, 1975.

———. *The Voluntary Nonprofit Sector.* Lexington, Mass.: Lexington Books, 1977.

I

PRIVATE NONPROFIT PRODUCTION OF PUBLIC SERVICES

1

The Private Provision of Public Services: A Comparison of Sweden and Holland

ESTELLE JAMES

This paper is part of a broader study that analyzes the determinants and consequences of the public–private division of responsibility for the provision of quasi-public goods, goods that yield a combination of private and social benefits, such as education, health, and cultural activities.[1] The private provision of these goods is often carried out through nonprofit organizations (NPOs), institutions that are legally prohibited from distributing a monetary residual and must therefore spend all their resources on organizational activities.[2] Therefore, this topic can be redefined as an exploration of the size and nature of the private nonprofit sector as a provider of quasi-public goods. I utilize a comparative economics perspective, drawing on the diverse experience of a variety of Western and Third World countries.

A case study of Sweden is presented in this chapter, but comparisons are also made with other countries, especially Holland; these two modern welfare states are polar cases with respect to their reliance on nonprofit production, Holland using it extensively and Sweden virtually not at all, for most services. Thus, in a sense, this paper is about a negative rather than a positive, the absence of something rather than its presence.

An earlier version of this paper was written while the author was a fellow at the Woodrow Wilson International Center for Scholars, Washington, D.C. It is based on published material as well as statistical data collected and interviews held with numerous scholars, government officials, private school headmasters, managers of adult education associations and other organizations, during a visit to Sweden in 1981. I wish to thank all of the people who were so generous with their time, in addition to the staff members at the Swedish Institute who arranged the interviews. My research assistant at the Wilson Center, James Sinclair, was very helpful in assembling the tables and performing related calculations. I also appreciate the financial assistance from the Social Science Research Council for this trip and the facilities provided by Arbetslivscentrum during my stay in Stockholm. Support was received from the Exxon Education Foundation, the National Endowment for the Humanities, the Program on Non-Profit Organizations at Yale University (PONPO), U.S.A.I.D., the Netherlands Institute for Advanced Study, the American Association of University Women, the Spencer Foundation, and the Department of Education, on broader aspects of this project.

Two sets of issues are considered. First, what insights does the Swedish experience provide on the preconditions for a large (or a very small) non-profit sector? Second, what can we learn from Sweden about the behavior of this sector as a producer of quasi-public goods? The object here is to analyze the choice between government and private provision, to examine some of the problems that arise and alternative methods of solving them, when the provision of public services is privatized—a topic under much discussion today. In my broader work some of the conclusions tentatively drawn from this case study are tested statistically across a larger set of developed and developing countries and supporting results are obtained.

With respect to the first issue, I view nonprofit organizations as "interest-based communities" that contrast with geographically based communities in providing quasi-public goods. In this sense, local governments and NPOs are competing institutional arrangements, and the choice between them is seen as depending on the degree of cultural heterogeneity and its geographic dispersion, the strength and diversity of religious organizations, and the disparate distribution of economic and political power.

With respect to the second issue, ideally we would like to compare the public and private sectors with regard to variables such as quantity, quality, cost effectiveness, distributive effects, and so on. Unfortunately, in most countries the available data does not allow us to do this directly. Particularly lacking are data on consumer characteristics in the two sectors; this is essential for calculations of value added because consumers (e.g., students and patients) are probably the most important input into the production of many quasi-public services. We can, however, investigate certain behavioral characteristics of nonprofit organizations, thereby indirectly throwing light on their desirability as providers of these services. For example, how do NPOs solve the entry problem and secure their venture capital, in the absence of the profit motive? What are their sources of entrepreneurship and labor? How fast do they respond to changes in demand? Are they large enough to benefit from economies of scale? What are the implications of privatization for social segmentation and equity, and how are these affected by government regulations? This chapter examines these questions with respect to the provision of educational services in Sweden.

Briefly, I find that both in Sweden and Holland quasi-public goods are financed mainly by the government, a common pattern in most Western countries. However, financing and production can be separated—as in the case of Holland, where cultural heterogeneity and strong religious groups have led to a system of service delivery dominated by private nonprofit (mostly religious) organizations. Sweden, however, lacks the preconditions for a large production-oriented nonprofit sector, and most service delivery has been delegated to local governments instead. Although the productive role of Swedish NPOs is small, they play a crucial informational and intermediational role in the Swedish political process, so their indirect influence on the provision of public goods is much greater than their direct output would imply. Representation and advocacy, then, are important functions for NPOs to perform, as "interest-based communities" in democratic welfare states.

The first part of this paper sets forth my major hypotheses regarding the determinants of the public–private division of responsibility for producing quasi-public goods and compares these hypotheses with the Swedish situation. Following that, I examine in greater detail the behavior of and problems encountered by private institutions in providing one quasi-public service, education, in Sweden, both currently and historically. The conclusion summarizes my findings about Sweden and compares it with earlier findings about the Netherlands. Despite vast differences in the size of the private sectors in these two societies, their nonprofit institutions behave in strikingly similar ways in many respects—leading me to believe that these may indeed be "universal" characteristics that will be found in many other countries, too.

THE SIZE OF THE NONPROFIT SECTOR: THEORETICAL PREDICTIONS AND SWEDISH DATA

Hypotheses

This paper views the nonprofit provision of quasi-public goods in the modern welfare state as a response to differentiated tastes about the quantity and kind of service preferred, a differentiation that is not accommodated for in government production.[3] It is also an indication that there are private suppliers who wish to provide the service, for reasons other than the pecuniary profit motive. In general, the more dispersed are peoples' preferences with respect to product variety, the greater the economic resources of people not accommodated by government services, the larger the supply of potential entrepreneurs, and the more the subsidy they are able to elicit from government, the larger I would expect the nonprofit sector to grow as a provider of quasi-public goods.

Hypothesis I
Heterogeneous preferences often stem from deep-seated religious and linguistic differences. Therefore, I would expect cultural heterogeneity to be positively associated with nonprofit provision. Three patterns may develop in heterogeneous societies, depending on the relationship between cultural diversity and political power: single group dominance; pluralism with geographic concentration; or pluralism with geographic dispersion.

If a single group dominates politically and wishes to impose its preferences on all others (Model A), we would expect to find uniform public provision together with policies that discourage NPOs. Examples would include the state provision of education in Holland and France and laws that suppressed Catholic schools, in the early nineteenth century.

If the various groups are geographically concentrated in different parts of the country and one group is not able or anxious to impose its preferences on others (Model B), we would expect to find public provision by local governments, each catering to a different constituency, as in Switzerland, where each canton runs and chooses the language for its own school system. The private sector would again be small. For similar reasons, residential segregation by class together with local government provision of quasi-public goods results in a relatively small private sector, as in the United States.

If the heterogeneous groups are geographically mixed and a pluralistic model is adopted (Model C), we would expect to find considerable provision through private nonprofit organizations, supplementing pure government production, as in Holland today.

Economic theory often assumes that Model B applies, that people will move to communities offering the kinds of services they prefer, that people with like preferences will therefore tend to congregate together and provide their quasi-public services through their local government. Model C, in contrast, assumes that barriers to mobility often stop the process at a point where considerable heterogeneity still exists, that governments are constrained to offer a uniform product (in order to maximize administrative simplicity or scale economies and minimize rationing problems), and that NPOs are then an alternative institutional mechanism for responding to diverse tastes without incurring movement costs or overcoming other movement barriers. The more uniform the government product, the more heterogeneous the tastes and the more intense are peoples' preferences, the greater will be peoples' willingness to seek other alternatives even if they must pay for them, and the larger will be the resulting private sector.

Hypothesis II

The nature of the service preferred depends on income as well as taste. In particular, the upper and lower classes may have different quantity–quality trade-offs, with the demand for quality highly income elastic. The dominant political class then determines the quantity and quality of the public sector, and other classes will resort to the private sector, if they have the economic resources to do so. Therefore, we would expect a complex relationship between the distribution of income and political power in a society and the size and nature of its private sector.

In a society with a high degree of income and political equality, the supply (quantity and quality) of public services will be correspondingly uniform and broad, hence there will be little demand for a private sector based on income differences. This is the egalitarian model.

At the opposite extreme we have a very nonegalitarian society, in which the locus of economic and political power is tightly concentrated in one small group. The government then provides services preferred by the upper classes (e.g., high culture and high quality selective education), while a private sector may arise to provide the services demanded by the lower classes and its size will depend on their ability and willingness to pay. Excess demand–driven private educational sectors in many developing countries are an example of this inequality model.

If the upper classes have maintained their economic wealth but do not control the political system or the provision of government services, they will resort to the private sector to satisfy their tastes. We would then expect to find an elitist private sector, not necessarily large but high in quality and influence, while government provides quantity for broader groups in society (as in Venezuela and Ecuador; see the Levy chapter in this volume). Thus, if the government provides high quality but low quantity, the private sector may grow large, whereas if public services are low in quality but high in quantity the private sector remains small but powerful. This is a model of disparate economic and political power.

Hypothesis III
The private production of quasi-public goods typically occurs in the nonprofit sector. Indeed, nonprofit status is often required for private providers of schools and other social services, particularly for those that receive government subsidies. And most of these nonprofit providers are religious organizations.

Religion was the basis for collective community action before secular states developed and this role continues in the private nonprofit sector today. Whereas most business firms are driven by the profit motive, religious organizations provide education, health, and other social services to maximize their members, socialize them, shape their tastes, and maintain group loyalty. Besides this nonpecuniary motivation, religious institutions are well suited to serve as NPO entrepreneurs: providing organizational ability, venture capital, and inexpensive labor (e.g., monks and nuns) to NPOs that serve their present and future constituencies. Their lower costs enable them to compete effectively against profit-maximizing firms as well as governments in those labor-intensive industries in which they choose to operate.

In addition to this supply effect, organized religious minorities may stimulate a demand for their particular "brand" of service (e.g., for parochial schools) among their members. Moreover, they may be politically powerful enough to secure government subsidies, via direct grants or indirect tax privileges, for NPO service providers. This suggests that NPO production will be greater in countries where several strong, independent religious organizations coexist and compete for members.

Hypothesis IV
The government may provide subsidies to nonprofit organizations as a way of lowering costs, accommodating diverse tastes, or as a response to pressure from religious organizations. I would expect a positive relationship between government subsidies and relative share of the private sector in producing quasi-public goods.

Predictions about Sweden

What would these hypotheses lead us to expect in the case of Sweden? Sweden is one of the most culturally homogeneous countries in the world. At least until the "guest worker" immigration of the 1960s, Swedes were united in language and religion.[4] If we posit the nonprofit sector as an institutional firm for accommodating differentiated tastes regarding quasi-public goods, there was no cultural basis for such diversity in Sweden.

Nor did the upper classes have an incentive to establish the private sector as their special domain since, until World War I, they closely controlled the public sector. High income and property requirements for voting were not eliminated until the period immediately surrounding World War I. Even after the labor-based Social Democratic Party was elected in 1932, the upper classes retained many of their preferred services. For example, an extremely selective system of public education, favoring children from high socioeconomic backgrounds, prevailed until the shift to comprehensive primary schools and integrated secondary schools in the 1960s and 1970s. By that time, when the shift to more uniform government services might have generated a demand for differentiated goods in the private sector among the wealthy elite, their financial ability had been substantially reduced by high tax rates, so that Sweden is now one of the most egalitarian countries in the world.[5] The income and related taste differentials that remain are (partially) accommodated by a pattern of residential segregation combined with local government provision of many public goods.

Nor has organized religion been a likely supply-side force for a thriving public sector. Ninety-five percent of the population belongs to the Church of Sweden, an established church closely tied to and financially dependent on the government since the Reformation, when the king became simultaneously head of church and state.[6] Until 1860 all Swedes were legally required to belong to the church. Even now, every Swede born to a church member is considered a member unless he or she explicitly declares otherwise. Schools are not needed as a proselytizing device in these circumstances.

Membership, however, is largely nominal; only 3 percent of the Church of Sweden members attend services and most consider themselves secular. The church receives almost all its financing from the government. For many years ministers' salaries were paid by the state; in effect they were civil servants. Since 1961 each parish has been responsible for clerical salaries but also has the right to levy a church tax that is collected as part of the local income tax.

In return for its access to government funding, the church has certain civic responsibilities, mainly maintaining population records (births, deaths, and marriages) and cemeteries. As will be discussed in the next part, until World War II public education was administered by the church. The church has also given up much of its autonomy in exchange for state funds. Decisions about ecclesiastical law, books for worship, appointments of top clergymen, and even the alcoholic content of communal wine are made jointly by government and church synod. The Church of Sweden is, in effect, part of the Swedish government and as such could hardly become the source of entrepreneurship for a competing nongovernment sector.

Finally, the Swedish government has never adopted a tax and subsidy policy favoring the private provision of quasi-public goods. Unlike the Netherlands, Swedish NPOs have not been given government grants for service production, except in narrowly specified areas. Unlike the United States, Swedish tax law does not grant deductions for contributions to NPOs. Most NPOs are not exempt from the property tax, must pay an income tax on sale of services to nonmembers, and are required to use up 80 percent of their current revenues (except for contributions) within five years; that is, large-scale saving and capital accumulation are discouraged. Although the negative attitude toward the private provision of quasi-public goods is consistent with the collectivist egalitarian ideology of the Social Democratic Party, which was in power from 1932–1976, a similar policy prevailed before 1932 when the upper classes and the Church of Sweden had much greater power over the public sector and therefore had no need for a private nonprofit sector.

Given its cultural and economic homogeneity, its lack of a strong independent church, and its delegation (with subsidy) of public service provision to local government rather than to NPOs, we would expect Sweden to have only a small private sector involved in the production of quasi-public goods. And that is exactly what we find.

Empirical Data about Swedish NPOs

Table 1.1 summarizes the available data on the role of the government and private sectors in providing quasi-public goods in Sweden. It is difficult to establish with precision the size of the nonprofit sector since no centralized data source exists.[7] Instead, information must be assembled from a variety of sources that use different definitions and are incomplete at best. Nevertheless, certain conclusions emerge sharply, and these are consistent with the hypotheses just presented.

First of all, it is clear that the private provision of public goods in Sweden is very small: in 1979 income and expenditures of NPOs totaled 6.8 billion kronor, barely 1.6 percent of GNP and 3.1 percent of direct government spending.

Second, the Swedish case supports the hypotheses that geographically based communities and NPO "interest-based communities" are competitors for the job of producing quasi-public goods. In Sweden, provision by local government has clearly won out: local governments do more direct spending than the nonprofit sector and central government combined.[8]

As in most Western countries, government funding is the major revenue source for NPO service providers; they flourish if and only if they have access to such funding. This means that NPOs play an important produc-

Table 1.1. Size and Revenue Sources of the Swedish Nonprofit Sector Compared with Government, 1979 (in billion kronor)

Activity	Sources of NPO Revenues			Total NPO Prod.	Central Govt. Prod.[a]	Local Govt. Prod.[b]
	From Central Govt.[a]	From Local Govt.	Private Revenues			
Education[c]	50%	25%	25%	2.356	6.406	27.619
Culture[d]	67%	23%	10%	1.046	.373	1.942
Sports[e]	19%	31%	50%	1.480	.022	3.670
Religion[f]	4%	NA	96%	.969	.010	3.271
Other[g]	100%			.937	75.768	100.965
Total	46%	19%	35%	6.788	82.579	137.467

[a]Data on central government subsidies to NPOs, direct expenditures by the central government, and central government transfers to local communities were assembled from material provided by the Riksrevisionsverket (National Audit Bureau), particularly *Budget redovisning för 1979–80*, which lists each appropriation in the 1979–1980 budget; a computer printout that assigns to each appropriation a purpose and type of recipient; *Statistiska meddelanden*, 1981:7, pp. 36–7, which groups all state expenditures by major purpose and type of recipient; and *Fördelningen av driftbudgetens utgiften efter ändamål*, 1981, which groups all state expenditures by major and minor purposes and type of recipient. The nonprofit sector was defined to include "associations" and "other official institutions." See note 7 for comments on this definition and related data.

[b]Data on local (municipal and county) expenditures were taken from *Kommunernas Finanser 1979*, Statistiska Centralbyrån, Stockholm, 1981, pp. 16, 56, 57, 59, 64, 66, 90, 94, 95. From this was subtracted local transfers to NPOs to obtain direct local spending. The distinction between central and local government production is somewhat arbitrary since the former heavily finances and evaluates the latter.

[c]Numbers for local subsidies and private sources of income for education are based on annual financial reports of adult education associations and interviews with their officials, both of which indicated that about 25 percent of their revenues came from local governments, 25 percent from participant fees, sales of materials, interest, and rent. Adult education is by far the largest NPO activity in the education category. Private primary and secondary schools probably get a higher proportion of their revenues from tuition fees and a lower proportion from municipalities, whereas the opposite is true for folk high schools.

[d]Local subsidies to cultural NPOs were derived from *Kulturstatistik*, published by Statens kulturråd och Statistiska centralbyrån, Stockholm, 1981, p. 107. Private revenues of cultural NPOs are my estimate, based on budgetary data for cultural organizations in *Kulturstatistik*, p. 123 and in *Utbildningsdepartementet*, Statsliggaren, 1980–1981 (containing line-by-line expenditures for the Education Dept.), which suggested that private sources account for approximately 10 percent of total revenues for cultural institutions.

[e]Local subsidies to recreational NPOs were derived from *Fritidspolitik and Samhällsstod*, National Youth Board, Stockholm, 1981, p. 76. According to this, p. 68, sports organizations are 50 percent self-financing. This was confirmed in an interview with an official of the National Sports Federation. Lotteries are a major source of private funding; membership dues and admission fees are secondary sources.

[f]Approximately 75 percent of expenditures on religion was derived from the "parish tax," collected by local government for the Church of Sweden. Since this is a state church financed by a special church tax determined by each parish, I am considering it part of the local government sector rather than the NPO sector. The Free Churches are treated as NPOs, but data on local government contributions to them were not available; however, this sum is very small. Data on private revenues for Swedish Free Churches are my estimate, based on the following information. According to my interview with church officials and perusal of their annual reports, there are approximately 300,000 Free Church members in Sweden, each of whom contributes an average of 3000 kronor. Also, the Svenska Missionforbundet, the largest Free Church organization in Sweden, had an income of 186 million kronor and approximately 20 percent of the Free Church members and finances in the country. Both of these methods yield a total private revenue to the churches of 900–930 million kronor, from which the percentages in this table were derived.

[g]This number was obtained from National Audit Bureau data. Because data were not available for private revenues of "other" NPO activities, these sums slightly understate the total revenues and expenditures of the Swedish nonprofit sector. However, the understatement is negligible, since all services for which NPOs are important providers are included.

tive role only in these areas where government explicitly wants nonprofit endeavors—culture, sports, and adult education.

For example, the government repeatedly stresses a preference for private over state production in the cultural field, to generate the pluralism and diversity of opinion, which they regard as a "public good" in a democracy. The reliance on private organizations in sports is seen as a means of encouraging volunteer labor and voluntary consumption. The more complex case of adult education, to which large subsidies are given, will be discussed later. The limited amount of government subsidies overall, for service production by private organizations, is the most immediate explanation for the small size of the Swedish nonprofit sector.

Closely related is the absence of voluntary contributions for quasi-public goods, which are heavily supported by government spending. Some voluntary contributions—much less than current levels of government expenditures—were made for these services by wealthy people in the nineteenth century, but philanthropy is now rare in Sweden. This observation is roughly consistent with a model in which voluntary contributions diminish (are "crowded out") as government spending on public goods increases, presumably satisfying peoples' demand. Those donations that remain now go overwhelmingly to the dissenting Free Churches, especially to their missionary work abroad, activities that are not supported by the government.

This brings us to our final point—that religion plays an important role in the Swedish nonprofit sector, although not as central as in most other countries. At least one-third of the educational, cultural, and recreational nonprofit organizations do indeed have a religious affiliation, many with the Free Churches, even in secular Sweden. Many of the others are tied to another ideological organization, the socialist labor union.

The Representational Role of NPOs

Although NPOs play a minor productive role in the Swedish economy, they play a major role as intermediaries between the government and the people, representing "interest-based communities" in the political process. Indeed, this representational role is used to justify the subsidies the government pays to cover the administrative (as opposed to production costs) of many NPOs. Whereas this type of activity is termed *lobbying* in the United States and is financed by the private groups who benefit from them, in Sweden the flow of information they provide is considered a public good from which society at large benefits and therefore should subsidize. Of course, this information often justifies public expenditures favored by the represented groups and by the Social Democratic government.

Specifically, umbrella organizations of workers, immigrants, handicapped people, youth, pensioners, and so on, through their government-subsidized administrative staff:

1. are represented on "committees of inquiry" that study issues before bills are formulated;

2. are part of the "remiss process" in which proposed bills are circulated to and discussed by all interest groups concerned, and consequently modified, before the final version is enacted;
3. sit on administrative boards, such as the national board of education or the various cultural councils, which oversee general policy and implement legislation in each area;
4. shape the opinions of their members in favor of policies that they have helped to formulate and collective consumption activities that they will help to administer; and
5. are often affiliated with political parties, so that their officials run for political office, are elected to Parliament, and are appointed to high administrative positions—blurring the line between the public and private sectors.

Thus, nonprofit organizations have a much greater impact on the Swedish economy and society than their direct production activities would indicate. They operate by influencing collective government actions and individual consumption patterns, serving as an intermediary between the two: this is their raison d'être in the Swedish model of a pluralistic democratic welfare state.[9]

PRIVATE NONPROFIT BEHAVIOR IN EDUCATION

I move on now to examine certain behavioral characteristics of NPOs in those few areas where they serve as producers of quasi-public goods, with particular attention to the field of education. The object is to understand better the possible consequences of privatizing public services, a topic under considerable discussion today. Some of the questions addressed are as follows:

1. How do private nonprofit institutions solve the entry problem? What is the source of entrepreneurship and venture capital in a sector where the profit motive is ruled out? This bears significantly on the ability of the nonprofit sector to increase output and the speed with which it will do so, in response to increased demand stemming from private or public sources.
2. How is labor attracted and compensated in NPOs? Are salaries low because of financing difficulties or do NPOs in fact engage in disguised profit distribution, by paying above-market salaries or other (nonpecuniary) forms of remuneration? If the former case holds, this would seem to limit their ability to attract labor for rapid expansion, when desired. If the latter case holds, this would mean that payments, including any public subsidies, are not all used for the intended purpose (i.e., to meet the real opportunity cost of the service provided).
3. Are voluntary donations of time and labor a viable way of financing private production of public services?
4. If government and nonprofit producers coexist in an industry, what is the difference between them? For example, in the field of education, are private schools better and costlier than public schools or are they less costly because of financial difficulties that force them to economize on input quantity, quality, and remuneration?

5. Does the private provision of public services lead to segmentation within society, along racial, religious, or class lines? In particular, in a system of privatized education do the wealthy elite pay for and secure a better education for their children, thereby perpetuating their advantaged socioeconomic position?
6. If the government subsidizes NPOs, how are the costs and benefits of the subsidy divided among consumers, workers, and society at large? Do government subsidies lead to government regulation? If so, does the private sector lose some of its unique characteristics, which made it preferable to government production in the first place? If not, how will accountability and social control over the use of public funds be maintained?

As we saw in the first part, the Swedish social, economic, and political environment is not conducive to a large nonprofit producing sector, and those organizations that provide services exist only in particularized areas. Therefore, in this section I examine some of the more interesting members of a small set, operating where they are the exception rather than the rule. Three groups of institutions that currently and historically have provided educational services are considered: private secondary schools for girls and their replacement by public schools in the early part of the twentieth century; private schools today, a rare exception to the government monopoly; and the growth of adult education produced by private associations, financed by the government, during the 1960s and 1970s. The final part summarizes some of the lessons that can be learned from these three cases and compares the Swedish and Dutch experience with NPOs.

Private Secondary Schools for Girls and the Historical Shift to a Public System

Secondary school education for boys in Sweden has long been the domain of the government rather than the private sector. As predicted earlier, cultural homogeneity, interdependence of church and state, and political control by the upper classes, all brought about a system of elite public education supplemented by relatively few private schools, in the nineteenth century. However, preferences about secondary education for girls were much more diverse, before World War I. As a result of this diversity, the private sector flourished, until an emerging consensus replaced it with a public system after 1927. These points will be elaborated upon.[10]

From the time of the Reformation until 1951, state responsibility for administering public education in Sweden was shared with the church. Sweden's first national educational ordinance was part of the ecclesiastical ordinance of 1571. The same person served as Minister of Education and Ecclesiastical Affairs, and the bishops were required to file with him annual reports on their schools. Although national policy was made by the Minister and the Riksdag (Parliament) on matters such as school structure, timing, and curriculum, regional and local administration were vested in the diocese and the parishes. For example, compulsory school attendance was decreed on a national basis by the primary education code of 1842,

Table 1.2.   Enrollment in Lower Secondary Schools, 1910–1959

Year	Higher Elementary & Local Realskolor[a]	State Secondary[b]	Municipal Girls' Schools[c]	Private[d]	Total	Percent Private	Percent of Age Group 10–19 Enrolled
Male							
1910	868	15,760		NA	16,628		
1920	5,003	20,026		2,517	27,546	9	4.7
1925	7,250	19,639		2,243	29,132	8	
1930	6,139	19,040		2,156	27,335	8	4.9
1940	7,857	24,484		1,390	33,731	4	6.7
1945	8,392	27,824		2,166	38,382	6	
1950	7,289	41,087		2,557	50,933	5	11.6
1959	14,738	54,155		2,687	71,580	4	12.0
Female							
1910	636	1,120		12,359	14,115	88	
1920	5,731	1,557		21,587	28,875	75	5.1
1925	8,602	1,507		22,465	32,574	69	
1930	8,121	5,299	578	20,218	34,216	59	6.3
1940	10,717	13,749	12,273	4,400	41,139	11	8.5
1945	11,206	18,419	14,101	3,298	47,024	7	
1950	9,139	33,311	18,213	3,151	63,814	5	15.0
1959	17,775	50,994	23,257	3,408	95,434	4	16.6

Source: *Elever I Icke-Obligatoriska Skolor, 1864–1970 (Pupils in Secondary Schools in Sweden, 1864–1970)*, Central Bureau of Statistics, Stockholm, 1977.
[a] See pp. 112–14, 117, 119, 174.
[b] See pp. 121–23, 174.
[c] See p. 142.
[d] See pp. 138–40, 147, 148, 174.

ondary schools as well as the universities, students were trained for the but the number of required years and weeks in the year, as well as the day-to-day operation of the classroom depended on local (parish) decisions. Clearly, there was no raison d'être for the church to start its own private educational system, since it controlled the public one.

Nor was there a reason for the upper classes to foster a private educational system for their sons in the nineteenth or early twentieth centuries, since they essentially controlled the state and the church. Hence, they were able to use the government apparatus as their entrepreneurial tool, the public schools as their own "elite cooperative." As a result, Sweden had the kind of differentiated educational system predicted by the "inequality model": high-quality selective public schools providing preuniversity training for upper class children, while low-cost "folkskolor" provided literacy and other basic skills to working class children. Most of the universities, too, were public, run by the state or municipalities for those few who had completed the gymnasium. As evidence of the narrow selectivity of this system, in 1920 less than 5 percent of all males aged 10–19 were attending school beyond the third grade level (see Table 1.2). In the academic sec-

learned professions, the clergy, and government service. Although a small number still resorted to private schools, this was an unnecessary expense for most of the elite. Public education was, clearly, the instrument of the church, the state, and the upper classes, and this trinity in fact constituted one small mutually self-reinforcing segment of society.

Although the upper classes had a common set of interests for their sons, which they achieved through their control of the government, the church, and the public schools, their preferences diverged concerning the proper education for their daughters. In particular, the belief that girls needed to be educated beyond the primary level was by no means universal within this group. The solution in the nineteenth and early twentieth centuries was for girls to be excluded from the state secondary schools and educated privately, often by religious groups, for those who wanted it. These private schools were supported by two main sources: the tuition fees paid by their consumers and the modest wages paid their staff—which was predominantly female, religious, and/or part-time, hence operating in a different and lower-paid labor market than teachers at the boys' secondary schools.

By the end of the nineteenth century, as more of the upper classes were sending their daughters for some secondary education, pressure developed for a partial state subsidy—indicative of a public interest that was growing but still was not large enough to cover the full cost. A state college for training girls' school teachers was established and central standards with inspection instituted. Nevertheless, the primary responsibility remained with the private sector, which was clearly filling in where there was insufficient consensus for public provision, among the dominant upper classes.

The ability of the private sector to respond under these circumstances is demonstrated by the fact that in 1910 (when a few state schools opened their doors to women) enrollments at private schools offering a specialized "girls curriculum" (12,359) were almost as high as state school enrollments for boys (15,760) at the lower secondary level (see Table 1.2). This suggests that, at least where capital and labor costs are low and the target consumer group is wealthy, a privatized system and an "elite cooperative" public system will reach a similar equilibrium quantity; the demand elasticity for education seems small for that group over the relevant range.

At the upper secondary level the enrollment disparity was much greater—only 516 women attended private gymnasium in 1920, less than 10 percent of the men at the state gymnasium (see Table 1.3). Partly, this resulted from the fact that gymnasium education was more standardized and costly than lower secondary education; more capital equipment was needed and fewer low-wage women teachers were available. But mainly, I believe, the lower enrollments of women reflected the remaining ambivalence toward their education.

This attitude was, however, rapidly converging in the early twentieth century. By 1925, female enrollments at the gymnasium level had quadrupled (relative to 1910) and was now 25 percent of male enrollments. At

Table 1.3.   Enrollment at Upper Secondary Levels, 1910–1959

Year	State Gymnasia[a]	Private[b]	Total	Percent Private	Percent of Age Group 10–19 Enrolled
Male					
1910	5,711	NA	5,711+	NA	
1920	6,236	1,411	7,647	18	1.5
1925	7,840	1,639	9,479	17	
1930	6,229	1,554	7,783	20	1.6
1940	8,883	1,753	10,636	16	2.6
1945	9,017	1,810	10,827	17	
1950	9,801	1,854	11,655	16	3.6
1959	22,112	2,740	24,852	11	5.2
Female					
1910	0	516	516	100	
1920	11	1,193	1,204	99	0.2
1925	406	1,920	2,326	83	
1930	1,090	1,244	2,334	53	0.5
1940	4,523	1,221	5,744	21	
1945	5,003	1,344	6,347	21	1.3
1950	6,940	1,489	8,429	18	2.1
1959	19,959	2,602	22,561	12	4.3

Source: Same as Table 1.2.
[a]See pp. 128–31, 146, 175.
[b]See pp. 145–48, 175.

the lower secondary level, female enrollments actually exceeded male. With a consensus emerging that girls as well as boys should be educated, there was no longer any reason for avoiding the government as the most expedient entrepreneur. In 1927 the Riksdag opened the state upper secondary schools to girls, and in 1928 the state decided to finance lower secondary municipal girls' schools as well, withdrawing its subsidies from private schools at the same time. In other words, a clear policy choice was made to favor government rather than private provision. From this point on we see a rapid decline in the share of the private sector, which could not compete with a public sector that provided a low-price elitist education for girls.

At the lower secondary level the main effect of the new policy was a displacement of private by public schools (see Table 1.2). Indeed, many of the formerly private schools remained intact but were simply municipalized. Until World War II girls' enrollment grew moderately, at about the same rate as for boys. This is consistent with the interpretation that enrollment parity between the two groups had been achieved before girls' schools were municipalized and the price elasticity of demand was low over the relevant range, so the shift to a public system for girls did not increase enrollments at the lower secondary level.

At the upper secondary level the picture looked quite different. Here, the number of girls enrolled increased dramatically, much faster than boys' enrollments, virtually all of it going to the public sector (see Table 1.3). Specifically, girls' enrollments in gymnasia rose from 2326 in 1925 to 6347 in 1945 and 22,561 in 1959, almost a tenfold increase, compared with a three-fold increase for boys over this period, so that by 1959 boy–girl parity had almost been achieved. The number of students enrolled in private gymnasia stabilized, its relative share dwindling from 83 to 12 percent.

Was this huge enrollment increase for girls due to the shift to a public system with tax financing, hence a lower price charged to consumers? Would it have been equally accommodated by expansion in the private system, as appeared to have been the case earlier at the lower secondary level? As noted earlier, the capital and labor for gymnasia were more costly and difficult to secure privately, and the price elasticity of demand may well have been greater over this range. However, it should be recalled that the take-over by the state was itself a response to changing tastes in girls' education; indeed, the rapid enrollment increase may have caused the take-over rather than vice versa. Thus, the actual price effect is indeterminate, impossible to disentangle from the positive taste and income effects operating at the same time, but it probably accounts for only a modest part of the total enrollment rise.

What, then, was the impact of the shift from a private to a public system of education for girls after 1927? This can be decomposed into the following four elements, for the period 1927–1957, during which the highly selective system remained intact:

1. some (probably modest) enrollment increase due to the lower price in a public system;
2. a transfer payment toward those who would have educated their daughters anyway, away from those who still did not but paid taxes;
3. higher wages for teachers of girls, who were now paid the same as boys' teachers, often in coed schools; part of the higher labor cost was due to a real opportunity cost of the rapid expansion in girls' enrollment, part a quality improvement, and part an inframarginal rent to teachers who otherwise would have worked for lower wages; and
4. correspondingly, a cost of education that rose faster than enrollment.

Whereas state provision of public services is often associated with the ideology of the Social Democratic Party in Sweden, it is important to note that this educational system was already firmly in place when they took over the government in 1932.

Private Schools Today

The Socialists did, however, have different class interests in mind. Consequently, the Swedish school system has undergone a major democratization over the past two decades, eliminating the elitist character described earlier. A 9-year compulsory comprehensive school was introduced in 1962, followed by an integrated secondary school in 1971. Specialization still occurs at the secondary level, where 22 different "study lines" are offered; however, students in the vocational as well as the academic tracks qualify for university admission.

The higher educational system also underwent a major expansion in the 1970s, with new recruitment procedures instituted to attract working class children. Specifically, employment experience became a substitute for academic qualifications as a criterion for admissions to universities, all of which (except for the Stockholm School of Economics) are public. As a result of these reforms, 90 percent of each cohort stays in school until age 18 and one-third eventually go on to higher education.[11] Thus, education, including the secondary and university levels, is no longer the preserve of the upper class. How have the private schools fared as these changes have taken place?

On the basis of the earlier predictions, one might have expected an escape by the elite to the private sector at the secondary school level, where they could obtain the differentiated product of their choice in the face of a relatively uniform public system geared toward the middle and working classes. However, this did not occur, mainly because the other preconditions necessary for a flourishing private sector were not present. I have already discussed many of these factors in general terms. Here I simply mention those additional points that pertain particularly to the provision of education.

First of all, by the time the educational system was changed the distribution of income in Sweden had also been changed, by a combination of tax and transfer schemes, labor market policies, and general development. By the mid-1960s Sweden was one of the most egalitarian countries in the world; the remaining upper class was small, its disposable monetary income available for spending on private education, limited.

Second, some opportunity still exists for differentiation within the public sector. This includes choice of study line, selection of schools offering demanding study lines, and residential segregation combined with local control over schools.

Moreover, one must look at the interconnection between the various levels of education, since greater selectivity at higher levels, based on academic criteria, increases the incentive for the upper classes to utilize elite private schools at lower levels. Viewed from this vantage point, there is little reason for the upper classes to send their children to elite secondary schools, since this will not help them get into the public universities, particularly in view of the new "democratized" criteria for admission.

Added to all of these demand-side factors was a government policy that discouraged the supply of privatized public services. Contributions to such institutions are not tax deductible in Sweden, as they are in the United States, and strong social disapprobrium is attached to their use. Many private school staff members expressed to me (during interviews) that they felt harassed by government inspectors. In 1962 the Riksdag required that for private schools to get official recognition they must offer the same range of facilities as the public ones; schools with a narrow curriculum or selective student body would not be approved. Taken together with the shift toward comprehensive and integrated schools occurring in the public system, this raised the subject variety, minimum effective size and capital requirements in the private sector. As a result of all these forces, the number of private schools and their share of total enrollments has declined, rather than risen, over the past two decades.

Currently, less than 1 percent of all primary school children (appropriately 6000) are enrolled in 35 private schools in Sweden. The comparable figure is 2 percent at the secondary level, most of them in vocational schools connected to and partially supported by particular trades or enterprises. There are only 19 private academic secondary schools.[12] Thus, education is virtually a state monopoly in Sweden, a pattern that, as we have seen and tried to explain, was established much earlier.

What can we learn about nonprofit sector behavior by studying the few remaining private schools? The importance of cultural heterogeneity and religion is underscored by their nature and location: of the 35 private primary schools, 9 have a religious affiliation, 11 follow a foreign curriculum and use a foreign language as the medium of instruction, 10 practice the special Waldorf pedagogy, and 24 are in the two largest cities, where the greatest diversity is found, Stockholm and Gothenburg.

Many people I interviewed maintained that the demand for private education has been increasing over the past 15 years, allegedly because of dissatisfaction with the teaching methods and secularization (and perhaps the increasing heterogeneity) within the public schools. Most of the existing private schools report a large excess demand for student places, which they ration mainly on a first-come, first-serve basis: both price and ability rationing are frowned upon socially and raise the probability of closure by the government. Existing schools have not expanded, partially because of the capital requirements and implied cost discontinuities. Fifteen new schools were started during the 1970s to meet this increased demand—almost all of them associated with a religious or Waldorf group, which helped provide the organizational ability.

Private schools can utilize three conceivable financial strategies to survive:

1. they can charge a high tuition, equivalent, for example, to the average cost of educating a child in the public schools—19,600 kronor in 1979;
2. they can keep their costs lower than in the public schools and charge a correspondingly lower tuition; or
3. they can acquire a subsidy from the government or other sources, to help cover costs in lieu of tuition.

To investigate which of these strategies were actually utilized, I interviewed and obtained financial statements from 14 of the 17 private primary schools in Stockholm. I found that option #1 was utilized by only one school—a school that was used mainly by foreign diplomats and executives, who passed the high cost back to their embassies and transnational corporations. Apparently, Swedish households are simply not willing to pay high tuition given the availability of free public schools, so this is not a feasible survival technique for a private school.

Most private schools relied on option #2, economizing heavily on costs. Cost savings can imply technological efficiency, lower quality, or reduced remuneration to teachers and other staff. All three of these were used as cost-saving techniques by the Stockholm private schools. Most claimed they cut wasteful administrative expenses (e.g., by simplifying procedures and having one person double as instructor and headmaster), took better care of their books and materials, which could therefore be reused, and had less equipment and fewer specialized teachers. Volunteer parental labor sometimes replaced expensive hired labor for painting and other tasks. Most important, the Waldorf and religious schools (including all those started within the past decade) typically paid their teachers significantly less than the public system, nonpecuniary rewards apparently being large enough to compensate for their lower wages.

Although the private schools generally perceive themselves to be operating in a hostile environment, it is nevertheless true that they all receive some government support. As educational institutions, they are not required to charge the value-added tax on their product price, and they are exempt from property, income, and legacy taxes that other private organizations, including many NPOs, must pay. Children ride to school in public buses on special student passes. The municipalities usually provide school lunches, textbooks, and often low-rent buildings as well. The liberal Swedish welfare program means that low-paid teachers are eligible for housing grants, child care allowances, and other social benefits—an indirect subsidy.

Beyond these tax privileges and other indirect subsidies, five Stockholm schools receive direct state support to cover most of their teacher salaries.[13] These schools are also closely regulated, with respect to curriculum, total school time and its allocation among subjects, teacher salary scales, facilities, tuition fees, and selection procedures. Recently the government even claimed the right to assign students to the private vocational schools that it supported; some of these schools, and the companies that also supported them, seemed willing to forego the state subsidy rather than lose their control over admissions and future employment.

However, nonsubsidized schools also feel closely regulated and inspected, in order to qualify as "acceptable" during the obligatory school-age period. Although their curriculum and time allocation may diverge somewhat from that in the public sector, private primary schools must prepare their students for the public secondary schools they will often attend, private secondary schools must prepare them for the public universities, and both must orient their teaching toward the national exams. Moreover, they all feel that high tuition and selectivity are frowned upon in Swedish society, and the perceived threat of government harassment or enforced closure forces them to observe this social norm. Thus, constraints are implicit as well as explicit, informal as well as formal, and extend to nonsubsidized as well as subsidized schools.

In summary, almost all the private primary schools served some clientele that is differentiated along cultural or ideological lines, they charge only a modest tuition fee—far less than the per capita cost of public schools—and, if not heavily subsidized, economize by paying low salaries to their teachers. All receive some amount of state support, often indirect, and are subject to some degree of state regulation. But a small number are heavily subsidized and heavily regulated, and these regulations raise their salaries and per capita costs to parity with the public schools, unlike the nonsubsidized schools but very much like the heavily subsidized schools in other countries.

Adult Education

The one major exception to the virtual monopoly of state schools occurs in the field of adult education.[14] Adult education is an integral part of the educational-cultural-welfare sector in Sweden, much of it carried out in "study circles"—small groups that meet weekly to learn informally about a variety of subjects. Study circles are financed largely by the government but produced exclusively by 10 private nonprofit associations, the educational arms of the labor unions, churches, and political parities. This section explores some of the reasons for and consequences of the use of NPOs in this area. Briefly, because of the complementarity between adult education and the primary interests of their parent organizations, study circles are profitable activities for these associations in both pecuniary and nonpecuniary ways, and for the same reason they were an effective mechanism for the government to use to stimulate voluntary demand and supply.

To elaborate, in the first half of the twentieth century, before the government became involved, the Swedish "popular movements" were informally educating their members using a familiar Scandinavian technique: study circles with volunteer leaders. The trade unions imparted skills relevant to organizing and bargaining; the churches engaged in Bible study and choir practice; the political parties discussed current events.

State subsidies for study circles were instituted on a small scale in 1947–1948. To qualify for these grants, the study circle merely had to have 5 to 20 participants who met 20 hours or more spread over at least 4 weeks to study an agreed subject methodically with materials and a leader approved by an authorized "adult educational association." The latter point was fundamental: the associations, not the government, determined the content and teacher of the course and audited their branches to determine whether the minimal requirements just mentioned were met. These criteria and procedures remain today.

The first effect of (and perhaps the first reason for) the subsidy system

Table 1.4. Study Circles and Subsidies

Year	Number of Subsidized Study Circles	Study Circle Hours	Participants[a]	Total State Subsidies (in m. kr.)
1948	17,800		221,000	
1957	62,400		650,000	
1963	100,000	2,500,000	980,000	15
1967	130,000	3,355,000	1,260,000	
1973	244,000	7,020,000	2,327,000	215
1977	321,000	9,779,000	2,997,000	537
1979	334,000	10,814,000	3,036,000	768
1981	300,000	9,600,000	2,700,000	782

Source: Interview with Sten Ljungdahl, National Board of Education, Stockholm, who quoted from past government documents; and *Folkbildningsarbetet, Special Issue on Study Associations* (June–July 1976). The 15 million kronor figure for 1963 is my estimate, based on actual data for the Stockholm branch of ABF, which receives about 4 percent of the total subsidy. Numbers for 1981 were an estimate, made in 1982.

[a]This number includes considerable double-counting since individuals who participate in two study circles are counted twice. The actual number of discrete participants is probably less than half this number.

was to transfer some costs to the government, thereby relieving the organizations financially. As a second effect, study circles grew modestly during the 1950s, reaching a total of about 100,000 circles, with 1 million participants by 1963 (see Table 1.4). The largest subsidy (one-third of the total) went to the Workers Educational Association (ABF), the educational arm of the labor unions, the cooperatives, and the ruling Social Democratic Party.

In 1963 the government began a major expansion of its adult education program, as an important component of the burgeoning welfare state. At the same time that elementary schools became comprehensive and compulsary for 9 years, secondary schools became nonselective and integrated, plans were laid for a more open university system, and opportunity was also provided for the less educated older generation to "catch up." Particular efforts were made to attract target groups, such as immigrants, housewives, the handicapped, and the elderly and to teach basic job-related skills such as Swedish, English, math, and civics. Given the voluntary nature of these courses and the reluctance of some of these groups to participate, provision through organizations that had other connections with them in their daily lives seemed most likely to induce a large demand. To induce a large supply, a funding scheme was devised that was profitable to the organizations both financially and ideologically. The explosion of adult education that occurred during the 1960s and 1970s suggests that this was, indeed, a successful strategy.

Specifically, the state agreed to pay 75 percent of teacher and material costs, up to a specified limit per hour, for an unlimited number of hours, plus a bonus for high-priority subjects and target groups. The municipalities, too, paid varying stipends, including an imputed rental cost for building space owned by the associations and used for study circles. This system meant that, in the aggregate, over the next two decades, approximately 50 percent of total association costs were paid by the central government and 25 percent by local government, leaving only 25 percent to be covered by course participants and other private sources.

In effect, the government subsidies covered the incremental costs of each course and also enabled the organizations to earn a marginal "profit" that could be applied toward their administrative overhead and buildings, which were used jointly for other unsubsidized activities. For example, the 1979 annual report of the Stockholm branch of the ABF, the largest single "adult education" organization, showed total study circle revenues of 40 million kronor and direct outlays of 28 million—a profit rate of over 40 percent relative to marginal costs, which covered the fixed costs of the ABF build-ing and staff.

Furthermore, each circle offered by a union, church, or political party could carry its own ideological message—a form of nonpecuniary profit as well. Typically, each association has its own publishing company and bookstore, which could produce and distribute inexpensive public rela-tions literature for the parent organization once its fixed costs were cov-ered by the captive audience of course participants. As a result of these pecuniary and nonpecuniary motivations, the associations vigorously com-peted for students (using personal contacts, organizational connections, and newspaper advertising) and rapidly expanded their study circle hours, with the number quadrupling between 1963 and 1979.

The organizations were successful in attracting participants partially be-cause they provided variety, choice, and specializations geared to the inter-ests of their constituents. Although many associations produced the same circles in subjects such as art and literature, ABF developed special com-petence in teaching Swedish for immigrants, English, and social studies; TBV (the educational association of white collar employees) in vocational training; the Free Churches in religion and pedagogy; the Church of Swe-den in liturgical music and services. Typically, a medium-sized town (of 20,000 inhabitants) would have at least five associations, each with an office, paid staff, and dozens of study circles. The associations would be differentiated by course specialization, ideological emphasis, and a self-selection of students and teachers.

A common reason given elsewhere for provision through NPOs is the hope that they will contribute some of the resources, hence the service will cost the government less money than would direct public production. Al-though this may have been a motivating force in Sweden initially, it does not seem to have been an actual effect.

First of all, we have seen that all (marginal) costs were covered by the government and, in some cases, profits were earned to support other non-subsidized activities. Second, the decentralization within each organiza-tion, the multiplicity of organizations within each town, and the need to plan and certify for subsidy numerous small study circles meant that the associations necessarily incurred high administrative expenses. For example, in the Stockholm branch of ABF, 30 percent of the total wage bill goes to administrators, and the proportions are similar for other associations.[15]

In addition, the 1960s saw the shift from volunteer leaders to a paid professional staff. In the early years of study circle activity volunteers were used heavily as leaders, giving the organizations an apparent cost advantage. To expand their offerings rapidly, however, they hired part-time and eventually full-time leaders, for whom the government ceiling on reimbursed wages quickly became a floor. The need to use paid professionals was crucial for language courses such as English and Swedish for immigrants, but it became customary in other areas as well. The associations had little economic rationale or market ability to resist this development. In effect, the government subsidy set a lower bound on the demand for (marginal productivity of) labor in study circles, and employment expanded until the supply price reached this level. Thus, the number of study circles grew quickly but total costs and central government subsidies grew faster still.

Aggregate date on revenue and costs unfortunately is not available. However, annual reports for the Stockholm ABF show that, between 1963 and 1979, the number of their study circle hours rose threefold, total income and expenditures rose 16-fold, administrative salaries rose 18-fold, state subsidies rose 33-fold, and total teacher salaries rose 36-fold! Whereas at the margin of output and quality the higher wages may have been a necessary accompaniment of a rapid expansion rate, an inframarginal rent was probably received by many workers who would have led study circles for much lower pay. The Swedish experience with adult education is consistent with other observations in this study that, as government financing replaces private financing of a quasi-public good, consumers benefit from lower prices and higher output but producer-workers also benefit from higher earnings.

An addendum: in the 1980s, the Swedish government is trying to cut back on its welfare expenditures by encouraging greater administrative efficiency, reduced teacher salaries, and a return to volunteerism. A new incentive scheme, implemented in 1981, gives the associations a flat fee per hour, for a limited number of hours, regardless of costs incurred. Therefore, the central office of each association must allocate its quota of hours among the various branches and subjects; they also face pressures to cut costs by merger and use of volunteers. Many association managers believe that centralization and mergers will in fact take place. However, the full-time study circle teachers, now unionized, constitute a newly created group with common interests and powers to defend them; they are still demanding pay increases and resisting replacement by cheaper personnel. Therefore, the process seems (at least partially) irreversible, a return to volunteerism is highly unlikely, once a sector has become subsidized and professionalized.

SUMMARY AND CONCLUSION: SWEDISH–DUTCH COMPARISON

In summary, the nonprofit sector has been found to play only a small role in Sweden as a producer of quasi-public services (i.e., services that provide private as well as social benefits). The Swedish outcome is consistent with my initial hypotheses about factors that determine the public–private division of labor. In particular, the cultural and economic homogeneity within Sweden, the absence of a strong independent church, and the distribution of political power would lead us to expect a large public, small private sector in producing such goods, and this is an accurate description of the situation.

In Holland, where very different conditions prevail, the public–private division of production responsibilities is reversed. The extreme cultural heterogeneity, in the form of intensely held religious cleavages (between Catholics, Calvinists, and liberal Protestants) that characterized Dutch society at the turn of the century led to a highly privatized system in which the nonprofit sector produces most of the country's quasi-public goods— albeit financed almost exclusively by the government. NPOs produce approximately 15 percent of Dutch GNP and, in areas such as education, health, culture, and social services, their output is greater than that of the central and local governments combined.[16] Thus, whereas Holland and Sweden are both modern welfare states at roughly the same stage of development, with similar per capita incomes and relative size of government budgets (roughly two-thirds of the GNP in both cases), their mode of delivering services is totally different.

Although NPOs carry on few production activities in Sweden, they play an important role in the political process. There, they are key instruments in the two-way flow of information between government and individuals, which is considered a public good. This is compatible with the view that NPOs should be considered "interest-based communities" that compete with the usual geographically based communities for various social tasks. In the Swedish case geographical communities have clearly won out in the production sphere, but interest groups play a major institutionalized role in the political sphere. Indeed, representation and advocacy may be one of the most important functions of NPOs in the modern welfare state.

What can we learn from the Swedish experience about the behavior of NPOs? I return now to the questions raised at the beginning of the preceding part and, in answering them, compare Swedish with Dutch NPOs, drawing on my earlier paper for the latter.

In both Sweden and Holland, the private sector did indeed respond positively to increased demand, suggesting it is a viable mechanism for providing services under certain circumstances.[17] We observed this in Sweden in the case of secondary education for girls at the turn of the century and adult education today, in Holland when public subsidies became available to private schools in 1917 and social services after World War II. In both cases, most of the entrepreneurship came from institutions that already existed for some other, more basic, purpose rather than from individuals or spontaneous groups. It is interesting to note that, even in a secularized country such as Sweden, organized religion still plays an important entrepreneurial role in its nonprofit sector, albeit not as important as in Holland. The role of Swedish labor unions and political parties in sponsoring NPOs is less universal and suggests that the source of entrepreneurship may vary among countries depending on their most important long-term economic and cultural institutions. In any event, it appears that service provision through NPOs may not be viable in societies that do not have strong, independent, ideologically based organizations, particularly religious organizations.

As for the source of venture capital to NPOs, this is indeed a problem in the absence of a profit motive or return, which probably helps explain why private organizations have functioned best in labor-intensive areas where capital requirements are low. In some countries, funds for the nonprofit sector have come from wealthy institutions, such as the church in Latin America, or from wealthy individuals who have funded buildings or established foundations that then finance operating NPOs, as in the United States. But large donations are actually discouraged in Sweden, since they imply a trade-off of pecuniary wealth for status and control that are frowned upon by the Social Democratic ethos.[18]

Instead, in Sweden the government is the main source of capital to NPOs and this is usually provided in kind rather than in money, with ownership remaining in the public domain. For example, many private schools occupy buildings made available to them at low rental by their municipalities. In Holland, where NPOs are stronger, the government goes further still, constructing buildings and then turning ownership over to each private school. Both in Sweden and Holland, sports facilities are constructed and maintained by local governments but used by nonprofit sports organizations.

More generally, NPOs are heavily subsidized in most Western countries, able to flourish only if they are sanctioned by government policy. In Sweden NPOs play a large production role only in the areas of culture, sports, and adult education, where they are subsidized by the government.[19] This suggests that even when NPOs are substitutes for governments in production, the two sectors are complementary from a budgetary point of view: nonprofit activities increase when government spending rises, rather than the reverse. And together with this budgetary dependency often comes regulations that determine how the service is to be produced, at what cost, and who will benefit from it.

NPOs providing quasi-public goods in Holland and Sweden are limited in their capacity to charge high prices because of government regulation or competition from free government services. Therefore, those without large subsidies tend to produce at low cost with little opportunity for disguised profit distribution. In particular, low-paid or volunteer labor is often used. For example, low wages were paid to teachers at girls' schools prior to 1927, at private schools today, and volunteer leaders were used in the early years of study circles. Workers will remain at such jobs only if broader markets are closed to them (e.g., women teachers at the turn of the century), if there are large nonpecuniary rewards (as in sports), or if they are, in fact, doing this as part of their job for some other organization (e.g., a trade union or church). Since the availability of workers in these categories may be limited, the ability of NPOs to expand may also be limited, in the absence of government subsidy.

When government subsidies are instituted, the pecuniary marginal productivity of labor rises, market wages can be paid (indeed, this is often required as a condition of the subsidy), and rapid expansion is facilitated. This process could be seen to take place in the field of adult education in Sweden and primary–secondary education and social services in Holland. However, the inframarginal workers gain a rent—the subsidy constitutes, in part, a redistribution of income to them. Thus, both consumer and producer interests are involved in government subsidies to NPOs. Whereas the economic efficiency arguments are usually couched in terms of the former, the latter is at least equally important in the political process that creates and maintains these subsidies.

As a result of the higher wages and factor inputs, NPO costs may start from a low base but rise much faster than output when subsidies are instituted. This happened dramatically in adult education; it is also consistent with the large cost differential between subsidized and nonsubsidized primary schools in Sweden and the absence of cost differentials between public and subsidized private schools in Holland today. Whether quality rises as a function of these subsidies and costs is, of course, a key question that, unfortunately, I am unable to answer.[20]

A major reason given for reliance on nonprofit organizations in many countries (e.g., see the Badelt chapter in this volume) is that by tapping private revenue sources and utilizing lower cost production methods, this will save money for the public treasury. The experience of Sweden and Holland suggests that reliance on NPOs often implies heavy government subsidies, professionalization, and higher salaries; hence the initial costsaving is illusory and disappears in the long run.

An important issue that always arises when the privatization of education or other services is discussed concerns the degree to which this would lead to a social segmentation of society, in particular, a segmentation along class lines. It is true that any system that permits choice (including choice among various government institutions such as public schools) will cause people with like tastes to be grouped together. For example, students and teachers self-select themselves among the various adult educational associations in Sweden, depending on their political and religious ideologies. The extensive reliance on private schools in Holland has reinforced the religious segmentation within that society.

The social segmentation that results from choice among private producers of public services need not correspond to economic class segmentation, however. For example, the few private schools that exist today in Sweden tend to charge relatively low tuition, which would not automatically stratify along class lines; they do not provide elite education. This is partly because of government regulation against high tuition (in the case of subsidized schools) and partly because of social pressure and market competition. The private sector has not become an elite sector, also, because other opportunities for product differentiation exist for the upper classes within the public sector and because the higher educational system does not reward elitism in secondary schools. We found exactly the same situation, for very similar reasons, in the Netherlands, where private schools have captured 70 percent rather than 1 percent of the primary and secondary school enrollments.

It is indeed significant that in these two countries, which are at opposite poles in their public–private division of responsibility for producing education and other quasi-public goods, the actual operation of their nonprofit sectors exhibits striking similarities in several of the dimensions examined: source of entrepreneurship and venture capital, role of volunteerism and cost differentials, influence of government funding and regulation, impact on social and economic segmentation. This lends credence to the argument that general forces are at work stemming from the nonprofit institutional form—its origins and its interactions with the public sector—rather than from the unique circumstances of particular countries.

NOTES

1. Other papers in this study include Estelle James, 'The Non-Profit Sector in International Perspective: The Case of Sri Lanka," *Journal of Comparative Economics* (June 1982); (see chapter 12); "How Nonprofits Grow: A Model," *Journal of Policy Analysis and Management* (Spring 1983): 350–65; "Benefits and Costs of Privatized Public Services: Lessons from the Dutch Educational System," *Comparative Education Review* (December 1984); "The Private Nonprofit Provision of Education: A Theoretical Model and Application to Japan," *Journal of Comparative Economics* (September 1986): 255–76 (see chapter 2); "The Nonprofit Sector in Comparative Perspective" in *The Nonprofit Sector: A Research Handbook,* ed. W. Powell (New Haven: Yale University Press, 1987); "The Public/Private Division of Responsibility for Education: An International Comparison," *Economics of Education Review* (1987): 1–14; "Excess Demand and Private Education in Kenya," Program on Non-Profit Organizations working paper (New Haven: Yale University, 1986); "Differences in the Role of the Private Education Sector in Developing and Modern Countries," Dijon, 1986; "Public Policies toward Private Education," World Bank Discussion Paper, 1987; Estelle James and Gail Benjamin, *Public Policy and Private Education in Japan* (London: Macmillan, 1988); "Educational Distribution and Redistribution Through Education in Japan," *Journal of Human Resources* (Fall 1987): 469–89.

2. Some of the reasons why nonprofit organizations predominate over profit-maximizing organizations (PMOs) in the provision of quasi-public goods are discussed in Estelle James and Susan Rose-Ackerman, *The Nonprofit Sector in Market Economies* (London: Harwood Academic Publishers, 1986). Briefly, the latter can operate efficiently where private benefits and fee financing predominate; the former have a comparative advantage where social (external) benefits and voluntary donations play an important role. It is often argued that informational assymetry between producer and consumer leads to provision by NPOs, which are

considered more trustworthy than PMOs. This paper concentrates on the division between the government and the private nonprofit sector, rather than the division between the private NPO and PMO sectors.

3. The importance of heterogeneous preferences as a determinant of the size of the nonprofit sector was originally stressed by Burton Weisbrod, *The Voluntary Nonprofit Sector* (Lexington, Mass.: Lexington Books, 1977) and "Toward a Theory of the Voluntary Nonprofit Sector in a Three-Sector Economy," in *Altruism, Morality and Economic Theory* ed. Edmund Phelps (New York: Russell Sage Foundation, 1975) pp. 171–91.

4. For example, in two indices of ethnic and linguistic fractionalization presented in Charles Taylor and Michael Hudson, *World Handbook of Political and Social Indicators,* 2d ed. (New Haven: Yale University Press, 1972), pp. 271–74, Sweden ranked 73 out of 111 and 107 out of 136, respectively.

5. For example, according to data on sectoral income distribution reported in Taylor and Hudson, *World Handbook,* pp. 263–65, Sweden had a Gini Index of 5.6 and 46.5 percent was the smallest percentage of the population with half the national income, ranking 2 out of 52 countries in degree of equality, using these measures. (The U.S. ranked 8, with numbers of 12.2 and 42 percent, respectively.).

6. For basic data, see *Fact Sheet on Religion in Sweden,* published by the Swedish Institute, Stockholm.

7. Data are most readily available on central government subsidies to NPOs, their major source of finance. The main problem here is that definitions used in different government publications are not always consistent. For example, the category of "official institutions" in *Statiska meddelanden,* assembled by the National Audit Bureau, includes most but not all organizations that are listed as *ideel forening* or *stiftelse* in *Kulturstatistick,* published by the State Cultural Council and the Central Bureau of Statistics. The former also includes a few organizations that are labeled by the latter as *aktiebolag* or (partially) state-owned joint stock companies, which may not be subject to a zero-profit constraint. In this case, however, I used the Audit Department's definitions, since this was the only complete set of data for central government expenditures and transfers. Likewise, data on local government expenditures on culture given in *Kommunernas finanser 1979,* Central Bureau of Statistics, and *Kulturstatistik* did not always agree. Here, I used the former, which was the most comprehensive source for local government spending. Comprehensive data on local government subsidies to NPOs and private revenues (e.g., contributions, sales, interest, and rental income) were not available. Instead, I used various sources and methods for estimating these amounts, including government publications and annual reports of large organizations, as indicated in the footnotes to Table 1.1. Most of the numbers given, therefore, are not exact. In view of the magnitudes involved, however, the main conclusions reached in the text are not affected by these data problems.

8. However, the decision-making power of local governments should not be overestimated. Although they have their own taxing authority, they are heavily dependent on transfers from the central government—and these transfers often come with tight strings attached. For example, approximately half of local expenditures on education are paid centrally; in return, the municipalities must accept the headmasters and teachers assigned to them by central authorities, salaries are determined by national negotiations between the teachers' union and the municipal association, curricula is planned, in-service training conducted, and local schools inspected by a central administration that occupies several square blocks in Stockholm.

9. For further discussion of this role see, for example, Gunnar Heckscher, "Interest Groups in Sweden: Their Political Role," in *Interest Groups on Four Continents,* ed. Henry W. Ehrmann (Pittsburgh: University of Pittsburgh Press, 1958), pp. 155–73.

10. For the data on which this section is based, see *Elever I Icke-Obligatoriska Skolor, 1864–1970 (Pupils in Secondary Schools in Sweden, 1864–1970)* (Stockholm: Central Bureau of Statistics, 1977.

11. For a summary of these facts and other basic information about the modern educa-

tional system in Sweden, see the following: Sixten Marklund, *Educational Administration and Educational Development* (Stockholm: Institute of International Education, University of Stockholm, November 1979); Sixten Marklund and Gunnar Bergendal, *Trends in Swedish Educational Policy* (Stockholm: The Swedish Institute, 1979).

12. For a summary of the current situation regarding private primary and secondary schools, see Eugene Ekvall, *De Enskilda Skolornas Ställning Inom Utbildningsväsendet*, Swedish Government (Education Dept.) Report Ds U 1978:6; and *Fristående Skolor för Skolpliktiga Elever*, Swedish Government (Educational Dept.) Report SOU 1981:34. These are important government reports dealing with the position of private schools in Sweden. Also see Sixten Marklund, *Educational Administration*. For a list of the private schools, their location, affiliation, and year of origin see *Fristående Skolor*, p. 23.

13. The issue of state subsidies to private schools has been hotly debated in recent years and an increase has been proposed. See *Fristående Skolor*. The controversy stirred up by this proposal is indicative of the suspicious way private schools are regarded in Swedish society. In addition to Swedish government support, lesser amounts were also received from foreign governments, by the schools teaching their curriculum and language (e.g., the German, French, British, and American schools).

14. This section is based upon *Folkbildningsarbetet: Special Issue on Study Associations* (June–July 1976); *Fact Sheet on Adult Education*, (Stockholm: Swedish Institute); as well as annual reports of several adult educational associations, interviews with their leaders, and meetings with government officials dealing with adult education.

15. Based on the 1979 annual report of ABF as well as the reports of other associations.

16. For a fuller discussion of the Dutch situation see Estelle James, "Benefits and Costs of Privatized Public Services: Lessons from the Dutch Educational System," *Comparative Education Review* (December 1984); an expanded version was reprinted in *Private Education: Studies in Choice and Public Policy*, ed. Daniel Levy (New York: Oxford University Press, 1986). For further data also see Estelle James and Susan Rose-Ackerman, *The Nonprofit Enterprise in Market Economies*, a monograph in the Fundamentals of Pure and Applied Economics series, eds. J. Lesourne and H. Sonnenschein (London: Harwood Academic Publishers, 1986).

17. This finding is also consistent with data from other countries. For example, West discussed the growth of private education in nineteenth century England. See E. G. West, *Education and the State*, 2d ed. (London: The Institute of Economic Affairs, 1970). Pryor concludes that the elasticity of substitution of private for public expenditures in education is approximately unity—since centrally planned economies with a larger share of public financing and market economies with a larger share of private financing tend to spend the same total amounts on education, ceteris parabus. See Frederick Pryor, *Public Expenditures in Communist and Capitalist Nations* (Homewood, Ill.: Richard D. Irwin, 1968), p. 204.

18. See, for example, "Private Charity Going out of Style in West Europe's Welfare States," *New York Times* (June 30, 1978), p. 1, which describes how a proposed donation of a million kronors from King Gustaf Adolph to a national association for the handicapped was refused by the intended recipient on grounds that this was appropriately a government responsibility.

19. The fact that subsidies in and of themselves do not guarantee a large nonprofit sector is indicated by the experience of Denmark, another homogeneous country, although not as much so as Sweden. The Danish government liberally supports private schools, paying most of their operating costs, yet, only 10 percent of Danish children attend private schools, most of them associated with religious, political (socialist), or Waldorf groups. Apparently the cultural heterogeneity and supply of nonprofit entrepreneurship in Denmark are relatively small, so the overwhelming majority use public schools, despite the willingness of the government to support private schools. See Ekvall, *De Enskilda Skolornas*, pp. 7–9 and *Fristående Skolor*, pp. 29–32.

20. Adding to the cost problem is the possibility of excess entry, with each production unit too small to benefit fully from economies of scale, as seemed to happen in Dutch primary

schools and Swedish study circles. The government can minimize this problem by an appropriately designed subsidy-incentive system that encourages fewer and larger units—but, as discussed in my paper on Holland, NPO managerial objective functions may lead to results that do not lie along the cost-quality frontier.

REFERENCES

Arsbok för Sveriges kommunen. Stockholm: Statistiska centralbyrån, 1981.

Budget redovisning för 1979–80. Stockholm: National Audit Bureau.

Cultural Policy in Sweden—An Introduction. Stockholm: Swedish National Council for Cultural Affairs, 1979.

Ekvall, Eugene. De Enskilda Skolornas Ställning Inom Utbildningsväsendet. Swedish Government (Education Dept.) Report Ds U 1978:6.

Elever I Icke-Obligatoriska Skolor, 1864–1970 (Pupils in Secondary Schools in Sweden, 1864–1970). Stockholm: Central Bureau of Statistics, 1977.

Fact Sheet on Adult Education. Stockholm: Swedish Institute.

Fact Sheet on Local Government. Stockholm: Swedish Institute.

Fact Sheet on Religion in Sweden. Stockholm: Swedish Institute.

Folkbildningsarbetet—Special Issue on Study Associations (June–July 1976).

Fordelningen av driftbudgetens utgiften efter ändamål. Stockholm: National Audit Bureau, 1981.

Fristående Skolor för Skolpliktiga Elever. Swedish Government (Education Dept.) Report SOU 1981:34.

Fritidspolotik and Samhällsstod. Stockholm: National Youth Board, 1981.

Geiger, Roger. Private Sectors in Higher Education: Structure, Function and Change in Eight Nations. Ann Arbor: University of Michigan Press, 1986.

Heckscher, Gunnar. "Interest Groups in Sweden: Their Political Role." In Henry W. Ehrmann, ed., Interest Groups on Four Continents. Pittsburgh: University of Pittsburgh Press, 1958.

James, Estelle. "The Non-Profit Sector in International Perspective: The Case of Sri Lanka." Journal of Comparative Economics (June 1982): 99–122. (Chapter 12 in this volume.)

———. "How Nonprofits Grow: A Model." Journal of Policy Analysis and Management (Spring 1983): 350–365. Reprinted in Susan Rose-Ackerman, ed., The Economics of Non-Profit Institutions: Studies in Structure and Policy. New York: Oxford University Press, 1986.

———. "Benefits and Costs of Privatized Public Services: Lessons from the Dutch Educational system." Comparative Education Review (December 1984); expanded version in Daniel Levy, ed., Private Education: Studies in Choice and Public Policy. New York: Oxford University Press, 1986.

———. "Differences in the Role of the Private Educational Sector in Developing and Modern Countries." Paper delivered to the International Conference on the Economics of Education, Dijon, 1986. Also distributed as "The Political Economy of Private Education," World Bank discussion paper.

———. "Excess Demand and Private Education in Kenya," PONPO working paper. New Haven: Yale University, 1986.

———. "The Private Nonprofit Provision of Education: A Theoretical Model and Application to Japan." Journal of Comparative Economics (September 1986): 255–76. (Chapter 2 in this volume.)

———. "The Nonprofit Sector in Comparative Perspective" in W. Powell, ed., The Nonprofit Sector: A Research Handbook. New Haven: Yale University Press, 1987.

———. "Public Policies toward Private Education." World Bank discussion paper. Geneva: World Bank, 1987.

————. "The Public/Private Division of Responsibility for Education: An International Comparison." *Economics of Education Review* (1987): 1–14. Reprinted in Thomas James and Henry Levin, eds., *Comparing Public and Private Schools: Institutions and Organizations,* vol. 1. London: Palmer Press, 1988.

James, Estelle, and Gail Benjamin. "Educational Distribution and Redistribution Through Education." *Journal of Human Resources* (Fall 1987): 469–489.

————. *Public Policy and Private Education in Japan.* London: Macmillan, 1988.

James, Estelle, and Susan Rose-Ackerman. *The Nonprofit Enterprise in Market Economies,* a monograph in the Fundamentals of Pure and Applied Economies Series and *Encyclopedia of Economics,* eds. J. Lesourne and H. Sonnenschein. London: Harwood Academic Publishers, 1986.

Kommunernas finanser 1979. Stockholm: Statistiska centralbyrån, 1981.

Kulturstatistik. Stockholm: State Cultural Council and Central Bureau of Statistics, 1981.

Marklund, Sixten. *Educational Administration and Educational Development.* Stockholm: Institute of International Education, University of Stockholm, 1959.

Marklund, Sixten, and Gunnar Bergendal. *Trends in Swedish Educational Policy.* Stockholm: Swedish Institute, 1979.

Nilsson, Nils. *Swedish Cultural Policy in the 20th Century.* Stockholm: Swedish Institute, 1980.

"Private Charity Going Out of Style in West Europe's Welfare States." *New York Times* (June 30, 1978), p. 1.

Pryor, Frederick. *Public Expenditures in Communist and Capitalist Nations.* Homewood, Ill.: Richard D. Irwin, 1968.

Statliga Bedraq Till Folkrörelsen och Organisationer. Kommundepartementet Ds Kn 1978:1.

Statistiska meddelanden. Stockholm: National Audit Bureau, 1981.

The Swedish Budget. Stockholm: Ministry of the Budget, 1981.

Taylor, Charles, and Michael Hudson. *World Handbook of Political and Social Indicators,* 2d ed. New Haven: Yale University Press, 1972.

Utbildningsdepartementet. Stockholm: Statsliggaren, 1980–1981.

Weisbrod, Burton. "Toward a Theory of the Voluntary Nonprofit Sector in a Three-Sector Economy." In Edmund Phelps, ed., *Altruism, Morality and Economic Theory.* New York: Russell Sage Foundation, 1975.

————. *The Voluntary Nonprofit Sector.* Lexington, Mass.: Lexington Books, 1977.

West, E. G. *Education and the State,* 2d ed. London: The Institute of Economic Affairs, 1970.

Annual reports of private schools, adult educational associations and other organizations in Sweden.

2

The Private Nonprofit Provision of Education: A Theoretical Model and Application to Japan

ESTELLE JAMES

Why do some countries provide education and other quasi-public goods through government production while others rely heavily on the private sector? When private provision is used, why does the nonprofit organization (NPO) often prevail over the for-profit form? Why do nonprofits concentrate on the provision of quasi-public human capital–enhancing goods, such as education, health care, and other social services? The purpose of this paper is to examine these interrelated questions. In the broader study of which this paper is one part, I also examine what difference the choice of public versus private nonprofit management makes with respect to variables such as method of funding, quality, cost, efficiency, and distribution of services.[1]

The first section argues that the relative size of the private (nonprofit) sector is determined by excess demand and differentiated demand for quasi-

I wish to thank the numerous people in the United States and abroad who helped me with different aspects of the study that has been summarized in this paper. I especially appreciate the capable data analysis carried out by my research assistants, R. S. Huang and K. S. Lee, and helpful comments by Paul Gertler on an earlier draft. I gratefully acknowledge the financial support received for various parts of this study from the Exxon Education Foundation, the National Endowment for the Humanities, the Social Science Research Council, the Agency for International Development, the Netherlands Institute for Advanced Study, the Spencer Foundation, the American Association of University Women, and the Program on Non-Profit Organizations at Yale University. An earlier version of this paper was presented at the American Economic Association Meetings, December 1984. This paper is part of a larger work on Japanese education by Estelle James and Gail Benjamin, *Public Policy and Private Education in Japan* (London: Macmillan, 1988). The field work and analysis for the longer monograph were done jointly with Gail Benjamin, whose contributions to the ideas contained in this paper are gratefully acknowledged. This is a slightly revised version of a paper that was originally published in *The Journal of Comparative Economics* (1986):255–77. Copyright © 1986 by Academic Press, Inc. Reprinted by permission.

public goods emerging from a collective choice process, and by the supply of religious entrepreneurship in the society and industry under examination. The demand-side variables, initially set forth by Weisbrod[2] and developed further in this paper, explain why a private market exists for quasi-public goods. The supply-side variables help determine the size of the private market and also help explain why nonprofits are able to prevail over for-profits in the provision of certain goods, specifically those preferred by religious (ideological) entrepreneurs. To fix ideas, the analysis focuses on the case of education.

The second section applies this theoretical model to one country I have studied intensively, Japan. Demand- and supply-side variables are used to analyze why the size of the private (nonprofit) sector in education varies widely across the 47 Japanese prefectures. The results are consistent with our hypotheses and also throw light on the political economy of public–private choices. More tentative evidence suggests that the same framework will help us understand the role of the nonprofit sector and the public–private division of responsibility in other industries and countries as well.

DETERMINANTS OF THE PRIVATE SECTOR IN EDUCATION

The relative size of the private sector in education varies widely across countries, from 1 to 100 percent at the primary level, and from 2 to 92 percent at the secondary level. The range at higher educational levels is also substantial, although not quite as wide.

How do we explain this great diversity? Is the choice of system by country a random event, or are there underlying forces that enable us to predict its choice? In this section I suggest two sets of demand-side variables, excess demand and differentiated demand, that throw partial light on this question. These demand-side explanations view the private sector as a market response to a situation where large groups of people are dissatisfied with the amount or type of government production. A supply-side variable, the availability of (religious) educational entrepreneurs, adds further power to our explanation of the differential growth of the private sector. It also sheds light on why much private production in education is nonprofit, and why much nonprofit production is in education.

Excess Demand

In separate papers I develop more rigorously a model of demand-side forces that lead to the private provision of education and other quasi-public goods. I show in those papers that two different patterns of private education have evolved, depending on whether it is motivated by excess demand or differentiated demand. The former is more likely to be the source of private sector demand in developing countries, and the latter in advanced industrial societies.[3]

Excess demand for education may exist when the capacity of the public school system, as determined by a collective choice process such as majority voting, is less than full enrollment. Weisbrod set forth this idea in earlier work on the nonprofit sector and I develop it for the cases of uniform tax shares, varying tax shares, and equal and unequal production costs for the two sectors. The basic idea is that each person will vote to expand the public school system so long as his/her probable (external plus private) benefits from an incremental space exceed his/her tax share and equivalent benefits cannot be purchased more cheaply in the private market.

If the majority of voters (or the dominant political group) choose a public school system large enough to accommodate the entire population, then there is no leftover demand for the private sector. On the other hand, if the majority prefer a smaller public sector, then some people with private benefits greater than tuition may be left out, particularly if nonprice rationing is used. These people, for whom benefits exceed tuition but who cannot obtain a public school place, constitute the excess demand to which this paper refers, and they will enter the private sector.

From the above we can see that it does not make sense to talk of an excess demand model in countries, such as the United States, which have open access schools where a space is guaranteed for everyone. In open access schools overcrowding may result as demand grows so that the desire for quality may impel people to move to the private sector, but no one is left out. However, many countries limit the number of places in their public systems so that excess demand, as described above, can exist. We can see that the groups voting to restrict public education are those with low benefits or high taxes; government provision redistributes away from such groups. In addition, the number of people preferring a small public sector is larger if public production is more costly than private production; this may be due, for example, to bureaucratic rules, above-market civil service wages, and the deadweight loss from taxation. My empirical studies of private educational sectors indicate that the excess demand model applies in developing countries, where political coalitions of people with low benefits (from rural areas) and high taxes (from urban areas) often restrict the supply of government schools, particularly at the secondary and higher levels.

Differentiated Demand

A second demand-side model views private production as a response to differentiated tastes about the kinds of services to be consumed. The private sector then grows larger if people's preferences with respect to product variety are more heterogeneous and intense, and if these preferences are not accommodated by government production.

The differential demand model appears to explain the development of private educational production in modern industrial societies. Desire for cultural homogeneity is likely to be greatest at the primary level, for this is the age at which linguistic ability and religious identification develop and values are formed. However, residential segregation in public systems may accomplish this purpose better at the primary than the secondary level, since the catchment area is often larger for the latter. The partially counteracting effect of these two forces is predicted to lead to similar private sectors at the primary and secondary levels in societies where differentiated demand is the raison d'être for private education. These predictions are consistent with the empirical evidence, which shows that the primary and secondary private sectors are highly correlated and roughly equal in relative size in modern industrial countries, in contrast to developing countries where excess demand and private supply are concentrated at the secondary level.[4]

Differentiated demand for quality may also lead to the development of a private alternative if one group in society demands and is willing to pay for a better product than the median voter choice. Analysis of the impact of public school quality on private school enrollments is complicated by the endogeneity of quality choices, by the correlation of public quality with other variables that directly determine private sector size, and by the fact that variations in quality may be expected to have different effects in excess demand countries and differentiated demand countries. I have analyzed this issue at length in a separate paper, and discuss it more specifically when I present my empirical results for Japan.

Private Supply: Why Nonprofit?

Thus, demand-side variables explain why a private sector develops for the production of education and other quasi-public goods even when public schools are available. I emphasize supply-side variables in explaining how large the private sector grows and why it often takes the nonprofit form.

Observations from the United States as well as from other countries indicate that most founders of private schools (and other NPOs) are ideological organizations: political groups, socialist labor unions, and first and foremost, organized religion. Universally across countries, religious groups are the major founders of nonprofit service institutions. We see this in the origin of many private schools and voluntary hospitals in the United States and England, Catholic schools in France and Latin America, Calvinist schools in Holland, missionary activities in developing countries, and in services provided by Moslem waqfs (religious trusts), etc. Usually these are proselytizing religions, but other religious/ideological groups often must start their own schools as a defensive reaction (e.g., the "independence schools" in Kenya and the caste-dominated schools in India were started partly to provide an alternative to the Western mission schools). Typically such schools' costs of production are lower than those of government schools for reasons that are briefly discussed below. Their lower cost and potentially more rapid supply response mean that people are more likely to vote for a smaller public sector, and that excess or differentiated demanders are more likely to find an outlet in the private sector in countries with strong independent, proselytizing religious organizations competing for clients.

This simple observation, that religious groups are the major founders of private schools and other NPOs, has important implications for nonprofit theory. It explains why nonprofits are concentrated in areas such as education and health, and it suggests a particular reason why the nonprofit form was chosen by the founders. Their object was not to maximize profits but to maximize religious faith or religious adherents, and schools were chosen as the vehicle because they are one of the most important institutions of taste formation and socialization. The nonprofit form was chosen because the main objective was often not compatible with profit-maximizing behavior. For example, religious schools set up to keep members within the fold and/or to attract new believers may have to charge a price below the profit-maximizing level in order to compete with government schools and entice the largest number of students, subject to the constraint of covering their costs. That is, in one simplified version, such religious schools' objective may be to choose P to maximize $Q(P)$ subject to $PQ - C(Q) = 0$, and if potential profits >0, this may yield a P below the profit-maximizing level.

Once these religious schools are founded they have a comparative advantage over the profit-maximizing alternatives. First, they have a semi-captive audience; as discussed in the previous section, parents may prefer to send their children to school with a particular religious orientation. The service suppliers, the religious group itself, may "advertise" that this is a good thing to do. This semi-captive audience reduces such schools' risk in comparison to that faced by profit-maximizing schools. Second, some people may trust such schools and hospitals precisely because they are run by religious groups (i.e., because of their religious label, not their nonprofit label). Third, religious groups have, in the past, had special access to low-cost volunteer labor (e.g., priests and nuns) and donated capital, which have allowed them to undercut their secular profit-maximizing rivals and compete with government schools, even for students who do not have religious motivations. Fourth, once a school or hospital has been in existence for some time it may develop a reputation which allows it to continue attracting a clientele even if it later loses its cost advantage. Finally, the religious group may be politically powerful enough to secure government subsidies and to require that only nonprofits be eligible for these subsidies. Thus, the religious motive provides a powerful supply-side explanation for where private schools are found, why the nonprofit form is used, and how these institutions may compete effectively with both public and private profit-maximizing alternatives.[5]

STATISTICAL TESTING OF DEMAND AND SUPPLY EFFECTS: THE CASE OF JAPAN

Statistical testing of the demand- and supply-side hypotheses presented above is not an easy task. Ideally, if we attempt to explain the differential size of the private nonprofit sector across a large number of countries, we should have information, for each country, on the amount of government and private production; the quality, religious and linguistic orientation, and differentiation of public schools; the various indicators of quantity and quality demanded; the degree of cultural heterogeneity within the population, including the strength of religious and linguistic identification; the availability of (ideological) entrepreneurs; and the amount of governmental subsidy to existing and prospective private schools. In practice, these data are exceedingly difficult to obtain. Data gaps and definitional differences from one county to another make cross-national statistical analysis problematic, in general. In this case, uniform data are often not available on the degree of (religious and linguistic) differentiation within the public system, or on government subsidies to the private system. In addition, objective measures do not exist for some of the subjective variables we would want to include, such as "intensity of preference" for religiously differentiated schools. Moreover, the definition of public versus private is by no means an unambiguous concept. We really have a continuum of public and private funding and control, with different countries representing different points on this continuum.

To reduce these problems in statistical testing, I have focused on differences in private sector size across states or provinces within several countries. Results for Holland and the United States, which have been summarized in another paper, support the differentiated demand model presented in Section 2. Religious and ethnic differences, together with ability to pay for differentiated private education, are shown to explain interstate differences in private enrollments. The excess demand model is more difficult to depict, since it requires us to model collective choices about quantity of public education; this choice process may vary depending on the political system and method of public finance in each country. In this paper I develop at some length the case of Japan, arguing that differences in relative roles of the private sector across Japanese prefectures are a function of differences in their excess demand.[6]

Description of Japanese System

Over one-quarter of all high school (upper secondary) students and three-quarters of those in universities attend private institutions in Japan. This private education surely did not arise in response to differentiated demand since culturally and ethnically, Japan is one of the most homogeneous countries in the world. Instead, Japan is unique among modern industrialized countries in the degree to which it fits the excess demand model.

While Japan can hardly be characterized as a developing country today, it has made the transition to modern industrial state more rapidly and more recently than most Western countries, and the large demand-driven private education sector may be a legacy of earlier periods. In addition, since the end of World War II, Japan has been controlled by the conservative Liberal Democratic Party (LDP), which has maintained the lowest rate of government expenditures and taxation among modern developed countries. This policy of limited government production, as applied to education, meant that only the minimum quantity deemed necessary for national purposes has been provided publicly, while everything else has been considered a consumer good and left to private enterprise.

Public high schools and universities are not open access in Japan; a space is not guaranteed for everyone, nor is attendance compulsory. Instead, public spaces are limited, rationed by competitive exams, and generally filled to capacity. However, during the postwar period, private rates of return were high so that demand far exceeded the restricted government supply, as evidenced by high application rates, low acceptance rates, and intense pressures to pass the entrance exams. Public schools and universities became increasingly selective while the huge excess demand went to the less prestigious and growing private sector. Thus, private funding and management of secondary and higher education flourished, particularly in the past three decades.

To throw more rigorous light on the determinants of the size and nature of the private sector, this paper presents the results of a regression analysis based on prefectural data. In Japan there are 47 administrative units, or prefectures, which have very different public/private divisions of responsiblity for education and very different advancement rates to secondary and higher education. While elementary and junior high school levels are compulsory, attended by almost 100 percent of the age group, and are almost completely public everywhere, the proportion of students continuing to high school varies from 75 to 96 percent, and the percentage of high school enrollments in private schools varies from 2.2 to 55 percent, across prefectures. Similarly, the proportion of private university enrollments ranges from 0 to 91 percent. How do we explain these large differences?

I focus on explaining prefectural differences in the relative size of the private sector in secondary education. This level was chosen because elementary and junior high schools are almost completely public while the university level is characterized by substantial interprefectural mobility; i.e., higher education operates in a national and not a local market, and I am looking for local explanations and differences. Secondary schools are local, and large public and private school sectors co-exist, but to varying degrees in different prefectures. The text represents a verbal expositon of my model and results while all equations referred to in the text are presented in the Appendix.

The Model

My hypothesis is that the private sector in education arose in response to excess demand, which varied across prefectures [Eq. (1)]. First and most important, demand for education is higher in prefectures with high per capita income [Eq. (2)]. My reasoning is that education has a positive income elasticity of demand, ceteris paribus. These differences in income and demand were even greater in earlier years, when the development of the private sector took place. In addition, demand is expected to be higher in more urbanized prefectures with larger proportions of the labor force in secondary and tertiary industries, and hence greater rates of return to (and more incentive to acquire) education.[7]

The supply of public school places relative to total population[8] in each prefecture is modelled as depending on its per capita public budget for high school education (HSEDBUDG) and on its quantity–quality tradeoff [Eq. (3)]. While I do not offer a generic explanation of public school capacity and its relationship to per capita income, the particular method of local public finance in Japan leads to a situation in which the supply of public school places is not higher in wealthier prefectures and may even be lower. This is explained at length in the next section. In other words, I hypothesize that excess demand is a positive function of prefectural per capita income and a negative function of public sector size.

Differences in the supply of (religious) entrepreneurship to the private nonprofit sector are seen as another important explanatory factor [Eqs. (4a) and (4b)]. Finally, I show that the resulting public/private division of responsibility for education, and its differences across prefectures, is consistent with the interests and location of the main supporters of the ruling party, the LDP, and that their votes reflect the fact that their interests are being served [Eqs. (10a), (10b), and (10c)].

Public Quantity and Quality

I now discuss in greater detail the determination of public school quantity. Decisions about spending in secondary schools in Japan are left largely to the prefectures, although the central government controls matters such as curriculum, texts, and teacher qualifications. The question is, how do prefectures make decisions regarding the supply of public school places? If all prefectures made the same decisions—e.g., if the quantities supplied were imposed by the central government and were uniform for all (relative to population)—then we would simply expect the prefectures with higher incomes to have higher leftover demands and hence larger private school sectors. On the other hand, if prefectures were responsive to local conditions, we might expect those with higher demands to have a larger public supply, and hence the proportion left over for the private sector would be the same across prefectures. In fact, we find considerable variation across prefectures in percentage private, the implication being that different prefectures have different kinds of responsiveness to the demands of their constituents. That is what we must explain on the public supply side of the model.

I hypothesize that the supply of public school places is not a positive function of income and may, in fact, be negatively related. My reasoning is that

1. prefectural budgets for spending on public goods are largely independent of prefectural income, because of the particular method of public finance in Japan [Eqs. (5a)–(d)];
2. per capita spending on public secondary education actually declines with income, indicating that high-income prefectures prefer to spend their public budgets on primary education or other public goods [Eq. (6)];
3. however, the quality of secondary education (as measured by expenditure per student) is higher for high-income prefectures [Eq. (7)];
4. therefore, because of the quantity–quality tradeoff in the face of relatively fixed local budgets, the supply of public school places is a negative function of prefectural income [Eq. (8)].

Prefectural Budgets versus Prefectural Income
As noted above, one might expect supply to be positively related to per capita income in the prefecture, since PCI determines its local tax base. However, this relationship may not hold because of the method of local funding in Japan. While this paper does not aim to explain this method in great detail, the following stylized facts are relevant. Basically, prefectural funds come from two sources: local taxes and central taxes which are shared with prefectures on the basis of need. The latter, whose usage is not earmarked, constitute almost 40 percent of total prefectural budgets and go mainly to low-income prefectures. Thus, the supply of public goods, including educational expenditures, depends on local tax plus shared tax, the former positively and the latter negatively related to per capita income, so that the net impact of per capita income on educational expenditures depends on the relative strength of these two factors. This is largely an empirical question, since there is no strong theoretical reason to predict on a priori grounds which of these two effects will be larger.

I examined this question empirically by estimating the statistical relationship between per capita income and per capita taxes [Eqs. (5a)–(5d)]. As expected, I found that per capita income has a significant negative effect on per capita shared taxes and a significant positive effect on per capita local taxes. The effect on the two taxes combined is not significantly different from zero and the trade-off between the two taxes is approximately -1. That is, as per capita income rises, the shared tax declines but the local tax increases just enough to substitute for it, so that the total prefectural budget, and hence the supply of public goods, is largely independent of per capita income. Wealthier prefectures will not, in general, have larger budgets for public goods despite their greater demand.

Relative Income Elasticity of Public Education

Of course, if higher-income prefectures spend a higher proportion of their public budgets on education, this could still imply a higher educational budget per capita and a positive relationship between prefectural income and supply of public school places. On a priori grounds, there is no reason to expect such an effect. Upon statistical testing [Eq. 6], I found that spending at the secondary level does not increase and may decline as per capita income rises. Evidently, high-income prefectures choose to spend more of their public budgets on other public services. This may be partially due to the fact that wealthy prefectures have fewer children per family, but is also consistent with my hypothesis that they leave much of secondary education, a quasi-public good, to the private sector.

Supply and the Quantity–Quality Trade-off

Even if they had the same educational budget, we might expect wealthier prefectures to spend more on public quality and less on public quantity because of the positive income elasticity of demand for quality combined with the fact that if quantity is not provided in the public sector it can be obtained in the private sector. In that case, the supply of public school places would be lower but the total demand for education and therefore the leftover demand for private school places would be higher in wealthy Japanese prefectures.

When I tested these relationships empirically, I found that higher per capita income indeed leads to greater spending per student (a measure of quality) but fewer places in the public schools. (Note that this quantity–quality trade-off is the opposite of the situation in open access school systems with zero excess demand such as that in the United States, where higher quality may attract more people to public schools and hence may lead to a larger public sector and a smaller private sector.) Not surprisingly, a movement to a higher educational budget, ceteris paribus, exerts a positive influence on both quantity and quality [Eqs. (7) and (8)].

Thus, I would predict that, other things remaining constant, excess demand and private sector size will be larger in wealthy prefectures and in those with a small public budget for high school education.

Private Supply

So far, this section has viewed the private sector as a passive responder to excess demand. However, private schools are legally required to be nonprofits in Japan (as they are in many other countries); i.e., they are prohibited from distributing a monetary residual to their owners, and ownership cannot be sold for monetary returns. This means that the private sector will respond only if there are sufficient entrepreneurs willing to start schools for motives other than dividends or capital gains. I therefore considered the possibility that the availability of nonprofit entrepreneurship varies among prefectures, helping to explain the variation in the role of the private sector. How can we measure this potential entrepreneurship?

In my broader study I have observed that in other countries organized religion, particularly Christianity, plays an important entrepreneurial role in the nonprofit sector, and this appears to also be true in Japan. Christianity has typically used education as a taste-formation instrument, an important proselytizing tool. Christian missionaries have historically provided the capital, cheap labor, and organizing skills necessary to start private schools at low cost, and have also served as role models for indigenous educational entrepreneurs. Approximately one-third of the private schools and universities in Japan have been started by religious organizations, most of them Christian. I would, therefore, expect the private educational sector to be larger in prefectures with a large Christian missionary influence.

Government Subsidies

In many countries private education is heavily subsidized; i.e., while production is delegated to the private sector, much of the financing is still provided by the government. The availability of subsidies is an important additional variable to explain and to take into account in international and interstate comparisons of the role of the private sector. In the case of Japan, subsidies were not introduced until recently (the 1970s) but now exist to similar extents in all prefectures, cover a relatively small proportion of total costs (less than 30 percent) and appear to be accompanied by an agreement to stabilize sectoral shares at presubsidy levels. Therefore, relative size of the private system across prefectures in Japan can be modelled as independent of government subsidies. Instead, the subsidies can be modelled as flowing to schools in those prefectures which had a large preexisting private sector, for other more basic reasons.[9]

Results

Thus, the equations estimated had percentage of total high school enrollments in the private sector (%PVT) as a major independent variable. It has been suggested that private schools are more likely to develop in urban areas, where demand is concentrated, tastes and income are diverse, and entrepreneurship prevalent. To test for this possibility, two alternative exogenous "urbanization" variables were included: population per square kilometer (DENS) and percentage of population in dense areas (%DENS). To measure the impact of private (religious) supply, two alternative measures of missionary influence were used: percentage of Christian clergy relative to population (CHRCL), and a dummy for the presence of two or more Christian high schools prior to World War II (CHRSCH).

In some equations PSS and/or HSEDBUDG were added as independent variables, indicating the educational budget constraint and the quantity–

Table 2.1. Percentage of Secondary School Enrollment in Private Schools (%PVT) as Dependent Variable

Adj. R^2/F	Const.	PCI	DENS	%DENS	CHR[a]	PSS	HSEDBUDG	PUB	%ACPUB
.64 (42.51)*	−16.7 (2.72)**	0.026 (5.89)*			6.1 (2.95)**				
.5 (24.34)*	18.0 (15.23)*		0.004 (3.54)*		8.7 (3.7)*				
.49 (22.7)*	9.9 (3.27)**			0.25 (3.25)**	5.7 (1.88)***				
.64 (27.75)*	−18.1 (2.06)***	0.027 (4.12)*	−0.0003 (0.23)		6.2 (2.93)**				
.64 (27.84)*	−16.0 (2.49)***	0.025 (4.39)*		0.03 (0.38)	5.6 (2.21)***				
.64 (27.7)*	−17.0 (1.88)	0.026 (5.79)*			6.1 (2.82)**	0.001 (0.04)			
.73 (41.45)*	17.2 (1.64)	0.017 (3.61)*			6.1 (3.36)*		−0.01 (3.75)*		
.8 (60.55)*	47.4 (3.95)*	0.008 (1.69)***			3.7 (2.27)***			−11.8 (5.8)*	
.81 (39.9)*	23.0 (2.54)***	0.01 (2.22)***			4.9 (2.99)**	0.05 (4.21)*	−0.02 (6.14)*		−0.15 (2.34)***
.81 (41.15)*	60.3 (4.45)*	0.01 (2.17)***			4.8 (2.95)**	−0.008 (0.87)		−12.4 (6.3)*	−0.14 (2.24)***

	(1)	(2)	(3)	(4)	(5)	(6)	(7)	(8)
	.62	−29.6	0.031	200	0.01			
	(25.8)*	(3.63)*	(7.6)*	(2.38)***	(.63)			
	.71	9.2	0.022	216		−0.01		
	(38.8)*	(.88)	(5.06)*	(2.95)**		(3.8)*		
	.83	49.3	0.008	216			−13.2	
	(75.6)*	(4.52)*	(1.92)***	(3.85)*			(7.36)*	
	.83	16.4	0.011	213	0.06	−0.02		−0.12
	(44.83)*	(1.97)	(2.53)**	(3.75)*	(5.45)*	(7.24)*		(2.02)***
	.84	59.2	0.01	224	−0.005		−13.9	−0.11
	(49.2)*	(4.73)*	(2.4)***	(4.1)*	(.62)		(7.75)*	(1.98)***
Sample means %PVT = 22.7	1442	594	45.4	.3	563	1761	3.1	64.7

* = significant at .1 percent level.
** = significant at 1 percent level.
*** = significant at 5 percent level.

Note: One tail tests were used, except for constant.

[a]CHR = CHRSCH for first ten equations; CHRCL for last five equations. Mean CHRCL = .02.

quality trade-off in the public sector. In other equations PUB was added to show directly how excess demand declines as PUB increases. Finally, I argued that the private sector arises mainly from excess demand for pre-university education. If this is so, %PVT should be smaller when the academic share of public school places (%ACPUB) is high and the vocational share low; I test this by including %ACPUB in my full equations. Appendix 2 gives some comments on my statistical methodology. What did I find? The key results are presented in Table 2.1.

First, per capita income is indeed positive and significant in all formulations. In the two-variable equation with PCI and CHRSCH or CHRCL, a high PCI signifies a high demand for education and also serves as a proxy for a low public supply stemming from a choice of quality over quantity. When PUB, PSS, and HSEDBUDG are added as explanatory variables, only the demand function remains for PCI, and its size and significance therefore decline.

Relatedly, the "urbanization" variables are significant when added as a second variable (to CHRSCH) but not when added as a third variable (to CHRSCH and PCI). We may infer, then, that density and urbanization do help to explain the development of a private sector in education but much of this operates through their correlation with per capita income, which also appears to be true in other countries I have studied.

As expected, PUB is always negative and highly significant.[10] The same is true (but to a slightly lesser extent) of %ACPUB. HSEDBUDG, too, is significant and negative, consistent with the prediction that a larger HSEDBUDG implies a larger supply of public school places, hence a smaller leftover demand for the private sector. The impact of PSS is somewhat more complicated. To the degree that some people opt for the private sector because of low quality in the public sector, PSS would be expected to exert a negative influence on %PVT. This appears to be the case, for example, in regressions run for the United States. On the other hand, it was argued earlier that the public sector in Japan is generally considered the high-quality sector and is usually filled to capacity; people do not opt out to get higher quality. Moreover, as seen, higher public quality is associated with lower public quantity, ceteris paribus. If this is so, %PVT would be expected to be a positive function of PSS if HSEDBUDG is controlled. But if HSEDBUDG is not controlled, a high PSS could either be a proxy for a high HSEDBUDG or could signify a choice of quality over quantity along a given HSEDBUDG, the former leading to a low %PVT, the latter leading to a high %PVT. So, if these two effects cancel each other out, the impact of PSS would not be significantly different from zero. Also, once PUB is controlled PSS should not have a significant effect. The results were consistent with these expectations. When HSEDBUDG was in the model, PSS was significantly positive, but when HSEDBUDG was taken out or PUB was put in, PSS became insignificant, as expected.[11]

As for the two "religion" variables, CHRCL and CHRSCH, these were considered as alternatives. CHRCL was usually significant, CHRSCH always significant, and their quantitative effects were very similar. In the two-variable models, CHRSCH yielded the highest R^2, but in the three- or four-variable models, CHRCL gave the best fit. CHRSCH, the existence of at least two Christian high schools before World War II, explicitly captures and emphasizes a historical element, suggesting that the private sector tended to perpetuate itself, if started early, before the rapid growth of government schools. We also experimented with percent of the population that is Christian as the "religion" variable. This did not turn out to be significant, although the presence of Christian clergy or early Christian schools was significant. Also, %PVT enrollments is a much larger number than percentage of the population that is Christian (about 1 percent). Both these observations are consistent with our interpretation that in Japan religion is operating as a supply-side rather than a demand-side variable. Several results with CHRSCH and CHRCL are presented in Table 2.1.

The two equations that are most enlightening and consistent with our model are:

$$\%PVT = 23.0 \ + \ 0.01 \ PCI \ + \ 4.9 \ CHRSCH \ - \ 0.02 \ HSEDBUDG$$
$$(2.54)^{***}(2.22)^{***} \quad (2.99)^{**} \quad\quad (6.14)^{*}$$
$$+ \ 0.05 \ PSS \ - \ 0.15 \ \%ACPUB \quad R^2 = .81$$
$$(4.21)^{*} \quad (2.34)^{***}$$

$$\%PVT = 59.2 \ + \ 0.01 \ PCI \ + \ 224 \ CHRCL \ - \ 13.9 \ PUB \ - \ .005 \ PSS$$
$$(4.73)^{*} \ (2.4)^{***} \quad\quad (4.1)^{*} \quad\quad (7.75)^{*} \quad\quad (.62)$$
$$- \ 0.11 \ \%ACPUB \quad R^2 = .84$$
$$(1.98)^{***}$$

(See Table 2.1 for significance levels denoted by asterisks.) These equations demonstrate that high demand (from PCI), low public supply (from a combination of PUB and %ACPUB or from HSEDBUDG and PSS), and a large supply of nonprofit entrepreneurs (from CHRSCH or CHRCL) all lead to a large private sector, as predicted. These results are also consistent with similar regressions we ran for the United States, Holland, and India, in which per capita income and religious variables always play a major role in explaining why the size of the private sector varies across states, and with cross-national regressions, in which stage of development, religious heterogeneity, and public supply explain differences among countries.

The Political Economy of Shared and Local Taxes

We return now to the crucial questions of (1) why the rich prefectures do not raise their taxes and thereby provide more public quantity as well as quality, and (2) why the poor prefectures are able to get so much transferred taxes for public goods from the central government. Several explanations occur, and the main ones are consistent with the collective choice model presented in Section 2 which argues that public/private outcomes are consistent with the interests of the dominant political group.

Regarding the first question, early development of the private sector may have served as an escape valve in wealthier prefectures, diminishing the political pressure for more public spending and production. Also, interprefectural mobility may limit the ability of one prefecture to raise its taxes relative to others; people in high tax brackets may simply be driven out of the prefecture if they value low taxes more than public goods. Moreover, wealthy prefectures may fear that a rise in local taxes and expenditures would increase the defined level of need elsewhere, and hence would increase the shared tax that is tranferred away from them. To the degree that the need for shared taxes is deemed to be inversely related to local taxes, there is little incentive to impose the latter.

Most important, as shown in another paper, educational expenditures in Japan represent a redistribution from the rich to the poor, i.e., the tax share of the rich is high and far exceeds their enrollment share.[12] The upper classes, therefore, would resent higher local taxes that would permit both quantity and quality. This group gains if taxes, and hence subsidies to others, are kept low, even if this means they must buy their own education privately. The fact that wealthier prefectures do not have larger public educational budgets suggests that the upper classes (e.g., top managers and proprietors) have enough political power to prevent large-scale income redistribution within their localities. The fact that quality is chosen over quantity in these prefectures is also consistent with their preferences; it enables the upper classes to use the public schools.

In contrast, our analysis of shared taxes shows that the poor prefectures, which tend to be rural, have enough political power to secure a redistribution from rich urban prefectures; their ability to do so is enhanced by the fact that they are overrepresented (relative to population) in the powerful Japanese Diet (Parliament). This redistribution allows them to provide education (and other quasi-public goods) publicly, at no cost to them, rather than privately. Conversely, since they have obtained the redistribution, one would expect them to be pleased with the central government. Therefore, we would expect support for the ruling party, the LDP, to be negatively correlated with prefectural income and with percentage private education, and positively correlated with per capita shared tax; indeed, this is the case. Regressions with "% voters supporting LDP in the 1980 elections" (%LDP) as the dependent variable, and with per capita income, %PVT, and per capita shared tax as the independent variables, have coefficients which are negative, negative, and positive, respectively. When all three variables were included in the same equation, each had the right sign but none was significant, although the combined R^2 was 0.44 and the F test indicated that the results as a whole were significant ($F = 11.36$)—a finding that is associated with collinearity. When they were run in three separate equations, all coefficients were highly significant—consistent with our view that these effects are strong, not additive, but simply different ways of saying the same thing [Eq. (10a)–(10c)].

Thus, the wealthy urban prefectures satisfy their demand for education and other quasi-public goods privately to limit redistribution within their borders, while the poorer rural districts provide their education publicly with "free" funds supplied by others, a beneficial arrangement which is consistent with their support of the party in power, the LDP. Ironically, the more conservative prefectures (i.e., those supporting the LDP) therefore end up having a relatively large public sector, while the less conservative prefectures have a larger private sector.

By the late 1960s, Japan's industrial base had developed, the LDP's agricultural stronghold had declined, and its elected majority had reached the lowest point since World War II. In effect, the median voter had shifted from countryside to city, the urban working class had increased, and to stay in power the LDP had to respond to a new set of political preferences. Spurred by these developments, the government undertook a major reexamination of its policies in the field of education and social welfare, culminating in a decision to increase expenditures in these areas. Both central and prefectural funding was involved. However, the increases in education took the form of subsidies to private high schools and colleges, rather than increased public production. In fact, the subsidies seem to have been accompanied by an implicit decision to stabilize sectoral shares. Since the subsidies covered only a part (up to 30 percent) of private sector costs but played a crucial role in keeping many institutions alive, a larger number of people reap their benefits than would have been the case if the same amount of money had been spent on the full funding of new public school places. Presumably, this was deemed to be in the vote-maximizing interest of the LDP.

CONCLUSION

This paper has addressed two related issues: which factors determine the public-private division of responsibility for quasi-public goods, and which factors determine the relative role of the nonprofit sector, across countries and industries? These questions are joined because the private supply of quasi-public goods, such as education and health care, is often nonprofit, nonprofits concentrate on the production of such goods, and the nonprofit sector tends to be large in countries with a large private sector providing such goods.

I have emphasized supply-side (entrepreneurship) variables in analyzing the industries in which nonprofits are found. Observations from the United States as well as from other countries indicate that many NPO founders were religious organizations whose objective was maintaining and increasing their adherents rather than maximizing profits. I argue that this simple observation goes far toward explaining why they chose the nonprofit form and why they operate in taste formation or in crucial life and death situations such as schools and hospitals. Their access to low-cost labor, e.g., priests and nuns, and their religious "brand name" gave them an advantage over secular PMOs once they entered these industries. Thus, a theory based on religious source and ideological motivation of entrepreneurship is offered in place of theories that stress lack of consumer information about output characteristics in explaining the services that nonprofits provide.

These services also tend to be quasi-public goods, i.e., goods which get parcelled out, yield both private and public benefits, and hence are often provided by government. Thus, the nonprofit entrepreneurs must compete with government services, which usually have a price advantage over NPOs. This paper argues that the private sector flourishes where excess demand exists, in the face of limited government production, or where intensely felt preferences over product variety (religious, linguistic) make people willing to pay a higher price in the private sector. I hypothesize that excess demand is particularly common in developing countries at the secondary and higher levels, while private education at the primary level, and in modern industrial societies, is often due to differentiated demand. These variables explain why and when a demand exists for the private production of quasi-public goods, and the differential availability of (religious) entrepreneurship explains further why the private supply response varies across countries, often taking the nonprofit form.

The empirical evidence from Japan, presented in this paper, is consistent with this model. While Japan is clearly a modern industrial state, it made the transition more rapidly and more recently than most Western countries and still exhibits some characteristics of a developing society, including a demand-driven private sector in education. In Japan we observed that a political coalition of low demanders and high taxpayers produced a policy of limited government spending, leaving an excess demand for education at the secondary and higher levels that was filled by the private sector. When differences across Japanese prefectures were analyzed, indicators of excess demand and religious entrepreneurship were found to be positively related to the relative role of private nonprofit production. Elsewhere I have reported evidence of differentiated demand-driven private education in the United States, Holland, and Sweden, with religious entrepreneurship again playing an important supply-side role. This model now needs to be tested within and across a larger set of countries, and that is my next step.

APPENDIX 1

List of Symbols and Data Sources

D   = total demand for education
DPRIV   = excess demand for education

URB = index of urbanization

SPRIV = supply of private school places

REL = index of religious entrepreneurship

%LDP = percent voters supporting LDP in 1980 election (*Japan Statistical Yearbook*. Tokyo: 1982).

PCI = per capita income, 1979, in thousand yen (*Japan Statistical Yearbook*. Tokyo: 1982, p. 545).

PCSHT = per capita shared tax, 1979, in thousand yen (*Japan Statistical Yearbook*. Tokyo: 1982, pp. 520–22).

PCLT = per capita local tax, 1979, in thousand yen (*Japan Statistical Yearbook*. Tokyo: 1982).

PCT = per capita shared plus local tax, 1979, in thousand yen (*Japan Statistical Yearbook*. Tokyo: 1982).

HSEDBUDG = spending in public high schools per hundred population, 1979 (*Japan Statistical Yearbook*. Tokyo: 1982).

PSS = per student spending in public high schools, 1979, in thousand yen (*Japan Statistical Yearbook*. Tokyo: 1982, p. 644). This is used as an index of quality.

%PVT = percent of total high school enrollment in private schools, 1980 (*Summary of Education Statistics*. Tokyo: Mombu tōkei yōran, Ministry of Education, 1982, pp. 126–81).

CHRSCH = dummy for presence of two or more Christian schools at junior high school level or above, prior to World War II (*Christian Education in Japan*. Report of the Committee on International Missionary Council, 1932).

CHRCL = percent of Christian clergy relative to population, 1980 (*Japan Statistical Yearbook*. Tokyo: 1982, pp. 16, 670–71).

DENS = population per square kilometer, 1981 (*Japan Statistical Yearbook*. Tokyo: 1982, p. 6).

%DENS = percent of population in densely populated areas, 1980 (*Japan Statistical Yearbook*. Tokyo: 1982).

PUB = number of public high school students (1980) per hundred population (1979) (*Summary of Educational Statistics*. Tokyo: Mombu tōkei yōran, Ministry of Education, 1982, pp. 120–23; and *Japan Statistical Yearbook*. Tokyo: 1982, p. 6).

% ACPUB = proportion of public school places in academic rather than vocational courses, 1981 (*Report on Survey of School Standards*. Tokyo: 1982, pp. 200, 201, 243, 250).

Note: All data are averages denoted by prefecture.

Equations

$$DPRIV = D\text{-}PUB \tag{1}$$
$$D = D(PCI, URB) \tag{2}$$
$$PUB = P(PSS, HSEDBUDG) \tag{3}$$
$$\%PVT = f(DPRIV, SPRIV) \tag{4a}$$
$$= g(PCI, URB, HSEDBUDG, PSS, REL). \tag{4b}$$

$$PCSHT = 286 \quad -0.13(PCI)$$
$$(12.18)^* \quad (8.3)^* \qquad R^2 = 0.61 \tag{5a}$$

$$PCLT = -58 + 0.11(PCI)$$
$$(4.54)^* \quad (12.18)^*$$
$$R^2 = 0.78 \quad (5b)$$

$$PCT = 207 - 0.01(PCI)$$
$$(8.48)^* \quad (0.6)$$
$$R^2 = 0.01 \quad (5c)$$

$$PCSHT = \frac{206}{(12.98)^*} \quad \frac{-1.1(PCLT)}{(8.9)^*}$$
$$R^2 = 0.64 \quad (5d)$$

$$HSEDBUDG = 2945 - 0.816(PCI) + 0.027(PCT)$$
$$(7.6)^* \quad (4.93)^* \quad (0.02)$$
$$R^2 = 0.36 \quad (6)$$

$$PSS = -17.16 + 0.22(PCI) - 0.225(PCT) + .173(HSEDBUDG)$$
$$(0.14) \quad (5.04)^* \quad (0.73) \quad (5.42)^*$$
$$R^2 = 0.45. \quad (7)$$

$$PUB = 3.12 - 0.001(PCI) + 0.001(PCT) + 0.001(HSEDBUDG)$$
$$(4.9)^* \quad (5.04)^* \quad (.81) \quad (4.94)^*$$
$$R^2 = 0.75. \quad (8)$$

$$\%PVT = 23.0 + 0.01(PCI) + 4.9(CHRSCH) - 0.02(HSEDBUDG)$$
$$(2.54)^{***} \quad (2.22)^{***} \quad (2.99)^{**} \quad (6.14)^*$$

$$+ 0.05(PSS) - 0.15(\%ACPUB)$$
$$(4.21)^* \quad (2.34)^{***}$$
$$R^2 = 0.81. \quad (9a)$$

$$\%PVT = 59.2 + 0.01(PCI) + 2.24(CHRCL) - 13.9(PUB)$$
$$(4.73)^* \quad (2.4)^{***} \quad (4.1)^* \quad (7.75)^*$$

$$- 0.005(PSS) - 0.11(\%ACPUB)$$
$$(.62) \quad (1.98)^{***}$$
$$R_2 = 0.84 \quad (9b)$$

$$\%LDP = 104 - 0.04(PCI)$$
$$(5.4)^*$$
$$R^2 = 0.35 \quad (10a)$$

$$\%LDP = 70 - 0.76(\%PVT)$$
$$(4.7)^*$$
$$R^2 = 0.33 \quad (10b)$$

$$\%LDP = 35 + 0.2(PSCHT)$$
$$(5.0)^*$$
$$R^2 = 0.36 \quad (10c)$$

Numbers in parentheses are t statistics. A single asterisk (*) indicates that the coefficients are significant at the .1 percent level or better; a double asterisk (**) indicates significance at the 1 percent level; and a triple asterisk (***) at the 3 percent level.

APPENDIX 2: STATISTICAL METHODOLOGY

One theoretical problem with estimating %PVT directly, using a linear probability model, is that the predicted value of %PVT may be >1 or <zero for some prefectures, even though the actual value can never be >1 or <zero. In reality this did not turn out to be a problem for me since it only occurred twice in all my regressions, and then only by very small negative amounts.

Because of this possible problem another technique, known as logit analysis, is sometimes used in situations where probabilities are being estimated. In logit analysis we estimate the log of the odds of %PVT, $LOP = \ln [\%PVT/(1 - \%PVT)]$. Then, the predicted value of $\%PVT = 1/[1 + e^{-E(LOP)}]$, which can never be >1 or <zero. I used both methods and found they gave very similar results.

I also found that a statistical problem known as heteroscedasticity was present in the logit model, which I corrected for using the weighted least squares method. This changed the coefficients slightly but it did not change any of the results regarding statistical significance. Heteroscedasticity was not present in the linear probability model.

In this paper, I present the results of my estimation of %PVT using the linear probability model. This is the most direct method and it happens to give the best fit in this case. Since practically none of the predicted values were out of bounds and since heteroscedasticity was not present, this method seems superior to the logit method for my purposes—but my basic conclusions would not change if I used the logit model, with either weighted or unweighted data.

NOTES

1. See Estelle James, "The Non-Profit Sector in International Perspective: The Case of Sri Lanka," *Journal of Comparative Economics* (June 1982): 99–122; "How Nonprofits Grow: A Model," *Journal of Policy Analysis and Management* (Spring 1983): 350–65; "Benefits and Costs of Privatized Public Services: Lessons from the Dutch Educational System," *Comparative Education Review* (December 1984); "The Nonprofit Sector in Comparative Perspective," in *The Nonprofit Sector: A Research Handbook*, ed. W. Powell (New Haven: Yale University Press, 1987); "The Public/Private Division of Responsibility for Education: An International Comparison," *Economics of Education Review* (1987): 1–14; "Excess Demand and Private Education in Kenya," PONPO working paper (New Haven: Yale University, 1986); "Institutional Choice in the Education Industry," paper delivered to the International Workshop on Institutional Choice, Vienna, 1987; "Public Policies Toward Private Education," World Bank discussion paper, 1987; Estelle James and Gail Benjamin, "Educational Distribution and Redistribution through Education," *Journal of Human Resources* (Fall 1987): 469–489; *Public Policy and Private Education in Japan* (London: Macmillan, 1988); Estelle James and Susan Rose-Ackerman, "The Nonprofit Enterprise in Market Economies," a monograph in the Fundamentals of Pure and Applied Economics Series (London: Harwood Academic Publishers, 1986).

2. See Burton Weisbrod, "Toward a Theory of the Voluntary Nonprofit Sector in a Three-Sector Economy," in Edmund Phelps, ed., *Altruism, Morality and Economic Theory* (New York: Russell Sage Foundation, 1975); *The Voluntary Nonprofit Sector* (Lexington, Mass.: Lexington Books, 1977).

3. James, "Public/Private Division of Responsibility,"; "Institutional Choice."

4. James, "Institutional Choice."

5. For further development of this point, see James, "Nonprofit Sector in Comparative Perspective"; James and Rose-Ackerman, "Nonprofit Enterprise."

6. The statistical analysis of Japan presented in this paper is based on a much larger study of the role of the private sector in Japanese education by James and Benjamin, *Public Policy and Private Education in Japan*. Results for other countries are summarized in James, "The Public/Private Division of Responsibility."

7. The demand for higher education is also positively related to income if higher education is a normal good. In this paper I do not attempt to explain perfectural differences in public and private university enrollments. Here I simply note that since the desire to attain college admission provides a motivation for attending a private high school if a public school place is not available, this demand for university education translates into a demand for private high school education in high-income prefectures.

8. It would have been preferable to define supply as number of public places per hundred in the relevant age group. However, this latter statistic was not available by prefecture. Prefectures with declining family size or with large inflow of working-age people would be seen

to have a larger supply relative to the relevant age group if this figure could have been obtained.

9. For further discussion of government subsidies in Japan, see James and Benjamin, *Public Policy and Private Education in Japan.*

10. PUB was interpreted here as an indication of public supply, since the full-time public high schools are filled to capacity, in contrast to the situation in open access systems, where PUB would indicate the demand for public education rather than the supply. Thus, in Japan the negative effect of PUB is interpreted as evidence of excess demand, whereas in open access systems it indicates differentiated demand. In either case, in a situation where most age-eligible students attend high school, a smaller attendance in public schools necessarily implies larger private enrollments, so the significance of PUB and the high R^2 in equations with PUB is not as interesting as the significance of other variables and high R^2 of other equations.

11. It is important to note that I have treated PSS as a positive indicator of quality, not a negative indicator of efficiency. It would have been useful to include in this regression an indicator of the relative costs of providing equal-quality public and private education. As shown in James and Benjamin, *Public Policy and Private Education in Japan,* expenditures per student in private schools have been 70 to 90 percent of those in public schools. According to the model presented in Section 2, the smaller is this percentage, the larger is the number of voters who would opt for a small public system if quality is the same in the two sectors. I could not include this efficiency indicator because data on PSS in private schools were not available by prefecture. In addition, a lower ratio of private to public PSS may indicate that private quality is less, not that efficiency is greater. See James and Benjamin for a fuller discussion of these issues.

12. James and Benjamin, "Educational Distribution and Redistribution."

REFERENCES

Goldberger, A. S., *Econometric Theory.* New York: Wiley, 1964.

James, Estelle. "How Nonprofits Grow: A Model." *Journal of Policy Analysis and Management* (Spring 1983): 350–65; reprinted in Susan Rose-Ackerman, *The Economics of Non-Profit Institutions: Studies in Structure and Policy.* New York: Oxford University Press, 1986.

———. "The Non-Profit Sector in International Perspective; The Case of Sri Lanka." *Journal of Comparative Economics.* (June 1983): 99–122. (Chapter 12 in this volume.)

———. "Benefits and Costs of Privatized Public Services: Lessons from the Dutch Educational System." *Comparative Education Review* (December 1984); expanded version reprinted in Daniel Levy, ed., *Private Education: Studies in Choice and Public Policy.* New York: Oxford University Press, 1986.

———. "Excess Demand and Private Education in Kenya." PONPO working paper. New Haven: Yale University, 1986.

———. "The Nonprofit Sector in Comparative Perspective." in W. Powell, ed., *The Nonprofit Sector: A Research Handbook.* New Haven: Yale University Press, 1987.

———. "Institutional Choice in the Education Industry." Paper delivered at the International Workshop on Institutional Choice, Vienna, 1987.

———. "Public Policies toward Private Education." World Bank discussion paper. Washington: World Bank, 1987.

———. "The Public/Private Division of Responsibility for Education: An International Comparison." *Economics of Education Review* (1987): 1–14; reprinted in Thomas James and Henry Levin, eds., *Comparing Public and Private Schools: Institutions and Organizations,* vol. 1. London: Falmer Press, 1988.

James, Estelle, and Gail Benjamin. "Educational Distribution and Redistribution through Education." *Journal of Human Resources* (Fall 1987): 469–489.

————. *Public Policy and Private Education in Japan*. London: Macmillan, 1988.

James, Estelle, and Susan Rose-Ackerman. *The Nonprofit Enterprise in Market Economies*, a monograph in the Fundamentals of Pure and Applied Economics Series and *Encyclopedia of Economics*, eds. J. Lesourne and H. Sonnenschein. London: Harwood Academic Publishers, 1986.

Japan Statistical Yearbook. Tokyo: Office of the Prime Minister, 1982.

Weisbrod, Burton. "Toward a Theory of the Voluntary Nonprofit Sector in a Three-Sector Economy." in Edmund Phelps, ed., *Altruism, Morality and Economic Theory*. New York: Russell Sage Foundation, 1975.

————. *The Voluntary Nonprofit Sector*. Lexington, Mass.: Lexington Books, 1977.

Zellner, Arnold, and T. H. Lee. "Joint Estimation of Relationships Involving Discrete Random Variables." *Econometrica* (April 1965): 382–94.

3

Evaluating Private Institutions: The Case of Latin American Higher Education

DANIEL LEVY

An evaluation of Latin America's private universities is pertinent to several current scholarly and policy concerns. Most central to this volume and book series is the comparison between private (nonprofit) and public institutions. That comparison is undertaken within a policy field, education, characterized by terrific disappointment over the performance of major institutions. Gone is the era of optimism with its broad confidence in both public and private schools and universities, in both the more- and less-developed nations.

At the higher education level, disappointment has been striking in Latin America. But as most criticism has focused on traditional public universities, formidable alternatives have arisen. Significant among these are private universities. From but a marginal existence a half century ago, the private sector has come to hold one-third of Latin America's enrollment. And the private universities are characteristically distinct from their public counterparts. Consequently, those interested in the role of universities in developing areas, as well as those interested in comparing organizational forms, may want to evaluate the performance of these private alternatives.

In international terms, the importance of Latin America's private models is clear. Most of the developed world, even excluding the communist world, relies almost exclusively on public institutions to perform higher education's tasks. Japan and the United States are the two major exceptions,

I thank the Program on Non-Profit Organizations, Institution for Social and Policy Studies at Yale University and the Andrew W. Mellon Foundation, respectively, for generous institutional and financial support.

This is a revised version of "Latin America's Private Universities: How Successful Are They?" *Comparative Education Review* 29, no. 4 (November 1985): 440–59, itself based largely, though not exclusively, on *Higher Education and the State in Latin America: Private Challenges to Public Dominance* (Chicago: University of Chicago Press, 1986). Copyright © 1986 by the University of Chicago. Reprinted by permission.

though the U.S. private share of total enrollment has plummeted from 50 percent in 1950 to just over 20 percent, below the contemporary Latin American percentage. Of special relevance here, most developing nations have also pursued publicly based models. Africa, most of the Middle East, and parts of Asia basically fit this generalization—as did Latin America for most of its history. But along with contemporary Latin America, several Asian nations now rely heavily on private higher education. Furthermore, many other nations, developing as well as developed, have considered establishing private sectors. Still others have considered introducing or augmenting some characteristics of private systems (e.g., tuition) within their nominally public sectors.

To evaluate the private experience of 20 Latin American republics in one brief chapter is a perilous undertaking. It must begin with qualifications. First, I write here in very general terms, either ignoring or merely hinting at what in fact are significant variations and exceptions. Although specific illustrations are included, few are fully elaborated. From this first qualification comes the second one. Although drawing freely and extensively on the substantiation developed in my recent book, I cannot include as many examples, data, and citations as I would like to substantiate my broad assertions (much less to prove them.)[1] The breadth of the subject matter also makes it difficult to develop a focused or cogent theme within such limited space. Nevertheless, I venture this: the private university has generally been successful in terms of its own goals, but these goals have been both restrictive and controversial.

I do not suggest that fulfillment of chosen goals is the single best context of evaluation, let alone the only one. It does, however, allow analysis of both the evolution and contemporary performance of private universities within a manageable and coherent evaluative framework. Moreover, I believe it is one very useful context of evaluation. It is important to deal with the goals, and institutional means to achieve them, of the powerful interests that are behind private (or public) growth. In any case, the focus on certain goals does not preclude identification of the limits and questionable aspects of those goals. By contrast, works dealing with the policy goals in Latin American higher education are frequently concerned with ideal–typical goals advocated by the authors themselves. Although such approaches have value, they obviously should not displace empirical investigation. A central proposition guiding the analysis here is that it is worthwhile to specify how and in what sense a university has or has not been successful. My hope is to find some patterns of private strengths and weaknesses that may be generalizable to broader private–public comparisons.

The chapter is divided into four major sections. First, after presenting basic data on private growth, it explores the goals behind three different "waves" of private growth, leading to distinguishable private subsectors. Thus, in the next section, each subsector is evaluated separately, in terms of the goals it fulfills and the interests and groups it serves. The section after that analyzes how the subsectors' successes pose normative problems

Table 3.1. Latin American Private and Total Enrollment, 1955–1975

	1955		1960		1965		1970		1975	
	N	%	N	%	N	%	N	%	N	%
Latin America	57,431		83,961		171,674		429,635		1,143,395	
	403,338	14.2	546,732	15.4	859,076	20.0	1,453,596	29.6	3,396,341	33.7
Without Brazil	23,977		41,407		103,480		192,875		442,824	
	329,763	7.3	450,000	9.2	703,295	14.7	983,123	19.6	2,323,793	19.1

Source: See note 4.
Note: The top row of numbers for each entry shows private enrollment; the bottom row, total enrollment (i.e., private plus public).

and are limited in scope. The final section deals with the tricky question of academic quality to illustrate some private advantages and their limitations.

GOALS STIMULATING PRIVATE GROWTH

At least two factors make the private growth in Latin America higher education particularly interesting for students of nonprofit organizations. One is that so little precedent could be found in Latin America, indeed in most of the world.[2] The other, related, factor is that this private growth clearly results from certain identifiable perceptions of "public failure." These failures go beyond merely not being involved in an activity (though they include those): private institutions grew largely because many groups and classes rejected public institutions that they once supported, sponsored, and attended. Why then has private higher education so dramatically emerged and grown in Latin America?

Growth of Private Universities

No private university existed in Latin America until the 1880s. Only Colombia and Chile deviated from the regional tradition by 1917. As late as 1930, probably less than 3 percent of total Latin American enrollment was in the private sector. Yet, by 1955, the figure had jumped to roughly 14 percent. By 1965 it reached 20 percent, growing to 30 percent in 1970, and 34 percent by 1975, then stabilizing.[3] These private percentages can be a bit misleading because of the great weight of the unusual Brazilian case, with its massive private sector. Table 3.1 therefore summarizes the trends with and without Brazil.[4]

With or without Brazil, the percentages reflect extraordinary private growth in proportional terms. Moreover, this growth occurred amid unprecedented public sector expansion, especially since 1960. In fact, although Latin America's private sector grew from under 60,000 in 1955 to over 1 million in 1975, its public sector grew from under 350,000 to well over 2 million. In the 1960s, for example, public growth was greater than private growth in absolute numbers, though not in proportional terms, in all except two of the countries that had dual sectors.[5]

One could argue that this private surge from a few percent to 34 percent of total enrollment is misleading. Perhaps private higher education is not a new phenomenon in Latin America. The main idea would be that colonial universities were church universities. Indeed, many were church universities; but they were also state universities. By various criteria (juridical ownership, founding authority, governance, finance, and mission), most universities were a complex mixture of private and public. For example, Argentina's only colonial university (the University of Córdoba, 1614) was created and owned by the state but run largely by the Jesuits, with papal authorization. Of course, seminaries also existed in many nations. In general, however, "private" and "public" were not separate concepts in the major current senses of those terms.[6]

When the church–state partnership finally weakened, the public university form emerged strongly. The influences of the Enlightenment, the French Revolution, and the Napoleonic university model were factors. All took on special importance in Latin America's Independence period (after 1810). "National" universities were created from colonial ones, as with Argentina's University of Córdoba, or were created anew. Church influence greatly diminished. The state assumed fundamental authority over the university in naming officials, fixing curriculum requirements, and other matters of governance; at the same time, it assumed full responsibility to finance the university. The university was charged to serve society and the state, not the church. Evidence exists for these transformations in nations such as Chile, Ecuador, Mexico, and Venezuela. Thus, for well over a century, the public sector would enjoy a near monopoly in Latin American university education. In Venezuela, for example, only three universities were created alongside the Central University in the nineteenth century, all on a similar public model. The public university was the state's representative in Latin American higher education, even sometimes (as in Chile) in all of education. Although such broad generalization warrants qualification, until the 1930s only Chile and Peru had created the kind of institution that would eventually undo the public monopoly in most of Latin America, the Catholic university.[7]

The First Wave: Catholic Universities

Catholic universities form the first wave of private universities. This occurred in Argentina, Bolivia, Brazil, Chile, Ecuador, Panama, Paraguay, Peru, and every Central American nation except Costa Rica. (More generally, it appears that religious institutions often led the way in the establishment of private nonprofit sectors.) For what purpose, then, were the Catholic universities created? They were created principally in reaction to the secularism of the public universities. A major component in Latin American colonial higher education, religion had been relegated or even roundly assaulted.

The creation of Catholic universities reflected the political power of the Right and was meant to buttress it. Conservative parties, as well as the church, were predictable promotors of the first wave, as with Venezuela's Andrés Bello University (1953). But the first wave also reflected, paradoxically, the declining power of the church. After all, Catholic universities arose to save the church after it was pushed out of the existing higher education system. Thus, Colombia's Javeriana University was opened shortly after the Liberal Party's 1930 victory threatened the church's traditional university role. Moreover, governments and even the Left were generally more willing to allow a special church role in *part* of higher education, once it was clear that the church and its Conservative backers no longer held the power necessary to control the bulk of the higher education system.

Consider Brazil, atypical in its second- and third- but not first-wave causes of growth. As a first choice, the church wanted to maintain its great influence in the existing universities. It feared that separate Catholic universities would be socially and academically marginal, preserving pockets of Christianity while abandoning most of society and politics to secular materialism. Only when its hopes of gaining prominence within the public universities faded did it campaign for its second choice, Catholic universities. It would be better to have pockets of Christian education than to have no Christian education. Similarly, the creation of Argentine Catholic universities in the late 1950s reflected the church's realization that it could not control the University of Buenos Aires, for example; and it reflected the state's view that Catholic universities would pose a lesser threat than they would have early in the century, when the state refused to legitimize the short-lived Catholic University in Buenos Aires.[8]

But religious goals were not the only ones that the founders of Catholic universities had in mind. The universities' conservative bent suggested a rejection of the leftist political thought and action often found in the public sector. An important corollary was the desire to maintain social conservatism and class privileges. These areligious goals assumed greater significance by the 1950s and 1960s, as the public sector expanded rapidly and became increasingly identified with leftist politics. One sees these mixed goals behind the creation of, for example, Bolivia's Catholic University (1967) and the Dominican Republic's Madre y Maestra University (1962). The goal of upholding church ideas amid an otherwise secular context had been more salient in the 1930s and 1940s, as seen in the establishment of Ecuador's Pontifical University (1946).

The Second Wave: Secular Elite Universities

A second wave of private universities could be called "secular elite," or "elite" for short. Here the desire for class privileges, conservatism, or just academic tranquility and prestige, comes to the fore. Religious identity is a marginal or nonexistent goal. In terms of perceived public failures, the second wave has its main roots in the profound dissatisfaction of elite actors with the public sector. For one thing, the public sector has lost its once elite character. In Venezuela, for example, public enrollment grew from 7000 in 1955 to 35,000 in 1965 to 175,000 in 1975—with no entrance requirements at the four traditional public universities.[9]

Critical throughout Latin America was the expansion of secondary education. Consider the growth in cohort percentages between 1960 and 1970 in five nations: Colombia 12.5 to 25.9 percent, Costa Rica 18.4 to 32.8, Ecuador 12.6 to 28.5, Mexico 11.9 to 22.5, and Peru 16.1 to 35.6, with an overall Latin American shift from 15.0 to 28.7, moving to 42.0 percent by 1975. The higher education transformation is then equally impressive, with respective figures of 1.7 to 4.7 percent in Colombia, 4.8 to 10.2 in Costa Rica, 2.6 to 7.6 in Ecuador, 2.6 to 6.1 in Mexico, and 3.6 to 11.0 in Peru, with a 3.1 to 6.8 change in Latin America overall, moving to 11.7 percent by 1975.[10] With this opening to the middle and lower-middle class, came a perceived decline in average academic quality or at least social prestige, leading many from the most privileged classes to seek an elite alternative. Public university degrees and credentials came to be worth less and less on the job market. Furthermore, industrialists and other businessmen became increasingly upset with the public university's failure to produce trained personnel for their enterprises. And overlapping these social and economic "failures" were the more purely political ones. Elites were unhappy with the increasing leftist activism of professors and even administrators, but mostly of students.[11]

In short, privileged classes, employers, and conservatives in general were unhappy over what they saw as a *loss* of elitism, order, efficiency, and job-market relevancy in the public institutions. Thus, they reacted principally to a perceived public-sector failure. In several nations, however, they also reacted to perceived failures in the Catholic universities: too many had been either too traditional and unbusinesslike, as in Argentina, or, worse yet, increasingly liberal and permissive in the aftermath of Vatican II. Therefore, the second wave was partly a reaction to the first wave. Examples include Venezuela's Metropolitan University (1965) after the Andrés Bello (1953). It was created by the nation's bourgeoisie and backed by industrialists associated with the Eugenio Mendoza Foundation. Other examples include Mexico's Anáhuac (1965) after the Iberoamericana (1943) and Guatemala's Francisco Marroquín (1971) after the Rafael Landívar (1961).[12]

The Third Wave: Excess Demand–Driven Universities

Neat, consistent, associations between private institutions and elite goals would be facile, however. Not all the private growth has been directed toward such goals. A third wave refers to nonelite secular institutions, often unselective in admissions. Some of the causes of growth are similar to those in the elite subsector. There is, for example, often a preoccupation to get job-related training and to avoid leftist politicization. Fundamentally, however, the third wave represents a reaction to a different perceived public-sector inadequacy: less to the excesses of social democratization than to its limits. That is, even the unprecedented public expansion has often been insufficient to meet the still more dramatic growth in student demand for higher education. The most extreme example is Brazil, where the enrollment boom occurred mostly while a conservative military held power and placed greater curbs on the public sector's ability to meet booming demand than generally seen in Latin America (at least until military rule transformed other South American systems in the 1970s). Outside Brazil, the third wave is not responsible for the majority of university enrollments but usually for either a majority of private university enrollments, as in Colombia and the Dominican Republic, or a substantial minority of private university enrollments, as in Venezuela.[13]

It is too easy to ignore the third wave, because of its lack of prestige and even influence. In fact, it has surely captured the bulk of private growth in the 1970s and 1980s, as no new Catholic universities have been created and as elite universities, almost by definition, can expand only so much. Meanwhile, fiscal crises in much of Latin America are placing critically increasing restrictions on public growth.

In sum, most Latin American private sectors have emerged from three relatively distinct waves, each with its distinct raison d'être. This is not to say that the waves are completely distinct or that variation is absent within each. These waves of growth are neither fully self-contained nor internally uniform. Nor do the universities produced in these waves always fit neatly into one category, especially as their goals and characteristics evolve. This is especially true when Catholic universities dilute or reinterpret their religious missions. Some, such as Venezuela's Andrés Bello, resemble elite universities in certain respects whereas others, such as some in Colombia, more closely resemble institutions produced by the third wave. Furthermore, there are several partial or fundamental exceptions to the three-wave rule: some nations have created no private sector (Cuba and Uruguay); others (Bolivia, Panama, Paraguay) have created private sectors composed of only a single Catholic university; Costa Rica until the 1980s had only a secular nonelite institution; Chile is exceptional in several ways.

But in most nations three waves are usefully discernible, with a strong though overlapping sequential flow. Consider Argentina and Peru. Argentina's Catholic university share of private enrollment declined from 74 to 47 percent, 1965–1977, with nonelite growth particularly strong in recent years. Peru's first wave began decades before any other private institutions were created. In the early 1960s both Catholic and elite private universities followed. Nonelite private universities did not appear until 1964, but they have dominated private growth since then.[14] As mentioned, no Catholic universities have been created in the 1970s or 1980s and the creation of elite institutions appears to have slowed recently, whereas the third-wave institutions continue to proliferate.

FULFILLING CHOSEN GOALS

Religion

Insofar as Catholic universities were created to promote strong religious identities, their performance might charitably be considered mixed. Few students specialize in religious study. Analysis of the fields of study in Venezuela's Andrés Bello University, for example, shows no religious specialization. It shows only 0.5 percent of the students in what may be the closest field, philosophy.[15] Nor do most Catholic universities have formidable religious course requirements for students specialized in secular fields. Meanwhile, a decreasing percentage of professors are priests. In fact, many of the part-timers also teach in secular universities or work in nonreligious jobs outside academia. Although the picture is different for administrators, even there the lay representation is high once we look below the top of the administrative structure. In Brazil's Catholic University of Rio, priests may account for 65–75 percent of the highest ranking administrators but only 29 percent of the university council members and 14 percent of the divisional council members.[16]

Nonetheless, the Catholic subsector has fulfilled many of its goals. Even on religious matters, its failures could easily be exaggerated. Certain institutions, such as the Catholic University of Argentina, have maintained some traditionally religious flavor. Others, such as Mexico's Iberoamericana, strive for a religious identity based more on the principles of Vatican II than traditionalism. Besides, almost all Catholic universities, no matter how much they fall short of their religious goals, approximate them much more than the non-Catholic universities do, especially where there has been outright hostility toward religion in the public universities. Finally, since some Catholic universities, especially if created in the 1960s, never intended to function fundamentally according to identifiably Catholic standards, it would, of course, be misleading to evaluate them too much by those standards.

In any case, the major failure in terms of original goals is related to a major success. The decline of traditional Catholic missions has been accompanied by the achievement of increasing academic openness and prestige. This is not merely a fortuitous by-product; it is a consciously pursued policy. In an obvious parallel to what Jencks and Riesman have called the "academic revolution" in the United States, the principal job of a Latin American Catholic university is increasingly to be a good university.[17] Vatican II and then subsequent Catholic university conferences have emphasized a move away from defensive dogmatic faith toward a more open pursuit of scientific truth, with academic freedom.

Prestige

The secular elite subsector has been strikingly successful when judged by
its own goals. The success is clear with regard to each of the major goals
for which it was created. Academically, the subsector enjoys a higher prestige than does any other, private or public. Socially, it tends to be the most
exclusive in class terms, drawing disproportionally on those groups able
to provide privileged opportunities, often including private secondary
schooling, for their children. Economically, graduates have the best prospects, particularly with private and multinational employers.[18] Politically,
these institutions sometimes explicitly promote conservative views. Whether
or not they do that, they consistently avoid the conflict and disorder so
characteristic of many public universities. Good examples of these elite
characteristics are found at institutions like Colombia's Los Andes University, the Dominican Republic's Technological Institute of Santo Domingo,
Mexico's Institute of Technological and Advanced Studies in Monterrey,
Peru's Pacífico University, and Venezuela's Rafael Urdaneta University.

Economic Returns

The third wave has also been largely successful in fulfilling its own goals.
Marketplace tests may illustrate this point. New institutions are still being
created at a brisk pace, while existing ones expand; few have failed and
closed. And the students attracted are paying students. Insofar as these
institutions were created to meet the demand not met elsewhere, they have
made substantial contributions. For example, Costa Rica's, Colombia's,
and Brazil's unprestigious private institutions have provided opportunities
for working youth who could not study in the times available in the public
sector. At the same time, some of these institutions have successfully linked
other students to the job market and most have provided politically tranquil atmospheres that again contrast to those often found in the public
sector.

By successfully pursuing their key goals, the three private subsectors have
usually gratified key constituencies. The ability to please their most concerned constituencies may be taken as another measure by which to evaluate private success. We have already seen that many Catholic and especially secular elite universities serve privileged student clienteles. It is equally
clear that major organizations have been served in several ways. To begin
with, the church must accept that the mixed performance of Catholic universities far surpasses what the church reaps from other universities. Less
equivocal gratification has been achieved by business organizations. They
are confident that the elite universities, and some Catholic ones, provide
efficient educations, spending donated money on relatively tranquil and
job-relevant educations. Compared to the public sector, the private sector
trains more students in desired fields of study. Consider these illustrative
contrasts of the percentage of total private versus total public enrollment

(1977–1978) in the fields of economics, business, administration, and communication combined: Bolivia, 42.5 versus 9.9; Colombia, 36.8 versus 10.3; Ecuador, 23.4 versus 18.2; Mexico, 35.3 versus 16.6; Peru, 47.2 versus 23.2.[19]

Benefits to the State

Less obvious, but no less important, are the ways in which the private sector has successfully served the state. The state has only sometimes made explicit its support for private growth (i.e., defined itself as a key constituency of the private sector), yet that support has been widespread—and generally rewarded. First, the private sector has satisfied social, economic, and political groups that are prominent constituencies of the state. The dissatisfaction of these groups could pose serious threats to the state's stability. Second, the private sector has increasingly provided personnel not just for private enterprise but also for the state. This is especially true for high-level technical and economic positions, as with those filled by graduates of the Autonomous Technical Institute of Mexico. It is also true, however, even for more strictly political positions, such as those obtained by graduates of Venezuela's Andrés Bello University and Peru's Pontifical University. All this pertains to the modernization, or "technification," of the state, favoring those trained efficiently for applied tasks. Third, the private sector has avoided the leftist political activism often characteristic of the public sector. The state enjoys a more quiescent private than public sector, without the difficulties of direct administration.

Costs to the State: Private Financing of Private Universities

Fourth, the private sector is basically self-financed. The state is thereby relieved of a major financial burden. The burden has been especially onerous since public sector enrollments have grown so rapidly. Governments have implored public universities to increase their nonstate income but have met with very little success. Major variation in public university income profiles have not involved mixes in private and public sources. Tuition is still almost always absent or nominal. Philanthropic giving to public institutions remains extremely rare in Latin America.

In contrast, the private institutions draw very little of their income from the state. Top Catholic universities draw the most within the private sector. For one thing, they tend to be the oldest private institutions and may lose some "privateness" over time. After decades of existence, Chile's and Peru's first Catholic universities were granted significant state subsidies. Two decades after its creation, Peru's first Catholic university received nearly 30 percent of its income from the state. Related to their age, some Catholic universities originally copied national university policies in nonreligious activities. Over time, some have forged political profiles that make them appear less "anti-public university" than the secular elite universities often

Table 3.2. Private Subsector Income Sources

	State	Donations	Tuition
Catholic	1[a]	2	2.5[b]
Secular elite	2	1	1
Third-wave	3	3	2.5[b]

[a] 1 = the subsector that receives the most income; 3 = least.

[b] My guess is that the average Catholic tuition is higher, but evidence is lacking.

do. Also over time, especially if they lost conservative business support, many Catholic universities could not sustain their improving quality without state aid. Donated services remain important but are insufficient. Finally, as in Bolivia, states have sometimes financed Catholic universities because (1) they have been furious over what they saw as public university failures and (2) it is cheaper to pay for part of a student's Catholic university education than all of his public university education (were some Catholic universities to fold).

Nonetheless, outside Chile no Catholic university has depended more on state than private funds. And the state has given very little to the two other private subsectors. For nonelite (third-wave) institutions, the most questionable exception concerns the tax breaks granted virtually all private higher education institutions. Some nonelite institutions violate at least the spirit of legal exemptions for nonprofit organizations as they funnel would-be profits toward noneducational purposes (e.g., into salaries for relatives who actually work very little at the institution). Still, even the culpable institutions depend overwhelmingly on tuition.

Secular elite universities have rarely even solicited state subsidies. Instead, they have boasted of their ability to attract paying students, contract research, and, partly breaking regional tradition, corporate and foundation donations. Rare is the corporation or even foundation that gives to different universities. But several have established and financed the growth or physical plant of a given university, "their" university. A good example is Venezuela's Eugenio Mendoza Foundation and its Metropolitan University. Additionally, secular elite universities along with some prestigious Catholic universities have been favored targets for international aid (from the U.S. government, multilateral agencies, and foundations). The attraction of domestic and international finance reflects perceptions of private success in meeting academic, social, economic, and political goals.

Table 3.2 gives a simplified comparative summary of how the private subsectors finance themselves. It shows, for example, that the secular elite subsector's base is stronger than the third-wave's base. But it should not obscure the fact that each subsector sustains itself chiefly on tuition. Nor should it obscure the broader fact of private sector self-financing versus public sector state subsidization.

CRITIQUE OF THE GOALS

I have thus far evaluated the private sector by how well it has fulfilled its own purposes. The picture has been positive, with qualifications, but this obviously has been a biased and limited evaluation. It underscores the importance of the criteria chosen or emphasized in evaluating "success." I give less space to the positive than the negative considerations not because the latter necessarily outweigh the former. Rather, it is that the negative features may be less readily identified.

Two fundamental kinds of negative evaluations can be made of the private sector, even by those who concede its general success in fulfilling its own goals. The first is normative. Observers need not approve of the goals. Beyond that, some may see their fulfillment as injurious to the public interest. The second kind of criticism is empirically based. Whether or not the private sector's contributions are regarded as good or bad, they are limited in scope. It is less that the sector performs tasks poorly than that it avoids many tasks. Illustratively, we would not generally regard most U.S. liberal arts colleges as failures for not doing research, when they never intended to, but we may nevertheless emphasize this omission if we compare their performance to those of other higher education institutions. Before identifying critical tasks that the private sector generally avoids, I first consider normative reservations about the private sector's pursuit of its own selected endeavors. Again I analyze privatization by subsector.

Educational Conservatism

Although those Catholic universities that once fulfilled their distinctive church-oriented roles could be called successes on their own terms, detractors could argue that they did not join other universities in social or political reform, indeed that they opposed such reform. By serving church interests they served traditional conservative interests. They could also be accused of squelching academic freedom in favor of dogma and "Truth." At the same time, the business-oriented Right could find fault with the Catholic universities' traditionalism, oriented to the church rather than to capitalist development. Then, beginning in the 1960s, the growing liberalism of many Catholic universities increasingly put them at odds with entrepreneurial and other conservative interests, as the second wave reaction to the first wave suggested earlier. These interests denounced actions once limited to the public sector, such as demonstrations for social change. For example, when El Salvador's Jesuit university associated itself with calls for social justice and negotiations between the guerrillas and the government, the Right was angered and the government threatened to close the institution. (The public university had already been closed.)

On the other hand, when Catholic universities have served modernizing capitalist interests, they have been targets of charges leveled principally against the secular elite universities. Naturally, the main charge against the latter is elitism, a charge sustained by data on tuitions. So one negative factor accompanying the advantages of self-financing is that such financing partly determines to whom opportunity is offered. Private-sector tuition contrasts sharply with a proud public-sector tradition of no tuition or nominal tuition. It is not uncommon for governments to subsidize student health care, housing, food, transportation, and social activities. Almost all of the governments that have tried to initiate public-sector tuitions have failed in the face of stiff opposition, though a few tuition-loan programs are in place.

Elitism and Access

The secular-elite universities are most vulnerable to charges of elitism in tuition, in that they set the highest rates. Academic prestige, related to social prestige and future economic reward, allows this. Third-wave institutions simply do not offer enough to warrant high charges. The same holds for unprestigious Catholic universities. Furthermore, some Catholic universities are truly restrained by concerns about equity. I would guess that the Catholics charge more on the average (as the prestigious ones certainly do) than do demand-absorbing institutions. Venezuela's Catholic Andrés Bello charges more than most or all of the nation's nonuniversity private institutions, but the elite Metropolitan and Rafael Urdaneta universities charge roughly 50 percent more than the Andrés Bello. When Colombia's top Catholic university, Javeriana, charged about $350/U.S. annually, the secular elite Los Andes charged over $600. Similarly, Argentina's Belgrano charged about double what was charged at the most expensive religiously inspired university (Salvador).[20]

Each private subsector charges tuitions that are high not only by comparison with the public sector but also by comparison with average national wages. And, again, tuition is the chief source of finance for each private subsector.

As data on tuition would suggest, private–public differences in access policy are broadly reflected in intersectoral socioeconomic differences. Data vary by nation, of course, but tend to sustain the basic pattern found in Colombia. Significant overlap between the private and public sectors notwithstanding, notably more private elitism is found. The most privileged socioeconomic group concentrates in the second-wave private institutions, followed closely by some Catholic universities. A few public universities (including Colombia's National and Antioquia universities) also draw from the pinnacle but simultaneously draw on a much wider, more heterogeneous, clientele than do the most prestigious private universities. Third-wave private institutions reach further down the socioeconomic ladder than do many leading public universities yet (although data are scarce on less-prestigious institutions) probably not as far down as do many provincial public universities.[21]

Not surprisingly, then, "intellectual elitism" overlaps with social class

elitism. The academically best prepared students come very disproportion-
ately from wealthier families and the most prestigious secondary schools,
often private secular ones. To illustrate, even when Colombian private
schools held fewer than one in five primary enrollments they accounted for
nearly 9 in 10 enrollments at the two most prestigious private universities
(versus a still impressive more than 6 in 10 at the public national university).[22]

Often connected with socioeconomic elitism is restrictive politics. Representatives of elite universities are fond of claiming to offer depoliticized
alternatives to the public sector. The claim has some validity. But virtually
all universities are politicized in some significant sense; that is, they serve
certain political interests more than others. This is evident in the elite universities tied to conservative political ideologies. Some manifest a marked
intolerance for expressions of leftist views. In the name of banning politicization, they may severely limit democratic participation. These limits are
themselves political actions, politically motivated. The elite universities often
represent the political-economic philosophies of the enterprises to which
they are related, just as some Catholic universities have represented the
church's political beliefs. In sum, one's evaluation of the elite universities
depends largely on one's attitude toward political quiescence and the dominant order upheld by both the state and powerful private interests.

Quality

Political restrictiveness, along with accommodation to dominant economic
structures, is also found in many nonelite institutions. But the principal
fault found with the third wave concerns the generally low academic quality that it has produced. As in Brazil and Peru, the quality can be disgrace-
ful, and some of the institutions are unconcerned about anything except
attracting students.[23] Instead, as suggested earlier, they may pursue financial rewards in ways that abuse the spirit of "nonprofit" educational status
(and tax exemptions).

Other third-wave institutions are at least concerned to provide their students with job-relevant skills. Even there, however, room for a normative
critique remains, and that critique would also involve the elite institutions.
It holds that there is a crucial difference between job-oriented "training"
and broader "education," with its emphasis on reflection, independent
thought, and criticism.

In short, one chief set of reservations about the private sector's self-
satisfying process is that it is accompanied by features that critics see as
highly negative. Another set of reservations, to which I now turn, concerns
the empirical limitations on the private sector's success story.

Limited Goals

To begin with, the private sector's success is based largely on the public
sector's burdens. The private sector can select comparatively limited goals,

whereas the public sector undertakes to fulfill many more goals, including more of the most difficult ones. Third wave institutions are most vulnerable on this point. Most set very modest goals. The "market test" of attracting students is not very challenging where demand for higher education easily outpaces the public sector's supply of openings. But limited undertakings also characterize the elite private universities and, though to a lesser extent, the Catholic universities. I concentrate here on two concerns—access and fields of study—where the private sector's comparatively limited scope is quantitatively demonstrable.

Restricted Admissions

Regarding access policy, data on tuition and on entering graduates from privileged schools have already suggested the elite restrictiveness found in the private sector. Access is frequently limited to the academically best prepared. Entrance exams have been much more common for private than public universities; in the latter they have often been blocked by students as "elitist" or "private" policies. In Ecuador, for example, all five private universities had entrance exams, whereas only one among many more public institutions did.

The public sector has generally accepted the principal burden of providing higher education for secondary school graduates. As Table 3.1 showed, the public sector accounts for 66 percent of all enrollment. Only in Brazil (and very recently in Colombia) has the private sector absorbed more than half of the total higher education enrollment. This broad private–public contrast holds despite the existence of the generally unselective third-wave private institutions, a few highly selective public universities (such as Venezuela's Simón Bolívar), and several comparatively selective faculties (e.g., medicine) within public universities that are not selective in most of their faculties. The public sector has often taken nearly all candidates while the private sector has selected only those students it wants. Moreover, restrictiveness in access policy is not limited to socioeconomic factors. More private than public institutions accept (and retain) only those students who are willing to comport themselves within certain political guidelines.

Restricted Course Offerings

Access is obviously limited to those students willing to pursue the fields of study that given private institutions offer. And here we see another example of the problems that accompany the advantages of self-financing. Self-financing means inadequate financing for many important university functions. Private universities usually concentrate on those fields that are relatively inexpensive to offer. Here is an important caveat to the private sector's factually accurate claim that it basically supports itself through voluntary payments, whereas the public university relies on the state's mandatory tax system: the private universities generally steer clear of activities that require heavy financing. *Some* institutions within the higher education system must offer the medical sciences, exact sciences, and engineering, but if public institutions do it then the private ones can avoid it. In other cases, it is less a matter of the freedom to avoid these courses than the financial inability to provide them.[24]

Several of the top Catholic universities are less vulnerable on this point about field restrictiveness than are their secular counterparts. But, first, these are precisely the private universities most likely to rely on some state subsidy. Second, even Catholic universities do not match the proportional enrollment (in the costly fields) found in public universities of comparable prestige. Most secular elite universities do not come close. The nonelite institutions rarely even feign an interest in such fields.

Let us return to data from the five nations considered earlier with regard to the distributions of students by field of study. Whereas the private sector could be credited for a substantial lead in business-related fields, we now see that the cost is another, powerful basis of private–public distinction. Table 3.3 compares private–public data for three of the least expensive fields against probably the three most expensive fields.

The private sector consistently and easily surpasses the public sector in proportional enrollment in the inexpensive "commercial" category. Its edge is statistically much less striking in the humanities and law, yet even equal private–public percentages would suggest that cost counterbalances the weight of possibly limited job utility (humanities) and strong public sector tradition (law). More striking, however, is the degree to which the private sector is underrepresented in the most expensive fields. This occurs in 13 of 15 cases. An exception is caused by just one unique institution, the Autonomous University of Guadalajara. It has almost two-thirds of Mexico's private university medical students, but thousands of these come from the United States.

For further evidence, I present full enrollment data for two more nations. In Argentina (1977) the private sector had 78 percent of its 82,911 college students in the humanities and social sciences, with only 18 percent in medicine, natural sciences, and engineering, versus respective figures of 48 and 50 percent for the public sector's 453,539 students. (The remainder in each sector is located in miscellaneous fields.) In Venezuela (1978), the private sector (25,756) had a 21 to 15 percent lead in engineering and architecture combined, whereas the public sector (239,915) had a 17 to 9 percent lead in teacher education, but most differences hypothesized on the basis of cost emerge clearly (despite the obscuring effects of the public sector's 30 percent in a "basic cycle," versus 7 percent for the private sector). The public sector maintained a 17 to 5 percent advantage in the medical and natural sciences, whereas it trailed by a telling 60 to 23 percent in the social sciences and humanities.[25]

ACADEMIC QUALITY AND PRESTIGE

Although several arguments have touched on the question of academic quality, I have held the major discussion aside to show at greater length an example of the simultaneous successes and limitations of privatization,

Table 3.3. Private–Public Comparisons by Field of Specialization (%)

Nation	Commercial		Humanities		Law		Medicine		Exact Sciences		Engineering	
	Private	Public	Private	Public	Private	Public	Private	Public	Private	Public	Private	Public
Bolivia	58	10	12	2	0	8	0	21	0	15	0	23
Colombia	37	10	5	7	16	4	4	9	4	12	17	26
Ecuador	23	18	9	6	6	6	1	11	3	5	8	17
Mexico	35	20	1	2	6	9	20	20	1	4	17	24
Peru	47	23	7	0	5	4	1	7	6	4	8	29

Sources: See note 19.
Note: Economics, business, administration, and communications are designated *commercial.*

including an example of where some limitations are not as obvious as the successes. In terms of our capabilities, we can establish invidious private–public patterns, which appear to be generalizable beyond our case, but those patterns are complex, full of qualifications, and insufficiently extensive to allow complete conclusions.[26]

However desirable it would be to determine the quality of institutions through systematic procedures, severe problems arise. In terms of statistical measures, one problem concerns the availability of data. Accumulating some national data is easier than finding broad cross-national data. Another problem is data reliability. Yet even more fundamental is the relationship between hypothesized indicators and quality.

One common indicator is the percentage of full-time professors. But this indicator is terribly confusing in Latin America generally. Many of the professors, judged by their ability to teach and to help place their students in good jobs, work principally in state ministries, hospitals, law firms, and so forth. A related measure is the student/teacher ratio, but this suffers from many of the same problems. Furthermore, data would have to be available in full-time equivalents, which is rarely the case. Moreover, compilers generally count twice those who teach in both sectors, regardless of how much time they spend in each. (For what it is worth, I found a private edge in 8 of the 13 nations I could investigate.) Nor is it easier to draw conclusions from data on expenditures per pupil. Higher ratios may indicate either quality *or* inefficiency—or student concentrations in fields that are expensive to teach, or diseconomies of scale, or major expenses on research.

Unable to establish statistically based conclusions on quality, I rely largely on the opinions of experts and "users" of higher education. This approach has obvious limitations, yet carries special weight when there is consensus—even amid great disagreement over the roots or desirability of the situation. Such is the situation in most of Latin America. More fruitful than a mere conclusion concerning which sector is superior, however, is the identification of patterns of perceived superiority and inferiority. In discussing perceptions, I am not pretending to deal with provable, objective quality but more with *prestige*. Even regarding prestige, however, I am uncomfortable with unqualified conclusions on which sector leads. The identifications should be sensitive to national, institutional, and subject-matter variation. It is more useful to show quilted patterns than to declare one sector superior. In most of our dual sector systems, the private sector is considered generally superior to the public sector. Yet much of what follows tempers that assessment.

Of the 20 nations I studied, 18 had dual sectors. Momentarily leaving aside systems with fewer than 100,000 students in 1975, a perceived private edge exists in 5 systems (Colombia, Ecuador, Mexico, Peru, Venezuela), rough parity in 2 (Argentina, Chile), and private inferiority in 1 (Brazil). Of the cases with under 100,000 students that I could bring in with reasonable confidence, 3 show private advantages (Bolivia, El Salvador, Honduras), whereas 1 shows private inferiority (Costa Rica). Most other small systems probably fit the private edge group, with Panama questionable. Summing up, the private sector may well hold a perceived edge in somewhere up to 14 of the 18 systems with dual sectors, whereas the public sector has a clear edge in only 2.

The private edge depends largely on the good reputation of most Catholic universities. This is especially true where the Catholic subsector constitutes a major part of the private sector, as in Ecuador. Even though not all Catholic universities have achieved the level of Ecuador's Quito or Guayaquil universities, Colombia's Javeriana or Biolivariana, Chile's Catholic University in Santiago, Peru's Pontifical, or Venezuela's Andrés Bello, most have achieved respectability. Bolivia's and probably Paraguay's Catholic universities do well within the context of their higher education systems. But the private sector's prestige rests increasingly on the secular elite as well as the Catholic subsector. Notwithstanding its Pontifical University, Peru's private sector prestige now probably depends more on the Cayetano, Pacífico, and other universities. Los Andes has the highest prestige in Colombia. I have found plentiful if scattered documentation of the standing of both Catholic and secular-elite private universities in terms of employment preferences in both private enterprises and the state; a small sample of such evidence was provided in the section on private successes.

A major factor diluting a generalized Spanish American private edge is the size of the demand-absorbing subsector. Most assessments of sectoral quality ignore this subsector, which is, after all, less important in most respects (economic and political) than in enrollment weight. Demand-absorbing institutions thus have something in common with U.S. nonprestigious private liberal arts colleges that are often overlooked when conclusions about private sector quality are based on the Harvards and the Dartmouths. If the private sector is evaluated by giving full weight (proportional to enrollment) to the demand-absorbing subsector, then the private edge is seriously diminished, or even thrown into doubt, in Colombia, Peru, and the Dominican Republic. Much obviously depends on the relative size of this subsector (fast growing) and on just how poor the quality is (e.g., probably worse in the Dominican Republic and Peru than in Argentina and Venezuela). Finally, this modification must be measured against the size of the *public* sector's demand-absorbing institutions. In fact, most public institutions have been partly demand-absorbing, driving down average quality, and many have been at least essentially demand-absorbing as those in the private sector. Illustrative are Colombia's departmental (regional) universities, offering few fields of study and lacking finances, laboratories, and libraries.

A national sketch may be helpful here. Venezuela illustrates general private sector superiority amid qualifications. The Catholic Andrés Bello is still quantitatively the most important bulwark of private quality, but the secular Metropolitana has probably overtaken it in prestige, and the secular Rafael Urdaneta and Tecnológica are also rising in stature. One of the public-experimental universities, the Simón Bolívar, shares the pinnacle with these private institutions; but the several other public experimental universities do not. Although there are both private and public nonuniversities of varying quality, the only nonselect private university is the Santa María. A private edge already came to be widely acknowledged by the 1960s, as the public sector was academically, socially, and politically transformed. On the other hand, despite an institutional slide based on trends in fields such as education and economics, the public national university (Universidad Central) maintains its position at or near the prestige pinnacle in fields such as dentistry and architecture. Moreover, a third wave of nonuniversity institutions has grown alarmingly in recent years, as economic crises drive the state finally to limit public growth.

We might imagine a relatively typical Spanish American system, with 20 percent enrollment in the private sector. Put another way, this is not so much a typical system (since no single model exists) as it is a composite picture based on an aggregation of Spanish America's systems (leaving aside Brazil with its massive private sector composed chiefly of third-wave institutions and by itself discrediting any notion of inherent private superiority). The system might be divided into (1) its pinnacle, of roughly the top 5 percent; (2) its prestige core, of perhaps the next 15 percent; (3) the mediocre bulk, of roughly 40 percent; and (4) the low-prestige bulk, of about 40 percent. The private sector would at least hold its own in the top category, probably better; it would achieve great overrepresentation in the second; it would be significantly underrepresented in the other two, though not as significantly as some would guess when they underestimate the size of the third wave. Again, then, two salient features are an average private edge and, on the other hand, significant private–public overlap.

Additional factors qualify the perceived private edge even in average quality. Examples include research and graduate education, both costly (undergraduate) fields of study. Assuming that some of the best graduates of secondary schools choose careers like medicine, we see a significant public advantage. Moreover, the private sector is often weak when it comes to the national treasure of fine arts and the basic, critical, social sciences. This last point underscores the subjective aspects of prestige. Economics is better in the private than the public universities if you represent most businesses, governments, and international agencies—but not if you favor Marxist over mainstream Western economics. In any case, the public sector often holds the edge in many fields of study, even where private universities overall are generally more prestigious than public ones.

Finally, we come to the distinction between perceived quality and the mainstream economists' definition of quality, "value added." One can easily concede that on the average the private universities graduate the better trained students but emphasize academic and financial selectivity (including student motivation and self-selectivity) in access. This of course has been a major issue in the debate over the quality of private versus public U.S. schools. In response, the prestigious private universities claim that their success is rooted largely in their own substantive policies and efficiencies. They are less tied to statist–bureaucratic constraints and have innovated more (e.g., departmentalization instead of traditional faculty structures) and have built better ties with employers. They do not sacrifice academics to political disruption or "hyperparticipation." In short, even if we can establish where the private sector achieves more prestige or boasts superior outputs, we cannot easily determine exactly what its contributions are.

CONCLUSION

The ability of Latin America's private universities to limit themselves to certain desired tasks, excluding others, is one fundamental reason for their success in achieving their own goals and satisfying their own constituencies. Thus, even if they fulfill their goals better than the public universities fulfill theirs, they need not be regarded as superior. Rather, they could be considered more focused, specialized institutions, fulfilling their functions well largely because they leave other, often tougher, functions to the public sector.[27] The argument might have been probed further, with evidence that private institutions often flourish still more directly—even parasitically— off the public sector. This occurs, for example, when the private universities hire, as part-timers, professors who draw their principal salaries in the public universities or in the state bureaucracy. In other cases, and to the private sector's credit, professors purged from repressive public universities have been hired by private universities. Examples include Brazil in the late 1960s and early 1970s, Bolivia in the early 1970s, and Argentina in the periods following the 1966 coup, the Peronist takeover of the early 1970s, and the 1976 coup. But perhaps the clearest ongoing way in which the private sector prospers directly at the public sector's expense is by drawing away many of the nation's finest students while public universities broaden their access.[28]

Therefore, private successes do not necessarily improve the higher education system overall. In terms of policy implications, even if one assumes that the private sector is generally superior to the public sector, it does not logically follow that proportional expansion of the private sector would make for a better system.[29]

Assessments of whether the expanding private sector has to date improved the higher education system depend greatly on one's priorities and normative perspectives. Fortunately, at least some of those priorities and perspectives can be informed by salient factual phenomena, be they adjudged favorable or unfavorable. Private universities have generally fulfilled the purposes for which they were created and grew. They have usually satisfied their chief constituencies both within the universities themselves and in society at large. They have done so largely by meeting needs or demands perceived by key actors to be unmet within a failing public sector. However, this private sector success is obviously not welcomed by those who disapprove of the very goals of these institutions and their constituencies. Furthermore, even those who approve of what the private sector does should acknowledge that, by choice or necessity, it generally undertakes tasks that are more narrowly defined, and frequently more easily attainable, than those undertaken by its public counterpart.

This chapter did not produce a simple verdict as to whether the private sector has been a success or a failure but analyzed in what ways, within what contexts, with what qualifications, and for whom the sector has been successful or not. Complex, multiple responses have emerged. Of course, even these responses have been general in nature, sacrificing to brevity the richness of qualifications, data, and substantiation that the central theses truly require. Still, some important outlines of the story were highlighted here and should be part of any overall evaluation. Thus, for example, evaluations should come to grips with enormous private–public differences. One may choose to extol or to condemn the private sector for its distinctiveness from the public sector, but it will not do to defend or to downplay the private sector for pursuing the same goals as the public sector. Surely universities in both sectors aim "to improve education" and "to serve society." But in many crucial respects, the private sector has defined and pursued such goals differently from the way the public sector has.

NOTES

1. Daniel Levy, *Higher Education and the State in Latin America: Private Challenges to Public Dominance* (Chicago: University of Chicago Press, 1986), especially parts of Chapters 2 and 7. However, many of the examples used in this article will not be found in the book, and the data and conclusions are developed in somewhat different ways. The book includes full chapter case studies on three nations (Chile, Mexico, and Brazil) but goes beyond them to consider Latin America inclusively in terms of the finance, governance, and functioning of private versus public sectors. Readers interested in private–public sectoral evolution might look also at comparisons drawn to the U.S. case: Daniel Levy,"The Rise of Private Universities in Latin America and the United States," in *The Sociology of Educational Expansion,* ed. Margaret Archer (London: Sage, 1982), pp. 93–132.

2. For an analysis of some non-Latin American cases see Roger L. Geiger, *Private Sectors in Higher Education: Structure, Function and Change in Eight Nations,* (Ann Arbor: University of Michigan Press, 1986).

3. For one well-known theoretical treatment of why nonprofit sectors arise, see Burton A. Weisbrod, "Toward a Theory of the Voluntary Nonprofit Sector in a Three-Sector Economy," in *The Economics of Nonprofit Institutions: Studies in Structure and Policy,* ed. Susan Rose-Ackerman (New York: Oxford University Press, 1986), pp. 21–44.

4. The 20 nations incorporated in the table are Argentina, Bolivia, Brazil, Chile, Colombia, Costa Rica, Cuba, The Dominican Republic, Ecuador, El Salvador, Guatemala, Haiti, Honduras, Mexico, Nicaragua, Panama, Paraguay, Peru, Uruguay, and Venezuela. The figures are documented and elaborated on fully in Levy, *Higher Education.* The single major source is the Organization of American States (OAS) and its various issues of *América en cifras.*

5. Based on Organization of American States (OAS), *América en cifras 1972* (Washington, D.C.: OAS, 1974), pp. 201–202. The gross data in Table 3.1 do not show the substantial

variation across nations. At the extremes, only Cuba and Uruguay now have no private sector, whereas Brazil's accounts for two-thirds of that nation's enrollment.

6. I believe that this point about private–public fusion and later separation has historical validity across many geographical and institutional fields.

7. Chief exceptions were Brazil and Haiti, where no university emerged in the nineteenth century, and Colombia and Guatemala, where *concordatos* preserved a joint government-church university presence.

8. Héctor Félix Bravo, *Las universidades privadas y el examen de habilitación para el ejercicio profesional* ((Buenos Aires: Universidad de Buenos Aires, n.d.), pp. 4–6.

9. Various issues of OAS, *América en cifras;* Consejo Nacional de Universidades (CNU), *Oportunidades de estudio en las instituciones de educación superior de Venezuela* (Caracas: CNU, 1978), pp. 24–36.

10. James W. Wilkie, ed. *Statistical Abstract of Latin America,* volume 20 (Los Angeles: UCLA Latin American Center Publications, 1980), p. 123.

11. For example, the extreme left attained majorities in student elections in Venezuela's three largest public universities six out of nine times, 1960–1968, whereas it usually received less than 5 percent of the vote in elections for national office. Daniel Levine, *Conflict and Political Change in Venezuela* (Princeton, N.J.: Princeton University Press, 1973), pp. 170–74.

12. This religious to secular shift within nonprofit sectors may be worth more cross-national and cross-field research. I believe that it is relevant to Latin American primary and secondary education and to other regions' educational systems as well.

13. The two most striking cases of nonelite private growth are found in Brazil and Colombia, probably followed by the Dominican Republic and Peru. The restrictiveness of public sectors in the first three is suggested by the low percentage of the cohort group in higher education in 1960, against a Latin American percentage of 3.1; Brazil 1.6, Colombia 1.7, and the Dominican Republic 1.3, but 3.6 for Peru (Wilkie, *Statistical Abstract,* p. 123).

14. Mark W. Lusk, *Peruvian Higher Education in an Environment of Development and Revolution,* Research Monograph 1 (Logan: Utah State University, Department of Sociology, 1984), pp. 91–92, and figures adapted from Consejo de Rectores de las Universidades Privadas, *20 años de universidades privadas en la República Argentina* (Buenos Aires: Editorial de Belgrano, 1978), p. 283. The absence of new universities does not preclude enrollment growth in the Catholic subsector. In Venezuela, for example, this enrollment increased from 3748 in 1965 to 8284 in 1977, all within one institution. See Unión de Universidades de América Latina (UDUAL), *Censo universitario latinoamericano* (Mexico City: UDUAL, 1967), p. 789 as well as p. 832 of the 1980 edition.

15. Consejo Nacional de Universidades (CNU), *Boletín estadístico* 1, no. 8 (Caracas: CNU, 1982): 301 (data from 1981).

16. Pontificia Universidade Católica—Rio (PUC-Rio), *Catálogo geral 1980* (Rio: PUC-Rio, 1980), pp. xii–xv.

17. Christopher Jencks and David Riesman, *The Academic Revolution* (Garden City, N.Y.: Doubleday, 1968). A good introduction to some of the evolving goals of Latin America's Catholic universities is found in Consejo Episcopal Latinoamericano (CELAM), *Iglesia y universidad en América Latina* (Bogota: CELAM, 1978).

18. See, for example, Arthur Liebman, Kenneth N. Walker, and Myron Glazer, *Latin American University Students: A Six-Nation Study* (Cambridge, Mass.: Harvard University Press, 1972), p. 55; and Orlando Albornoz, "Higher Education and the Politics of Development in Venezuela," *Journal of Interamerican Studies and World Affairs* 19 (August 1977): 309–13.

19. Calculated from UNESCO, *Statistical Yearbook, 1981* (Paris: UNESCO, 1981), p. 388; UDUAL, *Censo universitario latinoamericano* (Mexico City: UDUAL, 1980), pp. 270–404, 428–70, 713–97; Asociación Nacional de Universidades e Institutos de Enseñanza Superior (ANUIES), *Anuario estadístico 1978* (Mexico City: ANUIES, 1979), pp. 13–322.

20. Consejo Nacional de Universidades (CNU), *Oportunidades,* pp. 34–36; Edgardo

Boeninger, "Alternative Policies for Financing Higher Education," in *The Financing of Education in Latin America,* ed. Inter-American Development Bank (IDB) (Washington, D.C.: IDB, n.d.), p. 348. Private defense of tuition is formidable and widely shared by government officials, multinational organizations, and economists of education. Most important, the overwhelming majority of higher education students in *both* sectors are privileged compared to the majority of the general public that pays the taxes to finance universities, yet the students reap significant "private" or individual benefits from their university degrees.

21. Jaime Rodríguez Forero, "Universidad y estructura socio-económica," in *La universidad latinoamericana,* ed. Corporación Promoción Universitaria (CPU) (Santiago: CPU, 1972), pp. 225, 230–31; data from mid-1960s.

22. Ibid., p. 225.

23. See, for example, Luiz Antônio C. R. Cunha, "A expansão do ensino superor: causas e consequências," *Debate e Crítica* (5 (March 1975): 38–46.

24. An interesting conceptual question concerns the way and extent to which we see the private sector as limited because of choice or necessity. How much is it free to choose selectively or constrained to be limited? This chapter has emphasized choice but has cited financial constraints. Other constraints include legal-bureaucratic stipulations and tradition and timing. By *tradition and timing* I mean that the public sector typically preceded the private sector and established itself with networks and prestige in certain areas; consequently, private institutions would find it hard to enter these areas. On balance, however, I see Latin America's public universities as more constrained than their private counterparts when it comes to such factors as offering many fields of study, accepting students, responding to varied demands, spreading out across diverse regions, and so forth. Universities in both sectors are strongly and increasingly constrained financially but differently. Crucially, private universities with significant financial resources choose to be quite distinct from public universities in many respects and public universities created by governments to be distinct alternatives to their public predecessors have usually disappointed (victimized, for example, by public-sector unionization). Of course, I cannot provide a definitive answer on private versus public constraints but perhaps conclusions about which sector is more constrained are less interesting than the identification of contrasting patterns of constraints.

25. Calculated from Ministerio de Cultura y Educación (MCE), (*Estadísticas de la educación 1977* (Buenos Aires: MCE, 1977), pp. 7–8; Consejo Nacional de Universidades (CNU), *Matrícula estudiantil* (Caracas: CNU, 1978), p. 92. Crucially, in contrast to most public universities, even where private universities offer an expensive field they tend to specialize. Thus, roughly 60 and 70 percent, respectively, of Venezuela's Rafael Urdaneta and Metropolitan universities' enrollments are in engineering, whereas the public Central University has no more than 20 percent of its enrollments in any field. Calculations from CNU *Boletín,* pp. 133–34, 323, 333.

26. This section draws more closely than previous sections on Levy, *Higher Education* (pp. 280–91), and citations as well as further data can be found there.

27. I have argued that many such private–public comparisons characterizing Latin American higher education have parallels in other settings, such as U.S. elementary and secondary education. The private sector often outperforms the public sector on some conventional indicators of effectiveness like achievement levels and client satisfaction, but does so largely because of selectivity in clientele and missions. "A Comparison of Private and Public Educational Organizations," in *The Nonprofit Sector: A Research Handbook,* ed. Walter W. Powell (New Haven: Yale University Press, 1987), pp. 258–76.

28. Regional coverage offers another measure of private restrictiveness. For example, Brazil's public sector spreads out across the poorer regions much more than its private sector does, notwithstanding the abundance of nonelite private institutions. The prosperous southeast is home to 75 percent of the private institutions, versus 46 percent of the public ones. Ministerio da Educação e Cultura (MEC), *O ensino superior no Brasil 1974/1978* (Brasília: MEC, 1979), p. 22.

29. Similar points are crucial to the private–public debate in other settings. See, for ex-

ample, Richard J. Murnane, "Comparisons of Private and Public Schools: What Can We Learn?" in *Private Education and Public Policy*, ed. Daniel Levy (New York: Oxford University Press, 1986), pp. 153–69.

REFERENCES

Albornoz, Orlando. "Higher Education and the Politics of Development in Venezuela." *Journal of Interamerican Studies and World Affairs* 19 (August 1977): 309–13.

Associacion Nacional de Universidades e Institutos de Enseñanza Superior (ANUIES), *Anuario estadístico 1978*. Mexico City: ANUIES, 1979.

Boeninger, Edgardo. "Alternative Policies for Financing Higher Education." In Inter-American Development Bank (IDB) ed., *The Financing of Education in Latin America*. Washington, D.C.: IDB, n.d.

Bravo, Héctor Félix. *Las universidades privadas y el examen de habilitación para el ejercicio profesional*. Buenos Aires: Universidad de Buenos Aires, n.d.

Consejo Nacional de Universidades (CNU). *Boletín estadístico* Vol. 1, no. 8 (Caracuas: CNU, 1982).

———. *Matrícula estudiantil*. Caracas: CNU, 1978.

———. *Opportunidades de estudio en las instituciones de educación superior de Venezuela*. Caracas: CNU, 1978.

Consejo de Rectores de las Universidades Privadas. *20 años de universidades privadas en la Republica Argentina*. Buenos Aires: Editorial de Belgrano, 1978.

Consejo Episcopal Latinoamericano (CELAM). *Inglesia y universidad en América Latina*. Bogota: CELAM, 1978.

Cunna, Luiz Antônio C. R. "A expansão do ensino superior: causas e conseqüências," *Debate e Critica* 5 (March 1975): 38–46.

Geiger, Roger L. *Private Sectors in Higher Education: Structure, Function and Change in Eight Nations*. Ann Arbor: University of Michigan Press, 1986.

Jencks, Christopher, and David Riesman. *The Academic Revolution*. Garden City, N.Y.: Doubleday, 1968.

Levine, Daniel. *Conflict and Political Change in Venezuela*. Princeton, N.J.: Princeton University Press, 1973.

Levy, Daniel C. "The Rise of Private Universities in Latin America and the United States." In Margaret Archer, ed., *The Sociology of Educational Expansion*. London: Sage, 1982, pp. 93–132.

———. *Higher Education and the State in Latin America: Private Challenges to Public Dominance*. Chicago: University of Chicago Press, 1986.

———. "A Comparison of Private and Public Educational Organizations." In Walter W. Powell, ed., *The Nonprofit Sector: A Research Handbook*. New Haven, Conn.: Yale University Press, 1987, pp. 258–76.

Liebman, Arthur, Kenneth N. Walker, and Myron Glazer. *Latin American University Students: A Six-Nation Study*. Cambridge, Mass.: Harvard University Press, 1972.

Lusk, Mark W. *Peruvian Higher Education in an Environment of Development and Revolution*. Research Monograph 1. Logan: Utah State University, Department of Sociology, 1984.

Ministerio de Cultura y Educación (MCE). *Estadísticas de la educación 1977*. Buenos Aires: MCE, 1977.

Ministerio da Educacão e Cultura (MEC). *O ensino superior no Brasil 1974/197*. Brasília: MEC, 1979, p. 22.

Murnane, Richard J. "Comparisons of Private and Public Schools: What Can We Learn?" In Daniel Levy, ed., *Private Education and Public Policy*. New York: Oxford University Press, 1986, pp. 153–69.

Organization of American States. *América en cifras*.

Pontifícia Universidade Católica-Rio (PUC-Rio). *Catálogo geral 1980*. Rio: PUC-Rio, 1980.

Rodríguez, Forero, Jaime. "Universidad y estructura socioeconómica." In Corporación Promoción Universitaria (CPU) ed., *La universidad latinoamericana*. Santiago: CPU, 1972.

Unión de Universidades de América Latina (UDUAL). *Censo universitario latinoamericano*. Mexico City: UDUAL, 1980.

————. *Censo universitario latinoamericano*. Mexico City: UDUAL, 1967.

UNESCO. *Statistical Yearbook, 1981*. Paris: UNESCO, 1981.

Weisbrod, Burton A. "Toward a Theory of the Voluntary Nonprofit Sector in a Three-Sector Economy." In Susan Rose-Ackerman, ed., *The Economics of Nonprofit Institutions: Studies in Structure and Policy*. New York: Oxford University Press, 1986, pp. 21–44.

Wilkie, James W. *Statistical Abstract of Latin America*, vol. 20. Los Angeles: UCLA Latin American Center Publications, 1980.

4

Public Organizations: The Behavior of Hospitals in England and Wales

J. ROGERS HOLLINGSWORTH

and ELLEN JANE HOLLINGSWORTH

This paper compares the development and behavior of English and Welsh hospitals and discusses, in a broader context, the differences in the behavior of public and voluntary nonprofit organizations. The focus of the paper is on differences in the behavior of general hospitals during the twentieth century, but prior to the creation of the National Health Service.[1] The paper relies on existent theory as far as possible, but it also attempts to advance both the historical and the theoretical literature.[2]

The historical literature on Western Europe and North America has long reflected concern with the histories of public and voluntary organizations. Thus, there is a vast historical literature on schools and hospitals, for both the voluntary and public sectors. But there is very little empirical literature

We would like to express our appreciation to the Yale University Program on Non-Profit Organizations without the support of which the study would not have been possible. In addition, we gratefully acknowledge the support of the University of Wisconsin Institute for Research on Poverty and the University of Wisconsin Graduate Research Committee. We are indebted to many individuals for their suggestions and efforts: to Brian Abel-Smith, London School of Economics; Rudolph Klein, University of Bath; John Simon, Yale University; Robert Hanneman, University of California, Riverside; Michael Aiken, University of Pennsylvania; Odin Anderson and Burton Weisbrod, University of Wisconsin; Geoffrey Gibson, Mount Sinai School of Medicine; Elena De Costa, Indiana University of Pennsylvania; and Elliot Sprung of Sydney, Australia. To Nancy Williamson of Harvard University for her assistance with computer programming, and to Jane Mesler and Ruth Stewart for their typing, we also extend our thanks. And we are especially indebted to the librarians at the following institutions for making this study possible: the Department of Health and Social Security in London, the King Edward's Hospital Fund in London, the New York Academy of Medicine, and the Middleton Health Sciences Library at the University of Wisconsin. This is a revised version of an article that was originally published in the *Journal of Health Politics, Policy and Law* 10, no. 2 (Summer 1985): 371–93. Copyright © 1985 by Duke University. Reprinted by permission.

containing systematic comparisons of the way that public and voluntary organizations behave irrespective of country, time, or type of auspices.

The historical and social science literature on the study of voluntary and public sector organizations reflects the different research strategies of economists and historians. The few economists who have done empirical studies have compared the structure and behavior of voluntary organizations to those of public and for-profit organizations at one point in time.[3] However, historians have assumed that to understand the structure and behavior of organizations, one must first understand the historical processes that brought the structure into existence. The following analysis incorporates elements of both strategies. The historical circumstances out of which the structural arrangements of hospitals in the voluntary and public sectors emerged are briefly explained and a one-time-point comparison between the two sectors is presented. That time point, the late 1930s, is chosen because the Ministry of Health undertook a survey of all English and Welsh hospitals which focused on that period, and the data provide an excellent opportunity for comparing the behavior of public and voluntary organizations.

Specifically, the comparison we present answers the following questions:

1. Historically, why did quite different types of hospitals emerge in the voluntary and public sectors of England and Wales?
2. In what ways and to what extent were public and voluntary general hospitals different in England and Wales during the 1930s? While economists have tended to highlight differences between organizations in the public and private sectors, the economics literature does not always recognize that there is variation within the two sectors. However, our strategy will address this issue in some of the other questions guiding this research. Thus, other research questions are:
3. Among voluntary hospitals, what types of differences existed? In particular, how did teaching hospitals differ from other voluntary hospitals?
4. Among public hospitals, to what extent were local council hospitals, many separated from Poor Law administration for less than a decade, different from hospitals remaining under the auspices of the Poor Law?
5. How did the behavior of local council hospitals compare to that of voluntary hospitals? Did the 1929 Local Government Act result in voluntary and council hospitals that provided the same type of services?
6. Did the behavior of hospitals vary by their spatial distributions? Specifically, how did public and voluntary hospitals in London—both relatively well financed—compare with one another, and how did London hospitals in each sector compare with those in each sector in the provinces?

THEORETICAL AND HISTORICAL PERSPECTIVES

In a seminal paper, economist Burton Weisbrod has provided a theoretical explanation of why collective goods emerge in the private voluntary or the public sector.[4] He argues that most collective goods are developed first in the voluntary sector and only later does the public sector begin to provide the same services. While we are very indebted to Weisbrod for his substantial advancement of the literature, the theoretical perspective of this paper diverges somewhat from his work. Contrary to Weisbrod's argument, the historical record reveals that some collective goods are provided in the public sector before they emerge in the voluntary sector. For example, public hospitals in some societies developed before any emerged in the private sector. Thus, the theory must be refined in order to account for the emergence of services first in the public sector.[5]

Building on Weisbrod's work, the following theoretical perspective helps to explain the emergence of voluntary and public sector organizations. When only a minority of the population want specific types of collective goods (for example, hospitals, schools, parks, libraries) and are willing to pay for them, private voluntary organizations tend to develop in order to provide the services. In a heterogeneous society, especially one with a very inegalitarian distribution of income, there are many voluntary organizations that emerge in response to the demands of various minority groups. Because all minorities are not equally able to establish the same type of voluntary organizations, there will be considerable diversity concerning the type of services provided by voluntary organizations.

Over time, as the nature of demand for certain services becomes somewhat more homogeneous, voluntary organizations cannot meet all of the demand. Troubled by an increasing number of free riders, the voluntary sector is simply faced by too much demand relative to the funding available. To confront the problem, voluntary organizations resort to user fees, which become increasingly common as the overall wealth of the society rises with economic development. It is at that point that the public sector is likely to enter the arena of service provision. As the demand for services becomes widespread, and especially when this demand is combined with increases in per capita income, the state may become a provider in substantive areas previously dominated by voluntary organizations. In contrast to voluntary organizations, the state has greater power to discourage free riders by coercing payment through a tax system and by establishing rigid rules as to who may receive services and under what circumstances. Thus the public sector is somewhat more efficient in providing collective goods, as it can coerce payments.[6]

Once the public sector becomes a provider of services, the voluntary sector may well continue, though it will tend to be financed by minorities who are willing to pay for higher quality services than those financed by the state. Occasionally, the voluntary sector may even be successful in receiving public subsidies in order to provide services of a different quality from those provided by public organizations.

On the other hand, there are certain classes of public goods for which there may be no minority able or willing to provide financing (for example, defense, prisons, and welfare support for "undeserving" groups in the population). When this occurs, there may be demand that the state raise money to provide these services. In these circumstances, the voluntary sector historically does not precede the public sector. Moreover, if the society is relatively homogeneous, ethnically, racially, religiously, and in terms of wealth, then the demands for health, education, and similar services are likely to be relatively homogeneous. And in the face of homogeneously demanded goods, collective goods are likely to emerge first in the public rather than the private sector. For example, hospitals emerged first in the public sector in Sweden, for it was a country which industrialized very late, did not have highly skewed income, and was relatively homogeneous religiously and ethnically.

Thus far, the discussion has focused on why organizations emerge in the public or the voluntary private sector. But how do voluntary organizations behave relative to those in the public sector? We have argued that these two sectors behave differently because they respond to different environments. More specifically, public sector organizations tend to respond to the preferences of the majority, even though these preferences may not be clearly articulated, while voluntary organizations tend to respond to the preferences of minorities.[7] Relative to public organizations, those in the voluntary sector are somewhat more innovative, have a high level of technological complexity, are somewhat smaller, are less egalitarian in access to services, provide somewhat higher quality services, and spend more money on individual clients. Because public organizations, on the other hand, receive their funding from a much wider segment of society, they must provide a broader array of services, serve a larger constituency, and operate with fewer resources on a per client basis—all of which have implications for quality of and access to services, level of technological complexity, size, costs, types of case-loads, and the speed with which individual clients are processed.[8]

HISTORICAL BACKGROUND AND CHANGES IN THE 1930s

Although a full explanation of the circumstances leading to the development of English and Welsh general hospitals is beyond the scope of this paper, the broad historical outline as well as the major trends in the development of general hospitals during the 1930s are summarized below.[9]

English and Welsh hospitals, historically, were operated either under voluntary nonprofit auspices or under the public Poor Law authorities. Voluntary and public hospitals differed in origin, in staffing patterns, and in client load. Whereas the services of the voluntary hospitals were for the so-called "deserving poor," Poor Law institutions were for paupers, considered to be the "undeserving," and the elderly, who were presumed to be deserving. The tradition of English voluntarism, particularly with regard to hospitals, was strong from the seventeenth century onward. This tradition called for elites to make provision for the suffering of the "deserving poor," to provide respite for them through donations and subscriptions for hospitals. Donors and patrons "sponsored" patients for hospital admission.[10]

There was enormous variation in behavior among voluntary hospitals. Some voluntary hospitals were associated with rest and convalescent institutions; others were hardly more than converted residences. The large and prestigious teaching hospitals were renowned for their "honorary" consultants, their nursing schools, and their skill with complicated cases. Cottage hospitals, on the other hand, were often small and underequipped.

Doctors in the larger voluntary hospitals provided their services gratis, both because of their sense of social obligation and their recognition that wealthy patients preferred their physicians to be consultants who held honorary hospital positions. Elite doctors often became strongly identified with particular voluntary hospitals. Thus, many of the roots of voluntary hospitals were firmly in the tradition of charity for the deserving poor.[11]

There was somewhat less diversity in behavior among public general hospitals, probably because all were operated under the Poor Law. Designed for the "undeserving poor," Poor Law facilities developed in the public sector because there was no upper-income minority willing to provide services for what were considered to be the derelicts of society. While there was widespread recognition that aid to the "undeserving" was necessary, only the state with its coercive power was willing to provide such services. Over time, some of the wealthier Poor Law Unions provided Poor Law Hospitals, but more commonly, medical services were provided in Poor Law Institutions, where the ill were mixed with the senile, the orphaned, and the destitute. Poor Law inpatient medical services were more oriented to chronic services, not to acute care. The doctors who worked in Poor Law institutions and hospitals were full-time salaried physicians, but were expected to conduct administrative activities a considerable portion of their time.[12]

By the 1930s, the entire hospital industry was subjected to strong pressures for change. The most important pressure for change that the voluntary hospitals faced was the problem of rising costs. In the 1920s and 1930s, most voluntary hospitals (London hospitals in particular) experienced serious financial difficulties and pleaded anxiously for funds.[13] It was indeed expensive to acquire new complex technology and to provide the trained nursing appropriate to complicated surgery. The popularity of the automobile resulted in an increase in the number of accident victims needing emergency services that were costly to provide. As hospital costs rose, the traditional sources of hospital income from the voluntary sector were inadequate. The National Health Insurance plan, begun in 1911 to cover general practitioner services for the working class, had for all practical purposes provided no funding for hospital benefits.[14] During the interwar years, several important national commissions focused on the financial problems of hospitals.

Although both the number of voluntary hospitals and the number of beds in voluntary hospitals increased during the 1930s (see Table 4.1),

Table 4.1.   General Hospitals, 1911–1938

	1911	1921	1938
Number of general hospitals[a]	608	715	929
Number of beds in general hospitals	70,862	74,867	111,981
Number of voluntary general hospitals	554	641	696
Number of beds in voluntary general hospitals	29,935	37,027	58,007
Percent of all general hospital beds in voluntary general hospitals[b]	42.2	49.5	51.8

Source: Robert Pinker, *English Hospital Statistics 1861–1938* (London: 1966).

[a]The data in *Hospital Survey* for general hospitals differ somewhat from those in Pinker's study. See note 24.

[b]Prior to 1929, the hospital beds in general public hospitals were almost wholly reserved for the indigent.

there was grave concern about the survival of the voluntary system of hospitals. Slowly, society recognized that the voluntary sector could not meet the increased demand for, and cost of, hospital care. It was this recognition that led to change in the public sector. In the decade before World War II, a new type of public hospital emerged—the council hospital, controlled by local government and offering general services to all local residents regardless of age or income. For the most part, the council hospitals were former Poor Law facilities "appropriated" by local authorities after 1929.

In 1929 the Local Government Act provided for the dissolution of the Boards of Guardians and placed the administration of Poor Law facilities under the Public Assistance Committees of counties and county boroughs. Moreover, counties and county boroughs were given the authority to appropriate Poor Law facilities and operate them as local hospitals. Only Poor Law hospitals in which medical services could be separated from custodial care were eligible for appropriation, and parts of institutions (wards or blocks) could be appropriated.[15] Central government block grants to local authorities for a variety of health services were to be provided, and the Ministry of Health would reduce the intensity of its oversight of hospitals. The emphasis of the bill was on creating coordination among medical services at the local level. With local authorities already involved with provision of medical care for maternity cases, school children, and infectious diseases, it made sense for there to be a municipal provision of *general* hospital services, too.

The Local Government Act did not create a public hospital system with the stroke of a pen. The law did not mandate changes. Rather, it merely permitted local authorities to take action if they wished. And subsequently, the more progressive and prosperous local authorities moved rapidly toward implementation of the new law. For example, the London Common Council was the most efficient as it implemented during the 1930s a plan for the creation of council hospitals and reorganized the hospital functions of Poor Law facilities.[16]

Appropriation made possible the existence of council hospitals, but it did not ensure improvement in the quality of service provided. Previously, as Poor Law facilities, such hospitals had housed large numbers of tubercular and other types of chronically ill patients and did not have adequate facilities for acute care. And although facilities for acute care improved in those public hospitals that became council hospitals after 1929, acute facilities were relatively novel and difficult to finance in council hospitals. Also, full-time doctor-administrators were in short supply, and assisting doctors were generally nonexistent. Part-time consultants were rare because medical appointments in public hospitals offered little professional advancement and were not sought by ambitious younger doctors. Thus, in many instances, doctors who had presided over mixed institutions for many years, doing as much administrative work as medical work, found themselves called upon to deliver modern acute services in council hospitals.

Council hospitals modeled themselves as closely as possible after the well-established and esteemed voluntary hospitals. Physical facilities—heat, elevators, covered corridors—were improved. Operating rooms, pathology laboratories, and x-ray equipment were installed. Outpatient departments were created or strengthened. Council hospitals, in appointing their few part-time consultants, were doing just what voluntary hospitals had done, but unlike voluntary hospitals, council hospitals found it necessary to pay part-time consultants. Moreover, council hospitals offered nurses better salaries than did voluntary hospitals. In a few instances, totally new hospitals were built. For remodeled council hospitals, new names were chosen and the exteriors were altered and improved in order to lessen stigma.[17] Council hospitals, like those in the voluntary sector, also attempted to recover costs from patients, though their contributions covered only a very small fraction of actual costs.

Some Poor Law Hospitals continued in existence to serve paupers. This type of hospital could send acute cases to local voluntary hospitals. For this reason, Poor Law Hospitals, as distinct from council hospitals, did not develop acute care services and remained institutions for the treatment of the chronically ill.[18]

Inevitably there was disappointment with Local Authority responses to the 1929 Act. Some Local Authorities were too financially strained to appropriate institutions; other appropriated Poor Law hospitals and then could hardly afford to improve the facilities. Thus, the types of facilities and the quality of care in council hospitals varied greatly. Many council hospitals could offer only a few services.

Shortages of medical specialists and hospital beds in some areas were also salient issues in the 1930s. Specialists, for economic reasons, tended to locate in large voluntary hospitals or in specialty hospitals, both of which were in large urban areas. For many citizens, seeing a specialist involved the uncertainties and expenses of a long journey. Cottage hospitals tended to have only general practitioners, who were often confronted with cases beyond their competence.[19] Their options were to carry on with the case (hoping for the best) or to refer the patient to some distant facility. Neither alternative was highly palatable to the patient, and public outcry for better distribution of specialists was heard during the 1930s.[20] Council hospitals also needed specialists on their staffs to cope with acute cases, further exacerbating the shortage and distribution problems. Finally, even the rapid development of cottage hospitals during the previous 50 years and the inauguration of council hospitals had not brought enough beds to some areas.[21]

These were the main hospital issues on the eve of World War II, when there were 929 general hospitals in England and Wales.[22] It was widely recognized that the condition of voluntary hospitals varied enormously, and that they were at risk financially. Council hospitals were clearly, if unevenly, becoming an option for care, as the public sector assumed more responsibility for acute services previously rendered mostly in the voluntary sector. Despite the high level of public and government concern about hospitals, however, sources of accurate, complete information were few.

One outcome of World War II was that, for the first time, a systematic attempt was made to characterize hospitals in the prewar era. Fear of heavy bombing in London resulted in the dispatch of hundreds of doctors to hospitals in the provinces shortly after the war began. They found that hospitals, many mustered into the Emergency Hospital Service, often lacked the basics: x-ray equipment, operating rooms, and pathology laboratories.[23] Some hospitals were greatly understaffed and underequipped, and a massive effort to ensure at least minimum quality of care was launched. Finding so much variance in hospital accommodation and determined to obtain systematic information to facilitate postwar planning, the Ministry of Health in 1941 undertook a survey of every hospital in England and Wales. It is the data from that very large and careful *Hospital Survey*, completed in 1943 but not published until 1945–1946, which are used in the analysis below.[24] Because the survey focused on hospitals for the year 1938, much of the following analysis centers on hospitals during that year.

MEASURES OF HOSPITAL BEHAVIOR

The *Hospital Survey* data can be used to evaluate a variety of measures of public and voluntary hospital behavior. The various types of behavior are the subject of a sizeable literature, although limitations of data prevent our using several measures developed in recent years. There are interrelationships (or trade-offs) among the types of behavior that are discussed in that the presence of one type of behavior may inhibit another type.

The first measure is size—the total of general, special, and pay beds in each hospital. Total bed size has direct effects on the staff needed, the kinds of equipment provided, and the types of illnesses served.

Quality of service, the second measure, has been approached with a variety of techniques by different scholars and is the subject of a vast literature.[25] Obviously, the concept of quality is difficult to operationalize. Quality is concerned with the effect of care on the health of an individual. Numerous researchers have attempted to develop a reliable index of the quality of hospital care in terms of final outcomes, but thus far these endeavors have not been very successful. Partly for this reason, much of the scholarly literature simply ignores the issue of hospital quality. To confront this problem, a precedent has emerged for using inputs as a proxy for quality. However, there is no single input characteristic which is an adequate measure of the quality of hospital medical services, for the quality of medical services is a multidimensional concept. Thus, in this analysis (and consistent with some of the recent literature), we use three input measures—the number of nurses per bed, the number of qualified technical staff per bed (qualified technical staff include pharmacists, radiographers, physicists, laboratory assistants, massage staff, and chiropodists), and the number of doctors per bed. Unfortunately, case outcome data are unavailable for this period.

The third measure, cost of care, is the average cost of care per patient per week. These data are not available for many hospitals, either public or voluntary. Cost per patient per week data are available for 278 of the 656 voluntary hospitals (57.6 percent) and for 87 of 140 public hospitals (62.1 percent).

Technological complexity, the fourth measure, is the number of full-time and part-time medical *specialists* on the hospital staff. The number of specialists has been selected as a measure of technological complexity because the presence of highly specialized personnel represented one of the most, if not the most, important forms of medical technology, especially for the pre–World War II era. There were 16 types of specialists included in the analysis of technological complexity.[26]

Another important measure on which we compare public and voluntary hospitals is their technological equipment. For this purpose, we developed an index that includes whether the hospital had: (1) one or more operating rooms, (2) a pathology laboratory, (3) diagnostic x-ray equipment, and (4) therapeutic x-ray equipment.[27] These facilities were considered to be basic for hospital operation by those who carried out the hospital survey in 1942–43.

We also compare hospitals in terms of their patient loads and occupancy levels. More specifically, we compare public and voluntary hospitals in terms of (1) the percentage of all beds which were occupied, and (2) the number of outpatient visits per year. We also present data on the average number of people on waiting lists, although the meaning of waiting list data is not entirely clear. Voluntary hospitals occasionally developed long waiting lists in order to demonstrate to potential donors how greatly their services were needed, while public hospitals were not permitted to accumulate waiting lists. In addition, we compare the types of hospitals in terms of average length of stay. This variable is influenced by the relative

Table 4.2. Voluntary and Public Hospitals Compared in Size For the Year 1938

Total Number of Beds	Percent of Voluntary Hospitals	Percent of Public Hospitals[a]
Under 50 beds	54.3%	2.9%
50–99	17.6	.7
100–299	23.2	28.6
300–499	3.2	32.9
500 or more beds	1.7	34.9
Number of hospitals	656	140

[a]Both council hospitals and Poor Law hospitals are included in public hospitals.
Source: See note 24.

efficiency as well as the different types of case loads of the two hospital sectors. Finally, in order to compare accessibility to the two types of hospitals by social class and income group, we have collected data from various histories of individual hospitals and Ministry of Health reports.

FINDINGS

In what way and to what extent were public and voluntary general hospitals different in England and Wales during the 1930s?[28] Probably the most striking difference is the size of the institutions. As Table 4.2 shows, scarcely any public hospitals had fewer than 100 beds, whereas almost 72 percent of voluntary hospitals were of that size. The small hospital, with its often-attendant problem of providing highly competent medical staffing, was a voluntary hospital. Such a hospital, often a cottage hospital in a town or village, could offer only basic services. The public hospital, on the other hand, was very large, a result of the Poor Law mentality which required that institutions for the destitute be inexpensive, offering unspecialized and custodial services to masses of people. But as Table 4.3 indicates, the greater size of the public hospitals was not reflected in the presence of higher quality of services or greater number of specialists.

Public hospitals had less medical and support personnel for patient care than did voluntary hospitals. Of course, with a higher percentage of chronic patients as part of their case mix, public hospitals probably had less need for medical personnel and technologically complex facilities than did voluntary hospitals with their emphasis on acute care. Public hospitals spent less money weekly per patient, perhaps in part because they had fewer nurses, fewer doctors (both specialists and generalists), and fewer qualified technical staff.

Public hospitals appear to have been slightly more advanced than vol-

Table 4.3. Comparison of Types of Hospitals

Measures	All Hospitals			Voluntary Hospitals		
	Voluntary	Public	p^g	Teaching	Non-Teaching	p^g
Number of beds	87	472	***	451	71	***
Indicators of quality						
Nurses per 100 beds[a]	40	27	***	51	39	***
Doctors per 100 beds[b]	12	2	***	12	11	—
Qualified technical						
staff per 100 beds[c]	3	1	***	6	3	***
Cost (per patient per	£3-10-3	£3-4-2		£4-1-11	£3-9-3	
week)[d]	(N=378)	(N=87)	**	(N=28)	(N=350)	***
Technological complexity						
Full-time specialists per						
100 beds	.13	.05	—	1.45	.07	***
Part-time specialists						
per 100 beds[e]	10.0	1.8	***	7.0	10.0	—
Index of technological						
level of facilities[f]	2.4	2.5	—	4.0	2.4	***
Patient loads and						
occupancy level						
Percent of beds occu-						
pied	72.8	84.3	***	85.9	72.2	***
Average waiting list	78	0	***	717	51	***
Average days of pa-						
tient stay	16.5	38.9	***	16.4	17.9	—
Average outpatient visits	28,712	15,853	*	237,860	19,009	***
N	656	140		28	628	

[a]Nurses include all senior, staff, male, and assistant nurses, as well as student nurses and pupil mid-wives.

[b]Doctors include the following: full- and part-time physicians, surgeons, specialists, medical superintendents and deputies, registrars, chief assistants, and house physicians and surgeons. Three part-time persons are considered equal to one full-time person.

[c]The personnel included in qualified technical staff are listed above in the section on measures of hospital behavior. Three part-time qualified technical staff were considered to be equal to one full-time staff person.

[d]Data on weekly spending are not available for many smaller voluntary and public hospitals.

[e]Hospitals identified most specialists as part-time staff, but did not distinguish between doctors who saw patients almost every day in the hospital and those who had only one patient a year.

[f]The scale ranges from 0 to 4, with 4 being the maximum. The index is composed by tallying one point for each of the following: (1) having a pathology laboratory, indicated by the presence of a full- or part-time pathologist; (2) having one or more operating theatres; (3) having diagnostic x-ray capability, shown by the presence of a full- or part-time radiographer (support staff); (4) having therapeutic x-ray capability, shown by the presence of a full- or part-time radiologist or radiotherapist on the medical staff. Since this index does not distinguish between hospitals with one operating theatre and hospitals with several, its effect is to minimize some of the differences in technology.

[g]p = Level of statistical significance of the difference in values: * indicates $p < .05$; ** indicates $p < .01$; *** indicates $p < .001$.

untary hospitals in terms of technological equipment (see the index variable for technological facilities in Table 4.3). Yet, because public hospitals were much larger in bed size, the number of patients who used the equipment in public hospitals was much greater than the number of patients doing so in voluntary hospitals. Thus, it seems doubtful that public hospitals had any advantage in terms of technical equipment.

Public hospitals were both more and less accessible to the population than were voluntary hospitals. Only a fully occupied public hospital would turn away a patient, almost regardless of what the patient's ailments might be, whereas voluntary hospitals could—and did—refuse cases which they classified as uninteresting. Preferring acute cases, the voluntary hospital tended to turn away infectious diseases, the chronically ill, and the aged. Thus, voluntary hospitals had lower occupancy rates and shorter average lengths of stay (17 days compared to 39 days in public hospitals).

On the other hand, voluntary hospitals provided outpatient services much more actively than did public hospitals. On average, voluntary hospitals had almost twice as many outpatient visits as public hospitals. Many of these public outpatient services had arisen from demands resulting from work injuries.[29] However, accident cases were also brought to voluntary hospitals, especially in London. Although general practitioners complained that hospitals' free outpatient services siphoned off clients who could afford to pay doctors for assistance, voluntary hospitals staunchly defended their provision of outpatient clinics. They contended that outpatient voluntary clinics provided invaluable experience for training doctors and fulfilled an urgent social need.[30]

These findings seem to demonstrate quite graphically that on the eve of World War II, the two major hospital sectors had quite different contours. Most of the voluntary hospitals were struggling with providing sufficiently specialized services to handle patient demands while still servicing quite local markets (and therefore remaining small). Public hospitals struggled with problems of immense size and scarce resources. Voluntary hospitals tended to offer higher-quality services, and spend more per patient per week. Although they were less accessible to prospective inpatients, they were far more accessible to outpatients.

Among voluntary and public hospitals, what differences existed within each sector? Overall, there was greater variation in hospital characteristics among institutions in the voluntary sector. The origin of voluntary hospitals was much more mixed, and voluntary hospitals did not operate under public constraints that were comparable in all locations as was the case with public hospitals.

Students of English and Welsh hospitals have occasionally highlighted two main axes of differentiation among voluntary hospitals—whether the hospital was a teaching hospital or not, and whether it was located in London or the provinces. We will take up the second of these issues later, turning here to the differences between teaching and non-teaching hospitals.

In Table 4.3, the comparison between teaching hospitals and nonteaching hospitals is presented. On average, teaching hospitals were six and a half times larger than nonteaching hospitals. Teaching hospitals tended to have many more nurses, a few more doctors, and twice as many qualified technical staff per 100 beds; to spend more money on patient care; and to have more technological equipment. With its highly superior facilities and its enormous social prestige, the average teaching hospital had very high occupancy, a sizeable waiting list, and a quarter of a million outpatient visits per year.

The teaching hospitals were extremely skilled in their fund raising, seeking to build long waiting lists in order to demonstrate to potential donors how much their services were needed.[31] Meanwhile, they used their outpatient services in order to create good will among those of humbler origin.

Teaching hospitals had different styles of behavior in part because of their different revenue sources. The general pattern among voluntary hospitals was that the larger the hospital, the smaller the percentage of total receipts obtained from patients and their various "contributory schemes" and the larger the proportion from legacies and endowments.[32]

It is interesting to study the figures on doctors for the two types of voluntary hospitals. Teaching hospitals did not have many more doctors per 100 beds, even though the professional advantages of a teaching hospital appointment were considerable to a doctor.[33]

The *Hospital Survey* data overall indicate that teaching and nonteaching voluntary hospitals were very different in size, quality, cost, technological complexity, patient loads and occupancy levels. And, as indicated above, it was the teaching hospital that set the standard to which other hospitals aspired. Teaching hospitals were perceived, correctly, as very special places, both by persons in the health industries and by patients.

Public hospitals can also be examined on the basis of the extent to which council hospitals were different in behavior from public hospitals remaining under administration of the Poor Law. By 1939, most public general hospitals were council hospitals, although some had been taken over by local authorities only a year or two before World War II.

As Table 4.4 reveals, council hospitals (those open to the general public) were substantially larger than the public general hospitals remaining under the administration of the Poor Law. It was the larger and better public hospitals that local authorities had found most ready for conversion to general services for all residents. In one volume after another of the *Hospital Survey*, the wretchedness of the remaining Poor Law hospitals was noted. Thus, council hospitals spent significantly more for patients per week, not surprising in view of the acute care functions they were expected to provide. But in terms of staffing—particularly medical staffing—the council hospitals enjoyed only slightly better ratios of doctors to beds than the Poor Law hospitals. As mentioned earlier, public sector employment in hospitals had never been attractive to doctors, and evidently many council hospitals found that legacy difficult to overcome even if they could afford additional salary.

Two variables in Table 4.4 further illustrate the contrast between council hospital and Poor Law hospital behavior. The various indices measuring technological facilities were quite a bit higher in council hospitals, reflecting their increased attention to acute care, and their diminishing role

Public Organizations

123

Table 4.4. Comparison of Types of Hospitals

Measures	Council and Poor Law Hospitals			Council and Voluntary Hospitals		
	Council Hospitals	Poor Law Hospitals	p^g	Council Hospitals	Voluntary Hospitals	p^g
Number of beds	551	327	***	551	87	***
Indicators of quality:						
Nurses per 100 beds[a]	30	21	***	30	40	***
Doctors per 100 beds[b]	2	1	***	2	12	***
Qualified technical staff per 100 beds[c]	1	0	***	1	3	***
Cost (per patient per week)[d]	£3-8-9 (N=70)	£2-5-8 (N=17)	***	£3-8-9 (N=70)	£3-10-3 (N=378)	—
Technological complexity						
Full-time specialists per 100 beds	.05	.03	—	.05	.13	—
Part-time specialists per 100 beds[e]	1.9	1.6	—	1.9	10.0	***
Index of technological level of facilities[f]	2.9	1.7	***	2.9	2.4	***
Patient loads and occupancy level						
Percent of beds occupied	84.7	85.0	—	84.7	72.8	***
Average waiting list	—	—	—	—	78	—
Average days of patient stay	30.1	66.9	***	30.1	16.5	***
Average outpatient visits	22,951	1,938	***	22,951	28,712	—
N	93	46		93	656	

See Table 4.3 for notes.

in chronic care (which previously had loomed large in the caseloads of all public hospitals). Council hospitals also handled outpatients on a scale ten times as great as Poor Law hospitals, another evidence of the expectations placed on general hospitals. Outpatient services provided by Poor Law hospitals continued to be minimal, conceived in part in response to road accidents rather than to the needs of the general population.[34] Although council hospitals handled many more outpatient visits than did Poor Law hospitals, it is interesting to note that they handled only a few thousand more visits annually than the much smaller voluntary non-teaching hospitals. (See Tables 4.3 and 4.4). The new council hospitals had only partially moved into the role of providing outpatient services by 1939, and were they to be compared with same-sized voluntary hospitals, their provision of outpatient services would appear modest in the extreme.

The two types of public hospitals were virtually on a par in terms of their inpatient occupancy. Council hospitals were quite full, although their average length of stay (30 days) was considerably shorter than Poor Law hospital averages (67 days).

Although council hospitals were quite unlike Poor Law hospitals, the question that intrigued commentators in the late 1930s was how much they had become like voluntary hospitals. To what extent, during a decade of general economic hardship, did these approximately 100 general hospitals serve as a meaningful public alternative to the voluntary system?

Certainly the 1930s had seen vigorous changes in many council hospitals, as operating theaters were built, histology laboratories were added, mortuaries were cooled, waiting rooms were constructed, dispensaries and nurses' messrooms were created, chronic units were converted to acute care, hospital blocks were connected with concrete and glass bridges, and new entrances were opened.[35] But as Table 4.4 demonstrates, it was very difficult for public council hospitals to catch up with voluntary hospitals.

Even though council hospitals were often able to pay better salaries for nurses, they still had fewer nurses per 100 beds than voluntary hospitals. Both council and voluntary hospitals had an acute shortage of adequate accommodation for nurses. Similarly, willingness to pay consultants (a concession which voluntary hospitals had been unwilling to make), did not provide council hospitals with nearly as many doctors as there were in voluntary hospitals. There had been some consideration of allowing general practitioners to have access to council hospitals as part of the effort to get more medical staff, but for a variety of reasons, general practitioners were excluded. All in all, the council hospitals were usually understaffed, as they often had only one or two physician-administrators.[36]

During the 1930s, as during the early years of World War II, the acquisition of medical equipment by needy hospitals proved to be much easier than the redistribution of medical personnel. Although new equipment was often unsatisfactorily housed, medical personnel was simply impossible to muster as needed.[37] It was difficult to coax specialists to locate outside major cities, even for large voluntary hospitals, and the lower-status council hospitals faced grave difficulties in trying to recruit many kinds of specialists found in teaching hospitals and other fortunately situated institutions.[38]

Both council and voluntary hospitals tried to get patients to contribute to the cost of medical care. In the 1930s it was alleged that some patients avoided council hospitals because they mistakenly thought their obligations to pay for services there would be greater than in voluntary hospitals. But in neither type of hospital did most people pay for hospital services from personal savings. Most admittances were charity or near charity cases. Probably no more than 20 percent of patients actually paid out-of-pocket for hospital care. Nevertheless, revenue from patients was an important source of voluntary hospital revenue—London hospitals received 43.2 percent of their revenue from patients and provincial hospitals received 60.5 percent of their revenue from patient contributions. Much of this patient contribution came from two sources: subscription funds and the middle and upper-middle classes. Whereas many voluntary hospitals had entered into arrangements with subscription schemes for the supply of services, council hospitals had not done so on the same scale. Unfortunately, precise data are not available on the percent of public hospital revenue derived from patients, but secondary sources usually estimate it to have been substantially lower than for voluntary hospitals.[39]

Both council and voluntary hospitals had beds for full-paying patients, though they were much more evident in voluntary hospitals.[40] From hospital to hospital, pay-bed arrangements differed. Some hospitals provided separate, cheerful accommodations; others inaugurated semiprivate rooms. However, patients were expected to settle physicians' fees on a separate basis. There were many hard issues associated with pay beds: should pay-bed occupants have the right to be seen by their own doctors even if their doctors were not on the hospital staff? Was it appropriate that public hospitals have special facilities for upper-income patients? Should paying patients pay more than the cost of their care in order to subsidize the care of others? Although these matters were not resolved by the late 1930s, approximately 7 percent of all voluntary beds were pay beds, with nonteaching hospitals so designating 11 percent of their beds. Council hospitals had about 1 percent of their beds as pay beds.[41]

Of course, there was variation in the attainments of council hospitals—some had better locations to attract staff, larger budgets for purchasing and salaries, more years of experience with general services. Certainly council hospitals as a group compared favorably with Poor Law hospitals, if not so favorably with voluntary hospitals.

The differences between council hospitals and voluntary hospitals appear no less dramatic when controls for size are introduced into the analysis. Middle-sized voluntary hospitals (with 100–299 beds) provided higher-quality services, spent more money, exhibited more technological complexity, and provided more access than middle-sized council hospitals (see Table 4.5). Larger public and voluntary hospitals (over 300 beds) were also quite dissimilar. For example, professional staff were more numerous in voluntary hospitals, and there was more sophisticated equipment available.

These findings, with and without controls for size, make it abundantly clear that council hospitals were quite unlike voluntary hospitals. Handicapped by traditions of staffing, the large number of long-term patients, the lack of money, and cultural stigma, council hospitals provided much-needed services to the English and Welsh public, but they were not effective options for providing the highest-quality care.

Even in London (see Table 4.6), the new council hospital did not measure up to the voluntary hospital behavior. The London Common Council, in taking over London institutions from the Boards of Guardians, had assumed responsibility for a relatively well-administered set of institutions.[42] London public authorities had long been known for their ability to run good health care facilities.[43] Even so, the new council hospitals were inferior in quality to the voluntary hospitals, though equal in spending for patients. At the time of appropriation only 9 of the 28 London public

Table 4.5. Comparison of Council and Voluntary Hospitals, with Size Controls

Measures	Hospitals with 100–299 Beds			Hospitals with over 300 Beds		
	Council	Voluntary	p^g	Council	Voluntary	p^g
Number of beds	203	164	—	650	479	—
Indicators of quality						
Nurses per 100 beds[a]	25	42	***	31	49	***
Doctors per 100 beds[b]	3	8	***	2	9	***
Qualified technical staff per 100 beds[c]	1	4	***	1	5	***
Cost (per patient per week)[d]	£2-19-11	£3-8-9		£3-11-3	£3-18-5	
	(N=14)	(N=124)	***	(N=55)	(N=32)	—
Technological complexity						
Full-time specialists per 100 beds	0	.2	—	.1	1.2	—
Part-time specialists per 100 beds[e]	3.0	9.0	***	2.0	6.0	***
Index of technological level of facilities[f]	2.1	3.5	***	3.2	3.9	***
Patient loads and occupancy level						
Percent of beds occupied	78.5	82.7	—	86.0	85.4	—
Average waiting list	0	164	***	0	672	***
Average days of patient stay	34.7	18.0	***	29.5	17.5	***
Average outpatient visits	4,111	54,061	***	28,324	234,732	***
N	19	152		73	32	

See Table 4.3 for notes.

hospitals had outpatient departments.[44] Perhaps the achievements of the Guardians of London public hospitals have been somewhat oversold.

Council hospitals in the provinces also did not compare very favorably to voluntary provincial hospitals—that is, not any more than was the case in London. They, too, were tied to their unglamorous pasts and inhibited by the economic constraints of the 1930s.

London voluntary hospitals were quite different from their sister institutions in the provinces. Not only were they much larger, but they had staff for higher-quality services, more money to spend on patient care, greater technology and specialization, and higher occupancy. The same dissimilarity according to location was not found among council hospitals. London council hospitals appear to have been rather like provincial council hospitals as to size, quality, specialization, and technology.

CONCLUDING OBSERVATIONS

The history of voluntary and public hospitals in England and Wales supports the theory that collective goods will first be provided in the voluntary

Table 4.6.   Comparison of Types of Hospitals, with Location Controls

Measures	Hospitals in London		Hospitals in Provinces			
	Voluntary	Council	Voluntary	All Public	Council	Poor Law
Number of beds	229	606	76	446	531	327
Indicators of quality						
Nurses per 100 beds[a]	47	36	39	27	27	21
Doctors per 100 beds[b]	12	3	12	2	2	1
Qualified technical staff per 100 beds[c]	5	2	3	1	1	.4
Cost (per patient per week)[d]	£4-6-7	£4-7-6	£3-6-10	£2-13-8	£2-16-10	£2-4-8
Technological complexity						
Full-time specialists per 100 beds	1.0	.03	.08	.05	.07	.03
Part-time specialists per 100 beds[e]	13.0	2.0	10.0	2.0	2.0	2.0
Index of technological level of facilities[f]	3.4	3.0	2.4	2.4	2.9	1.7
Patient loads and occupancy level						
Percent of beds occupied	79.9	86.1	72.5	84.5	84.2	84.9
Average waiting list	206	0	69	0	0	0
Average days of patient stay	17.9	30.2	16.4	42.8	29.0	66.9
Average outpatient visits	132,795	39,075	20,612	10,232	16,406	1,895
N	46	27	611	111	65	46

See Table 4.3 for notes.

sector if only a minority of citizens have enough wealth to express demand for the goods. If the demand for a collective good becomes increasingly homogeneous throughout the society, the public sector will begin to provide the services. When there are groups for which no one is willing to assume the financial responsibility but for whom the society accepts moral responsibility, the state must provide services. This was the case with Poor Law institutions and hospitals.

In addition, the foregoing data analysis has highlighted several strongly related patterns of hospital behavior:

1. Hospitals in the public and voluntary sectors behaved very differently. As suggested by the theory, relative to hospitals in the public sector, those in the voluntary sector were somewhat more innovative, had a somewhat higher level of technological complexity, were much smaller, were somewhat less egalitarian in access to care, provided somewhat higher-quality services, and spent more money on individual clients.
2. Within the ranks of voluntary hospitals, teaching hospitals—the quintessential voluntary institutions—were very different from non-teaching hospitals.
3. Council hospitals behaved quite dissimilarly from Poor Law hospitals.

4. Council hospitals, as a group and with controls for size and location, differed substantially from the voluntary hospitals on which they tried to pattern themselves.
5. Location had more effect on the behavior of voluntary hospitals than on that of council hospitals.

The differences discussed above between voluntary and public hospitals, including council hospitals, can be explained at a theoretical level in terms of the preferences and strengths of groups involved in decision-making about hospitals. At a conceptual level, there are three main groups with which we should be concerned: (1) higher-income consumers, (2) lower-income consumers, and (3) providers. Government bureaucrats and regulators did not seriously affect hospital behavior in the 1930s.[45]

Upper-income consumers provide the most important keys to understanding the behavior of voluntary hospitals. Upper-income groups in England and Wales tended to be the traditional supporters (and founders) of voluntary hospitals, especially hospitals with more than 50 beds. Historically, these hospitals, created originally for the "deserving poor," were thought by donors and founders to be places to which they personally would never go. During the twentieth century, as hospital care was increasingly used by all classes, upper-income groups insisted that voluntary hospitals—to which they had given their allegiance historically—provide high-quality care and technologically complex service. Relatively unconcerned about providing access to hospital services for the mass of the population, upper-income groups placed their emphasis on sophistication and quality, not on general services.

The upper-income consumers were not willing or able to provide funding sufficient to supply hospital services for everyone who wished them. Once the public sector began to provide general hospital services, upper-income groups remained loyal to the voluntary institutions to which they had historically given allegiance and funds. Although by 1938 about half of the income for voluntary hospitals came from payments by patients, a large percentage of income was still based on legacies, endowments, and gifts. The well-to-do were still quite important in shaping the behavior of voluntary hospitals.[46]

Middle-income groups, many of whom belonged to friendly societies and paid small weekly or monthly amounts for hospitalization benefits, also expected particular kinds of services. After all, they argued that they were paying for it (in fact, their subscriptions underwrote only a small part of the costs of the care received). Their concern was to obtain the best possible service for themselves, and their interest in egalitarian access for all comers was low.

The working class looked at the provision of hospital services quite differently. Their concern was to secure access to "free" services. If services were too elaborate or complex, payment might be required of patients, and lower-income groups would be shut out. For them, institutions that provided basic, "free" care were the desiderata. And public hospitals met these criteria. Prior to 1929, public hospitals had provided "free" care, but only if patients accepted the stigma of Poor Law classification to receive services. Once the Local Government Act was enacted and hospital administration under the public health law became possible, the lower-income consumer was able to secure free services without stigma.

After 1929, public hospitals were supported almost wholly by public funds. Because local ratepayers, accustomed to low taxes to support Poor Law institutions, would not support high rates, publicly supported hospitals were under constant pressure to keep costs low but at the same time to be open to all. The only way to accomplish both of these goals simultaneously was to emphasize very basic services and to ration professional care and special services (which were costly).

Council hospitals had to accept the chronically ill, the elderly, and other patients not welcome at voluntary institutions. Since, at the same time, council hospitals were developing acute care services, the loads on them were enormous, much greater than the loads on voluntary hospitals.

Council hospitals, with their lower costs, unspecialized services, and access for all, tended to suit taxpayers, and to be acceptable also to the low-income population. In exchange for obtaining free care without stigma or delay, low-income groups were willing to give up some of the refinements found in the larger voluntary hospitals. The fact that public taxation, which affected everyone, supported public hospitals meant that majoritarian constraints were imposed on council hospital behavior. Thus, the source of funding was directly linked to the amount of funding.

For the most part, upper-income groups had little interest in council hospitals. They were not going to go there, and their doctors did not work in them. Council hospitals had evolved from the Poor Law and were inextricably associated with the stigmatized indigent even if they were administered by county boroughs and counties rather than Poor Law unions.

Providers in the different types of institutions took their cues from their work situations. In council hospitals, doctors were expected to see hundreds of patients, many suffering from chronic diseases associated with poverty. Doctors, however well intentioned, were overwhelmed with patient cases. Full-time positions in public hospitals had historically recruited doctors who prized security highly and were not strongly motivated professionally. Often their administrative duties and abilities were as important as their medical skills. Cut off from the mainstream of the profession, and unable to rely on influential clients for prestige and income, they were ineffective voices in addressing what council hospitals should do and how they might be reorganized to permit different behavior. Some doctors involved with public health were interested in providing better health care in hospitals, of course, but overall the providers in the public system lacked the resources to create a better set of institutions rapidly. Since doctors in public hospitals were more or less permanent public servants, there was limited circulation of medical personnel in and out of public hospitals, so that information about conditions in them and suggestions for change were limited. Even though private consultants sometimes saw patients in council hospitals, they tended to remain more involved with voluntary hospitals than with their new-found affiliates, and did not serve to induce much change in hospital behavior. The medical staff in council hospitals, then, though hard working, did not function as a significant force for upgrading their institutions.

Providers in voluntary hospitals were in quite different situations. Most of them (86 percent) worked part-time in the hospitals, and were dependent on their dispensaries and surgeries for the bulk of their income. The fact that a doctor was a consultant, or in training to be a consultant, enhanced his reputation and drew clients to him outside the hospital. Being a doctor with an appointment at a voluntary hospital assisted him with attracting high-status and high-paying clients outside the hospital, and these high-status clients in turn increased his ability to shape hospital policy. Providers were more concerned with interesting cases than with ascertaining and meeting the medical needs of the society. Basically, the behavior of larger voluntary hospitals was influenced by an alliance of upper-income groups and high-status physicians, and the behavior of these hospitals tended to reflect the preferences of these two groups.

There were various reasons for the lack of public concern about the divergence in the behavior of voluntary and council hospitals. Most importantly, local authorities were very much constrained by inadequate funding, whereas voluntary hospitals had more flexible, varied, and occasionally more lucrative sources of funding. Moreover, voluntary hospitals had no interest in narrowing the gap between public and voluntary hospitals. Furthermore, the management of voluntary hospitals believed they had little to gain by emphasizing the development of a well-coordinated hospital system, in which resources and clients would be more equitably distributed and in which their policies might be subject to periodic public scrutiny.

Despite the tradition of solid ministerial reports on medical care, there were inefficient sources for assessing the behavior of public and voluntary hospitals. Nonprofit organizations (the British Hospital Association, the King Edward's Fund for London, the Nuffield Trust) concentrated on the behavior of a select group of voluntary hospitals only, and there were no countrywide efforts to measure hospital achievements and service capacity. Ironically, as indicated above, it was the anticipation of World War II devastation and the redeployment of well-trained and influential doctors during the war that provided the public with information about how different the public and voluntary hospitals were. Before the war, however, public and voluntary nonprofit hospitals differed substantially in their behavior because they were constrained by the influence and/or preferences of different sets of interest groups and because they received their funding from different sources. And because of these constraints, hospitals in the two sectors spent different sums of money, had different types of patient loads, varied in their quality of care, and served different strata of society.

As historians and economists continue to compare the behavior of public and voluntary nonprofit organizations, they are likely to find that organizations in the two sectors behave differently as long as they receive their funding from different sources and as long as they are constrained by interest groups with quite different preferences.[47]

NOTES

1. The literature on individual British hospitals is fairly voluminous and thus cannot be fully cited here. Three bibliographies helpful to readers seeking literature on hospitals in England and Wales are the *Cumulative Index of Hospital Literature* (Chicago: American Hospital Association, 1945 to the present); the *Bibliography of the History of Medicine* (Washington, D.C.: U.S. Department of Health and Human Services, Government Printing Office, 1964 to the present); and *Hospital Abstracts* (London: Her Majesty's Stationery Office, 1960 to the present). The best single work on British hospitals is Brian Abel-Smith, *The Hospitals, 1800–1949* (London: Heinemann, 1964). This source has been extremely helpful.

2. For some of the best literature, see Burton A. Weisbrod, *The Voluntary Nonprofit Sector* (Lexington, Mass.: Lexington Books, 1977); Marc Bendick, Jr., "Education as a Three-sector Industry" (Ph.D diss., University of Wisconsin—Madison, 1975); Mark Pauly and Michael Redisch, "The Not-for-profit Hospital as a Physicians' Cooperative," *American Economic Review* 63 (1973): 87–99. A complementary perspective is expressed in the stimulating study by James Douglas, *Why Charity? The Case for a Third Sector* (Beverly Hills, Calif.: Sage Publications, 1983).

3. Joseph P. Newhouse, "Toward a Theory of Nonprofit Institutions: An Economic Model of a Hospital," *American Economic Review* 60 (1970): 64–74; Bernard Ferber, "An Analysis of Chain-operation For-profit Hospitals," *Health Services Research* 6 (1971): 49; Weisbrod, *Voluntary Nonprofit Sector*.

4. Weisbrod, ibid., pp. 51–76. Also see Douglas, *Why Charity?*

5. For Weisbrod's use of the term *collective good*, consult *Voluntary Nonprofit Sector*. Briefly, a collective good is one that, if consumed by one person in a group, cannot be withheld from other group members. Those who do not purchase or pay for the good can share it. See Mancur Olson, *The Logic of Collective Action* (Cambridge, Mass.: Harvard University Press, 1965).

6. See Susan Rose-Ackerman, "United Charities: An Economic Analysis," *Public Policy* 28 (Summer 1980); 323–50.

7. Weisbrod, *Voluntary Nonprofit Sector,* pp. 51–76, and Douglas, *Why Charity?* The view was developed at length in J. Rogers Hollingsworth, *A Political Economy of Medicine: Great Britain and the United States* (Baltimore: Johns Hopkins University Press, 1986); also see J. Rogers Hollingsworth and Ellen Jane Hollingsworth, *Controversy About American Hospitals: Funding, Ownership and Performance* (Washington, D.C.: American Enterprise Institute, 1988).

8. Hollingsworth, *Political Economy of Medicine.*

9. General hospitals were utilized for acute care, especially care related to surgery. Although specialty and infectious disease hospitals were also numerous, they were not the objects of public debate and discussion that general hospitals were.

10. E. G. Thomas, "The Old Poor Law and Medicine," *Medical History* 24 (1980): 1–19; Hollingsworth, *Political Economy of Medicine;* Abel-Smith, *Hospitals;* Harry Eckstein, *The English Health Service: Its Origins, Structure, and Achievements* (Cambridge, Mass.: Harvard University Press, 1958), pp. 35, 66–67; Acton Society Trust, *Hospital and the State, Hospital Organization and Administration under the National Health Service* (London: Author, 1955), pp. 10–11.

11. W. K. Jordan, *Philanthropy in England, 1480–1600* (London: George Allen and Unwin, Ltd., 1959); F. N. Poynter, ed., *The Evolution of Hospitals in Britain* (London: Pitman Medical Publishing Company, Ltd., 1962); Abel-Smith, *Hospitals;* Jeanne M. Peterson, *The Medical Profession in Mid-Victorian London* (Berkeley: University of California Press, 1978).

12. P. J. Watkin, *Lambeth Hospital: Fifty Years Retrospect* (London: Lambeth Hospital, 1954), pp. 4–13; Sidney Webb and Beatrice Webb, *The State and the Doctor* (London: Longmans, Green and Co., 1910), pp. 121–29, 228–61.

13. British Hospitals Association, *The Hospitals Yearbook, 1931* (London: Nursing Mirror Limited, 1931); *The Hospitals Yearbook, 1938* (London: Central Bureau of Hospital Information, 1938), pp. 56–57.

14. Sir Heneage Ogilvie, "The Practitioner and the Hospital Service," *British Medical Journal* 26 (September 1953): 707–11; King Edward's Hospital Fund for London, *Statistical Report of One Hundred and Thirteen London Hospitals for the Year 1921* (London: King Edward's Hospital Fund for London, 1922), pp. 12–13; Herman Levy, *National Health Insurance* (Cambridge: Cambridge University Press, 1944).

15. Political and Economic Planning, *Report on the British Health Services: A Survey of the Existing Health Services in Great Britain with Proposals for Future Development* (London: Political and Economic Planning, 1935. Hereafter cited as *PEP*); Rudolf Klein, *The Politics of the National Health Service* (London: Longman, 1983); Ministry of Health, *Ninth Annual Report of the Ministry of Health, 1927–1928* (London: His Majesty's Stationery Office, 1928), pp. 162–66; R. C. Wofinden, *Health Services in England* (Bristol, England: John Wright and Sons, Ltds., 1947), p. 23.

16. Alan R. Neate, *The St. Marylebone Workhouse and Institution, 1730–1965* (London: St. Marylebone Society, 1967), pp. 32–35; Watkin, *Lambeth Hospital;* London Voluntary Hospitals Committee, *Joint Survey of Medical and Surgical Services in the County of London: Part 1: Voluntary Hospitals, Clinics and Dispensaries* (London: P. S. King and Son, Ltd., 1931), p. 7; London County Council, *The London County Council Hospitals: A Retrospect* (London: Author, 1949), pp. 11–20, 53–60.

17. Ministry of Health, *Twentieth Annual Report of the Ministry of Health, 1938–1939* (London: His Majesty's Stationery Office, 1939), pp. 65, 77, 245–47; George Hurrell, *The History of Newcastle General Hospital* (Newcastle upon Tyne, England: Hindson and Andrew Reid Ltd., 1967), pp. 13, 114; British Hospitals Association, *The Hospitals Yearbook, 1932* (London: Central Bureau of Hospital Information, 1932, pp. 15–16; A. E. Clark-Kennedy, *The London: A Study in the Voluntary Hospital System.* Volume 2. *1840–1948* (London: Pitman Medical Publishing Co., Ltd., 1963), pp. 216–17; G. H. Jennings, "Early Memories of the Edgware General," *Nursing Mirror* 145 (1977): 25–27.

18. George Fairbairn and Arthur Bailieu, *Statement Concerning Hospital Matters in Britain* (London: G. Harmsworth and Co., Ltds., 1925), p. 10; Joint Council of the Order of St. John and the British Red Cross Society and the British Hospitals Incorporated, *The Hospitals Yearbook, 1940* (London: Central Bureau of Hospital Information, 1940), pp. 31–43.

19. Richard M. Titmuss, *Problems of Social Policy* (London: His Majesty's Stationery Office, 1950), p. 69; Ogilvie, "The Practitioner," pp. 707–11; A. W. Haslett, "Britain's Cottage Hospitals," *Hospitals* 21 (1947): 65.

20. Rosemary Stevens, *Medical Practice in Modern England* (New Haven, Conn.: Yale University Press, 1966), Chapter 3 and 4.

21. *PEP*, pp. 257–59.

22. Robert Pinker, *English Hospital Statistics, 1861–1938* (London: Heinemann, 1966), p. 57.

23. Abel-Smith, *Hospitals;* Titmuss, *Problems of Social Policy,* Chapter 11.

24. Nuffield Provincial Hospitals Trust, *The Hospital Survey: The Domesday Book of the Hospital Services* (London: Oxford University Press, 1946). The *Hospital Survey* was taken in 1942 and 1943 by the Ministry of Health with the assistance of the Nuffield Provincial Hospitals Trust. The survey covered general hospitals, special hospitals, infectious disease

hospitals, and convalescent homes. Each institution was asked to complete a standard form with information on types of beds, number of inpatients and outpatients, full- and part-time medical staff, nurses, and other assistants. In addition, information on medical technology was obtained. Many general hospitals at the time were in the Emergency Hospital Service and therefore were asked to report bed counts both for the time of the survey and for December 31, 1938. This latter data point is used in this study.

Approximately 825 general hospitals were listed in the survey, including approximately 20 recovery homes attached to hospitals. These have been excluded from our analysis because they lacked separate staffing. Because the *Hospital Survey* did not include individual hospital data for the Monmouthshire and South Wales area, general hospitals in that area also are omitted from the study (approximately 55 general hospitals, with 4200 beds).

Data were collected for all public general hospitals and for all voluntary general hospitals with 75 or more beds. Voluntary hospitals with fewer beds were sampled as follows: 60 hospitals each were chosen from among the 210 with fewer than 25 beds, from the 151 hospitals with between 25 and 49 beds, and from the 81 hospitals with between 50 and 74 beds. The sample hospitals were weighted in the statistical analysis, so that the statistical results represented the whole general hospital universe.

These data have been supplemented by information from the *British Hospitals Yearbook, 1938* and *1939*, which are the sources for data on hospital expenditures and for sorting public hospitals into council and Poor Law categories.

25. For a good discussion of quality of medical care as a concept, see Avedis Donabedian, *The Definition of Quality and Approaches to Its Assessment*, Volume 1: *Explorations in Quality Assessment and Monitoring* (Ann Arbor, Mich.: Health Administration Press, 1980). For some of the other literature on the subject, see Mary Goss, "Organizational Goals and the Quality of Medical Care," *Journal of Health and Social Behavior* 11 (December 1970): 255–68; Newhouse, "Toward a Theory of Nonprofit Institutions"; and Burton A. Weisbrod and Mark Schlesinger, "Public, Private, Nonprofit Ownership and the Response to Asymmetric Information: The Case of Nursing Homes" (unpublished paper, November 1983).

26. The types of specialists are anaesthetists; dental surgeons; dermatologists; ear, nose, and throat surgeons; neurologists; obstetricians and gynecologists; ophthalmic surgeons; orthopedic surgeons; pathologists; pediatricians; physiotherapists; medical staff in psychological medicine; radiologists; radiotherapists; medical staff for tuberculosis and venereal disease. In Tables 4.3 through 4.6, part-time and full-time specialist figures are presented separately because of the difficulties of determining the proper equivalent between full- and part-time personnel.

27. The presence of a pathology laboratory was indicated by the presence of a full- or part-time pathologist. The existence of diagnostic x-ray equipment was indicated by the presence of a radiographer, and the existence of therapeutic x-ray equipment by the presence of a medical staff radiologist or radiotherapist.

28. Most data reported below are drawn from Ministry of Health, *Hospital Survey*, 10 volumes (London: 1945–1946). Hereafter the *Hospital Survey* is cited as *HS*, with the geographical area indicated: northwestern (NW); Yorkshire (Yorks); southwestern (SW); London and surrounding (London); Berkshire, Buckinghamshire, and Oxfordshire (BBO); eastern (East); northeastern (NE); Sheffield and East Midland (SEM); West Midlands (WM). The Monmouthshire–South Wales volume is not cited (see note 24).

29. *HS*:NW, pp. 22–23.

30. Abel-Smith, *Hospitals;* Frank Honigsbaum, *The Division in British Medicine* (New York: St. Martin's Press, 1979).

31. See *HS*:NW, p. 13, for a discussion of waiting lists.

32. King Edward's Hospital Fund for London, *Statistical Summary of the Income, Expenditure, Work and Costs of One Hundred and Forty-Six London Hospitals for the Year 1938* (London: King Edward's Hospital Fund for London, 1939), pp. 5–49; *PEP*, p. 233.

33. This finding may be attributable to the data source used in this study. Unfortunately, the *Hospital Survey* data capture only the distinction between part-time and full-time doctors,

without indicating what proportion of time a part-time doctor spent in hospital service. There are indications from the survey that, in some hospitals, doctors who had not seen a patient in the hospital for over a year were listed on the medical staff. Provincial hospitals, the surveyors implied, wish to present the best possible picture of their resources. Thus, the number of specialists per 100 beds, and the number of doctors per 100 beds may not be, as they appear, indicators of roughly equivalent medical staff time for patients in teaching and nonteaching hospitals. We do not have adequate data with which to resolve the issues. Surveyors and other students of English and Welsh medical services during the 1930s believed that teaching hospitals had more and better doctors than nonteaching voluntary hospitals.

34. Sir Allen Daley, "British Hospitals as They Were before 1948," *British Medical Journal* 2 (September 10, 1960): 758–59; Norman Wilson, *Municipal Health Services* (London: George Allen and Unwin, Ltd., 1980), pp. 142–55.

35. London County Council, *LCC Hospitals,* pp. 34–35; Janet Gooch, *A History of Brighton General Hospital* (London: Phillimore, 1980), pp. 142–50.

36. Brian Abel-Smith, *A History of the Nursing Profession in Great Britain* (New York: Springer Publishing Company, Inc., 1960); *HS:NW,* p. 10; *HS:Yorks,* p. 20; *HS: SW,* pp. 21–22; Wilson, *Municipal Health,* p. 91; Honigsbaum, *Division in British Medicine,* pp. 137–49; Stevens, *Medical Practice,* p. 61; Abel-Smith, *Hospitals,* pp. 375–77; "An Extensive Survey," *The Hospital* 41 (May 1956): 139, 143.

37. *HS:NW,* p. 10.

38. *HS:NW,* p. 14.

39. Wilson, *Municipal Health,* p. 87; Abel-Smith, *Hospitals.*

40. Peter Speck, with Mick Fines, Chris Hinton, and Pauline Whitear, *The Institution and Hospital at Fir Vale, Sheffield: A Centenary History of the Northern General Hospital* (Sheffield, England: Northern General Hospital, 1978), p. 28.

41. Daley, "British Hospitals," pp. 758–59.

42. London County Council, *LCC Hospitals.*

43. Gwendolyn Ayers, *England's First State Hospitals and the Metropolitan Asylums Board, 1867–1930* (London: Wellcome Institute of the History of Medicine, 1971).

44. King Edward's Hospital Fund for London, *Report of the Committee Appointed to Inquire into Out-patients Methods of London Voluntary Hospitals as Affecting Suitability of Patients and Time of Waiting* (London: Geo. Barber and Son, Ltds., 1932), pp. 2–28; Abel-Smith, *Hospitals,* pp. 379–80.

45. See Hollingsworth, *Political Economy of Medicine* for detailed documentation of this perspective.

46. Clark-Kennedy, *The London: A Study in the Voluntary Hospital System.*

47. For an economic and historical analysis of this view, see the study on American hospitals during the twentieth century, Hollingsworth and Hollingsworth, *Controversy about American Hospitals.*

REFERENCES

Abel-Smith, Brian. "An Extensive Survey." *The Hospital* 41 (May 1956).

———. *A History of the Nursing Profession in Great Britain.* New York: Springer Publishing Company, Inc., 1960.

———. *The Hospitals, 1800–1948.* London: Heinemann, 1964.

Acton Society Trust. *Hospital and the State, Hospital Organization and Administration under the National Health Service.* London: Author, 1955.

Ayers, Gwendolyn. *England's First State Hospitals and the Metropolitan Asylums Board, 1867–1930.* London: Wellcome Institute of the History of Medicine, 1971.

Bendick, Jr., Marc. "Education as a Three-Sector Industry." Ph.D. diss., University of Wisconsin—Madison, 1975.

Bibliography of the History of Medicine. Washington, D.C.: U.S. Department of Health and Human Services, Government Printing Office, 1964.

British Hospitals Association. *The Hospitals Yearbook, 1931, 1932 and 1938.* London: Nursing Mirror Limited.

Clark-Kennedy, A. E. *The London: A Study in the Voluntary Hospital System.* Volume 2: *1840–1948.* London: Pitman Medical Publishing Co., Ltd., 1963.

Cumulative Index of Hospital Literature. Chicago: American Hospital Association, 1945 to the present.

Daley, Sir Allen. "British Hospitals as They Were before 1848." *British Medical Journal* (September 1960): 758–59.

Donabedian, Avedis. *The Definition of Quality and Approaches to Its Assessment,* Volume 1: *Explorations in Quality Assessment and Monitoring.* Ann Arbor, Mich.: Health Administration Press, 1980.

Douglas, James. *Why Charity? The Case for a Third Sector.* Beverly Hills, Calif.: Sage Publications, 1983.

Eckstein, Henry. *The English Health Service: Its Origins, Structure, and Achievements.* Cambridge, Mass.: Harvard University Press, 1958.

Fairbairn, George, and Arthur Bailieu. *Statement Concerning Hospital Matters in Britain.* London: G. Harmsworth and Co., Ltd., 1925.

Ferber, Bernard. "An Analysis of Chain-operation For-profit Hospitals." *Health Services Research* (1971).

Gooch, Janet. *A History of Brighton General Hospital.* London: Phillimore, 1980.

Goss, Mary. "Organizational Goals and the Quality of Medical Care." *Journal of Health and Social Behavior* (December 1970): 255–68.

Haslett, A. W., "Britain's Cottage Hospitals." *Hospitals* (1947).

Hollingsworth, J. Rogers. *A Political Economy of Medicine: Great Britain and the United States.* Baltimore: Johns Hopkins University Press, 1986.

Hollingsworth, J. Rogers, and Ellen Jane Hollingsworth. *Controversy About American Hospitals: Funding Ownership and Performance.* Washington, D.C.: American Enterprise Institute, 1988.

Honigsbaum, Frank. *The Division in British Medicine.* New York: St. Martin's Press, 1979.

Hospital Abstracts. London: Her Majesty's Stationery Office, 1960–present.

Hurrell, George. *The History of Newcastle General Hospital.* Newcastle upon Tyne, England: Hindson and Andrew Reid Ltd., 1967.

Jennings, G. H. "Early Memories of the Edgeware General," *Nursing Mirror* 145 (1977): 25–27.

Joint Council of the Order of St. John and the British Red Cross Society and the British Hospitals Incorporated. *The Hospitals Yearbook, 1940.* London: Central Bureau of Hospital Information, 1940.

Jordan, W. K. *Philanthropy in England, 1480–1600.* London: George Allen and Unwin, Ltd., 1959.

King Edward's Hospital Fund for London. *Statistical Report of One Hundred and Thirteen London Hospitals for the Year 1921.* London: King Edward's Hospital Fund for London, 1922.

————. *Report of the Committee Appointed to Inquire into Out-patient Methods of London Voluntary Hospitals as Affecting Suitability of Patients and Time of Waiting.* London: Geo. Barber and Son, Ltds., 1932.

————. *Statistical Summary of the Income, Expenditure, Work and Costs of One Hundred and Forty-six London Hospitals for the Year 1938.* London: King Edward's Hospital Fund for London, 1939.

Klein, Rudolf. *The Politics of the National Health Service.* London: Longman, 1983.

Levy, Herman. *National Health Insurance.* Cambridge: Cambridge University Press, 1944.

London County Council. *The London County Council Hospitals: A Retrospect.* London: London County Council, 1949.

London Voluntary Hospitals Committee. *Joint Survey of Medical and Surgical Services in the County of London:* Part I, *Voluntary Hospitals, Clinics and Dispensaries.* London: P. S. King and Sons, Ltd., 1931.

Ministry of Health. *Ninth Annual Report of the Ministry of Health, 1927–1928.* London: His Majesty's Stationery Office, 1928.

———. *Twentieth Annual Report of the Ministry of Health, 1938–1939.* London: His Majesty's Stationery Office, 1939.

———. *Hospital Survey,* 10 volumes. London: Author, 1945–46.

Neate, Alan R. *The St. Marylebone Workhouse and Institution, 1730–1965.* London: St. Marlebone Society, 1967.

Newhouse, Joseph P. "Toward a Theory of Nonprofit Institutions: An Economic Model of a Hospital." *American Economic Review* 60 (1970): 64–74.

Nuffield Provincial Hospitals Trust. *The Hospital Survey: The Domesday Book of the Hospital Services.* London: Oxford University Press, 1946.

Ogilvie, Sir Heneage. "The Practitioner and the Hospital Service." *British Medical Journal* (September 1953): 707–11.

Olson, Mancur. *The Logic of Collection Action.* Cambridge, Mass.: Harvard University Press, 1965.

Pauly, Mark, and Michael Redisch. "The Not-for-profit Hospital as a Physicians' Cooperative." *American Economic Review* 63 (1973).

Peterson, Jeanne M. *The Medical Profession in Mid-Victorian London.* Berkeley: University of California Press, 1978.

Pinker, Robert. *English Hospital Statistics, 1861–1938.* London: Heinemann, 1966.

Political and Economic Planning. *Report on the British Health Services: A Survey of the Existing Health Services in Great Britain with Proposals for Future Development.* London: Political and Economic Planning, 1935.

Poynter, F. N., ed. *The Evolution of Hospitals in Britain.* London: Pitman Medical Publishing Company, Ltd., 1962.

Rose-Ackerman, Susan. "United Charities: An Economic Analysis." *Public Policy* (Summer 1980): 323–50.

Speck, Peter, with Michael Fines, Chris Hinton, and Pauline Whitear. *The Institution and Hospital at Fir Vale, Sheffield: A Centenary History of the Northern General Hospital.* Sheffield, England: Northern General Hospital, 1978.

Stevens, Rosemary. *Medical Practice in Modern England.* New Haven, Conn.: Yale University Press, 1966.

Thomas, E. G. "The Old Poor Law and Medicine." *Medical History* 24 (1980): 1–19.

Titmuss, Richard M. *Problems of Social Policy.* London: His Majesty's Stationery Office, 1950.

Watkin, P. J. *Lambeth Hospital: Fifty Years Retrospect.* London: Lambeth Hospital, 1954.

Webb, Sidney, and Beatrice Webb. *The State and the Doctor.* London: Nursing Mirror Limited, 1931.

Weisbrod, Burton A. *The Voluntary Nonprofit Sector.* Lexington, Mass.: Lexington Books, 1977.

Weisbrod, Burton A., and Mark Schlesinger. "Public, Private, Nonprofit Ownership and the Response to Asymmetric Information: The Case of Nursing Homes." Unpublished paper, November 1983.

Wilson, Norman. *Municipal Health Services.* London: George Allen and Unwin, Ltd., 1980.

Wofinden, R. C. *Health Services in England.* Bristol, England: John Wright and Sons, Ltds., 1947.

II

GOVERNMENT FUNDING AND ACCOUNTABILITY

5

Purchase of Service in England

KEN JUDGE and JILLIAN SMITH

Seebohm and Title XX were key words that symbolized the transformation of the personal social services in England and the United States, respectively, during the 1970s. The changes that took place in the United States, however, are often unfavorably contrasted with the post-Seebohm provision in England. The phenomenon about which most concern has been expressed in the United States is the dramatic expansion of purchase of service contracting (POSC).[1] What is often forgotten, however, is that POSC remains an important feature in the landscape of the English personal social services as well. One of the reasons for this oversight is that few scholars, with the exception of visiting Americans such as Mencher[2] in the 1950s and Kramer[3] in the 1970s, have concerned themselves with this topic. In fact, despite the many cultural differences between the two countries, the English experience of purchase of service closely parallels that of America in many respects.[4] Our aim is not to compare the overall operation of POSC on either side of the Atlantic, but to take a single particularly interesting aspect of the common experience of POSC—the rationale for the purchase of social care—and examine it in a specifically English context.

First, we present a brief review of the salient U.S. literature. Second, we discuss the subjective perceptions of managers in English Social Services Departments (SSDs) about the reasons for purchasing services rather than providing them directly. Finally, attempts are made to test various hypotheses that might account for the substantial variations in the purchasing behavior of SSDs. In particular, we will report the results of a statistical investigation of POSC spending in England in 1978–79. Before proceeding, though, there are three points about POSC in England worth

We are grateful to our colleagues Ben Knox and Spyros Missiakoulis for making available their logit and tobit computer programs and to Martin Knapp for advice and encouragement. This article was originally published in the *Social Service Review*, 57 (1983): 209–23. Copyright © 1983 by The University of Chicago. All rights reserved. Reprinted by permission.

emphasizing: those aspects with which we are particularly concerned, the relative imprecision of the term, and its scale.

Fiscal transfers associated with SSDs vary along three critical dimensions. First, the type of agency with which the relationship is established can be another local authority, a voluntary organization, a profit-making agency, or an individual. Second, the resources involved can be both capital and current expenditure, or transfers in-kind such as accommodation. Finally, the transfers can flow in both directions; the SSD is a provider and recipient. For the purposes of this article, however, the use of the term POSC will be restricted to refer to financial transfers by SSDs on current account, and, although this includes purchases from other local authorities, we shall concentrate primarily on fiscal relations between SSDs and nonstatutory agencies. This represented about 71 percent of all POSC spending in 1978–79.[5]

Even within this restricted context, it is essential to emphasize that POSC is not a very precise concept on either side of the Atlantic. In the United States, Wedel has put forward the clearest definition. "A contract may be defined in general terms as an agreement between a governmental agency (the contracting agency) and another organization or individual (the contractor) for the purpose of providing care or services to clientele of the governmental agency."[6] But there is an important qualification to this definition because the financial relations between public and private agencies are best considered as a continuum where clearly expressed contracts are at one pole and unrestricted grants not unlike gifts are at the other. As Beck pointed out, "It is difficult . . . to limit discussion of government by contract to instances where there is an actual contract, since the key issue seems to be the expectations of the public body, whether embodied in a statement of a grant or in a statute or a letter of understanding or an actual contract. Yet in some instances of public support for private agencies the expectations of government are so vaguely formulated that there is little similarity to contract."[7]

Moreover, as the most recent studies have shown, POSC is best seen as an umbrella term embracing different modes of partnership between public and private agencies. For example, Gurin et al.[8] distinguish between purchase of service and block contracting, whereas Pacific Consultants[9] identify forms of contracting with other public agencies, private organizations, individual vendors, and via-client reimbursement.

The situation in England is very similar, and at least four types of POSC can be identified. The most common is vendor reimbursement for units of client-specific services, such as a place in a residential home or foster care. Quasi contracting usually involves the payment of substantial grants to voluntary agencies on the assumption that services will be provided that substitute for SSD provision but where the expectations of both sides are rather vague. In certain instances, clearer contractual obligations do exist when SSDs reimburse delegate agencies that provide services on their be-

Table 5.1. POSC and the Personal Social Services in Britain and the United States

Country	Purchases from Private and Voluntary Agencies as a Proportion of Total Expenditure			
	Minimum (%)	Mean (%)	Maximum (%)	Coefficient of Variation (%)
Britain, 1978–79	.8	8.2	20.9	50.7
United States, 1978	.1	34.2	68.2	41.2

Sources: Department of the Environment, *Revenue Outturn Statistics Forms RO3A-E* (London, 1980); American Public Welfare Association, *A Study of Purchase of Social Services in Selected States* (Washington, D.C.: APWA), appendix B.

half. Finally, almost all SSDs distribute a large number of small grants to numerous organizations in support of general community development.

The final point worth making about POSC in England is that although the relative level of expenditure is smaller than in the United States, as shown in Table 5.1, it can be substantial. Of course, there are wide variations among individual local authorities, but some SSDs make very extensive use of voluntary organizations, and it is not unusual to find such authorities contracting-out all of their expenditure on certain services such as residential accommodation for the mentally and physically handicapped, meals on wheels, day nurseries, and day centers for the elderly.

THE AMERICAN CONTEXT

The decisions made by public agencies in the United States about whether to provide social services directly or purchase them from private organizations have been among the most controversial and hotly debated in the field of social care during the 1970s. As Sharkansky wrote, "Contracting does not proceed quietly. It has warm supporters and intense opponents. There are stories of beautiful successes and horrible failures, each mingled with simple ideology, myth, and personal stakes." [10]

Despite the considerable interest in and importance attached to POSC, however, there is a remarkable absence of firm evidence with which to evaluate the various arguments advanced for and against contracting out. One of the consequences of the paucity of good evaluative material is that there has been little other than faith and prejudice to guide policymakers in their POSC decision making. Benton states that "since . . . state and local decisions are nearly always based on intuition rather than formal judgement, it is not surprising that there is tremendous variation among jurisdictions across the United States in the actual pattern of purchased versus direct service delivery. . . . In many jurisdictions, no rationale other than tradition and the accumulated legacy of past decisions can explain the relationship between direct and purchased services."[11] Despite this there is no shortage of normative arguments in favor of POSC. Most of them fall into four distinct categories: it is more economic, it offers greater flexibility and consumer choice, it provides more scope for innovation and specialization, and it improves management and evaluation. The economic arguments for POSC are probably the most common, and the starting point is the set of widespread beliefs about the inefficiency of the public sector. For example, Savas writes that "government is very inefficient in delivering services, due to a host of factors, including absence of management skills, lack of motivation, political interference, patronage, rigid civil service system, public employee unionism . . . lack of agreement on goals of government programs, the difficulty of measuring performance (particularly in many of the 'softer' services), and the monopoly structure . . . of many public services."[12]

In contrast, Fitch[13] and Fisk et al.[14] suggest that the adoption of POSC introduces the advantage of competition among suppliers which may produce, via economies of scale and specialization, lower unit costs and improvements in the quantity or quality of services. Terrell supports this view by quoting the views of public officials who described the various economic advantages to government "in terms of the 'multiplier effect' secured when private agencies increase the efficiency of public dollars through the use of 'volunteer support, mixed funding and donated capital.' "[15]

Another frequently cited advantage of POSC is that it permits greater flexibility and choice in planning and delivering social services, and it offers an "escape from the rigidities of personnel, budgetary, and other central controls imposed by general government agencies."[16] A more positive argument is that purchasing and contracting offer clients more choice and better access to services from a wider range of providers. If public agencies provide incentives for many suppliers to enter the market, including community groups with limited independent resources, it is possible it might "improve the access of some clients to needed services, since they would present themselves to providers who were very close to them both physically and in other ways."[17] Similarly, Terrell[18] and Kramer claim that POSC "can be an effective way of serving hard-to-reach or controversial groups, cultural minorities or widely-dispersed populations whom government may be obligated to serve, but where fear or stigma prevent utilization."[19] It also offers a way of obtaining specialist skills that are only needed infrequently,[20] and Terrell reports that "the decision to buy services also grew from the belief that the private sectors could provide better innovative programs."[21] Finally, a number of commentators have suggested that POSC will improve the management and evaluation of social programs. Fisk et al.[22] suggest it will provide improved management information, such as comparative data on the effectiveness and efficiency of different suppliers. Manser believes that it will encourage "agencies participating in purchase of service contracts to develop more sophisticated and objective costing procedures and to create refined standards of quantity and quality of services."[23] Kramer thinks that POSC offers government agencies the opportunity to influence standards in, and coordinate the activities of, various contractors.[24] Last, Fitch points out that it promotes the development of desirable management devices, such as incentive reimbursement schemes.[25]

Whatever the merits of the normative arguments, the limited empirical evidence available about the criteria that influence POSC decision making supports the general view that "there are no consistent policies governing purchase of services."[26] This is confirmed by both Wedel and research teams from the Urban Institute, Pacific Consultants, and the American Public Welfare Association (APWA), who conducted surveys of key local actors to obtain information about the factors that influenced their decisions about POSC.

Wedel's data were collected by sending a mail questionnaire to the chief executives of state public assistance agencies in 1972–73. The questionnaire included 23 statements encompassing arguments justifying the use of POSC as well as some of the problems. Respondents were asked to rate the influence of each statement about POSC decision making on a six-point scale. The results were rather disappointing. The statements that were suggestive of an improvement in managerial efficiency, such as greater cost effectiveness, flexibility, and specialization due to POSC, were not considered to be very influential. On the other hand, they lend little support to the view that POSC has deleterious consequences. In fact, Wedel concludes that his results "will come as little surprise to those who hold that the purchase of service policy has been interpreted in an opportunistic fashion,"[27] and "that the potential hazards and benefits identified in the literature play a secondary role in decisions concerning the practice."[28]

The Urban Institute survey was conducted in 1977 as part of their general evaluation of the implementation of Title XX, and questions were addressed to private suppliers as well as public agencies requiring services. Once again, however, the picture obtained was a mixed one. The two most common reasons given for deciding to purchase services were the lack of qualified public employees and tradition, although lower costs were also important to a smaller number of respondents.[29]

The third study was carried out in six states in 1978. Pacific Consultants asked state managers to rank seventeen factors about POSC decision making in order of importance. The results show that three factors were consistently identified as very influential. First, increases in demand were greatest for the "hard" services historically provided by private agencies, and this inevitably increased POSC. Second, the availability of nonprofit agencies with the resources to provide the 25 percent match for federal funds in the early years of Title XX meant that they were easily assured of obtaining renewable contracts. Finally, once providers were locked into the system they had a vested interest in applying political pressure to maintain their position. In contrast, it was reported that information about comparative costs had not been a significant factor in choosing POSC because of the absence of reliable data.[30]

The final survey was carried out by the APWA in five states during the winter of 1980–81. The purpose of the study was to identify and analyze factors influencing POSC. The main research instrument was a structured questionnaire that asked respondents to rate the importance of 25 factors in terms of their influence on decisions to purchase social services. A rather odd aspect of this procedure was that two potentially important factors were deliberately excluded: "One of them was political influence . . . while the other was tradition or historical precedent. . . . The respondents could have brought up these factors as having high influence upon the purchase decision of any of the study services. . . . As it turned out, however, only a few respondents identified these factors as having anything to do with purchase decision."[31]

The validity of this procedure is certainly open to question. Nevertheless, the finding that "no factor/cluster area emerged as a consistently high influence factor across all service categories and all states"[32] is consistent with the earlier studies. Bearing these findings in mind, we now turn to a discussion of POSC in England so as to investigate to what extent the American experience is duplicated across the Atlantic.

SUBJECTIVE REASONS FOR POSC IN ENGLAND

During 1980 members of the Personal Social Services Research Unit (PSSRU),[33] to which the authors belong, interviewed a sample of directors of SSDs in England about their perceptions of the fiscal pressure facing their authorities.[34] One of the topics discussed with them was purchase of service in general and collaboration with the voluntary sector in particular. Subsequently, we went back to three of these authorities (a rural nonmetropolitan county, a large metropolitan district with a very deprived inner-city area, and a suburban London borough) and interviewed many of the people within the SSD most closely involved with POSC.[35] One of the most important questions we put to SSD Managers and directors was why they chose to purchase services rather than to provide them directly. As we expected, the answers varied considerably, but the most common reasons given for POSC were as follows: private agencies have traditionally been available; they provide specialized but essential services; their costs are lower; they provide better value for money; they are more flexible, innovative, and participative; and they promote consumer choice and better access to patients. We shall elaborate upon each of these reasons separately, but it should be recognized that in practice they are neither exhaustive nor mutually exclusive.

Traditional Supply

The most common reason given for POSC by representatives of local authorities is tradition. In general, this means that because of the traditional availability of different kinds of services, many SSDs have developed their own provision around that supplied by voluntary organizations. Also, in some areas, religious affiliation and the development of denominational services helped to establish a powerful sense of civic pluralism. For example, in two of the authorities we visited there was no doubt about the historical importance of a strong Roman Catholic presence.

The importance of the availability of voluntary provision, especially residential places, was emphasized on numerous occasions in both a positive and a negative sense. One assistant director stated that "if a voluntary organisation exists and it's providing a satisfactory service then we support them . . . there are voluntary homes up and down the country providing perfectly adequate accommodation at a cost that is relatively cheap. Why should the local authority go around creating places and building places when that facility exists?"

In contrast, the director of another authority explained that the lack of alternative provision accounted for the local public response: ". . . if you are elderly and you have to go into a residential home you would like to be sufficiently near to your relatives so that you can be visited, and since there are no private homes here of any kind whatsoever then the logic of the situation is that the local authority will provide homes within this area . . . in certain parts of the country there are voluntary homes . . . but in our instance the short answer as to why we provide homes ourselves is that there are no voluntary homes in existence."

Specialized Services

Nearly all SSDs have at least some clients with special needs in circumstances that make it uneconomic for the local authority to provide a suitable service themselves. One senior manager told us that his SSD used the voluntary sector "basically to fill in gaps, not to duplicate what is available but to go outside when there is a special need really." This is particularly common with respect to residential provision for certain groups of children and the mentally and physically handicapped. One social work manager explained why voluntary services had been purchased for a particular client in his area. A teenage girl who had been in foster care had "graduated to a bedsitter and just wasn't coping and obviously needed something between the foster home and the bedsitter, somewhere where there was some supervision but some ability to have freedom as well. We had no hostel provision locally but the Children's Society have a House which is set up for this type of child where there is quite a lot of supervision and support available, but it's not enforced as it were, the children have bedsitter type accommodation and it seemed ideal for this particular lass."

At different times and in other parts of the country various other considerations apply. Often, for example, delegate agencies are sponsored because of the special nature of their provision, which is reinforced by a historical involvement in meeting the needs of a particular client group. The assistant director of a small northern SSD explained that his authority delegated responsibilities to the local Deaf Society because it was a well-established organization with considerable expertise.

Lower Costs and Better Value

There is almost no evidence to support the view that sectoral cost comparisons play a significant part in POSC decision making. One of the reasons why costs are not of central importance is that, as in the United States, there are relatively few directly comparable services provided in the public and voluntary sectors. Either the nature and quality of service provision and/or the characteristics of clients varies between the two sectors. For example, it is widely recognized that levels of client dependency and associated staff costs are much lower in voluntary than in local authority homes for the elderly.[36]

It is true that the observable unit costs of nearly all residential provision in the voluntary sector are lower than SSD provision, but the existing discussion of these cost variations is rather simplistic.[37] In fact, it is safest to assume that lower unit costs in the voluntary sector are attributable to such factors as the traditional treatment of capital costs and poorer conditions of service for staff. Neither of these factors are constant, and with average costs rising fast in the voluntary sector, it is probable that, standardizing for client characteristics, the long-run marginal costs of residential provision are very similar in both sectors. The same conclusion might be widely applicable to many other, professional services. For example, one influential director was adamant that in his experience "the professional voluntary organizations are able to do the job no more cheaply or effectively than the local authority and to have a voluntary organization doing part of our work only adds to the problems of communication and co-ordination. For example, a national child care organisation wished to start a family center, but the cost to us would have been greater than the cost of our own very effective center. If money had been available it would therefore have been preferable for us to open our own family center rather than ask a voluntary organization to do so."

As far as residential provision (which dominates POSC) is concerned, the results of our interviews suggest that positive placement decisions are very rarely made on the basis of cost comparisons. If residential care is thought to be appropriate, then the assessed needs and/or preferences of the client are generally paramount. Insofar as costs enter into the decision-making process at all, our impression is that they have an increasingly negative influence. For example, the impact of fiscal pressure in many local authorities means that SSDs are adopting more constraints and stricter criteria about the sponsorship of elderly people in voluntary and private homes because this is a relatively easy part of their budget to control.

Although it is very common for claims to be made that voluntary services are cheaper than their statutory equivalents, there is a lack of evidence to support such propositions. In fact, one of the few careful evaluations to have been undertaken produced rather mixed results. Two of our colleagues have demonstrated that although voluntary day centers for the elderly can be cheaper, ceteris paribus, than local authority provision, this is crucially dependent upon the scale of operation. "Small voluntary units, certainly enjoy a cost advantage, but larger voluntary units are unlikely to be cheaper, and are probably more expensive, than local authority units of a similar scale." [38]

Nevertheless, a more plausible variant to the theme that voluntary provision is cheaper than public is the argument that voluntary organizations provide better value for money. They do so for two main reasons. First, as in the United States, voluntary organizations subsidize the services that they provide on behalf of SSDs. For example, Mencher reports that in 1954 the Home Office specifically suggested to local authorities that they should seek a 25 percent subsidy for each child placed in a voluntary home. [39] Similar practices continue to the present day. Second, contracting-out to voluntary organizations often results in the provision of supplementary assistance aside from the basic services. In his study of Birmingham, for example, Newton cites the following observation by a local government officer: "If we find an organization that does our job more cheaply then we support them. We might make a grant of, say, £1,000, but we get £5,000 worth of work out of them." [40] This proposition is well supported by evidence from different parts of the country and is particularly applicable to informal but labor-intensive preventive services.

Flexibility, Innovation, and Participation

Some of the many advantages often claimed for voluntary agencies are that they are more flexible, innovative, and participatory than SSDs. These views were supported by a number of local authority representatives, but they emphasized that they were rarely the primary reasons for POSC. It is true that voluntary organizations can often be more flexible than SSDs can choose or afford to be. For example, in some areas a local authority might decide to support a voluntary day center for the elderly in a temporarily converted church hall. Such a service might be regarded as far from ideal, but it is easier to justify support for something that might not otherwise exist in any form if the SSD is not directly responsible for service provision. Voluntary agencies can also be used to enable the local authority to escape other constraints, such as restrictive practices. Collaboration with the voluntary sector can also generate more positive advantages. One director told us about the way in which the meals on wheels service had been extended. "Because we have the meals delivered by a voluntary organization we can combine it with the books on wheels service . . . if it was a local authority service it would be very unlikely that you could generate something like books on wheels because economically it would be lost before it started but, because it's the voluntary sector, instead of taking

ten meals you might take eight meals and four households of books. . . .
There is lots of flexibility you can get through using the voluntary sector."

There is little evidence to support the proposition that voluntary organizations are necessarily more innovative than SSDs, but they are often
useful vehicles for experimental action. One local official confirmed that
"there are times when a voluntary agency can do things experimentally
and innovatory in a way that a local authority might have a little more
difficulty with . . . especially when the finance is made available through
something like Urban Aid and the authority wishes to avoid being locked
into long-term service delivery."

Finally, the participatory advantages of POSC are widely recognized. A
community liaison officer identified two of them: "If you are using voluntary organizations then it involves members of the community becoming
involved in their own social services and I think that's to be welcomed
because that has spin-offs in the community. Secondly, a number of these
projects involve a degree of self-help amongst client groups, that too I
think is to be commended."

Consumer Choice and Access

The last reason given to explain POSC that was mentioned with any frequency by local authority representatives is that it enables some clients to
have a degree of choice about, and improved access to, the appropriate
social services that they want or are thought to need. Indeed, part of the
basic philosophy in some authorities is the belief that alternatives to SSD
provision are essential ingredients in a pluralist welfare system. Another
common argument is that there are always groups of clients that the SSD
finds hard to reach for one reason or another, and so certain kinds of
voluntary agency can be more effective service providers for, say, battered
wives, alcoholics, and West Indian youths. A reassuring feature of such
agencies is that "they do not carry the social services label or a professional label. . . . I think, for example, that there are certain clients who
would go to Marriage Guidance Counsellors precisely because they are a
non-statutory body, they wouldn't be seen dead inside an SSD office. . . .
Another example is the Samaritans, I mean someone who is suicidal is not
going to ring up their Social Services Department."

Overview

It is not our intention to suggest that the reasons for POSC as stated above
represent an exhaustive list, but they do give an indication of the considerable variety of local authority opinion about purchasing services rather
than providing them directly. In particular, the cumulative effect of the
evidence we accumulated from various local authorities largely confirms
the picture presented in the American literature: no consistent and unambiguous rationale for POSC emerges. In the circumstances, therefore, it is

worth investigating whether any statistical relationships, which have a degree of causal plausibility, can be identified so as to improve our understanding of the observed variations in POSC between SSDs.

VARIATIONS AMONG SSDs IN ENGLAND

One of the characteristic features of POSC in England is the considerable variation in purchasing behavior among SSDs. The purpose of this section, therefore, is to present a preliminary statistical investigation of the underlying reasons that account for the observed patterns of spending in the English personal social services. The analysis is necessarily speculative at this stage, although it is hoped that a current investigation of the characteristics of volunteers will provide "training" data to enable us to specify improved models, with the help of synthetic estimation,[41] in the future. In the meantime, we hope to improve the limited understanding of POSC by examining various hypotheses that purport to account for the purchasing of services in England.

The financial statistics relating to POSC are complex and not entirely satisfactory for our present purpose. The revenue outturn statistics collected by the Department of the Environment provide information about spending by SSDs on purchases from, and grants to, private and voluntary agencies for about 40 different categories of service.[42] Unfortunately, SSDs are not consistent with each other in the distinction they make between purchases and grants, and so more reliable results can be obtained by aggregating the two categories into an overall measure of POSC. Our purpose is to examine variations among areas in spending on this overall measure of POSC for different services. We standardize levels of expenditure by taking as the dependent variable levels of spending per head of the population. Moreover, as we do not have space to report explanatory models for all of the personal social services, we have concentrated attention on the selection shown in Table 5.2. The extent of variations among SSDs for this subset of services is illustrated in Table 5.3.

Hypotheses

Our primary intention is to report the results of our attempts to test the strength of causal arguments derived from the relevant literatures and interviews that we discussed earlier. First, we will outline the primary arguments and show how they can be operationalized.

Labour Ideology
It is widely assumed that Labour-controlled local authorities are less enthusiastic about POSC than their Conservative counterparts. This is largely a by-product of the fact that the Labour Party seems to have "more faith in the merits of municipal enterprise."[43] "Labour," therefore, represents

Table 5.2. POSC and the Personal Social Services in England, 1978–79

Services	Total Expenditure[a] (£ Thousands)	Purchases from and Grants to Private and Voluntary Agencies (£ Thousands)	POSC as a Percentage of Service Expenditure (%)
Homes for the elderly	317,559	21,355	6.7
Residential care for children	206,143	33,064	16.0
Other residential care	77,657	26,607	34.3
Meals on wheels	17,956	1,829	10.2
Day care for the under fives	43,379	2,634	6.1
Day centers for the elderly	19,017	2,013	10.6
Subtotal	681,711	87,502	12.8
All other services[b]	608,910	18,955	3.1
Total	1,290,621	106,457	8.2

Source: Department of the Environment, *Revenue Outturn Statistics Forms RO3A-E* (London, 1980).
[a] Staff and running expenses.
[b] Including social work, administration, and domestic help.

the proportion of council seats held by the Labour Party in each local authority in 1978. We expect to find a negative relationship between this and most of the dependent variables.

Economies of Scale
One of the most common arguments advanced to account for POSC is the need for public agencies to purchase specialized services. The capacity to provide these services is directly related to the scale of a public agency's service delivery system. It follows, therefore, that the smallest authorities with the fewest resources might have the greatest difficulty in providing a

Table 5.3. POSC Variations between SSDs in the Personal Social Services in England, 1978–79

Service	Maximum (%)	Mean (%)	Minimum (%)	Coefficient of Variation (%)
Homes for the elderly	39.8	7.4	.0	99.3
Residential care for children	52.4	16.7	.0	65.7
Other residential care	92.7	33.8	.0	49.9
Meals on wheels	100.0	18.1	.0	166.5
Day care for the under fives	100.0	10.7	.0	215.7
Day centers for the elderly	100.0	15.7	.0	175.1
Subtotal	33.3	13.0	1.5	49.2
All other services	13.5	2.9	.0	104.0
Total	20.9	8.2	.8	50.7

Source: Department of the Environment, *Revenue Outturn Statistics Forms RO3A-E* (London, 1980).
Note: POSC as a percentage of service expenditure.

full range of services. Davies et al. state: "There is much empirical evidence that large authorities enjoy potential advantages in the provision of services. . . . Much of this shows the existence and importance of what economists would call 'indivisible' capital equipment—physical (for instance, specialized institutions) and human (for instance, manpower with special skills and functions)—which can be provided economically only when shared by a larger number of recipients than need them in smaller authorities."[44] "Size" is the total population of a local authority area in 1978, and it is employed as a proxy for the scale of operation. We anticipate finding a negative relationship between this variable and capital-intensive residential services in particular.

Population Density
It is often asserted that the population density of an area will have a powerful influence on decisions about POSC. "Density" is the number of people per hectare in each local authority area. We expect to find this variable having opposing effects depending on the service in question. In the most densely populated cities where development land is scarce and prices are high, there is a powerful financial incentive to purchase rather than build expensive residential provision. This is particularly true in London, where the demand for available land has had historic influence on prices. We have included in our analyses, therefore, dummy variables representing London as a whole ("London") as well as the inner ("InLondon") and the outer boroughs ("OutLondon"). We expect to find a positive relationship between "Density" and/or the London dummy variables and all residential services. In contrast, however, a negative relationship between "Density" and day and community services is a possibility. Transport costs are such an important component of welfare provision in the more sparsely populated rural areas that significant cost savings can be obtained by relying on voluntary agencies to provide more informal services, such as meals on wheels and day centers for the elderly.

Levels of Spending
The relationship between the overall spending by a public agency and the proportion used for POSC is a potentially contradictory one. On the one hand, the normative literature suggests that the search for economy, or a perception of fiscal pressure, provides a powerful incentive toward POSC in the expectation that it will promote greater cost effectiveness. If there is any substance to this belief, one would expect to find a negative relationship between "Spend" (total public expenditure on personal social services per capita) and measures of contracting-out. A variant of this argument suggests that similar relationships will exist between POSC and "Budgetary Slack." The concept of budgetary slack is derived from the organizational sociology literature and is directly analogous to some key features of nonprofit agencies in the United States identified by Young and Finch: ". . . some agencies are more comfortably positioned than others in terms

of resources, reserves, and external obligations to indulge their own internally conceived goal structures. . . . Such slack is characteristic of organizations that have internal reserves or other means that permit them to become insensitive to their (economic) environment."[45]

For our present purposes we have drawn upon recent work at the PSSRU, which has made substantial progress in the development of territorial need indicators for the allocation of financial resources in the personal social services, to give some practical meaning to the concept. "Budgetary Slack" is defined as the ratio of actual spending to the assessed need for expenditure.[46]

These normative arguments are based on the belief that fiscal pressure encourages hard-pressed SSDs to use POSC as a way of obtaining more cost-effective services than would be possible through direct provision. However, the clear impression we obtained from interviewing key actors in SSDs is that in many respects purchases from private and voluntary agencies are supplements to, rather than substitutes for, direct provision. This view is supported by other commentators who have remarked that it is the higher spending SSDs that purchase the most services.[47] If this alternative belief has any general validity, therefore, we should expect to find positive rather than negative relationships between various measures of POSC and either "Spend" or "Budgetary Slack."

Traditional Supply
Evidence gathered on both sides of the Atlantic suggests that historic variations in the pattern of voluntary and private provision exert a considerable influence on contemporary POSC policies. In simple terms, this means that public agencies will take advantage of existing suppliers within their areas provided that the quality of service is satisfactory. Unfortunately, satisfactory data are only available to test this hypothesis for one service—residential homes for the elderly. But even in this case some caveats need to be introduced. First, most local authorities have always been very wary of placing clients in proprietary homes. Only 1.6 percent of local authority supported residents were in such homes in 1978, compared with 11.2 percent in voluntary homes. Second, as we do not have adequate historical records about the balance of provision between sectors within areas, we must assume that the existing ratio broadly reflects the pattern over time. Finally, although we would prefer to use the number of places in homes in different sectors to estimate the balance of provision, the form in which the data are available for the elderly means that we have to refer to the number of residents. "Tradition," therefore, is the ratio of the number of residents in voluntary homes for the elderly to those in local authority homes. We expect to find a positive relationship between this proxy supply measure and local authority purchasing behavior.

Sectarian Pluralism
The final hypothesis about POSC is probably the most difficult to test with existing data sources. In principle, given the historic importance of sectar-

ian influence on the local development of welfare provision, one might expect to find a positive relationship between POSC and the strength of minority religious affiliation. We cannot measure sectarian pluralism directly, however, and the only variable easily available is a possible proxy for only one example, albeit an important one, of denominational influence. "Catholic" is the proportion of Irish people in the population of each area, and although this is an extremely crude measure, it might be expected to have a positive relationship with POSC.

Exogenous Controls

There is always the danger in investigating variations in local authority behavior that biased or spurious results will be obtained unless a set of control variables representing the general economic and social characteristics of areas is included in the models. A widely used and convenient set of data suitable for this purpose has been extracted by Imber from the 1971 census.[48] For ease of exposition, we have reduced 22[49] of Imber's 23 census variables to 4 factors that between them account for more than 80 percent of the variation in the original data set.

For our present purpose, "Factors 1–4" have no substantive interest in themselves; they are included solely as a precaution to reduce the probability of making false causal inferences.

Results

Most of the substantive results of our models are derived from the ordinary least squares (OLS) regression equations that are summarized in Table 5.4. These models correspond to the selection of services shown in Tables 5.1 and 5.3 with one exception. The three nonresidential services on which we have focused attention are not suitable for OLS analysis because of the relatively large number of zero observations for each of the dependent variables. We attempt to respond to this difficulty below by employing more suitable statistical methods. However, at this stage, we have aggregated the data to produce a new dependent variable—total POSC on nonresidential care. Overall, the models were selected on the basis of a priori reasoning and statistical significance, and we report the standardized beta coefficients to indicate the relative importance of the variables. As explained above, the results should be regarded as illustrative rather than definitive, and the greatest reliance should be placed only on those arguments that are supported in models for more than one service.

The most important independent variables are "Labour," "Spend," and various measures of population density. The results confirm the impression given in the earlier literature that Labour-controlled authorities have the greatest faith in the virtues of municipal enterprise. There are significant negative relationships between "Labour" and all of the residential variables. Not surprisingly, a similar relationship is identified with the total POSC variable because contracting-out is dominated by residential provi-

Table 5.4. Multiple Regression Models of Variations in POSC

Independent Variables	Homes for the Elderly	Residential Care for Children	Other Residential Care	Nonresidential Care	Total POSC
	Dependent Variables				
Labour	−.292 (3.02)	−.498 (3.78)	−.439 (7.17)	—	−.246 (4.80)
Size	−.100[a] (1.68)*	—	—	—	—
Density	—	.414[a] (3.62)	.776 (7.49)	.459 (3.14)	.521 (6.67)
London	.196 (2.26)	—	—	—	—
InLondon	—	.435 (2.91)	.338 (3.57)	—	—
OutLondon	—	.246 (2.57)	.136 (2.20)	—	—
Spend	.478 (4.05)	.613 (3.36)	—	.281 (1.93)*	.593 (7.06)
Budgetary slack	—	—	—	—	—
Tradition	.348 (6.35)	—	—	—	—
Catholic	.097 (1.33)*	—	—	—	—
Factor 1	.191 (1.59)*	—	—	—	—
Factor 2	—	.480 (4.76)	—	—	—
Factor 3	—	−.258 (3.30)	—	—	—
Factor 4	—	−.118 (1.87)*	—	—	—
R^2	.80	.68	.78	.52	.86
$\bar{R}^2$	.78	.66	.77	.51	.86
F	54.2	25.8	86.7	54.3	212.4
N	105	105	105	105	105

Note: Numbers are standardized beta coefficients; t-statistics are in parentheses.
[a]In these equations we have substituted the logarithm of the variable.
* Coefficients not significant at the 95 percent confidence level.

sion. It is interesting to note, however, that no significant statistical relationship exists with nonresidential care. This adds further strength to the belief that not only have Labour councils had a historic faith in public provision but they have wanted to see tangible evidence of their achievements, preferably in the form of bricks and mortar.

The regularity and strength of the positive relationship between the independent variable "Spend" and four out of five of the dependent variables support the hypothesis that one of the primary reasons for POSC is to supplement existing services rather than substitute for them. In addition, the notion that rational searches for the most cost-effective solutions to service delivery needs are not uppermost in the minds of key decision makers might well be supported by no significant coefficients emerging for "Budgetary Slack" in any of the models. The absence of statistical relationships between this variable and spending on POSC, however, is not particularly surprising. It reflects the fact that it is derived from a normative assessment of the objective needs of areas that is not commonly perceived by local decision makers and does not, therefore, exercise a powerful influence on their actual behavior. Of course, the question remains as to whether it should.

The third set of crucial independent variables—"Density" and the associated dummy variables—is positively related to all of the dependent variables. In general, the results are as predicted with "InLondon" having a more powerful influence than "OutLondon" in the two models where they are included. In one case, the relationship between "Density" and residential care for children is a nonlinear one, but this is perfectly acceptable. Unexpectedly, however, a positive relationship also emerges with nonresidential care. One of our colleagues has suggested that a possible explanation for this finding is that informal voluntary action is difficult to promote in sparsely populated areas because of physical communication difficulties. Hence a positive association with "Density" should be expected. However, it is also possible that the observations on the aggregate nonresidential dependent variable are particularly subject to measurement error. For example, the largest single item of expenditure on POSC that is included is for children in care who are boarded out. Many authorities are known to have supplied misleading data for this item, and there may be other systematic biases. Nevertheless, we will investigate the relationship between "Density" and some representative nonresidential services below.

As far as the other independent variables are concerned, the one most worth drawing attention to is our proxy for "Tradition." The availability of alternative suppliers appears to exercise a powerful influence on local authority POSC behavior with respect to residential homes for the elderly. This confirms our impression of the importance of traditional influences in our interviews and supports the conclusions of the early American literature, but questions the design assumptions of the APWA study discussed above. There is very little evidence in our models to support the view that POSC is an important means of achieving economies of scale. "Size" is of limited importance in only one of the models. Similarly, "Catholic," our proxy for sectarian pluralism, is only significant at the 80 percent level in one of our models, although in this case it probably reflects at least as much the inability of the variable to capture what is intended as it does the true absence of any underlying causal relationship.

There are a number of difficulties in attempting to model any of the nonresidential social services, primarily because in most cases the extent of POSC is very small. This is exacerbated by the fact that a substantial number of authorities do not contract-out service provision for many of their services at all. As a result, conventional OLS regression analysis is not a suitable statistical technique. Instead, we must turn to what have been described as "qualitative response models" and their close relatives.[50] One possibility is to transform the data into a dichotomous dependent variable, where an authority takes the value of one if it uses POSC and zero if it does not, and use logit. However, this technique wastes a good deal of information about the variations in POSC among those SSDs that do contract-out. An alternative approach, therefore, that bridges the gap between logit and multiple regression is required, and this is provided by the tobit method.[51] In fact, we make use of both logit and tobit to investigate whether the hypotheses outlined earlier help to account for variations among SSDs in POSC for three nonresidential social services—meals on wheels, day care for children under the age of five, and day centers for the elderly. Although our primary purpose is not to predict levels of POSC that might be expected for particular services, we must emphasize that even less reliance can be placed on the coefficients in the logit and tobit models than applied to the OLS results. In the circumstances, to avoid unnecessary complexity and improve readability, we report the asymptotic t-statistics and the signs on the coefficients only. Even so, these models do allow us to investigate whether any of the hypotheses have sufficient strength to establish a degree of statistical significance. The models were selected on the usual criteria of significance, parsimony, and common sense. For the logit models, we are able to compare the results against a constant-only model, but the computer program available to us did not offer this facility for the tobit equations. The findings, shown in Table 5.5, are far from being unambiguous, but they do tend to lend support to some of our hypotheses and in part reinforce the regression results outlined above. "Labour" is negatively associated with POSC and the provision of meals on wheels and day centers for the elderly, but a positive relationship emerges with day care for children. The possible explanation for this unexpected finding is that ideological support for the program swamps any adverse concern about the form of provision. More than 58 percent of the POSC expenditure in this area is for preschool playgroups, which are largely provided informally through voluntary groups in almost all areas; if they are to be supported, therefore, it is difficult to avoid POSC spending.

Along with "Labour," the other most important independent variables once again are "Spend" and "Density." On this occasion, however, the negative signs on "Spend," together with "Budgetary Slack" in one model, suggest that POSC is used as a substitute for direct service provision. Why there should be such a marked difference in the apparent rationale for POSC between our selection of nonresidential and residential services is not immediately clear and merits further investigation.

On the face of it the "Density" results are similarly confusing, with a negative sign in one model and positive signs in the others, but here there is a more satisfactory intuitive explanation. The negative relationship in the logit model for meals on wheels reflects the economic incentive to use volunteer drivers to deliver meals in sparsely populated areas where trans-

Table 5.5. Logit and Tobit Models of POSC Variations

Independent Variables	Meals on Wheels		Day Care for Children Under 5		Day Centers for the Elderly	
	Logit	Tobit	Logit	Tobit	Logit	Tobit
Constant	3.01	3.20	.69*	−1.9	2.38	1.1*
Labour	−2.20	−1.14*	1.22*	—	−1.91	—
Size	−1.55*	—	1.75	—	—	—
Density	−2.92	—	—	6.1	—	2.0
London	—	—	—	—	—	—
InLondon	—	—	—	—	—	1.0*
OutLondon	—	—	—	−2.9	—	1.2*
Spend	—	−1.93	−1.10*	—	—	−2.4
Budgetary slack	—	—	—	—	—	−1.1*
Catholic	—	—	—	—	—	1.7
Factor 1	1.79	—	—	—	—	—
Factor 2	—	—	−1.61*	−2.4	—	—
Factor 3	1.21*	—	—	—	—	−2.3
Factor 4	—	—	—	—	−1.61*	—
Log likelihood	−61.4	25.6	−47.9	−8.1	−67.9	−33.1
LRTS[a]	22.6	—	6.3	—	7.6*	—
SIGMA	—	.082	—	.22	—	.26
N	105	105	105	105	105	105

Note: Numbers are asymptotic t-statistics.
[a] Likelihood ratio test statistic.
* Not significant at the 90 percent confidence level.

port costs are a potentially high proportion of total costs. In contrast, the positive association between "Density" and POSC for the two day care services might reflect the fact that the capital requirements of the program in terms of their needs for buildings raise the same kind of problems of high land costs as for residential services. There are only a few other results worthy of note. The negative and positive signs for "Size" and "Catholic" in the logit and tobit models for meals on wheels and day centers for the elderly, respectively, provide some minimal supporting evidence for the economy of scale and sectarian pluralism hypotheses. In contrast, the positive association for "Size" in the logit model and the negative sign on "OutLondon" in the tobit model for day care for children both defy explanation.

CONCLUSION

The purpose of this article has been to investigate why public agencies purchase services rather than provide them directly. Contrary to popular belief, one of our conclusions is that the British experience of POSC is remarkably similar in many respects to that reported in the American literature. In particular, the reasons given by key actors in SSDs are as varied as those in the United States. The general impression given in both countries is that the beliefs and prejudices of local decision makers and the historical experience of different patterns of welfare provision in particular areas weigh much more heavily than any rational consideration of the arguments contained in the normative literature on the subject. Purchase of service seems to be much more a response to circumstances and events outside the direct control of public agencies than a conscious choice. Even where rationality does intrude, it appears to be relatively marginal. There is almost no evidence that public agencies on either side of the Atlantic take advantage of purchasing opportunities to plan an efficient mixed economy of social care applicable to their local areas.

One of the dangers of relying on the subjective perceptions of managers about the rationale for POSC is that their ex post facto impressions inaccurately reflect the underlying causes of the variations in purchasing behavior. As an antidote to this approach, therefore, we have presented the results of a preliminary statistical investigation of variations in POSC. The results outlined here must be regarded as tentative, but it is worth noting that few of the hypotheses derived from the literature and interviews are supported by the results. Even taking account of the undoubted deficiencies in the data, they add credence to the view that intuition rather than deliberation is what has guided the actions of POSC decision makers. As far as comparisons between England and America are concerned, the most interesting finding is the strength of political partisanship. Ideology seems to play a much larger role in accounting for POSC variations in England. It would be interesting to know how the other particularly significant result compares with American experience—that POSC is more of a supplement to, rather than a substitute for, direct provision.

NOTES

1. See, e.g. Alfred J. Kahn and Sheila B. Kamerman, "The Course of Personal Social Services," *Public Welfare* 36 (Summer 1978): 29–42.

2. Samuel Mencher, "Financial Relationships between Voluntary and Statutory Bodies in the British Social Services," *Social Service Review* 32 (1958): 138–51.

3. Ralph M. Kramer, *Voluntary Agencies in the Welfare State* (Berkeley: University of California Press, 1981).

4. Ken Judge, "The Public Purchase of Social Care: British Confirmation of the American Experience," *Policy and Politics* 10 (October 1982): 397–416.

5. Ken Judge, "The Mixed Economy of Welfare: Purchase of Service Contracting in the Personal Social Services." Mimeograph, Personal Social Services Research Unit Discussion Paper no. 195 (Canterbury: University of Kent, 1981).

6. Kenneth R. Wedel, "Contracting for Public Assistance Social Services," *Public Welfare* 32 (Winter 1974): 57–62, quote on p. 57.

7. Bertram M. Beck, "Governmental Contracts with Non-profit Social Welfare Corporations," in *The Dilemma of Accountability in Modern Government*, ed. Bruce L. R. Smith and D. C. Hague (London: Macmillan Publishing Co., 1971), pp. 214–15.

8. Arnold Gurin, Barry Friedman, Natalie Ammarell, and Carole Sureau, "Contracting for Service as a Mechanism for the Delivery of Human Services: A Study of Contracting Practices

in Three Human Services Agencies in Massachusetts," mimeograph (Waltham, Mass.: Florence Heller Graduate School for Advanced Studies in Social Welfare, Brandeis University, June 1980), p. 9.

9. Pacific Consultants, *Title XX Purchase of Service*, Vol. 2, *The Flexibility of Comparing Costs between Directly Delivered and Purchased Services* (Berkeley, Calif.: Pacific Consultants, 1979), pp. 13–14.

10. Ira Sharkansky, "Policy Making and Service Delivery on the Margins of Government: The Case of Contractors," *Public Administration Review* 40 (March–April 1980): 116–23, quote on p. 118.

11. Bill B. Benton, "Questions for Research and Development," in *Social Services by Government Contract*, ed. Kenneth R. Wedel, Arthur J. Katz, and Ann Eick (New York: Praeger Publishers, 1979), p. 81.

12. E. S. Savas, *Alternatives for Delivering Public Services* (Boulder, Colo.: Westview Press, 1977), p. 2.

13. Lyle C. Fitch, "Increasing the Role of the Private Sector in Providing Public Services," in *Improving the Quality of Urban Management*, ed. Willis D. Howley and David Rogers (Beverly Hills, Calif.: Sage Publications, 1974), p. 551.

14. Donald Fisk, Herbert Kiesling, and Thomas Muller, *Private Provision of Public Services: An Overview* (Washington, D.C.: Urban Institute, 1978), p. 6.

15. Paul Terrell, *The Social Impact of Revenue Sharing* (New York: Praeger Publishers, 1976), p. 87.

16. Fitch, "Increasing the Role," p. 551.

17. Gurin et al., "Contracting for Service," p. 247.

18. Terrell, *Social Impact*, p. 86.

19. Kramer, *Voluntary Agencies*, p. 8.

20. Fisk et al., *Private Provision*, p. 6.

21. Terrell, *Social Impacts*, p. 6.

22. Fisk et al., *Private Provision*, p. 7.

23. Gordon Manser, "Implications of Purchase of Service for Voluntary Agencies," *Social Casework* 53, no. 6 (June 1972): 335–40, quote on p. 336.

24. Kramer, *Voluntary Agencies*, p. 8.

25. Fitch, "Increasing the Roles," p. 551.

26. Bill B. Benton, Tracey Field, and Rhona Millar, *Social Services: Federal Legislation U.S. State Implementation* (Washington, D.C.: Urban Institute, 1978), p. 113.

27. Wedel, "Contracting for Public Assistance," p. 59.

28. Kenneth R. Wedel, "Government Contracting for Purchase of Service," *Social Work* 21 (March 1976): 101–105, quote on p. 102.

29. Benton et al., *Social Services*.

30. Pacific Consultants, *Title XX Purchase of Service*, pp. 51–56.

31. American Public Welfare Association, *A Study of Purchase of Social Services in Selected States* (Washington, D.C.: Author, 1981), p. 10.

32. Ibid.

33. The Personal Social Services Research Unit (PSSRU) is sponsored by the Department of Health and Social Security to conduct studies of resource allocation in the field of social care. Further details are available from the authors.

34. Ewan Ferlie and Ken Judge, "Retrenchment and Rationality in the Personal Social Services," *Policy and Politics* 9 (1981): 311–30.

35. Ken Judge, "Mixed Economy of Welfare."

36. See R. A. Darton and P. V. McCoy, "Survey of Residential Accommodation for the Elderly," Mimeograph, Personal Social Services Research Unit Discussion Paper no. 186 (Canterbury: University of Kent, 1981).

37. Stephen Hatch and Ian Mocroft, "The Relative Costs of Services Provided by Voluntary and Statutory Organisations," *Public Administration* 57 (Winter 1979): 397–405.

38. Martin Knapp and Spyros Missiakoulis, "Inter-sectoral Cost Comparisons: Day Care for the Elderly," *Journal of Social Policy* 11 (July 1982): 335–54, quote on p. 335.

39. Mencher, "Financial Relationships," pp. 141–42.

40. Kenneth Newton, *Second City Politics* (London: Oxford University Press, 1976), p. 72.

41. See E. P. Erickson, "A Regression Method for Estimating Population Changes of Local Areas," *Journal of the American Statistical Association* 69 (1974): 867–75.

42. Purchases are defined as "services provided by voluntary organisations and registered private persons" and grants as "general contributions to voluntary organisations."

43. Bleddyn Davies, Andrew Barton, Ian McMillan, and Valerie Williamson, *Variations in Services for the Aged* (London: G. Bell & Sons, 1971), p. 133.

44. Ibid., p. 21.

45. Dennis R. Young and Stephen J. Finch, *Foster Care and Nonprofit Agencies* (Lexington, Mass.: D. C. Heath & Co., 1977), pp. 50, 229.

46. A. C. Bebbington and Bleddyn Davies, "Territorial Need Indicators: A New Approach, Part 2," *Journal of Social Policy* 9 (October 1980): 433–62.

47. Bob Holman, "The Place of Voluntary Societies—Past, Present and Future," *Community Care* 12 (November 1981): 16–18.

48. Valerie Imber, *A Classification of the English Personal Social Services Authorities*, Department of Health and Social Security (DHSS), Statistical and Research Report Series no. 16 (London: Her Majesty's Stationery Office, 1977).

49. The excluded variable is "Catholic."

50. Takeshi Amemiya, "Qualitative Response Models: A Survey," *Journal of Economic Literature* 19 (December 1981): 1483–1536.

51. James Tobin, "Estimation of Relationships for Limited Dependent Variables," *Econometrica* 26 (1958): 24–36.

REFERENCES

Amemiya, Takeshi. "Qualitative Response Models: A Survey." *Journal of Economic Literature* (December 1981): 1483–1536.

American Public Welfare Association. *A Study of Purchase of Social Services in Selected States.* Washington, D.C.: Author, 1981.

Bebbington, A. C., and Bleddyn Davies. "Territorial Need Indicators: A New Approach." *Journal of Social Policy* (October 1980): 433–62.

Beck, Bertram M. "Governmental Contracts with Non-profit Social Welfare Corporations." In Bruce L. R. Smith and D. C. Hague, eds., *The Dilemma of Accountability in Modern Government.* London: Macmillan Publishing Co., 1971.

Benton, Bill M. "Questions for Research and Development." In Kenneth R. Wedel, Arthur J. Katz, and Ann Eick, eds., *Social Services by Government Contract.* New York: Praeger Publishers, 1979.

Benton, Bill M., Tracey Field, and Rhona Millar. *Social Services: Federal Legislation U.S. State Implementation.* Washington, D.C.: Urban Institute, 1978.

Darton, R. A., and P. V. McCoy. "Survey of Residential Accommodation for the Elderly." Mimeograph, Personal Social Services Research Unit Discussion Paper no. 186. Canterbury: University of Kent, 1981.

Davies, Bleddyn, Andrew Barton, Ian McMillan, and Valerie Williamson. *Variations in Services for the Aged.* London: G. Bell & Sons, 1971.

Erickson, E. P. "A Regression Method for Estimating Population Changes of Local Areas." *Journal of the American Statistical Association* (1974): 867–75.

Ferlie, Ewan, and Ken Judge. "Retrenchment and Rationality in the Personal Social Services." *Policy and Politics* (1981): 311–30.

Fisk, Donald, Herbert Kiesling, and Thomas Muller. *Private Provision of Public Services: An Overview.* Washington, D.C.: Urban Institute, 1978.

Fitch, Lyle C. "Increasing the Role of the Private Sector in Providing Public Services." In

Willis D. Howley and David Rogers, eds., *Improving the Quality of Urban Management*. Beverly Hills, Calif.: Sage Publications, 1974.

Gurin, Arnold, Barry Friedman, Natalie Ammarell, and Carole Sureau. "Contracting for Service as a Mechanism for the Delivery of Human Services: A Study of Contracting Practices in Three Human Services Agencies in Massachusetts." Mimeograph. (Waltham, Mass.: Florence Heller Graduate School, Brandeis University, 1980).

Hatch, Stephen, and Ian Mocroft. "The Relative Costs of Services Provided by Voluntary and Statutory Organizations." *Public Administration* (Winter 1979): 397–405.

Holman, Bob. "The Place of Voluntary Societies—Past, Present and Future." *Community Care* (November 1981).

Imber, Valerie. *A Classification of the English Personal Social Services Authorities*. Department of Health and Social Security (DHSS), Statistical and Research Report Series No. 16. London: Her Majesty's Stationery Office, 1977.

Judge, Ken. "The Mixed Economy of Welfare: Purchase of Service Contracting in the Personal Social Services." Mimeograph, Personal Social Services Research Unit Discussion Paper No. 195. Canterbury: University of Kent, 1981.

———. "The Public Purchase of Social Care: British Confirmation of the American Experience," *Policy and Politics* (October 1982): 397–416.

Kahn, Alfred J., and Sheila B. Kamerman. "The Course of Personal Social Services." *Public Welfare* (Summer 1978): 29–42.

Knapp, Martin, and Spyros Missiakoulis. "Inter-sectoral Cost Comparisons: Day Care for the Elderly." *Journal of Social Policy* (June 1982): 335–54.

Kramer, Ralph M. *Voluntary Agencies in the Welfare State*. Berkeley, Calif.: University of California Press, 1981.

Manser, Gordon. "Implications of Purchase of Service for Voluntary Agencies." *Social Casework* (June 1972): 335–40.

Mencher, Samuel. "Financial Relationships between Voluntary and Statutory Bodies in the British Social Services." *Social Service Review* (1958): 138–51.

Newton, Kenneth. *Second City Politics*. London: Oxford University Press, 1976.

Pacific Consultants. *Title XX Purchase of Service*, Vol. 2, *The Flexibility of Comparing Costs between Directly Delivered and Purchased Services*. Berkeley, Calif.: Pacific Consultants, 1979.

Savas, E. S. *Alternatives for Delivering Public Services*. Boulder, Colo.: Westview Press, 1977.

Sharkansky, Ira. "Policy Making and Service Delivery on the Margins of Government: The Case of Contractors." *Public Administration Review* (March–April 1980): 116–23.

Terrell, Paul. *The Social Impact of Revenue Sharing*. New York: Praeger Publishers, 1976.

Tobin, James. "Estimation of Relationships for Limited Dependent Variables." *Econometrica* (1958): 24–36.

Wedel, Kenneth R. "Contracting for Public Assistance Social Services." *Public Welfare* (Winter 1974): 57–62.

———. "Government Contracting for Purchase of Social Service, *Social Work* (March 1976): 101–105.

Young, Dennis R., and Stephen J. Finch. *Foster Care and Nonprofit Agencies*. Lexington, Mass.: D. C. Heath & Co., 1977.

6

Government versus Private Provision of Social Services: The Case of Austria

CHRISTOPH BADELT

During the last few years debates on the future patterns of social policy in Austria have increasingly focused on the role of nonprofit organizations. At the same time there is still only little knowledge of the Austrian voluntary nonprofit sector and its economic relevance. This paper (1) summarizes the economic arguments and political hopes that are associated with nonprofit organizations (NPOs) in the field of social services, (2) gives an overview of empirical facts on the institutional mix in the provision of social services in Austria, and (3) outlines the relations between various Austrian government institutions and private nonprofit organizations from a socioeconomic point of view. One of the main elements in this discussion concerns the actual and projected role of volunteer labor in the provision of social services. The use of NPOs by government and volunteer labor by NPOs are seen as ways to simultaneously economize on costs and improve the quality of output.

THE POLITICAL DEBATE IN AUSTRIA

The political discussion of NPOs in Austria must be seen against the background of the frequently quoted "crisis of the welfare state."[1] At first sight this crisis is conceived as a purely financial problem, in particular with regard to financing the traditional social security system. Although it is obvious that retirement pension systems, health care, and unemployment insurance can only be financed in the future if substantial changes are implemented in the structure of benefits and contributions, indirectly these potential changes challenge the organizational patterns of social service provision.

The rapidly increasing expenditure of social security is only one important reason for the large deficits in public budgets. More generally, in Austria as elsewhere, the government is searching for a variety of ways to reduce the responsibility—and the financial burden—of the public sector. "Privatization" has become a guideline for public policy in many areas. Due to prevailing political values a far-reaching privatization of social services in the sense of for-profit firms taking over formerly public tasks seems to be out of the question. Consequently, a stronger engagement of NPOs is proposed as a possible political compromise between the two extremes of government and for-profit provision. This is not to say that such a policy would be explicitly declared as a compromise. It is more an implicit consequence of positions currently held by opposing political groups.

Statements like "Not everything can be done by a public authority," "We have to remember the big potential of private charity," "It is much more humane to provide social services informally than through public bureaucratic institutions," and so on, are made quite often by representatives of both sides of the political spectrum.[2] A more thorough analysis of the current political debate illustrates that a number of different hopes are associated with NPOs as providers of social services.

The first and most obvious expectation is that a stronger involvement of NPOs would help reduce expenditures by governments at all levels of the Austrian political system (i.e., federal, provincial, and local). Although the political Left often alleges that a "demolition of the Welfare State" is the true (albeit not revealed) goal of the Christian Democrats and right wing parties, there is no empirical evidence that such a policy is actually under serious consideration in Austria. The political rationale relies more on long-term considerations: well functioning NPOs would help to reduce the demand for public social services in the future.

This line of argument can be illustrated by the example of public hospitals. If NPOs provide a network of home care in case of sickness or illness, this would help to reduce the length of necessary hospitalization. Since one reason for the deficit of (public) hospitals is that too many beds are used for nursing purposes, which need not be done in a hospital, the activities of NPOs could enable governments to reduce the number of beds in hospitals and, thus, to economize on costs.

The political hope, therefore, rests on at least two assumptions: (1) NPOs would provide a different product or use a different technology from public hospitals, probably using volunteers; and (2) government would not or could not provide the same product or apply the same technology as NPOs do. In the political arena the validity of these assumptions is not seriously debated. From the economic perspective they are questions whose empirical validity is far from clear.

The second argument is closely linked to the cost-saving issue. It is pointed out that in most European welfare states "new" social needs have emerged, making it necessary to search for innovative institutional forms to meet them. Examples are the increasing isolation of senior citizens, the rising demand for counseling by "marginal groups" in society such as drug addicts, handicapped people, guest workers, and so on, and specific educational needs (in particular in adult education) that are not covered by the regular public school system. Many of these problems cannot simply be solved by the system of monetary transfers, which is typical of the social security system. The problems usually require social services to work on solutions, and it is increasingly doubted whether government bureaucracies can provide the necessary services in a satisfactory way.

This line of reasoning obviously refers to the ties between institutional form, technology, and output mentioned earlier. There is no doubt that NPOs have been successful in these areas, in particular with self-help groups in health care and related fields. Still, it remains an open question as to whether government institutions could not be reorganized to achieve similar effects. This possibility often is not considered in the political debate.

The third main argument in favor of NPOs is purely political. NPOs are seen as a possible means for decentralizing power in Austrian society, which is generally characterized by a very broad influence of the state and a few well-established interest groups. Private welfare organizations as well as small self-help groups or community organizations strengthen the element of pluralism in Austrian society. A process of "privatization" in the sense described earlier could help to support efforts toward democratization and stronger political and social participation by individual citizens. Of course, this goal is not generally accepted in Austrian political life. There are also groups (like parts of the "Green" movement) that might identify with the goal but doubt whether it can be reached through any form of privatization. Nevertheless, ignoring this dimension would mean leaving out an important aspect of the role of NPOs in Austria.

This brief recapitulation illustrates the variety of hopes that are associated with NPOs in the political debate. However, the theoretical or empirical basis for these hopes is rather vague. There is very little knowledge of the size of the voluntary sector in Austria or of its potential to take on new tasks. Knowledge of their specific means of production, their criteria for output distribution—in short, knowledge of their strengths and weaknesses—is still far from reliable or empirically validated.

Indeed, the "voluntary nonprofit sector," as conceived in the Anglo-American economic and social policy literature, is hardly a category of thought in Austria. One cannot even find an equivalent German word for this English term. The terms used in the scientific world (particularly by economists) are *Freiwilligensektor, autonomer Sektor, Dritter Sektor,* or *Nonprofit-Sektor.*[3] But these terms differ in their exact connotation, and none of them would be used in everyday language. This remark should not be viewed as a digression into linguistics but as an illustration of the missing consciousness concerning a "voluntary sector" as such.

It follows from this confusion that the exact institutional form as well as the role of volunteer labor are not determined when the role of NPOs, "private initiative," or similar categories are emphasized in the current political debate, thereby obscuring many potential conflicts between advocates of such a policy. If one tries to summarize the suggestions that are

scattered over the political landscape the following types of nonprofit organizations can be identified:

1. traditional and well-established voluntary organizations in the sense of social
   welfare organizations *(Wohlfahrtsverbände)*, some of them affiliated with
   churches, some of them purely secular in nature; examples are the Red Cross,
   or the Caritasverband, which is the largest welfare organization of the Catholic
   Church (these organizations usually employ both paid and volunteer labor);
2. local associations *(Vereine)* that are not necessarily branches or affiliates of the
   big welfare organizations (they may either be independent, or can be completely
   tied to political parties or interest groups);
3. decentralized grass-roots groups with a rather parochial character, sometimes
   organized around political civic action (these groups arrange a variety of services in a local community; they try to keep their political independence and
   employ exclusively volunteer labor);
4. volunteer labor outside any form of permanent organization ("informal volunteer work"), done on an individual basis, in particular, social services provided
   by friends, neighbors, and so on.

Category 1 has its definite place in the Austrian system of social services,
on the state and federal levels. NPOs of category 2 may play an important
role in certain provinces and some local communities, where cooperative
efforts between government and voluntary services have been tried. Category 4, of course, is part of the everyday social structure in rural and
urban areas. One of the most remarkable developments in local social policy is the attempt to integrate categories 3 and 4 with publicly produced
services in order to improve the total network of social services.

The following sections will review the status of NPO activities in Austria, hoping that this will serve to illuminate the current political debate.
The section that follows provides some macro data on the role of the nonprofit sector, particularly volunteer labor, and the next section discusses
cooperative arrangements between governments and various NPO categories.

NPO ACTIVITIES IN AUSTRIA: SOME QUANTITATIVE EVIDENCE

As indicated in the preceding section, there is little empirical knowledge
on the size and structure of the voluntary sector in Austria. In the field of
social services data are available in two areas: the provision of preschools
for children and senior citizen or nursing homes for the elderly. Moreover,
survey data give hints on the order of magnitude of volunteer labor in
Austria.

Nursery Schools and Kindergartens

Preschool education for children is a traditional working area of NPOs,
although the public sector has increased its activities in this field. Unlike

Table 6.1. Nursery Schools and Kindergartens
(Anstalten des Kindergartenwesens) in Austria 1984–1985

	Institutions		Classes (Groups)		Children	
	Number	Percent	Number	Percent	Number	Percent
Total	4,326	100	8,125	100	196,129	100
Public sector						
Total	3,069	70.9	5,752	70.8	140,714	71.7
Federal level	31	0.7	65	0.8	1,364	0.7
Provincial level	833	19.3	1,383	17.0	35,806	18.3
Community level	2,205	51.0	4,304	53.0	103,544	52.8
Voluntary nonprofit sector						
Total	1,054	24.4	2,057	25.3	49,317	25.1
Secular NPOs	300	6.9	485	6.0	9,693	4.9
Catholic church	728	16.8	1,505	18.5	38,231	19.5
Protestant church	26	0.6	67	0.8	1,393	0.7
For-profit organizations	203	4.7	316	3.9	6,098	3.1

Source: Calculations based on Österreichisches Statistisches Zentralamt (O.S.Z.), *Die Kindergärten (Kindertagesheime) Berichtsjahr 1984/85* (Vienna: O.S.Z., 1985).

other social services, preschool education is statistically well documented through data of the Austrian Statistical Office, which are summarized in Tables 6.1 and 6.2.

As can be seen from Table 6.1, the voluntary nonprofit sector accounts for about 25 percent of Austrian preschool education, measured either in the number of schools, the number of groups, or the number of children. Within the nonprofit sector the most prominent role is played by the Cath-

Table 6.2. Employment in Nursery Schools and Kindergartens
(Anstalten des Kindergartenwesens) in Austria, 1984–1985

Province	Public Sector		Private Sector (NPO & For-profit)		Total Employment
	Number	Percent	Number	Percent	
Burgenland	414	79.8	105	20.2	519
Kärnten	579	66.2	295	33.8	874
Niederösterreich	2,665	94.7	150	5.3	2,815
Oberösterreich	1,726	56.9	1,308	43.1	3,034
Salzburg	758	74.4	261	25.6	1,019
Steiermark	1,640	74.5	562	25.5	2,202
Tyrol	907	81.9	201	18.1	1,108
Vorarlberg	465	92.3	39	7.7	504
Vienna	3,540	66.4	1,791	33.6	5,331
Austria	12,694	72.9	4,712	27.1	17,406

Source: Calculations based on Österreichisches Statistisches Zentralamt (O.S.Z.), *Die Kindergärten (Kindertagesheime), Berichtsjahr 1984/85* (Vienna: O.S.Z., 1985). Disaggregation between the nonprofit and for-profit sectors is not available.

olic Church, which educates nearly 20 percent of Austrian preschoolers, while secular NPOs provide services to about 5 percent. The public sector, mostly on the community level, has taken over the vast majority of preschool education (71 percent), while for-profit organizations are only of marginal importance. This general picture is also mirrored on the input side, where 27 percent of the relevant personnel are found in the private sector.

It is especially interesting to note the regional differences in the relative role of the private sector. Vienna, simultaneously the capital of Austria and a separate province, has an above average portion of private preschool education, whereas in other provinces, such as Niederösterreich and Vorarlberg, the public sector comes close to a monopoly position. From a political point of view this is surprising, since Niederösterreich and Vorarlberg have strong conservative majorities, while in Vienna the Social Democrats hold a majority. From an economic standpoint the greater variety of preschool education in Vienna can be explained more easily: it reflects the greater heterogeneity of demand that can be met by variegated private organizations in a large city, whereas in smaller communities, a natural monopoly situation may exist, leading to state ownership.

However, the differences observed cannot be attributed completely to differences in demand structures and scale economies in rural and urban areas. More generally, the relative role of NPOs cannot be explained by economic arguments alone. In some provinces the establishment of a (public) nursery school has become an explicit goal and a symbol of success for politicians in their competition for votes. The public finance argument that such goods could be produced by the private sector, even if publicly financed, is hardly considered in this context, since political credit is more likely to accrue if the nursery school is government run.

Another interesting aspect of these data concerns the role of secular versus religious nursery schools. Most nursery schools are run by the (Catholic) church, whose sponsorship is widely seen as a signal of quality; the well-known "trustworthiness" argument seems to apply. To some degree this is also true for secular NPOs, which are usually cooperatives or "associations" tied to specific pedagogical ideologies and run by parents who are willing to engage themselves in the school in order to have their children educated in a particular way. Since the parents work for their own benefit the nonprofit form seems appropriate. A few for-profit nursery schools also exist, guaranteeing parents, through price-rationing, that their children will be in an environment of high-income upper class families. In other words, the different type of output provided by each form explains the institutional mix in this industry.[4]

Senior Citizen Homes and Nursing Homes

NPOs have also played an active role in caring for the elderly, in senior citizen and nursing homes. Table 6.3 presents data on the sectoral struc-

Table 6.3. Senior Citizen Homes and Nursing Homes in Austria, 1983

	Number of Institutions	Available Places	
		Number	Percent
Public sector			
Total	343	37,130	76.1
Provinces	61	8,273	17.0
Communities	226	22,897	46.9
Groups of communities			
(Sozialhilfeverbände)	56	5,960	12.2
Voluntary nonprofit sector			
Total	137	9,601	19.7
Secular NPOs	24	1,487	3.0
Church-affiliated NPOs	113	8,314	17.0
For-profit institutions	30	1,876	3.8
Total	510	48,807	100.0

Source: Compiled out of the information brochure of the Österreichischen Komitees für Sozialarbeit (ÖKSA), Heime für alte Menschen, Ausgabe 1983 (Vienna: ÖKSA, 1983).

ture of this industry. About 20 percent of all places in senior citizen homes are provided by NPOs. Again, in this industry the for-profit institutions play only a marginal role, leaving more than three-quarters (76.1 percent) of the market to the public sector. Again, the (Catholic) church dominates the supply within the voluntary nonprofit sector. Arguments of trust and product differences that have been elaborated for the nursery school industry also apply here.

Volunteer Labor

Both from the political and theoretical perspective volunteer labor is one of the most interesting phenomena in the voluntary nonprofit sector. Although volunteer labor is not strictly confined to NPOs, the voluntary nonprofit sector has been identified as most attractive to volunteers. As indicated earlier the availability of volunteer labor also is emphasized when NPOs are suggested as providers of social services. Social services provided by volunteers in NPOs are often said to have a very special quality that is appreciated by clients: volunteers may be more grass-roots oriented than employees of government institutions. They may have better sources of information than would a civil servant (for example, because they are living in the same neighborhood as the client), they may share similar experiences as a client (which is a typical rationale for self-help groups), or they may be willing to spend more time with a client than a paid worker would.

Although nearly everybody has "anecdotal evidence" about the importance of volunteer labor, only recently has there been a serious effort to estimate the order of magnitude of this phenomenon, thus providing a basis for evaluating its economic relevance. In Austria this was done only

Table 6.4.   Volume of Volunteer Labor in Austria, 1982

	Number of Volunteers	Weekly Number of Hours	Full-time Equivalents		
			Total	"Formal"	"Informal"
Personal social services	426,887	4,537,812	113,445	9,533	103,912
Culture and entertainment	195,442	1,119,885	27,997	16,798	11,199
Environmental and recreational services	118,294	842,254	21,056	9,571	11,485
Emergency services	66,862	244,714	6,118	5,591	527
Religious services	108,008	351,025	8,776	7,236	1,540
Political work	128,580	691,760	17,294	16,354	940
Neighborhood help	221,159	1,731,671	43,292	1,671	41,621
Total			237,978	66,754	171,224
% of labor Force			7.4%	2.1%	5.3%
% of labor force employed for wages			8.5%	2.4%	6.1%

once, in 1982.[5] The survey covered individuals between the ages of 16 and 70 and investigated actual participation and time inputs in volunteer labor. In accordance with Anglo-Saxon practice volunteer labor was defined as "productive work" done without direct monetary compensation ("unpaid work"), with the output used by people outside the volunteer's own household.[6] The borderline between production and consumption was drawn along the "criterion of the third person,"[7] in which "productive" work leads to outputs that can also be produced by others (for example, cooking, or taking care of elderly people; as counterexamples, fitness training or learning a foreign language). People may engage in volunteer work because they hope for nonmonetary rewards, because they gain direct utility from the *process* of work per se in addition to its output, and so on.[8]

It is obvious that definitions and measurements of this kind are based on heroic assumptions. The activity must be empirically observable and it also must be possible to transform such definitions into a questionnaire that is answered by noneconomists. In the survey this was done by presenting an extensive list of examples of volunteer work. The main results of a very cautious estimate of volunteer labor[9] for the whole population, disaggregated into seven categories or industries, are presented in Table 6.4.

The total volume of volunteer labor in Austria is estimated at about 238,000 full-time equivalent workers. This amounts to 7.4 percent of the Austrian labor force or 8.5 percent of the volume of work done by employed persons.[10]

Out of the seven categories that have been defined, personal social services represent by far the most important field in which volunteer labor takes place. With a total volunteer labor force of 113,000 full-time equivalents this "industry" is responsible for about 48 percent of total volunteer labor in Austria. With 55,000 individuals employed for wages in social service professions, the number of full-time equivalent people in the social service volunteer labor force is roughly double the paid labor force. This supports the hypothesis that volunteer labor is of significant economic relevance and possibly an important element in the formulation of social policy.

A second interesting result also deserves attention: the division between "formal" and "informal" volunteer labor. *Formal volunteer labor* was defined as work done within organizations, whereas *informal volunteer labor* was defined as taking place outside of organizations. In total, volunteer labor outside of organizations is about 2.5 times as large as formal volunteer work. In the social services, this ratio is even more extreme: more than 10 to 1.

At first sight, these ratios do not seem plausible. Yet, they are supported by data that exist for a few—quantitatively important—nonprofit organizations such as Caritas (Welfare Organization of the Catholic Church) or the Red Cross. Although these organizations employ large numbers of volunteers, their total volunteer time input is very small compared to the paid work done in them. Obviously the vast amount of informal helping relations between households accounts for the large size of the informal volunteer labor force in the personal social services shown in Table 6.4.

Traditional "Institutionalized" Services versus "New" Needs

Although the empirical picture of the Austrian voluntary sector just presented is obviously incomplete, it can still help us gain insight into the role of NPOs, particularly with regard to the economic and political discussion reviewed in the first section. At present, the well-established voluntary organizations (category 1), especially those run by the Catholic Church, play an important role in highly organized social services such as preschool education and institutionally organized care for the elderly. Although this role is often emphasized in the public debate, NPOs are still a minority supplier in these areas. It is very unlikely to be the intention of the political parties currently in power (Social Democrats and Christian Democrats) to fundamentally change the division of responsibilities between the sectors. Also, many of the economic arguments in favor of NPOs—in particular, those stressing access to volunteer labor—are only of limited relevance, since most of the services of category 1 NPOs are provided by paid labor.

The advantages of "privatization" in the field of social services seem to focus much more on the "new" kind of needs mentioned in the first section than on the institutionalized forms of social services. Although complete and reliable data are not available, experience indicates that, in the "new" needs area, the types of organizations providing service are much more variable. These are the fields of activity not only for NPOs of category 1, but particularly those of categories 2 and 3. Examples include home care for elderly and handicapped people; self-help groups for those with all kinds of medical and social problems; Meals on Wheels services; family counseling; care for alcoholics and drug addicts; and certain forms of preventive medicine (such as nutrition and exercise classes). In Austria, most of these services are under the jurisdiction of the provincial or local governments. Governments have the power to organize the provision of these services. They can behave passively, provide the services themselves, or arrange any other form of institutional solution.

Since some of these services are typical users of volunteer labor, NPO activities of categories 3 and 4 gain increasing importance. Thus, politicians may appear to be talking about NPOs in general, while in reality they are talking about (unpaid) volunteer labor, especially work that is done outside of any organization.

FORMS OF COOPERATION BETWEEN GOVERNMENT AND NPOs

During the 1970s the Austrian provinces *(Bundesländer)* have started to reorganize the legal basis of the personal social services and social welfare programs. Following these legal rearrangements a variety of institutional experiments have been set up, involving cooperation between government and NPOs.[11]

Contracting Out of Social Services

In Vienna, social services such as Meals on Wheels, family help, visiting services, and so on, are regularly contracted out. With very few exceptions contracts are made with NPOs, most of which would fall under categories 1 and 2. The city of Vienna is divided into a number of areas, and a specific NPO takes over the responsibility in each.

The city pays the NPOs on a fee per client basis, with fees set by negotiations in which the city has monopsony power. The NPOs typically use labor that is paid, but on a part-time basis, which allows them to avoid regular employment contracts and keep their labor costs low.

From an economist's standpoint it can be asked why the city usually cooperates with NPOs and not with for-profit firms. The "institutional choice" process of the city illustrates that, besides efficiency considerations, political preferences play an important role. Political restrictions against employing for-profit firms are very strict. Since the city not only regulates fees but also sets and monitors quality standards for the suppliers, market failure arguments (such as asymmetrical information) do not seem to apply. Finally, the solution is determined more by the value judgment that social services *should* be provided by nonprofit forms of institutions.

Even the concrete arrangement made with NPOs can primarily be explained by political arguments. Rather than open competition among the NPOs, which might be economically efficient, we find a well-balanced market-sharing arrangement among organizations with different political-religious affiliations. As mentioned previously, NPOs of category 1 are often linked with the church, whereas NPOs of category 2 are sometimes affiliated with political parties. In practice, therefore, the market-sharing arrangement implies a division of spheres of political influence. This also implies that it is in the interest of those political and religious groups to have social services provided by NPOs and not by for-profit firms.

In contrast to this situation in Vienna, in the province of Vorarlberg many social services (such as counseling, preventive health services, rehabilitation services, etc.) are organized through two NPOs that are under the influence of the province administration and the local interest group of the physicians. The NPOs employ all necessary professionals and are financed on a fee per service basis by the government. This can be interpreted as an alternative form of public service provision in which the strict rules of a public bureaucracy need not be applied. The legal form of an NPO allows far more flexibility than the strict bureaucratic rules of a government organization and therefore serves as a tool to bypass or modernize the organizational structure of public administration.

Another model that has recently been launched in Vorarlberg is the provision of ambulatory psychiatric care through a for-profit enterprise. This firm has been founded as a partnership between physicians and management experts, and social workers are cooperating with the firm on a self-employed basis. The fees are again paid and regulated by government. The government hopes that this model will generate incentives to increase quality and reduce costs, since the disadvantages of asymmetric information can be offset through public regulation. However, this model is heavily criticized by the Social Democratic opposition party pointing out that, for moral reasons, psychiatric services should not be provided through profit-oriented firms.

Government Cooperation with Grass-Roots Self-Help Groups and Volunteers

Some Austrian provinces have also started to search for organizational models in which NPO activities of categories 3 and 4, grass-roots groups and informal volunteer work, can be integrated into a local network of social services for which governments hold the final responsibility.

A first model that has worked in several provinces for some years, for example in Niederösterreich, is the so-called *Sozialstation*.[12] Such an organization, usually organized as an NPO, is constructed as an umbrella to coordinate social and medical services provided by for-profit firms (e.g., self-employed physicians), local NPOs (e.g., church-run welfare groups), and individual volunteers. In most cases the emphasis is on home care for ill people and senior citizens, family help in case of emergencies, and on the development of a network of social contacts.

The NPO usually hires experts (nurses, social workers), sometimes on an hourly basis. It can also pay small amounts to persons who serve as "volunteers," thus generating an interesting hybrid between paid and unpaid work. The idea behind the *Sozialstation* is to delegate the responsibility for a network of social services to an NPO that is politically and economically responsible for an entire community. Although the NPOs that organize the *Sozialstation* are typically NPOs of category 2, one of their main tasks is to integrate individual volunteers and local NPOs (category 3) into the network of services being coordinated. In practice, however, they often concentrate on the (easier) organization of paid services.

Another form of cooperation between the local Social Service Administration and individual volunteers is practiced in the province of Burgenland. There, social workers search for volunteers who are willing to take over the responsibility for a neighbor who needs help on a regular basis, usually because of sickness. The volunteer enters into a "contract" with the provincial government, agreeing to take over these duties and, in return, getting small monetary compensation, an amount small enough that no federal income taxes have to be paid. The "volunteer" is paid by the government and supervised by the social worker.

The logic of this neighborhood care system is to provide care and nursing services at a higher quality and lower cost than would obtain in institutionalized forms of care. For every client who can stay home because of this service and need not be transferred to a nursing home, the provincial government is saving a considerable amount of money. At the same time most clients prefer being taken care of in their own neighborhoods.

While the Burgenland model focuses on cooperation between social workers and individual volunteers, a new organizational form is currently being tested in several communities of the province of Vorarlberg. In the model Gesunder Lebensraum Vorarlberg a network of activities in the field of social services and preventive medicine is organized by an umbrella volunteer group *(Aktivgruppe)*, according to needs which are revealed by the residents of the community, usually in public meetings. The programs are run mainly by individual volunteers, but sometimes also by NPOs of type 2 and 3 and occasionally by self-employed therapists on a paid basis.

A particular feature of this venture is the organizational help the *Aktivgruppe* gets from a for-profit firm that specializes in counseling and community development. The government is willing to pay for these services because it feels that volunteer activities can only be reliable with professional help. Such help is not provided by government employees in order to prevent the impression that local volunteer groups are being used as "vehicles" for government policy. The result is an interesting institutional hybrid combining government institutions, NPOs of all kinds, and for-profit firms.

CONCLUSION

These examples illustrate the broad variety of institutional patterns in which NPOs are integrated into the provision of social services by local and provincial governments. We have shown that the following factors may be involved in the choice of institutional form:

1. Arguments, about the economic advantages of NPOs that are seen as conceivable but unproved in the scientific discussion, are simply taken for granted in the political debate. This is particularly true of the cost-saving issue, on which there is no sound empirical test so far.
2. The Catholic Church is the main nonprofit provider of services in areas such as child care and homes for the elderly. This suggests that nonprofit institutions are most likely to develop in areas where religious organizations have an interest and religious ideology or identification may be one component of their outputs.
3. Many advantages that are usually ascribed to NPOs can be traced back to characteristics that are neither necessary nor exclusive to the volunteer sector.[13] For example, improvements in the provision of social services that are due to decentralization, better methods for gaining information on the needs of clients, more flexible organizational structures, and so on, might also be achieved by altering the institutional structure within the government sector.
4. Because of their "trustworthiness," NPOs have better access to volunteer labor than other institutions. This is one reason why NPOs may use specific technologies and may produce higher quality in their production process. There are, however, also disadvantages to these technologies. Volunteer labor may have less training and reliability. Therefore, experiments with cooperation between government institutions and NPOs often make use of "semi-volunteers" or combinations of volunteers and professionals, trying to combine the advantages of paid and unpaid work while avoiding the disadvantages.
5. The actual institutional mix in social service industries is heavily influenced by political preferences and not simply by economic considerations. For example, on moral grounds, for-profit enterprises are often excluded from supplying social services or from receiving government fees for their services. Since the demand for many social services is financed directly or indirectly by governments, the work of for-profit firms can readily be impeded in this manner. Political preferences also explain the varying arrangements in the provision of social services among different provinces within Austria.

NOTES

1. Organization for Economic Cooperation and Development (OECD), *The Welfare State in Crisis* (Paris: OECD, 1981); *Social Expenditure 1960–1990, Problems of Growth and Control* (Paris: OECD, 1985).

2. See, e.g., E. Matzner, *Der Wohlfahrtsstaat von morgen* (Vienna: Österreichischer, 1982), pp. 164–86; B. Weissel, "Das System der Sozialen Sicherheit," in *Perspektiven 90, Sozialdemokratische Wirtschaftspolitik*, ed. E. Nowotny and H. Tieber (Zürich: Europaverlag, 1985), p. 320; J. Hawlik and W. Schüssel, *Staat lass nach, Vorschläge zur Begrenzung und Privatisierung offentlicher Aufgaben* (Munich: Herold, 1985).

3. C. Badelt, *Politische Okonomie der Freiwilligenarbeit, Theoretische Grundlegung und Anwendungen in der Sozialpolitik* (Frankfurt: Campus, 1985); Matzner, ibid.; K. Gretschmann, *Steuerungsprobleme der Staatswirtschaft* (Berlin: Duncker & Humblot, 1981).

4. NPOs may also be preferred in cases where consumer immobility causes local monopoly or oligopoly situations. In some instances, disguised profit distribution (e.g., through above-

market wages or contracts) may imply that apparent nonprofits are, in reality, operated for profit.

5. Badelt, *Politische Ökonomie,* pp. 158–88.

6. See, for example, P. Menchik and B. A. Weisbrod, "Volunteer Labor Supply in the Provision of Collective Goods," in *Nonprofit Firms in a Three-Sector Economy,* ed. M. J. White (Washington, D.C.: Urban Institute, 1981), p. 166; Gallup Organization, *Americans Volunteer 1981* (Princeton, N.J.: Gallup, 1981).

7. O. Hawrylyshyn, "Towards a Definition of Non-Market Activities," in *Review of Income and Wealth,* Series 23 (1977): 79–96.

8. Badelt, *Politische Ökonomie,* p. 9.

9. The calculation in this version is based only on the time inputs of respondents doing volunteer labor on a regular basis (not just occasionally).

10. At a 95 percent level of significance the respective confidence intervals would be between 5.5 percent and 9.3 percent, and 6.3 percent and 10.7 percent, respectively. The level of significance is much higher in the field of social services. Details can be found in Badelt, *Politische Ökonomie,* pp. 178–79.

11. J. Dezsy, *Gesundheitsreport II, Alter-Krankheit-Pflegefall* (Bern: Wilhelm Maudrich, 1987), pp. 92–97.

12. See, e.g., H. Lutz, *Hauskrankenpflege in Österreich* (Vienna: Kommunalpolitische Vereinigung der ÖVP, 1986).

13. C. Badelt, "New Concepts for the Supply of Government Services," in *Public Finance and the Quest for Efficiency,* ed. H. Hanusch (Detroit: Wayne State University Press, 1984), p. 276.

REFERENCES

Badelt, C. "New Concepts for the Supply of Government Service." In H. Hanusch, ed., *Public Finance and the Quest for Efficiency.* Detroit, Mich.: Wayne State University Press, 1984, pp. 267–78.
———. *Politische Ökonomie der Freiwilligenarbeit, Theoretische Grundlegung und Anwendungen in der Sozialpolitik.* Frankfurt: Campus, 1985.
Dezsy, J. *Gesundheitsreport II, Alter-Krankheit Pflegefall.* Vienna: Wilhelm Maudrich, 1987.
Gallup Organization. *Americans Volunteer 1981.* Princeton, N.J.: Gallup, 1981.
Gretschmann, K. *Steuerungsprobleme der Staatswirtschaft.* Berlin: Duncker & Humblot, 1981.
Hansmann, H. "The Role of Nonprofit Enterprise." *Yale Law Journal* 89 (1980): 835–901.
Hawlik, J., and W. Schüssel. *Staat lass nach, Vorschläge zur Begrenzung und Privatisierung öffentlicher Aufgaben.* Vienna: Herold, 1985.
Hawrylyshyn, O. "Towards a Definition of Non-Market Activities." *Review of Income and Wealth,* Series 23 (1977): 79–96.
Lutz, H. *Hauskrankenpflege in Österreich.* Vienna: Kommunalpolitische Vereinigung der ÖVP, 1986.
Menchik, P., and B. A. Weisbrod. "Volunteer Labor Supply in the Provision of Collective Goods." In M. J. White, ed., *Nonprofit Firms in a Three-Sector Economy.* Washington, D.C.: Urban Institute, 1981.
Matzner, E. *Der Wohlfahrtsstaat von morgen.* Vienna: Österreichischer Bundesverlag, 1982.
Organization for Economic Cooperation and Development (OECD), *The Welfare State in Crisis.* Paris: OECD, 1981.
———. *Social Expenditure 1960–1990, Problems of Growth and Control.* Paris: OECD, 1985.
Rose-Ackerman, S., ed., *The Economics of Nonprofit Institutions: Studies in Structure and Policy.* New York: Oxford University Press, 1981.

Weisbrod, B. A. *The Voluntary Nonprofit Sector: An Economic Analysis.* Lexington, Mass.: D. C. Heath, 1977.

Weissel, B. "Das System der Sozialen Sicherheit." In E. Nowotny and H.Tieber, eds., *Perspektiven 90, Sozialdemokratische Wirtschaftspolitik.* Vienna: Europaverlag, 1985, pp. 311–27.

7

The Function of Mellow Weakness: Nonprofit Organizations as Problem Nonsolvers in Germany

WOLFGANG SEIBEL

In recent years, several important West German nonprofit organizations have been involved in scandals and criminal cases. The case of the union-owned housing corporation, Neue Heimat, and the tax evasion of charitable associations sponsoring political parties are the best known examples of organizations cited for offenses against the legal prescriptions for private charities, sometimes with the full consciousness of their managers.

Although these specific occurrences have limited significance, it is not accidental that weakness of guidance and control is a frequent phenomenon in the "third sector." One may argue that nonprofit organizations beyond a certain size have a special inclination toward a loss of responsibility, accountability, or organizational liability.[1] NPOs are not as intensively guided by legal authority and organizational hierarchy as public bureaucracies are nor by economic competition as is the case with private enterprises. In addition, they are often short of professional staff.

On the other hand, it may be argued that these classical mechanisms of guidance and control are substituted for in the nonprofit sector by other types of social coordination: altruism, solidarity, professionalism, polyarchical structures, and so on.[2] In fact, recent studies show that ideology and relatively complex networks of interpersonal and interorganizational networks are influential in shaping the organizational behavior of NPOs.[3]

However, even if it is true that the behavior of NPOs relies on alternatives to markets and hierarchies, they cannot escape totally from the market nor from public responsibility. This poses a dilemma: they must maintain their own basic ethos—solidarity, religion, nonprofessional altruism, face-to-face contacts, networks of middle class elites or semipublic decision makers—and they must survive in an environment of markets and government authorities requiring professionalism and impersonal, formal structures of organizational liability. The necessity to deal with this dilemma has often been described as a crucial challenge to NPOs and similar types of "third sector" organizations.[4] Put another way, they must "walk a tightrope"[5] between organizational identity and organizational efficiency, and their ability to walk this tightrope also determines their ability to solve problems where profit-making enterprises and government bureaucracies have failed.

This view of NPOs, however, contains certain inherent contradictions. If NPOs have deep-seated weaknesses regarding efficiency and control, how can they also have a comparative advantage in providing collective goods or private goods characterized by informational asymmetry.[6] In an effort to improve their efficiency, why do they not become formal organizations similar to business firms and public bureaucracies? In other words, how do we explain the durable persistence of nonprofessionalism, altruism, nonselfish solidarity, and so on? This chapter argues that the durability of these characteristics becomes easier to explain if we characterize "third sector" organizations as providers of very special goods—symbols and illusions of problem solving that stabilize a given political system while actually problem nonsolving—and organizational weakness is not an obstacle but a prerequisite to their ability to provide these special services. To develop this argument, I start with three case studies on organizational failure in the nonprofit sector:

1. The "Autonomous Women's Houses" (*Autonome Frauenhauser*, AFHs), houses for battered women and their children, have been created in West Germany as a consequence of the women's movement and sustained by a spirit of independence and autonomy, but in fact they are totally dependent on public subsidies, which poses an ideological conflict between the organization's commitment to autonomy and its need to account for public grants.
2. The semipublic system of hospital funding in West Germany has been "improved" four times since 1972, the last time with the explicit objective of reducing costs by negotiations between the quasi-public hospital owners and the health insurance system—an attempt that failed because of the diffused authority inherent in such mixed third sector arrangements.
3. The "Workshops for Handicapped Persons" (*Werkstatten fur Behinderte*, WfBs) are obliged to pursue both the reintegration of handicapped persons into the labor market and their own economic success, allowing a certain independence from public subsidies—an attempt that requires a nonexistent entrepreneurship and a reduced influence of public grant givers on the workshop's managing board.

In each case I will explain how failure is caused by typical behavioral characteristics of nonprofit organizations—"solidarity," "charity," "pluralism," and so on—and how, at the same time, these characteristics provide the "organizational slack" that enables the nonprofit sector to serve as a shunting-yard for social and political problems that, basically, cannot be solved.

AUTONOMOUS WOMEN'S HOUSES: THE SELF-FULFILLING
PROPHECY OF BUREAUCRATIC AUTHORITARIANISM

Since the mid-1970s more and more houses for battered women have been founded in West Germany and particularly in West Berlin. The philosophy of political feminism strongly influenced both the founding and the organizational behavior of those institutions. As is indicated by the title *Autonomous Houses,* the philosophy underlying these houses, emphasizes autonomy, which means, after all, independence from government authorities. Further, the Autonomous Women's Houses emphasize several principles of self-guidance such as job rotation and the rejection of formal hierarchy and professionalism. Finally, they want to be "political" institutions, not only providing help for the women and their children but also struggling against patriarchal structures in society that are associated with the oppression of women.

The conflict between the guiding idea of an autonomous, nonhierarchical organization and the necessities of organizational goal attainment is clearly observed in this case. Goal attainment requires traditional forms of organizational fitness and efficiency as well as financial support from public authorities. The Autonomous Women's Houses must struggle for survival and support, but their own ideology weakens their position and provokes just those phenomena of governmental overcontrol that should have been avoided by organizational "autonomy." However, the Autonomous Women's Houses did not fall from the tightrope, they did not even try to walk it.

The conflict between the basic ideology and the necessity of a certain organizational tightness has its external and internal sides. The external aspect is shaped by the endeavor to get sustained funding. Although most of the Autonomous Women's Houses have been founded by voluntary associations, almost all of them are dependent on public subsidies. But public subsidies come in an enormous variety, regarding the sources as well as the amounts. The subsidies come from government authorities at the federal, the state, and municipal levels. The more conservative state governments and municipalities in the south of West Germany tend to restrict the subsidies or to prefer the Women's Houses run by traditional Welfare Associations. There has been a long conflict between the representatives of the Autonomous Women's Houses and the federal and state governments on the amount and structure of funding. At the core this is also a conflict between traditional and "alternative" forms of social welfare.

The federal government (as well as the established welfare associations) prefer to fund the Women's Houses under the Federal Social Help Act (Bundessozialhilfegesetz, BSHG), which allows financial support to all "establishments" of social welfare. However, this funding model is rejected by the Autonomous Women's Houses, which argue that it would individualize the social problem of women's oppression and that the declaration of Autonomous Women's Houses as "establishments" of social welfare would undermine their status of autonomy. Similar conflicts shape the funding of the Autonomous Women's Houses at the state and municipal level. Meanwhile, most of the eleven states have issued special enactments regulating the funding of Women's Houses and most of the municipalities where Women's Houses are located subsidize these institutions. The conflict there stems from the unwillingness of the Autonomous Women's Houses to accept the formal prescriptions of accountancy linked with the provision of these public subsidies. Although these prescriptions are more or less rigid in the different states and municipalities, the Autonomous Women's Houses try to escape from any formal control at all. They desire the squaring of the circle: a public funded independence.

This attitude is due to the philosophy of autonomy as well as to the rejection of formal hierarchy and professionalism (for instance, the subsidies depend on the responsibility of personal representatives "leading" the institution and, in case of contribution to wages, require formal credentials for the staff). However, this attitude provokes a permanent conflict with the grant giving authorities. Accordingly, payments are seriously delayed and important energy is absorbed in endless quarrels. These conflicts are very intensive also in those states or municipalities where public authorities are relatively openminded and willing to improve the situation of the Autonomous Women's Houses. The closed ideology of the Autonomous Women's Houses leads to a self-fulfilling prophecy: every requirement or reaction of the public authorities is perceived a priori as "bureaucratic" (oppressive) behavior that has to be rejected. If, consequently, the authorities refuse to do this or that or even stop the payments, this only proves the initial suspicion. And, of course, this causes a vicious circle: since the Autonomous Women's Houses turn out to be "dubious" and "untrustworthy," the public authorities feel obliged to exert even more rigid control.

Regarding the internal side of the conflict, the tension between the rejection of professionalism and formal hierarchy and the need for continuity and organizational accountability is the crucial problem. Job rotation and fluctuating employment of staff members have a frustrating impact on the spirit of work. The more frustration, the more fluctuation among the staff—another vicious circle.

These problems sometimes provoke conflicts between the staff and the board of an Autonomous Women's House. Whereas the staff tends to a rigorous rejection of formal professionalism and hierarchy, the board often emphasizes a certain organizational soundness and solidity as a prerequisite for successful work and successful dealing with public authorities. Needless to say, such behavior of the board is criticized by staff members as "bureaucratic" or even "authoritarian."

These tensions stem in part from the different social backgrounds and, consequently, from the different value orientations and prevailing behavioral attitudes of board members and staff members. The staff members are the true bearers of the ideology of autonomy and self-guidance. Most of them are well-qualified young social workers who have only limited chances to get durable employment in the current labor market. The Autonomous Women's House provides them both a job (even if not well paid) and an ideological backing that is vaguely oriented against a society apparently refusing social security. In contrast, the board members usually belong to the "new middle class," composed of young teachers, lawyers, physicians, or the spouses of well-established people. Their value orientation is shaped by charity and solidarity, but their behavioral attitude relies more or less on traditional norms of problem solving by organizational efficiency and professionalism.

Thus, conflicts within the Autonomous Women's Houses are the more probable the more distinctive is the social gap between the staff and the board members. It is obvious that these internal conflicts weaken once more the position of the Autonomous Women's Houses. The attempts of the board to strengthen or defend the position of the house by greater efficiency and accountability often provoke quarrels with the staff. This is another type of ideological self-paralysis.

WEST GERMAN HOSPITAL FUNDING: POLYARCHICAL POLICY MAKING AND MESO-CORPORATISM

In most Western industrialized countries hospitals represent a major part of the "third sector," with a mixture of public and private elements. What is peculiar to the West German situation is the tripolar system of funding with hospitals, insurance companies, and state agencies as permanent negotiators. Thus, this case does not deal with a single nonprofit organization but with a semipublic system of polyarchical cooperation (i.e., cooperation among a set of nonhierarchical organizations), which is, in different variants, a frequent phenomenon in the nonprofit sector.[7]

In 1972, the Hospital Funding Act was celebrated in Germany as a "centennial act" that gave a general guarantee for public hospital funding. Hospital funding was solemnly recognized as a public duty. The aim was a high standard of health care and the modernization of the hospital industry. Thereafter, all *Lander* (states) had to set up general plans for regional hospital facilities. Hospital funding itself is doubletracked: the government pays for the buildings and the equipment, while the health insurance companies pay the wages of staff and the costs of medicine by lump sum according to the duration of the patient's hospital treatment. Initially, the government subsidies were shared between the *Lander* and the *Bund* (federal government)—a type of mixed-funding *(Mischfinanzierung)* that is intensively disputed in West Germany. The core of that funding system was full cost reimbursement; that is, the guarantee that all hospital costs would be covered.

Obviously, this funding system had no internal brakes to stop the cost explosion. On the contrary, it provided incentives for new expenses. Since reimbursement for costs of staff and medicine depended on the number of patient days, long-term treatment was profitable for the hospitals. Since all expenses were paid, there was no incentive for hospital management to economize. So long as beds were filled, the hospital had no incentive to diversify its services to meet new needs. Finally, the physician had no incentive to take costs into account in decisions on medical treatment.

Not surprisingly, expenses in the whole health sector dramatically increased during the 1970s. This led to serious problems for the insurance companies. Consequently, the public debate was dominated by the insurance companies' point of view. Their interest was to reduce expenses by nearly all means—despite the lack of incentives for hospitals and doctors to do so. Further, responsibility for the hospital industry had shifted from the Ministry for Health Care to the Ministry of Labor and Social Welfare, which also was mainly interested in alleviating the insurance burden. As a result of this debate, in the early 1980s the federal government proposed a change in the system: to shift the responsibility for general planning from the state to a self-governing board of hospitals and insurance companies, to subsidize only that standard of hospital equipment stipulated both by hospitals and insurance companies, to differentiate the system of lump sum payments according to the peculiarities of the medical treatment, and to abandon the principle of covering costs in favor of prospective budgeting as a binding guideline for the hospital's planning as well as to introduce (slight) entrepreneurial incentives into hospital management.

At that point, the *Lander* saw a chance to suspend the mixed funding of hospital costs. The claim for abolition of mixed funding, then, became a necessary element in the compromise for all eleven *Lander*. In fact, this was the first element of the federal government proposal that was enacted. On the other hand, the *Lander* were not willing to give up their influence on hospital planning within the general provision of public health care. Consequently, the initial concept of hospital–insurance company self-government was reduced to a model of negotiations on the size of lump sum payments. At the core of this model a commission of arbitration was installed, with the power to decide if the hospitals and the insurance companies did not agree. It was and is composed of representatives of the hospitals, the insurance companies, the states (the *Lander*), and an "independent chairman." If the commission cannot find a compromise, the central government must decide. In any event, agreements between hospitals and insurance companies as well as decisions of the arbitration system had to be approved by government.

In addition to this reform, the system of lump sum payments was differentiated and the hospitals now are obliged to draft a binding budget. The right to retain profits from cost savings was established but limited to a period of one fiscal year. Neither the initial draft of the federal government nor the final compromise between the federal government and the *Lander* contained a cost reducing incentive for physicians. Nevertheless, this compromise was praised as a device to reduce cost augmentation by deregulation and the strengthening of self-government by the hospitals and insurance companies.

However, just the opposite came to pass and costs continued to increase. The root of this failure is the continuation of the irrationalities and ambiguities inherent in the Hospital Funding Act of 1972, which embodies shared responsibilities between central and regional governments and the absence of incentives for hospitals all linked together in a noncompetitive system of hospital health care. From the beginning, the government authorities—both at the state and the federal levels—lacked sufficient devices to assure a hospital system that took into account both needs and financial capabilities of public authorities and health insurance companies. Since there is no real competition between the hospitals, no freedom of contract between the hospitals and insurance companies, nor a system of internal incentives for cost reduction within the hospitals, the only cost limiting mechanism remains the bargaining between the hospitals and the insurance organizations.

But this, too, is ineffective, partially because the hospitals have no rational way to ensure cost reduction. In particular, there is no link between the hospital's profit or loss and the personal income of the leading physicians, who make many of the expenditure decisions. On the contrary, the more medical treatment given by the hospital, the more profitable it is for the physician. Furthermore, any general incentive to cut down services and personnel without differentiation will impede the adjustment of the hospitals to new health care needs, including gerontology, drug problems, and so on. Apparently neither the more differentiated lump sums nor the possibility of retaining a potential surplus for one year can compensate for these disadvantages.

The system of bargaining between hospitals and insurance companies offers few strong incentives to come to an agreement, so a large number of cases come to the commission of arbitration. However, the interests represented in the commission are nearly the same as those in the negotiation. Consequently, many of the arbitration procedures end with a stipulation by the government. But now, due to differentiation within the lump sum system, the state has much greater authority to impose on the hospitals special modes of equipment and reimbursement than in former times. This increases government involvement and sometimes also raises costs. What turned out, thus, was just the opposite of what had been intended by the reform. And it is difficult, given this complex multiorganizational structure, to place the responsibility for the continuing problem.

WORKSHOPS FOR HANDICAPPED PERSONS: RENT-SEEKING AND QUASI-NEPOTISM

The so-called Workshops for Handicapped Persons were established by the act in favor of Gravely Handicapped Persons *(Schwerbehindertengesetz)* in 1974. The purpose of these workshops was to combine personal care for handicapped people with the improvement or reinstatement of their labor skills in order to integrate them into the labor market. The target groups are physically and mentally handicapped persons. The workshops are non-profit organizations, charitable associations, or charitable corporations. The idea was that the workshops would be partially sustained by public subsidies but mainly funded by their own entrepreneurial activity. This double-tracked funding system, thus, combines two different types of external incentives for organizational behavior. The public subsidies themselves come from different authorities according to the different purposes of the workshop. Whereas grants for the sustainment of the workshop itself come from the municipal social welfare authorities, grants for their educational training activities come from the federal labor administration.

Self-funding by the sale of products never became an important part of the general sustainment of the workshops. "Entrepreneurial activity," including competitive behavior, marketing, and sales strategies never has been developed. In fact, all the workshops are completely dependent on public subsidies. Thus, the simulation of market forces in order to familiarize handicapped persons with the requirements of the labor market does not work. And, labor within the workshops is extremely poorly paid (120–300 marks, or $70–170, per month).

One may argue that this failure is due to the depressed economic situation since the mid-1970s, which could not have been taken into account when the legal frame for the workshops was established in 1974. When the general rate of bankruptcies for small and medium-sized enterprises is already high, there is hardly any chance to integrate handicapped people into the labor market. This question will be picked up in a later section of this paper. However, there are peculiarities of a nonprofit organization that characterize the way the workshops tried to cope with unfavorable economic circumstances. This is true for the recruitment and managerial capability of the staff as well as for the composition and influence of the workshops' boards.

As to the staff, the Act for Gravely Handicapped Persons prescribes a double-qualification of the workshop's manager: he or she must have an economic as well as psychological or pedagogical education. However, the psychological or pedagogical qualification might be sufficient if the economic capability of the workshop's management has been earned on the job, elsewhere. In fact, only half of the workshops' managers in the *Land* Hessen had the double qualification in 1984.[8]

The main feature of the workshops' boards is their involvement in the network of public and semipublic social welfare agencies. Notables of charitable organizations (including churches) and representatives of grant giving authorities usually form the board. This composition might be legitimized by the quest for control by the subsidy giving authorities; however, these representatives apparently do not exert control. The behavior of the boards is characterized by a general social welfare philosophy and, especially, by an identification with the workshop as a social welfare institution. The objective of the board members, thus, is to get sufficient subsidies from the authorities they represent. In addition, the general climate is shaped by a close network of personal relationships and even nepotism and disguised profit taking. In a particular case I examined, the workshop's manager was closely acquainted with a member of the *Land*'s government, the head of the division for pedagogic care was the son-in-law of the Prime Minister, and the head of the division for general administration was the spouse of the director of the county's social welfare authority (responsible, itself, for public grants and their control).

In general, internal management as well as external control of the workshop is weak. The lack of economic skills of the managers and the overrepresentation of public grant givers on the workshop's board together with the network of personal relationships and quasi-nepotism make illusive any hopes of entrepreneurial behavior. The workshop's behavior is entirely shaped by expectation of funding from the public grant givers. Instead of an entrepreneurial spirit, a mentality of "rent seeking" is noticed.

ORGANIZATIONAL AMBIVALENCE AND ORGANIZATIONAL FAILURE

These three case studies illustrate organizational failure in different areas of the public economy. In doing so, several peculiarities of organizational behavior have been revealed that seem to be typical of the "third sector"; that is, of organizations, such as NPOs, that lie between the market and the government. What again are these peculiarities? Why should they be typical of the nonprofit sector?

First of all, deviances from the modern type of private or public organization, based on formal authority and professionalized staff, are crucial factors for the failure of guidance and control in each of the cases we have examined. One may argue that such deviances belong to the everyday life of any public bureaucracy or private firm as well. However, they occur there as an empirical fact without any official legitimacy. Executives both of private firms and of public bureaucracies must be well aware of these deviances but must not encourage them.[9] On the contrary, deviances—or, more enthusiastically, "alternatives"—to hierarchical and professionalized organizations are often the core of identity and self-consciousness of nonprofit organizations or other institutional arrangements in the third sector. Values like "solidarity," "charity," "unselfish altruism," the individualistic ethics of professional groups (physicians, priests, nurses, academics) as well as political concepts like "autonomy," "pluralism," or even "federalism" have a strong influence on the legitimacy of everyday decision making in the nonprofit sector.

In the case of the Autonomous Women's Houses the hermetic ideology of "autonomy" and the rejection of any "bureaucratic" form of cooperation with the subsidy-providing authorities led to a vicious circle of organizational weakness and public overcontrol. In the system of West German hospital funding, the paralytic polyarchy between the authorities and hospitals or insurance companies, as well as the general indulgence to a cost-increasing rationale of leading physicians, eliminated both public planning and private competition. In the case of the Workshops for Handicapped Persons close personal relationships among a handful of notables and civil servants within the workshop's board led to oligarchical decision making and even to quasi-nepotism, which favors rent seeking instead of entrepreneurship and undercuts supervision by the subsidy-giving authorities.

None of these phenomena is very flattering for the affected NPOs or could serve as an example of the superiority of "alternative" mechanisms of guidance and control. However, they are caused by those deviances from the "normal" hierarchical and professionalized forms of organization, deviances that elsewhere are praised as important advantages of nonprofits in comparison with for-profit organizations or public administration.

The "solidarity" among women, amplified by feministic aspirations and political aims to surmount patriarchical structures regresses to the "closed minds"[10] of staff members in the Autonomous Women's Houses, unable to understand the necessity of organizational accountability in order to promote their own purposes and justify the spending of public money. The ideals of decentralized policy making, true federalism, institutional pluralism, and self-government as well as the physician's professional ethic cause the pathology of West German hospital funding. The idea of "altruism" instead of public authority and competitiveness legitimizes the renunciation of entrepreneurship and effective external control and forges the small community of closely interconnected givers and rent seekers in the Workshops for Handicapped Persons.

At first glance, this is merely another perspective on the "ambivalence" that Robert K. Merton has described for organizational leaders and, especially, for voluntary organizations.[11] However, if the reported case studies are reinterpreted by generalizing Merton's basic assumption for voluntary organizations—the dilemma of instrumental versus group maintaining functions—the organizational behavior of NPOs is seen to weaken the instrumental functions of goal attainment, efficiency, liability, accountability, and professionalism in favor of the basic spirit that shapes organizational identity and consciousness. If this is true, the attempt "to walk a tightrope" will lead to continuous misfortune.

It might be argued that in all these cases the failure of formal guidance and control can be explained by special circumstances. In what follows, I will not disprove that but I will argue that the political function of the nonprofit sector, its use as a resource for the stabilization of the political system, leads to valuing organizational weakness rather than tightness. In other words, "voluntary failure" is necessary for the political functionalism of "third party government," the alliance between NPOs and the state, just described.[12]

ORGANIZATIONAL SLACK AND THE FAILURE OF TIGHTROPE WALKING: NONSOLVING OF PROBLEMS AS THE POLITICAL FUNCTION OF NONPROFIT ORGANIZATIONS

If it is true that the case study failures of guidance and control are para-digmatic for organizational weakness in the nonprofit world, what conditions would strengthen nonprofit organizations? What would a wise and skillful tightrope-walking manager of an NPO (in the Merton sense) try to do? The NPO manager would try to tighten formal liability and profes-sionalism without undermining voluntarism or intrinsic motivation of the staff and other members of the organization. He or she would try to mo-bilize the ideological spirit or the structural flexibility of the organization without endangering its efficiency and accountability. In doing so, the manager would try to combine several entrepreneurial roles.[13] In short, the NPO manager would try to do what all clever organizational leaders are trying to do.

However, if NPO managers are doing what all managers do, an iso-morphic effect on organizational culture would be the long-range result. In fact, some scholars argue that this has happened.[14] But what then ex-plains the persistence and, perhaps, the growing importance of the non-profit sector with its reliance on ideologies, polyarchical networks, per-sonal trust, amateurism, individual altruism, solidarity, oligarchy, and nepotism, in contrast to more formal private and public organizations? Why should suppliers with notorious problems of coordination and trans-action costs survive in the long run?

All the common attempts to explain the existence of an organizational behavior within the nonprofit sector suppose that the task of NPOs is to solve problems and to provide goods with external benefits or informa-tional asymmetries. However, things may be more easily explained if we suppose that the function of NPOs is the nonsolving of problems. *The competitive advantage of NPOs, then, is not to do things better but to disguise better how poorly things are being done.* Most of the organiza-tional peculiarities of NPOs described in this article are appropriate to disguise as well as to mitigate the failure of problem solving—even those failures unveiled by curious academic scholars. They serve as a shunting yard for problems that none of the three sectors—private, public, non-profit—can solve but that are more easily cushioned by the mellow weak-ness of nonprofit organizations than by the relative tightness of profit-making organizations or public authorities. Governments can appear to be doing something about these problems and the failure of their success can then be blurred and if necessary, blamed on the peculiar functioning of nonprofit organizations.

By regarding the nonprofit sector in this way, the weakness of control, absence of general public attention, dubious accountability, renunciation of professionalized staff, paralytic polyarchy, oligarchy, nepotism, and ide-ological indolence appear on stage with a new decor. The weakness of formal structures is the strength of political functions. This kind of "loose coupling" here has transmuted to a macropolitical equivalent of the "organizational slack" that has been described by Cyert and March.[15] It impedes goal attainment of specific units but it improves the survival of the system as a whole. It is indeed "third party government"—but a government that is successful by its own failure. *The nonprofit sector, then, provides an institutional arrangement that enables complex societies to cope with social and political problems that cannot be solved.* Thus, it discharges government from responsibilities that could lead to unbearable risks for the general legitimacy of the political system.

The elegance of this type of problem nonsolving lies in a combination of structural and ideological mechanisms. The diversity and institutional pluralism of the nonprofit sector darkens the transparence of its failures for the general public and even for particularly interested people. The ideological halo of many NPOs, that sustains the spirit and identity of the organization and is necessary for the motivation of voluntary members, weakens formal liability and also mitigates disappointment when goals are not achieved.

If we now refer to the case studies, the hypothesis of problem nonsolving by NPOs becomes more evident. The semipublic–semiprivate institutions examined provide a modus vivendi for social and political problems that, for different reasons, cannot be solved. The patriarchical structure leading to general detriment for women and even to violence cannot be overcome within a "bearable" period of time. However, the Autonomous Women's Houses strive for that goal by separating themselves from the core institutions of public policy making and by developing an ideological shelter against all the inevitable disappointments in that struggle. The new "self-government" within West German hospital funding is a compromise that does not satisfy anyone but that absorbs the lion's share of political energy for slight changes within a basically irrational system of funding, since a general reform is judged to be unattainable. The reintegration of handicapped people in the labor market today is a useless attempt. However, the Workshops for Handicapped Persons live quite comfortably in these times, since the public subsidies produce the everyday illusion that "something is going on"—even if it is without any results.

The remaining risk of this type of problem nonsolving is the scandal. Once the unavoidable lack of efficiency, accountability, professionalism, and so on has exceeded a certain degree, it can only be treated as "unacceptable deviance"—regardless of the general political functionalism of such "deviant" organizational behavior. The instances cited in the first paragraph of this chapter are all cases where wasteful or self-serving behavior exceeded acceptable norms and therefore received public attention, but the argument of this paper is that they were only the tip of a much larger iceberg.

CONCLUSION AND FUTURE RESEARCH

This chapter has stressed that the nonprofit sector plays a special role as a third sector beside the market and the state. This is not a question of formal independence (which does not exist between the market and the state either) but of the importance, if not dominance, of particular mechanisms of social coordination: religion and other types of ideology, personal trust instead of formal control, solidarity, individual altruism, voluntarism and amateurism, polyarchical networks, nepotism, and so on. These are very influential factors in shaping the organizational behavior of nonprofit organizations and, in particular, their guidance and control. In this way, the thesis of this chapter does not harmonize with the theory of an institutional isomorphism in modern societies but does conform to the concept of a particular form of "third party government."

The weakness of organizational liability and accountability so often to be met in the nonprofit sector is due, to a large extent, to the "alternative" mechanisms of social coordination shaping the organizational behavior of NPOs. So, it makes sense to acknowledge a common phenomenon of "voluntary failure." However, talking about "failure" implies the necessity or, at least, the possibility of improvement. From this point of view, there must be a way to "walk the tighrope": to balance the contradictory requirements of organizational identity, on the one side, and efficiency, accountability, liability, and so on, on the other side.

Moreover, if the nonprofit sector is regarded as an institutional mechanism for providing certain goods in better quality than the two other ones (public and private for-profit) one must assume either an "institutional isomorphism" or that organizational failure does not greatly affect the quality of goods provided by NPOs. I have disputed the first of these predictions but the second allows for further consideration. If organizational failure does not necessarily affect the quality of goods provided by NPOs, the goods in question probably will not be articles or services but symbols and illusions.

Especially important is the role of political symbols and illusions. This is of crucial importance in cases where social and political problems cannot be solved and where it is impossible to treat them as individual problems. An unavoidable failure of problem solving is more easily cushioned in weak instead of tight organizational structures, and it is less risky for politicians if it does not appear in the core of public administration but in the semipublic periphery of the state. In this respect, the lack of liability and accountability of NPOs, the diversity of institutional structures, and the absence of general public attention favor a "symbolic use of politics" and the illusion that something is going on even if hardly anything happens.[16] This illusion may be sustained by influential self-encouraging ideologies strengthening the identity of NPOs as well as by cyclic political praises of the nonprofit sector's dignity.[17] Regarding the nonprofit sector in this way provides a comprehensive explanation for the necessity of a "third sector" as a sociopolitical buffer zone as well as for the persistence of its "alternative" mechanisms of social coordination and the unavoidable organizational weakness of NPOs.

If the function of a third (nonprofit) sector with durable peculiarities of organizational behavior is to stabilize the political system, this does not mean that nonprofit institutions are used by a ruling class in full consciousness. Even if there is an a posteriori political payoff for the ruling class elites, this is rather the result of self-protection of social action: the nonprofit sector provides an institutional arrangement that enables modern societies to cope with problems that, basically, cannot be solved.[18]

The following research questions are suggested by this analysis. To what extent do NPO staff members acknowledge the inherent organizational ambivalence of NPOs? What are the value orientations of NPO members and how do they compare with the political function of the nonprofit sector? Is there a different political functionalism for different types of NPOs? And, what is the relationship between the historical waves of increasing and decreasing importance of the nonprofit sector, changes in the magnitude of "unsolvable" problems, and the consequent need for sociopolitical stabilization in Western societies?

NOTES

1. Lester M. Salamon, "On Market Failure, Voluntary Failure and Third Party Government: Toward a Theory of Government—Nonprofit Relations in the Modern Welfare State," *Journal for Voluntary Action Research* (Spring 1987): 11–15; Cecil C. Selby, "Better Performance from 'Nonprofits.' The Unique Characteristics of Voluntary Organizations Should Be Source of Strength, not Weakness," *Harvard Business Review* 56 (1978): 92–98.

2. For a comparison of several types of guidance and control systems see Robert A. Dahl and Charles E. Lindblom, *Politics, Economics, and Welfare. Planning and Politico-economic Systems Resolved into Basic Social Processes* (New York: Harper and Row, 1953).; Franz-Xaver Kaufmann, Giandomenico Majone, and Vincent Ostrom, *Guidance, Control, and Evaluation in the Public Sector,* The Bielefeld Interdisciplinary Project. (Berlin: Walter de Gruyter, 1986).

3. Estelle James and Susan Rose-Ackerman, *The Nonprofit Enterprise in Market Economies* (London: Harwood Academic Publishers, 1986); Melissa Middleton, "Nonprofit's Board of Directors: Beyond the Governance Function," in *The Nonprofit Sector. A Research Handbook,* ed. William W. Powell (New Haven, Conn.: Yale University Press, 1987): 141–153.

4. For example, see Ralph M. Kramer, "The Future of the Voluntary Agency in a Mixed Economy," *Journal of Applied Behavioral Science* 21 (1985): 377–91; Robert K. Merton, "Dilemmas in Voluntary Associations," *Sociological Ambivalence and Other Essays* (New York: The Free Press, 1976), pp. 145–55; and Lester M. Salamon, "On Market Failure."

5. Merton, ibid., p. 105.

6. Burton A. Weisbrod, *The Voluntary Nonprofit Sector. An Economic Analysis* (Lexington, Mass.: Lexington Books, 1978); Henry B. Hansmann, "The Role of Nonprofit Enterprise," *Yale Law Journal* 89 (1980): 835–98.

7. Ralph M. Kramer and Bart Grossman, "Contracting for Social Services: Process Management and Resource Dependencies," *Social Service Review* (1987): 32–55.

8. Jurgen Hildebrandt, "Soziales Leistungsunternehmen Wekstatt fur Behinderte?" Mimeograph (Kassel, 1984).

9. John W. Meyer and Brian Rowan, "Institutionalized Organizations: Formal Structure and Myth and Ceremony," *American Journal of Sociology* 83 (1977): 340–63.

10. Milton Rokeach, ed., *The Open and Closed Mind. Investigations into the Nature of Belief Systems and Personality Systems,* (New York: Basic Books, 1960).

11. Merton, "Dilemmas in Voluntary Associations."

12. Also see Lester M. Salamon, "Rethinking Public Management: Third-Party Government and the Changing Forms of Public Action," *Public Policy* 29 (1981): 255–75; and "On Market Failure."

13. Dennis R. Young, *If not for Profit, for What? A Behavioral Theory of the Nonprofit Sector Based on Entrepreneurship* (Lexington, Mass.: Lexington Books, 1983), pp. 55–74.

14. Paul J. DiMaggio and Walter W. Powell, "The Iron Cage Revisited: Institutional Isomorphism and Collective Rationality in Organizational Fields," *American Sociological Review* 48 (1983): 147–60.

15. See Mark S. Granovetter, "The Strength of Weak Ties," *American Journal of Sociology* 78 (1983): 1360–80; Robert Glassman, "Persistence and Loose Coupling," *Behavioral Sciences* 18 (1973): 83–98; Richard M. Cyert and James G. March, *A Behavioral Theory of the Firm* (Englewood Cliffs, N.J.: Prentice-Hall, 1963); and Salamon, "Rethinking Public Management," for an elaboration of these concepts.

16. Murray Edelman, *The Symbolic Uses of Politics* (Urbana: University of Illinois Press, 1964).

17. Wolfgang Seibel, "Der Staatsstil fur Krisenzeiten: 'Selbststeuerung; offentlicher Aufgabentrager und das Problem der Kontrolle," *Politische Vierteljahresschrift* 28 (1987): 197–222.

18. Robert F. Arnove, *Philanthropy and Cultural Imperialism: The Foundations at Home and Abroad* (Boston: Hall and Co., 1980); Barry D. Karl and Stanley N. Katz, "Foundations and Ruling Class Elites," *Daedalus* 116 (1987): 1–40; Robert K. Merton, "The Unanticipated Consequences of Social Action," *Sociological Ambivalence and Other Essays,* pp. 145–55.

REFERENCES

Arnove, Robert F. *Philanthropy and Cultural Imperialism: The Foundations at Home and Abroad.* Boston: Hall and Co., 1980.

Cyert, Richard M., and James G. March. *A Behavioral Theory of the Firm.* Englewood Cliffs, N.J.: Prentice-Hall, 1963.

Dahl, Robert A., and Charles E. Lindblom. *Politics, Economics, and Welfare. Planning and Politico-Economic Systems Resolved into Basic Social Processes.* New York: Harper and Row, 1953.

DiMaggio, Paul J., and Walter W. Powell. "The Iron Cage Revisited: Institutional Isomorphism and Collective Rationality in Organizational Fields." *American Sociological Review* 48 (1983): 147–60.

Edelman, Murray. *The Symbolic Uses of Politics.* Urbana: University of Illinois Press, 1964.

Glassman, Robert. "Persistence and Loose Coupling." *Behavioral Science* 18 (1973): 83–98.

Granovetter, Mark S. "The Strength of Weak Ties." *American Journal of Sociology* 78 (1973): 1360–80.

Hansmann, Henry B. "The Role of Nonprofit Enterprise." *Yale Law Journal* 89 (1980): 835–98.

Hildebrandt, Jurgen. "Soziales Lesitungsunternehmen Wekstatt fur Behinderte?" Mimeograph, Kassel: 1984.

James, Estelle. "How Nonprofits Grow: A Model." *Journal of Policy Analysis and Management* 2 (1983): 350–60; reprinted in Susan Rose-Ackerman, *The Economics of Nonprofit Institutions. Studies in Structure and Policy.* New York: Oxford University Press, 1986.

James, Estelle, and Susan Rose-Ackerman. *The Nonprofit Enterprise in Market Economies.* London: Harwood Academic Publishers, 1986.

Karl, Barry D., and Stanley N. Katz. "Foundations and Ruling Class Elites," *Daedalus,* 116 (1987): 1–40.

Kaufmann, Franz-Xaver, Giandomenico Majone, and Vincent Ostrom, eds. *Guidance, Control, and Evaluation in the Public Sector.* The Bielefeld Interdisciplinary Project. Berlin: Walter de Gruyter, 1986.

Kramer, Ralph M. "The Future of the Voluntary Agency in a Mixed Economy," *Journal of Applied Behavioral Science* 21 (1985): 377–91.

———. *Voluntary Agencies in the Welfare State.* Berkeley: University of California Press, 1981.

Kramer, Ralph M., and Bart Grossman. "Contracting for Social Services: Process Management and Resource Dependencies." *Social Service Review* (1987): 32–55.

Krashinsky, Michael. *Transaction Costs and a Theory of the Non-Profit Organization.* Program on Non-Profit Organizations, Institution for Social and Policy Studies, Working Paper No. 84. New Haven, Conn.: Yale University, 1984.

Merton, Robert K. "Dilemmas in Voluntary Associations." In *Sociological Ambivalence and Other Essays.* New York: The Free Press, 1976, pp. 90–105.

———. "The Unanticipated Consequences of Social Action." In *Sociological Ambivalence and Other Essays.* New York: The Free Press, 1976, pp. 145–55.

Meyer, John W., and Brian Rowan. "Institutionalized Organizations: Formal Structure and Myth and Ceremony." *American Journal of Sociology* 83 (1977): 340–63.

Middleton, Melissa. "Nonprofit's Board of Directors: Beyond the Governance Function." In William W. Powell, ed., *The Nonprofit Sector. A Research Handbook.* New Haven, Conn.: Yale University Press, 1987.

Rokeach, Milton, ed. *The Open and Closed Mind. Investigations into the Nature of Belief Systems and Personality Systems.* New York: Basic Books, 1960.

Rose-Ackerman, Susan, ed.. *The Economics of Nonprofit Institutions. Studies in Structure and Policy.* New York: Oxford University Press, 1986.

Salamon, Lester M. "On Market Failure, Voluntary Failure and Third Party Government: Toward a Theory of Government–Nonprofit Relations in the Modern Welfare State." *Journal of Voluntary Action Research* (Spring 1987): 11–15.

———. "Rethinking Public Management: Third-Party Government and the Changing Forms of Public Action." *Public Policy* 29 (1981): 255–75.

Seibel, Wolfgang. "Der Staatsstil fur Krisenzeiten: 'Selbststeuerung' offentlicher Aufgabentrager und das Problem der Kontrolle." *Politische Vierteljahresschrift* 28 (1987): 197–222.

Selby, Cecil B. "Better Performance From 'Nonprofits.' The Unique Characteristics of Voluntary Organizations Should Be Source of Strength, not Weakness." *Harvard Business Review* 56 (1978): 92–98.

Weisbrod, Burton A. *The Voluntary Nonprofit Sector. An Economic Analysis.* Lexington, Mass.: Lexington Books, 1978.

Young, Dennis R. *If not for Profit, for What? A Behavioral Theory of the Nonprofit Sector Based on Entrepreneurship.* Lexington, Mass.: Lexington Books, 1983.

8

Intersectoral Differences in Cost Effectiveness: Residential Child Care in England and Wales

MARTIN KNAPP

One important feature of the search for efficiency or "value for money" in public policy has been a consideration of the contributions to be made by the for-profit (private in the British terminology) and nonprofit (voluntary) sectors. Despite the emphasis on "privatization" in Britain and most Western economies, there is actually very little evidence on the relative efficiency of the sectors. Privatization, of course, takes many different forms, most usefully analyzed in terms of the move away from solely public responsibility for funding, production, or regulation. In this chapter, "privatization of production" is the primary focus, although clearly it is not sensible to completely ignore either the source of funding or the question of regulation since both have efficiency implications. How do the three sectors compare in terms of production technologies and what are their relative efficiencies? In particular, what are the efficiency implications of the policy of increased contracting out or purchase of services contracting (POSC) advocated by governments? These questions will be examined in the context of residential child care services in England and Wales.

A number of reasons have been posited for contracting out public sector production responsibilities.[1] One factor is simply tradition. Public authorities plan and organize their own provision around the services already produced by nonpublic organizations. They seek to avoid unnecessary du-

This chapter is based on a paper, "The Relative Cost-Effectiveness of Public, Voluntary and Private Providers of Residential Child Care," presented to the joint UK–Nordic Health Economics Study Group, Vadstena, Sweden, 1985, and published in A. J. Culyer and B. Jönsson, ed., *Public and Private Health Care* (London: Basil Blackwell, 1986). It has gone through so many changes since its first draft that I forget who suggested what, and when. I am grateful to Tony Culyer and Estelle James for their important suggestions, and I apologize to those I have forgotten. Reprinted by permission.

plication. A second reason is specialization. Most local authorities or municipalities are unable to provide the full range of services required to meet the variety of needs displayed by their populations. They therefore purchase specialized care from other local authorities or from nonpublic agencies. This is common in child care.

It is widely believed that nonstatutory organizations have greater flexibility and innovative capacity, although it would be wrong to view public authorities as particularly deficient in this regard.[2] Arguments that for-profit organizations are less responsive to the needs of the community than nonprofit organizations could be argued to be irrelevant in the POSC debate,[3] and anyway these arguments are not borne out by recent British experience. A fourth factor is the belief that the existence of alternatives to public services allows the consumer or client to exercise choice. Certainly it could be argued that the provision of suitable care services for minority ethnic or religious groups is more likely within a mixed economy of welfare.

Bendick[4] argues that POSC ("the empowerment of mediating institutions") stimulates growth in the social care sector through two important links between production and financing. First, "by unlinking the popular charitable instinct from the politically unpopular governmental establishment," POSC offers the U.S. voting public precisely what it appears to desire. Second, POSC draws "service suppliers into the political constituency advancing and defending public programs."

Finally, it is often argued that nonpublic organizations or providers can produce services at lower cost and better value for money. Principally this last argument for POSC, the "efficiency" or cost effectiveness argument, is examined in this chapter. Is it the case that governments simply "promote the *myth* of the super-effectiveness of voluntary effort"[5] or are there *real* efficiency gains to be reaped from contracting out?

EXAMINING INTERSECTORAL DIFFERENCES: THE COST FUNCTION APPROACH

At the root of many of the arguments about comparative efficiency lies an (untested) assumption that the three sectors produce services (intermediate outputs) and affect the well-being of clients (final outputs) in essentially different ways: they employ different production technologies in the face of different constraints and respond to different sets of incentives. Much of the discussion of the intersectoral question is focused on comparative cost or cost effectiveness. Given the difficulties of final output measurement and the development of unidimensional output scales and also given the need to ensure that like is compared with like, the *cost function* technique is probably the most useful basis for examining such arguments. "The fundamental problem in making a valid comparison of the relative costs of local authority and voluntary homes lies in deriving the costs per child for similar types of establishments providing similar types of care to children with similar difficulties."[6]

In public policy contexts, an estimated cost function represents the "average" relationship between cost and output, and residuals indicate deviation from the average degree of efficiency. The function is actually derived from an assumption of cost minimization.[7] If producers do not attempt to minimize costs, the cost function loses a little but certainly not all of its appeal. Hanushek[8] argues in a related context that nonminimization allows economic inefficiency but does not invalidate the cost or production function "unless resources are also wantonly squandered." The fitted function can be interpreted as a behavioral rather than a technical relationship. Of course, there are strong arguments for believing cost minimization might not be such an unrealistic assumption after all. The exhortations of central and local governments and the realities of recession in recent years may be held to have encouraged a more diligent search for cost minimization by the public sector. Escalating costs and falling "POSC demand" have certainly sharpened the cost consciousness of voluntary and private agencies.

Most previous intersectoral cost comparisons, in Britain and elsewhere, have either taken inadequate account of factors known to be associated with differences in cost or have erroneously included staffing levels or ratios as explanations of these differences.[9] By starting from a clear conceptual base these errors of omission and commission are less likely to arise.

The approach adopted in the research reported here is based on the broad, multidisciplinary *production of welfare* framework, developed and updated over a decade and empirically examined in a variety of service contexts from a number of different disciplinary and policy perspectives.[10] The production of welfare approach starts with production at the level of the *individual client* and moves toward an understanding of the behavior of producers at the "plant" and "firm" level. The production of welfare model provides a valid conceptual base for the empirical examination of intersectoral efficiency differences. The implications of the approach for specification of cost functions have been discussed elsewhere.[11] The sources of cost variations in child care contexts are likely to be differences in input prices, volume of output, rate of production, specialization and "case mix," characteristics of children, quality of care (dimensions of the physical and social environment), staffing characteristics, location, and aspects of efficiency. The cost function approach has been employed only rarely in British intersectoral studies.[12] It was, however, used in two earlier studies by me, and the research reported in this should be seen as a development of that work.[13]

In the first study a single cost function, with suitable sector dummies, was estimated for day care services for the elderly.[14] The study found, inter alia, that the costs of day care varied with the dependency characteristics of users, the activities of units, and attendance levels, and these factors went some way in explaining intersectoral cost differences. Although day care in units run by nonprofit organizations was on average cheaper than in local authority units this was not the case at all scales of operation. Once the influences of user dependency, unit activities, and treatment modes were removed, units with an annual attendance in excess of 18,800 (or 360 per week) were run more cheaply by local authorities than by nonprofit organizations, although the cost differential between the sectors was not outside the range defined by the prediction errors. Nevertheless, it is unlikely that nonprofit day care in *larger* units is actually cheaper than local authority care, partly because large nonprofit units are no more successful than comparable local authority units in attracting and retaining unpaid staff and partly because the economical informality of small scale cannot be retained.

The second study fitted separate explanatory equations to samples of public and for-profit old people's homes—a cost function for the public sector and a "fee function" for the for-profit sector.[15] The intersectoral comparison involved the standardization of costs and fees for differences in resident dependency, home design and scale, occupancy and area factors, and the computation of cross-sector predictions. The two sectors adopted fairly different "care technologies" and for-profit home charges were clearly lower than local authority costs after standardization. These analyses, and interviews conducted with proprietors of 50 homes, suggested that the technology differences and the cost-fee difference could be attributed to the long hours worked by proprietors, the low rate of return on capital, lower wage rates (often in return for more flexible working hours), and a less cautious (and less costly) way of managing dependency.

The conclusions from both previous studies must be hedged with caveats—the absence of final output measures, the conflation of cost and mark-up relationships into a "fee function," the focus on short-run rather than long-run cost or fee functions, and the neglect in each study of one of the sectors. The study of residential child care reported in this chapter also harbors a number of inadequacies, although it represents an improvement along some of these dimensions. The most serious inadequacy is the inability to measure final outputs, although a range of intermediate output and quality of provision indicators are employed.

EMPIRICAL STUDY OF COSTS IN THREE SECTORS

Data Base: A National Survey of Children's Homes

The empirical basis for this study is a nationwide (English and Welsh) survey of 789 children's homes in the three sectors. Data were collected from the broad spectrum of residential services, including highly specialized therapeutic communities for disturbed adolescents and short-stay homes for severely mentally handicapped children. A "census" was conducted on March 2, 1983, with questionnaires completed by heads of homes and supplemented with financial, occupancy and other data (for some but not all homes) for the 12-month period ending March 31, 1983. We did not attempt to collect cost information from the private sector or from homes run by smaller nonprofit organizations, principally because we were not confident of obtaining reliable and consistent accounting information across the sample but also because we knew any such request would lower the response rate. Anyway, fees are the more relevant data for some aspects of the POSC debate since local authority contractors will be concerned about the costs to *them* (which are the fees charged by nonpublic homes) rather than the costs to these agencies. All participating local authorities, nonprofit organizations, and for-profit homes were self-selecting. Nevertheless, the public and nonprofit sector samples are representative of the national picture.[16] It is not possible to examine the representativeness of the sample of for-profit homes, for there was no national register of these homes at the time of the survey with which to compare the sample.

Home features, child characteristics, costs and fees—and, indeed, the pressing intersectoral policy issues—vary quite markedly among different home designations (see Table 8.1). Where possible it is sensible to examine designation groups separately. For a variety of reasons this chapter focuses on *community homes* and *hostels*. (The cost structure and functions for these two types of home are indistinguishable.) These are the least specialized forms of residential provision for children in need of care, although they are a far cry from the "ordinary" children's homes of the early postwar period, accommodating as they do some very "difficult" and disturbed children—most of them adolescents. There is a fairly considerable local authority demand for places in nonpublic community homes and hostels, and this demand is almost always a *local* demand. Thus, in trying to understand differences and relations between sectors, it is useful to look at nonprofit and for-profit homes within a particular local context. For more specialized forms of residential care, particularly community homes with education and homes for mentally or physically handicapped children, the demand for nonpublic care is potentially nationwide. Significant changes in patterns of provision and philosophies of care in recent years have led local authorities to reduce their reliance on residential care, and they have begun to look more critically at the "value for money" of their contracted-out placements—particularly in nonspecialist establishments.

It was immediately clear from preliminary examinations of the data that homes in the public, nonprofit, and for-profit sectors differed sufficiently to warrant separate investigation. In each case, the aims of investigation are to shed light on the production technology underlying the delivery of residential care, and to account for variations in costs or fees. At a second stage the technologies and circumstances of production can be compared and contrasted for the purposes of policy discussion.

Public Sector Costs

The estimation of a cost function for public sector children's homes proceeded in two stages and is described in more detail elsewhere.[17] In the

Table 8.1. Survey of Children's Homes: Sample Size and Home Characteristics

Sector & Characteristic[b]	Home Designation[a]							
	COMM	ADOL	HOS	CHE	MPH	OAC	Other	All
Public								
Number of homes	434	20	22	29	36	57	2	600
Number places	11.8	14.3	10.2	49.2	15.4	23.0	11.0	14.8
Percent occupancy	77.0	68.4	71.7	81.6	68.5	73.3	73.3	75.9
Percent single rooms	20.6	45.7	60.0	22.6	28.1	25.9	58.3	24.1
Percent with day care	16.8	35.0	4.5	43.6	55.6	49.1	100.0	24.7
Time in home[c]	19.4	8.0	6.8	8.5	35.2	3.3	21.2	15.6
Average cost[a]	169	352	184	304	274	301	153	197
Nonprofit								
Number homes	105	5	10	8	23	0	1	152
Number places	21.6	12.2	9.4	40.4	21.3	—	14.0	21.4
Percent occupancy	73.1	60.5	72.8	81.1	87.0	—	42.9	74.9
Percent single rooms	25.0	47.0	56.2	29.5	13.5	—	71.4	26.6
Percent with day care	21.9	20.0	10.0	62.5	43.5	—	0.0	26.3
Time in home[c]	37.6	26.7	8.3	14.9	53.8	—	18.7	36.7
Average cost[d]	125	176	140	298	215	—	450	154
For-profit								
Number of homes	18	1	2	11	5	0	0	37
Number places	13.2	25.0	10.0	24.8	25.8	—	—	18.1
Percent occupancy	72.1	76.0	75.0	81.8	83.8	—	—	76.5
Single rooms	20.2	36.0	62.5	15.5	7.4	—	—	20.7
Percent with day care	33.4	0.0	0.0	18.2	25.0	—	—	25.0
Time in home[c]	42.2	12.9	10.7	19.0	81.3	—	—	33.0
Average fee[e]	117	250	163	238	159	—	—	165
All								
Number of homes	557	23	34	48	64	57	3	789
Number places	13.7	14.3	9.9	42.3	18.3	23.0	12.0	16.2
Percent occupancy	76.1	67.1	72.2	81.6	75.8	73.3	63.2	75.7
Percent single rooms	21.4	45.6	59.0	22.1	21.4	25.9	62.7	24.4
Percent with day care	22.3	30.8	5.9	50.0	49.2	49.1	66.7	25.0
Time in home[c]	25.3	11.1	7.6	11.1	47.5	3.3	19.9	21.9
Cost/fee[f]	NA	NA	NA	NA	NA	NA	NA	NA

[a] Abbreviations: COMM (community homes—nonspecialist accommodation), ADOL (adolescent unit), HOS (hostels), CHE (community homes with education), MPH (homes for mentally or physically handicapped children), OAC (observation and assessment centers).

[b] Apart from the number of homes, all other tabulations are the average (mean) values for each characteristic within the relevant sector and designation.

[c] Average number of months since last admission to home for all children resident on night of survey.

[d] Average operating cost per child per week, financial year 1982–1983, using average number of residents over the *year* as the denominator.

[e] Average weekly fee per child per week on day of survey.

[f] For all homes it is not considered appropriate to average over costs and fees.

first stage I included indicators of most of the hypothesized cost-influencing factors, employing the usual statistical criteria and omitting those that were not held to be sufficiently reliable or clear in their influences. I did not have data on final output and in the case of some other hypothesized influences my indicators were not ideal. Having found a satisfactory empirical cost function (estimated by ordinary least squares), I examined (at the second stage) the cost-raising characteristics of the social environment and indicators reflecting the stated objectives of homes. I employed this two-stage method for a number of reasons. First, more observations on the social environment and objectives questions were missing than on other factors, and exclusion of the former allowed fitting the cost function to a larger number of homes. Second, I had greater confidence in the reliability of the first set of variables as indicators of hypothesized cost-influencing factors. Third, I had more confidence in the sources of any significant relationships for the first stage variables than for the second. The level of understanding of the influences of social environment on cost is still at too early a stage to allow satisfactory policy conclusions to be drawn from any established relationships.

Seventy percent of the observed variation in average operating cost (staff cost plus other items of revenue expenditure but excluding capital cost) was "explained" by the estimated cost function, which is reported in the Appendix to this chapter and discussed elsewhere.[18] Significant factors included a labor cost index, scale of home, average percentage of available places occupied over the year, proportion of beds in single rooms, ownership, rental or otherwise of a vehicle for use by the home, provision or otherwise of after-care, emergency day-care and preventive services, staff social work responsibilities outside the home (for residents or nonresidents), mean age of residents, gender proportion of residents, and the proportion mentally handicapped.[19]

This estimated public sector function has a number of policy implications. The ability of the function to explain some of the variations in average cost has relevance both for the auditing of local authorities (and especially the interauthority comparisons made by the Audit Commission) and for the allocation of equity-based central government grants to local governments. The variables measuring scale and occupancy have implications for the design of community homes and their usage within a system of care. The estimated function also includes among its explanatory variables a number of indicators of child characteristics and the range of nonresidential services offered, each of them of interest in the context of present policy trends in residential child care. We return to some of these issues later.

For-Profit Sector Fees

Until recently for-profit children's homes were subject to relatively little control by the public sector. The Children's Homes Act of 1982 tightened up these controls. At the time of the survey the size of the sector was difficult to gauge with any precision, partly because the new registration procedures were not then in force and partly because many other establishments—boarding schools, residential special schools, and homes for mentally handicapped children—often provide similar services to similar residents but are registered under different acts of Parliament. There is no doubt, however, that the for-profit sector is very much smaller than the other two sectors.

The mean fee across the full sample of for-profit homes (of all designations) was £165, although this hides considerable variation. In principle, the fee charged by homes can be represented as the outcome of two effects: the *demand* for places from families and (more important) from local authorities, and the *supply* of residential care of a particular variety and standard. The supply effect works through two constituent effects: the cost to provide a residential place in a home[20] and the markup added to the cost to arrive at the advertised fee. The markup is, of course, influenced by both supply and demand factors. Thus, it is assumed that a home calculates its weekly charges, in the light of experience as to the demand for places. My empirical investigations of for-profit homes focused predominantly on the supply side. Local demand indicators, of the kind described later and employed in the analyses of the nonprofit sector, have been examined but were not of importance. This result should not be interpreted as saying that demand influences are negligible, for the data available for analysis do not permit such a strong conclusion. Most of the for-profit homes covered by our survey are clustered in the southeast of England, so that area-based proxies for local authority demand show little variation across the sample. Furthermore, many for-profit homes—and especially those with some specialized care functions—clearly saw their market as a *national* market, so that local demand indicators were not relevant.

The weekly fee in each of the private homes was taken as the dependent variable in a series of multiple regression analyses, employing a weighted average fee in the small number of homes with multiple charges.[21] All designations of home were included in the study to provide enough observations for estimation. Although it was not possible to examine the influence of some of the hypothesized demand-side factors or to examine indicators of managerial style, the estimated equation "explained" 60 percent of fee variation (see these results in the Appendix to this chapter.) The significant influences on fees were the percentage of residents receiving full-time education or training within a home, the proportion of beds in single or double rooms, the staff's social work responsibilities outside the home, the availability or otherwise of volunteer car services, and the mean number of previous placements in care for residents of the home.[22]

Nonprofit Sector Fees, Costs and Markups

The nonprofit child care sector has always been larger than the for-profit sector and more closely integrated with the public sector. The present "crisis" in the welfare state has arguably hit it hardest. Many nonprofit organizations have diversified, but at the time of our survey, in terms of both human and capital resources, most remained heavily committed to the provision of residential care. Furthermore, almost all of the residential care they supplied was (and still is) provided under contract to local authorities.

In the last few years, with professional preferences swinging away from residential care, this has meant a considerable drop in the numbers of children placed in nonprofit homes, in turn creating financial and professional difficulties. Local authority demand has not only fallen but changed in emphasis, with the consequence that a much higher proportion of the children now placed outside the public sector have behavioral, emotional, physical, and other difficulties. These changes in the characteristics of residents have been one source of the escalating cost of nonprofit sector care, and this escalating cost has possibly contributed to a further fall in the demand for "contracted-out" places in a climate of fiscal pressure.[23] One result has been a marked degree of specialization within the spectrum of child care. Much of the specialization has reflected the behavioral, educational, or physical needs of children, but there has also been specialization by religious denomination—the great majority of nonprofit homes are run by organizations with clear denominational orientations—and, less often, "specialization by industrial sector." (The Railcare Centre, formerly the Southern Railwaymen's Home for Children, and the British Seamen's Boys Home were still open at the time of our survey, whereas the Actors' Orphanage and the home run by The Society of Licensed Victuallers had long since closed.) In 1984 about 4000 children were in nonprofit children's homes in England and Wales, 90 percent of whom had been placed there by a local authority. About 5 percent of all children in local authority care were in nonprofit homes.

Two data sets were used in the analyses: the register of information collected annually by the DHSS from each nonprofit home, and the Personal Social Services Research Unit (PSSRU) survey. The former has the advantage of covering the population, whereas the latter is a sample, albeit a representative one. On the other hand, the PSSRU survey data set includes both cost and fee data for some homes and a wealth of child, home, and staff data for all sample homes. The production technologies and "marketing strategies" of voluntary homes were investigated by combining the two data sets. The empirical analysis focused on the estimation of four relationships: a fee equation, a cost function, a proportional markup equation,[24] and an equation explaining variations in public sector purchase or utilization of places.

For many nonprofit homes the markup is negative; that is, the homes charge fees less than average operating cost. For other homes, fees exceeded average operating cost. In most such cases the fees would not have been sufficient to cover capital or overhead costs,[25] and even if they were, these homes—or their parent organizations—are subject to the "nondistribution constraint."[26] A fee equation was estimated using the Department of Health and Social Security (DHSS) register data, although the cost and markup equations could be fitted to only the subsample of homes covered by my own survey for which I had reliable information on operating costs. The subsample of voluntary homes used to estimate these two equations is biased toward the larger organizations, and I found from the estimation of fee variations that organizational scale is positively associated with the fee charged. The utilization equation models the local authority demand for nonprofit places from the supplier's perspective; it is not a "pure" demand schedule.

Full details of the four estimated equations are given elsewhere.[27] I will not discuss the utilization equation any further in this chapter. The other three equations can be briefly summarized. Fees were found to be influenced significantly by a labor cost index, home and organizational scale, occupancy rate, ages of children resident, religious denomination of organization (Catholic, Protestant, or other), home type, and political complexion of the local authorities with which a home principally contracts. Cost-influencing factors were a labor cost index, scale, proportion of places occupied, proportion of beds in double rooms, ages of children and their previous care placements (particularly the proportion coming to the home from a foster family breakdown), proportion of children spending most of the day in the home (that is, not attending school or not employed), provision or otherwise of day care and after-care services, and staff social work responsibilities outside the home. Finally, the proportional markup varied with labor cost, home and organizational scale, occupancy proportion, whether the home was of "assisted" status, the proportion of beds in single rooms, ratio of nonprofit to public sector costs in the area, and the supply of other nonprofit places in the area.

DIFFERENCES BETWEEN THE SECTORS

The estimated cost and fee functions for the three sectors, which are summarized in Table 8.2 and the Appendix, reflect the underlying production technologies and marketing strategies of different residential child care providers, subject of course to the usual errors of measurement and prediction. The estimated functions have numerous "within-sector" implications that are not considered here. What *are* considered are four intersectoral comparisons of particular interest: economies of scale, the London effect, the "cost–difficulty gradient," and market responsiveness.

Economies of Scale

The Curtis Committee Report, which provided the blueprint for the Children Act of 1948 and was thus the first postwar statement of the British central government philosophy of child care, proposed that large institutions be abandoned in favor of small "family group" homes with no more than 12 children. This emphasis on small scale, particularly in the public sector, has characterized the postwar period. In 1983 the average size of these "ordinary" public sector homes is almost exactly that recommended by the Curtis Committee (see Table 8.1). The estimated local authority

Table 8.2. Summary of Significant Variables in the Estimated Equations

Explanatory Variables (and Groups)	Public (cost)	For-profit (fee)	Nonprofit (cost)	Nonprofit (markup)
Labor cost index	X	X	X	X
Number of child residents[a]	X		X	X
Proportion of places occupied[a]	X		X	X
Single or double bedrooms[b]	X	X	X	X
Vehicle availability and ownership[c]	X	X		
Day care services offered[c]	X		X	
External social work responsibilities[c]	X		X	
Daytime activities of residents[a,c]		X	X	
Ages of residents	X		X	
Gender proportion of residents	X			
Proportion of children with mental handicaps	X			
Previous care histories of residents[c]			X	
Organizational size and status				X
Ratio of home cost/regional public cost				X
Market share				X
Sample size	411	34	68	58
Percentage of variance in dependent variable explained by equation	70%	69%	72%	77%

Note: Full details of these equations are given in the Appendix to this chapter. X indicates inclusion (and statistical significance).
[a] Including higher and lower powers.
[b] Introduced in various combinations.
[c] Introduced in aggregate and distinguishing individual components.

operating cost function indicates that the cost–scale relationship is U-shaped. Operating costs are minimized at approximately 12 places (assuming 80 percent occupancy), although there is relatively little cost variation around this cost-minimizing scale except at the extremes of the home size range. The cost–scale association for nonprofit homes is very different. Average operating cost rises monotonically with scale but at a decreasing rate. In fact, from around 15 places increases in scale make little difference to average cost. This reflects the different staffing arrangements required by larger homes. Small homes are generally run by highly motivated married couples with only part-time assistance (if any). Most would see themselves as little different from salaried foster parents providing a family environment. Larger scale brings organizational and perhaps also motivational complications that raise unit cost. Bringing in capital costs, either as depreciation figures or preferably as replacement cost annuities, does not significantly alter the scale relationship in either the public or nonprofit sectors. Scale is directly associated with proportional markup in the nonprofit sector. Thus, not only are average costs higher in larger nonprofit homes, but fees charged to local authorities are also *proportionately* larger. There is no scale evident in the for-profit sector.

The London Effect

The major resource in residential child care is labor—73.5 percent of direct noncapital expenditure during 1982–83 was on personnel. Labor markets for residential home staff members are likely to be localized; excess demand will generate competition among employers through internal and external labor markets, pushing up salaries and nonpecuniary advantages (such as accommodation or less disruptive hours), more paid overtime, the employment of lower quality staff, or the regrading of posts. I did not have data on input prices in this study but instead have used a *labor cost index* constructed by the Department of the Environment as a proxy. The index takes the value one for almost all local authorities outside London and a higher value for London boroughs; it is essentially picking up the higher labor costs within London.

If this labor cost index were behaving purely as an input price indicator I would expect a coefficient of unity (subject to measurement and estimation error) in the cost functions. If, as has been argued, this index undervalued interauthority variation in labor costs, particularly between London and the rest of the country, then a slightly larger coefficient would pick up the pure input price effect.[28] I found that the coefficient in the local authority function is substantially greater than unity. I examined a number of home-level indicators (such as home size, child characteristics, and nonresidential service provision) that might explain the marked cost differences between London and the rest of the country over and above the labor cost difference but did not find any such explanation. This absence of any satisfactory explanation of the London differential is particularly interesting in the context of intersectoral comparisons, for the estimated labor cost coefficient in the nonprofit sector equation is subtantially smaller than in the public sector equation, although again greater than unity. The difference between the two sectors could therefore reflect either missing variables (particularly indicators of the "difficulty" of children) or organizational slack.

To date no evidence has been presented to support the first reason for the marked public–nonprofit difference—missing "difficulty" effects. Even if this were the case it would not necessarily justify the reluctance of London boroughs to contract out more residential care to the nonpublic sectors, for the nonprofit and for-profit sectors appear to have a cost advantage at all levels of "difficulty."

The "Cost–Difficulty Gradient"

One of the most telling criticisms of bare cost comparisons is that they ignore differences in the characteristics of children between homes, authorities, services, and sectors. Our postal survey included a number of questions designed to gather information on those characteristics of children that might have an influence on the cost of care, although it was not possible to gather information on all characteristics hypothesized to have a cost-raising influence. The characteristics covered by the questionnaire were age, sex, length of time in the home since last admission, place of previous residence, number of placements during present care episode, and the presence or otherwise of mental and physical handicap. Only three of the child characteristics entered the public cost function: the average age of children, the proportion of girls, and the proportion of mentally handicapped residents. Overall, the cost–difficulty relationship appears *not* to be of importance in public homes. This conclusion must be qualified. First, my data collection did not include indicators of some of the principal dimensions of difficulty. Second, local authorities may not have increased the resources available to homes in line with the rising difficulty of residents. Anyway many of the more difficult children are accommodated in "more specialized" residential establishments (such as community homes with education, adolescent units, observation and assessment centers, or homes for mentally or physically handicapped children) so that the cost–difficulty gradient can be properly seen only by examining all designations together.

However, these qualifications must themselves be qualified in the light of the results for the nonpublic sectors. Nonprofit costs are higher in homes with a narrower age range, where children have had more placements in care prior to admission to the home, where more children are in the home during the day (a nonlinear effect), and where a larger proportion of children were admitted to the home following a foster placement breakdown. In the for-profit sector the only significant child characteristic is the mean number of previous placements in care, which raises the average fee. Included in these two functions, therefore, are commonly cited "difficulty" indicators. For example, although important in explaining cost variations in the nonprofit sector, the proportion of children who last resided in a foster placement does not alter local authority cost. This cannot be interpreted as implying that these children are no more expensive than other children in the provision of public sector care. Rather, it suggests that local authorities do not adjust—or feel they do not *need* to adjust—the supply of resources to homes in response to changes in difficulty characteristics. Fixed budgets and increasing levels of difficulty could thus result in the downgrading of quality of care relative to the two nonpublic sectors. The limited evidence collected in our survey on social environmental characteristics of homes and information from other research[29] does not, however, suggest any marked or pervasive differences between the sectors.

There are lessons here for advocates of increased contracting out of residential child care. If the cost difference between public and nonpublic sectors is, in part at least, a reflection of differences in cost effectiveness, then the increasingly difficult population of children in residential care will have a greater inflationary effect in the two nonpublic sectors, for there would appear to be a degree of slack in the public sector that can be taken up without pushing up costs.

Market Responsiveness

In considering the privatization of production and the efficiency implications of POSC the primary concern is the cost to a public agency of the services it purchases. For the reasons set out earlier, principally revolving around the limited geographical spread of the sample, it has not yet been possible to identify any demand-side influences on the fees charged by the for-profit sector. However, there are a number of ways in which the nonprofit sector appears to respond to market pressures. The determinants of the fee–cost markup for nonprofit homes reflect the market pressure effects. They fall into four groups: scale, relative prices, pressure of demand, and market penetration. These four do not represent the totality of associations between the sectors, partly because in common with all other empirical studies, we can never be sure that all possible influences have been included in the analysis and partly because some of the links between the sectors are already appearing in the cost function. These include the difficulty of children and the provision of nonresidential services, both of which will alter in response to local authority demands.

The size of a home (as measured by the number of places provided) and the size of a nonprofit organization (as measured by the number of homes) are each positively associated with fees. The influence of the former works through two channels: larger homes incur higher costs (other things being equal) and add a proportionately larger markup. The effect of organizational scale may be mirroring the finding in industrial settings of a positive relation between firm size and profitability, and it is now relatively well accepted that "small business proprietors" of old people's homes expect and extract a low return on capital, at least in the short run.[30] The lack of association between cost and organizational scale also conforms with previous work.[31] Homes run by larger organizations are charging higher fees not, therefore, because of a cost difference but because of an ability to add a larger markup (or less willingness to subsidize public sector responsibilities).

A number of relative price and cost variables were examined; the indicator in the equation is the ratio of operating cost in the nonprofit home (the baseline for the fee calculation by the supplier) to the average operating plus capital (depreciation) cost of local authority community homes and hostels (the baseline for the POSC decision by the demander) in the planning area in which the nonprofit home is located. If nonprofit costs are high relative to public costs there will be a lower proportional markup, suggesting that nonprofit organizations are responding to relative costs. If their objective is to survive, and that means in almost all cases surviving by attracting sufficient numbers of "contracted-out" children, they must subsidize such placements out of charitable donations, capital sales, and other income sources. Few organizations are keen to use their non-POSC income in this way, partly because administrative and capital expenditures have to be covered, partly because they feel no moral commitment to subsidize the public sector, and partly because the diversification of services (as a necessary response to the falling residential child care population) is rarely funded by public agencies until well-established and of proven effectiveness.

Finally, there are a number of influences on markup that might loosely be termed *market pressure effects*. The proportion of available places in a nonprofit home occupied over the year is directly related to markup. A home is less inclined to subsidize local authority responsibilities when it is successful in filling its available places. The ratio of places in the home to *all* nonprofit sector places in the area has a negative effect, which is at first counterintuitive. However, this result mirrors similar findings in U.S. health care studies of a positive association between price and supplier density. Greenhut et al.[32] explain this in terms of hidden costs, particularly associated with distance. Thus, "full price" (fee plus hidden costs) rather than fee determines demand, and a falling number of nonprofit homes in an area will not only shift the supply curve but also affect the demand curve and its elasticities. They argue that the conditions under which this will occur are not unreasonable. The other variable of interest here is the labor cost index. We have already noted that costs are higher in nonprofit homes in London than elsewhere. Organizations respond to this by forgoing some of their "profit" (or accepting the burden of a larger subsidy to the public sector) in an attempt to maintain their competitiveness. There is probably some regional cross-subsidization within organizations in order to achieve this as well as to reduce the amount of fee variation.

Cross-Sector Predictions of Costs and Fees

The figures in Table 8.1 suggest that for-profit community homes are cheaper than nonprofit, and nonprofit homes are cheaper than public homes. However, the technologies of care clearly differ between the sectors, and the characteristics of children and homes are also different. What is the relative effect of each, and what would be the effect on average cost of, say, the nonprofit sector taking on the salient characteristics of the public? In order to examine this effect, the variables appearing in the nonprofit cost function need to be set at the mean values for the *public* sector. The difference between observed average cost in the nonprofit sector and predicted cost calculated in this way is thus the weighted sum of differences between nonprofit and public sector means, the weights being the estimated coefficients in the nonprofit function. Thus, holding constant the technologies (the estimated regression *coefficients*) provides an indication of the effects of different cost-raising or fee-raising circumstances among sectors, and holding constant the characteristics of children and homes (the observed regression *variables*) provides an indication of some of the cost-effectiveness implications of POSC.

There are essentially four complications here: the inclusion or exclusion of capital cost and its measurement, the measurement of some of the vari-

Table 8.3.   Cross-Sector Predictors of Average (Operating plus Capital) Cost and Fee

	Circumstances/Characteristics Observed for		
Functional Base for Predictions	Public Sector	Nonprofit Sector	For-profit Sector
Public cost function plus capital	185[a]	203	235
Nonprofit cost function plus capital	144	151	147
Nonprofit cost function plus markup[c]	134	140[b]	92
For-profit sector fee function[d]	130	138	124

Note: Costs and fees are expressed to the nearest pound sterling per child week, 1982–1983 prices.

[a] Mean observed operating cost was £170 for the sample used for cross-sector comparisons (i.e., with observations on all variables needed for all calculations in this table) to which was added the calculated annuitized replacement cost of capital.

[b] The nonprofit sector mean fee of £140 is less than the operating plus capital cost (£151) because of the mean negative markup (i.e., the subsidy from the nonprofit to the public sector).

[c] In the markup function some variables are not available (or even sensible) for public and for-profit homes. The following assumptions have therefore been made. The labor cost index, number of places, and the occupancy rate have been allowed to vary (they *are* available) for both the public and for-profit sector predictions. For the public sector, predictions all other variables have been set to their nonprofit sample mean values except for the assisted homes dummy, which is set to one. For the for-profit sector, the assisted home dummy is set to zero and other variables set to their nonprofit sector sample mean values.

[d] The for-profit sector fee function was estimated over *all* designations. However, all calculations in this table are restricted to community homes and hostels.

ables appearing in one sector's function that do not have exact equivalents in the other sectors, the designations of homes over which the estimated functions have relevance, and the different geographical spreads of homes in the two sectors. A number of alternative comparisons are possible, depending upon the particular solutions chosen to circumvent each complication. For simplicity only one set of calculations is presented here:

- capital costs are included (calculated as annuitized replacement costs assuming 60 year lifespans, 5 percent interest rates, DHSS recommendations for cost limits, and thus varying only with respect to the number of places and the occupancy proportion);
- suitable proxies are chosen for missing values (the measurement of occupancy in the for-profit sector, and the public and for-profit sector treatment of some of the variables in the nonprofit markup function),
- all comparisons are restricted to community homes and hostels (even though the private fee function was estimated over a broader range of designations); and
- all homes, including London homes, are included.

Alternative assumptions *do* alter the cross-sector predictions but not the general tenor of the conclusions. The results of the cross-sector predictions are presented in Table 8.3. Consider the public–nonprofit comparison of *costs*. The observed mean costs are £185 (public) and £151 (nonprofit), a difference of £34 per child week. Standardizing for the characteristics of children, homes, services, and locations does *not* narrow the difference. The difference, after standardization, is either £41 (= £185 − £144, calculated using public sector characteristics as base, or £52 (= £203 − £151, using nonprofit sector characteristics as base). Similarly, the cost–fee difference between the public and for-profit sectors does not narrow after standardization. On the other hand, comparing fees in the two nonpublic sectors, the observed difference of £16 does disappear after standardization when nonprofit characteristics are used as base but appears to widen with private sector characteristics as base. In other words, only the difference between the two nonpublic sectors can be attributed in part to differences in child characteristics, home design, service diversification, and location—and then only tentatively.

CONCLUSION: THE SOURCES OF THE DIFFERENCES BETWEEN SECTORS

The *tentative* conclusion to be drawn from the comparison of costs and fees (and their predictive equations) is that, in the privatization of *production,* the two nonpublic sectors are more cost effective than the public sector in the sense that they employ more efficient "technologies" of care. This conclusion is subject to certain qualifications.

Data limitations have meant that the intersectoral comparisons have not been able to take account of final outputs (the effects, particularly the long-term effects, of services on children and their families, together with relevant externalities). If intermediate and final output can be monitored or regulated by the public sector this may not be such an important omission, except that such regulation is itself costly. Most children in nonprofit and for-profit homes have been placed there by local authorities, and each child will remain on the caseload of a local authority social worker who has a statutory obligation to remain in regular contact. It is unlikely, therefore, that there can be markedly inferior quality care in nonpublic homes, particularly since there is rarely a shortage of available residential placements from which to choose. Of course, it could be argued that what social workers perceive to be "good quality care" may not be quite as good when tested against its impact on client well-being. There are a number of drawbacks to this argument. First, it assumes a naivety among a group of service professionals that is at odds with reality. Second, there is as yet no comprehensive body of valid evidence on the relationship between quality of provision and final outputs with which to dispute the judgment of social service staff members. Third, it assumes that social workers are mistaken only when placing children in nonpublic homes and not in public homes.

It is sometimes suggested that local authority homes are accommodating the most difficult children. The measures of difficulty available for this study were limited, but they did not suggest any marked cost effect. Further, within this set there are many dimensions of "difficulty" that are commonly held to impose additional burdens on staff but that do not appear to raise the cost of public provision. Because they *do* raise costs in the nonprofit sector it was earlier argued that there may be a greater degree of organizational slack in the public than in the nonprofit sector. Certainly, the empirical results presented here are consistent with the idea that *competition* is a prime reason for the efficiency difference.[33] The falling numbers of children in the care of local authorities, in residential accommodation, and in nonpublic homes have heightened competition both within and between sectors. But competition will mean—and is already meaning—that some long-established voluntary organizations outside the public sector must either move out of residential provision or risk their complete demise, particularly if they have already pared down their costs to remove "organizational slack."

There are other reasons for believing that in the long run the cost of efficiency differences between sectors may be reduced. One is the continuing ability of nonprofit (and some for-profit) organizations to attract staff members at salaries below those in the public sector. Hatch and Mocroft[34] felt that the most important reason for intersectoral cost differences was "the greater commitment that a voluntary (nonprofit) organization can in some circumstances elicit from its staff, and their consequent willingness to work harder and/or for less money than the equivalent staff in a statutory organization." The differential motivations between sectors and the longer hours worked by nonprofit home care staff members (respective means of 40 hours and 59 hours per week in March 1983) ensure that nonprofit homes are cheaper than their local authority counterparts. However, with the trend toward the provision of residential accommodation for only the most "difficult" children in care, many of the heads of these small homes are finding their chosen careers unattractive. This raises questions about the long-run supply response of such highly motivated individuals. The supply is likely to dwindle with the trend toward residential provision for only the more difficult, disturbed, and perhaps delinquent children in the care of local authorities. Already care staff turnover in the nonprofit sector exceeds that in the public,[35] and this is likely to remain the case so long as organizations offer relatively poor terms of employment.

A final qualification to the tentative conclusion posited earlier concerns the "hidden" costs of provision. These include *contracting costs, regulation costs,* and *support service costs.* The first of these is almost certainly the smallest and yet is probably the only one to vary between sectors. The hidden support costs of residential child care—associated with field social work support, NHS, and other services—do *not* vary between sectors,[36] and although they all fall to the public sector this is of no importance in a POSC context. There is no reason in principle, either, to expect any marked intersectoral differences in the costs of regulation and inspection. *All* sectors are in need of careful monitoring.

The key to the long-run efficiency differences, particularly between public and nonprofit producers, would seem to be the ability or willingness of nonprofit bodies to continue to subsidize local authority placements by charging fees less than their average operating costs (and probably substantially less than their aggregate costs), due to donations of money and, even more, staff time. Whether this can continue is debatable.

APPENDIX

Appendix Table 8.1. Public Sector Cost Function

Variable	Coefficient	t statistic
Constant term	-526.619	-6.247[c]
Labour cost index	8.518	12.895[c]
Average number of residents in the home during the year	3.317	4.938[c]
Reciprocal of average number of residents	324.528	9.419[c]
Occupancy rate (average no. residents/no. places)	-196.683	-13.949[c]
Proportion of bedroom places in single rooms	15.865	1.674[a]
DV (dummy variable): 1 = vehicle owned by home; 0 = not	13.935	1.718[a]
DV: 1 = vehicle hired from commercial organization, 0 = not	9.414	1.984[b]
DV: 1 = home provides after-care and home-on-trial support as day care; 0 = not	21.443	1.307
DV: 1 = home provides emergency day care; 0 = not	32.743	2.053[b]
DV: 1 = home provides preventive/at risk day care; 0 = not	56.372	2.829[c]
DV: 1 = staff have social work responsibilities outside home (for residents or non-residents); 0 = not	13.733	3.390[c]
Average age of children resident on survey day	-17.029	-2.600[c]
Square of average age of children	0.757	2.824[c]
Proportion of residents who are girls	-62.250	-2.513[b]
Square of proportion of residents who are girls	54.761	2.237[b]
Proportion of residents who are mentally handicapped	-59.455	-1.796[a]
Square of proportion who are mentally handicapped	151.540	2.714[c]

$R^2 = 0.703$ Adjusted $\overline{R}^2 = 0.691$ $F = 54.806^c$ $n = 411$

Significance levels: [a] $0.10 \geqslant p > 0.05$.
[b] $0.05 \geqslant p > 0.01$.
[c] $0.01 \geqslant p$.
Dependent variable: average operating cost per child week (Sterling), 1982–1983.

Appendix Table 8.2.   For-profit Sector Fee Equation

Variable	Coefficient	t statistic
Intercept term	60.13	2.28[b]
Percentage of residents receiving full-time education (or training) within the home	1.47	6.22[c]
Proportion of bedrooms with just one or two beds	41.90	1.77[a]
Dummy variable taking value 1 if home staff have "outside care duties," and 0 otherwise	36.52	1.98[a]
Dummy variable taking value 1 if home has benefit of volunteer car service or similar, and 0 otherwise	−49.70	−1.95[a]
Mean number of previous placements in care for residents of the home	15.33	1.70[a]

$R^2 = 0.69$ $\bar{R}^2 = 0.64$ $F = 12.59^c$ $n = 34$

Significance levels: [a]$0.10 \geqslant p > 0.05$.
[b]$0.05 \geqslant p > 0.01$.
[c]$0.01 \geqslant p$.
Dependent variable: average fee per child week (Sterling), March 1983.

Appendix Table 8.3.   Nonprofit Sector Cost Function

Variable	Coefficient	t statistic
Constant	111.058	1.13
Labour cost index	2.110	2.25[b]
Reciprocal of average number of residents	−281.522	−3.68[c]
Occupancy rate	−356.609	−4.28[c]
Square of occupancy rate	173.106	3.63[c]
Proportion of bedroom places in rooms with two beds	45.203	2.81[c]
Range of ages of residents	−4.310	−5.02[c]
Mean previous placements in care per child	5.520	2.42[b]
Proportion of residents spending most of day in the home	179.738	4.32[c]
Square of proportion of residents spending day in home	−151.168	−3.28[c]
Square of proportion of residents whose last residence was in a foster home	80.220	2.38[b]
Dummy variable for home providing any day care facilities	18.858	2.07[b]
Dummy variable for home with staff having after-care duties outside the home	−27.792	−2.433[c]
Dummy variable for home providing any other social work tasks outside the home	−13.390	−1.75[a]

$R^2 = 0.720$ Adjusted $\bar{R}^2 = 0.653$ $F = 10.679^c$ $n = 68$

Significance levels: [a]$0.10 \geqslant p > 0.05$.
[b]$0.05 \geqslant p > 0.01$.
[c]$0.01 \geqslant p$.
Dependent variable: average operating cost per child week (Sterling), 1982–1983.

Appendix Table 8.4. Nonprofit Sector Proportional Mark-Up Equation

Variable	Coefficient	t statistic
Constant	1.808	3.32[c]
Labour cost index	−0.017	−3.27[c]
Reciprocal of number of places	−3.384	−4.90[c]
Occupancy rate	0.330	3.56[c]
Proportion of bedroom places in single rooms	−0.142	−1.72[a]
Dummy variable for assisted community homes	0.260	3.31[c]
Voluntary organization size	0.009	4.52[c]
Ratio of home average operating cost to average operating and capital cost of local authority community homes and hostels in the "planning area"	−0.608	−5.45[c]
Places in the home as a proportion of all voluntary home places in the planning area	−0.521	−1.90[a]

$R^2 = 0.771$ Adjusted $\overline{R}^2 = 0.733$ $F = 20.575^c$ $n = 58$

Significance levels: [a] $0.10 \geqslant p > 0.05$.
[b] $0.05 \geqslant p > 0.01$.
[c] $0.01 \geqslant p$.
Dependent variable: (fee − average operating cost)/average operating cost.

NOTES

1. Recently reviewed in Martin Knapp, Eileen Robertson, and Corinne Thomason, "Public Money, Voluntary Action: Whose Welfare?" Personal Social Services Research Unit Discussion Paper 514 (Canterbury: University of Kent, 1987). See also Ken Judge and Jillian Smith, "Purchase of Service in England," *Social Service Review* 57 (1983): 209–33.

2. Ralph Kramer, *Voluntary Agencies in the Welfare State* (Berkeley: University of California Press, 1981).

3. Neil Gilbert, *Capitalism and the Welfare State* (New Haven, Conn.: Yale University Press, 1983).

4. Marc Bendick, "Privatizing the Delivery of Social Welfare Services." Mimeograph (Washington, D.C.: Urban Institute, 1985).

5. Peter Westland, "The Year of the Voluntary Organisation," *Community Care* (November 19, 1981): 14–15.

6. Evidence submitted by the Department of Health and Social Security to the House of Commons Social Services Committee, report on *Children in Care*, HCP 360, session 1983–1984 (London: Her Majesty's Stationery Office, 1984).

7. For an account of cost functions, see Martin Knapp, *The Economics of Social Care* (London: Macmillan, 1984).

8. E. A. Hanushek, "Conceptual and Empirical Issues in the Estimation of Educational Production Functions," *Journal of Human Resources* 14 (1979): 351–88.

9. For example, see Francis Gladstone, *Voluntary Action in a Changing World* (London: National Council for Social Service, 1979); and Stephen Hatch and Ian Mocroft, "The Relative Costs of Services Provided by Voluntary and Statutory Organisations," *Public Administration* 57 (1979): 397–405.

10. Bleddyn Davies and Martin Knapp, *Old People's Homes and the Production of Welfare* (London: Routledge and Kegan Paul, 1981); Knapp, *Economics of Social Care*.

11. Knapp, ibid., Chapter 9.

12. See, for example, Robert Millward and David Parkin, "Public and Private Enterprise: Comparative Behaviour and Relative Efficiency" in Robert Millward et al., eds., *Public Sector Economics* (London: Longman, 1983).

13. A further study is now underway in the international domain. The relative costs, observed and standardized, of old people's homes in England and Catalunya (Spain) are com-

214 Government Funding and Accountability

pared between sectors and countries. See Martin Knapp, Julia Montserrat Codorniu, and Robin Darton, "Cross-Sector, Cross-Country Comparisons: Old People's Homes in Catalunya and England," Personal Social Services Research Unit Discussion Paper 513 (Canterbury: University of Kent, 1987).

14. Martin Knapp and Spyros Missiakoulis, "Inter-Sectoral Cost Comparisons: Day Care for the Elderly," *Journal of Social Policy* 11 (1982): 335–54.

15. Ken Judge and Martin Knapp, "Efficiency in the Production of Welfare: The Public and Private Sectors Compared," in Rudolf Klein and Michael O'Higgins, eds., *The Future of Welfare* (Oxford: Basil Blackwell, 1985); Ken Judge, Martin Knapp, and Jillian Smith, "The Comparative Costs of Public and Private Residential Homes for the Elderly," in Ken Judge and Ian Sinclair, eds., *Residential Care for Elderly People* (London: Her Majesty's Stationery Office, 1986).

16. Martin Knapp, *Economics of Social Care*.

17. Martin Knapp and Jillian Smith, "The Costs of Residential Child Care: Explaining Variations in the Public Sector," *Policy and Politics* 13 (April 1985): 127–54.

18. Ibid.

19. In all but one case, provision of after-care services, the coefficients on these variables attained statistical significance at the 90 percent level (sample size 411). See Knapp and Smith, ibid.

20. Costs were hypothesized to vary with input prices, scale, and so on, as with the public sector analysis.

21. Full details in Martin Knapp, "Private Children's Homes: An Analysis of Fee Variations and a Comparison with Public Sector Costs," *Policy and Politics* 15 (October 1987): 221–34.

22. Martin Knapp, ibid.; and Martin Knapp, "The Relative Cost-Effectiveness of Public, Voluntary and Private Providers of Residential Child Care," in Anthony Culyer and Bengt Jönsson, eds., *Public and Private Health Care* (Oxford: Basil Blackwell, 1986).

23. Martin Knapp, Andrew Fenyo, and Barry Baines, "The Demand for Contracted-out Residential Child Care," Personal Social Services Research Unit Discussion Paper 411 (Canterbury: University of Kent, 1986).

24. A proportional markup was chosen as the dependent variable because my interviews with senior managers in some of the larger nonprofit organizations suggested that this accorded most closely with practice.

25. But recall that these capital and overhead costs were also excluded from the local authority cost analyses.

26. Harry Hansmann, "The Role of Nonprofit Enterprise," *Yale Law Journal* 89 (April 1980): 835–908.

27. Martin Knapp and Andrew Fenyo, "Fee and Utilisation Variations within the Voluntary Residential Child Care Sector," Personal Social Services Research Unit Discussion Paper 378/2 (Canterbury: University of Kent, 1986).

28. Ian Begg, B. Moore, and J. Rhodes. "The Measurement of Inter-Authority Input Cost Differences," Mimeograph (Cambridge: Cambridge Economic Consultants, 1984); Robin Darton and Martin Knapp, "The Costs of Local Authority Old People's Homes: The Effects of Dependency, Design and Quality of Care," *Aging and Society* 4 (1984): 157–83.

29. David Berridge, *Children's Homes* (Oxford: Basil Blackwell, 1985).

30. Judge and Knapp, "Efficiency in the Production of Welfare."

31. For example see Dennis Young and Stephen Finch, *Foster Care and Nonprofit Agencies* (Lexington, Mass.: D. C. Heath, 1977).

32. M. L. Greenhut, C. S. Hung, G. Norman, and C. W. Smithson, "An Anomaly in the Service Industry: The Effect of Entry on Fees," *Economic Journal* 95 (March 1985): 169–77.

33. Robert Sugden, "Voluntary Organisations and the Welfare State," in Julian Le Grand and Ray Robinson, eds., *Privatisation and the Welfare State* (London: Allen and Unwin 1984).

34. Stephen Hatch and Ian Mocroft, "Relative Costs of Services," p. 404.

35. Martin Knapp, "The Turnover of Care Staff in Children's Homes," *Research Policy and Planning* 3 (November 1985): 19–25.

36. Martin Knapp and Barry Baines, "Hidden Cost Multipliers for Residential Child Care," *Local Government Studies* 13 (July 1987): 53–73.

REFERENCES

Begg, Ian, B. Moore, and J. Rhodes. "The Measurement of Inter-authority Input Cost Differences." Mimeograph. Cambridge: Cambridge Economic Consultants, 1984.

Bendick, Marc. "Privatising the Delivery of Social Welfare Services," Mimeograph. Washington, D.C.: Urban Institute and Bendick and Egan Economic Consultants, Inc., 1985.

Berridge, David. *Children's Homes*. Oxford: Basil Blackwell, 1984.

Darton, Robin, and Martin Knapp. "The Costs of Local Authority Old People's Homes: The Effects of Dependency, Design and Quality of Care." *Ageing and Society* 4 (1984): 157–83.

Davies, Bleddyn, and Martin Knapp. *Old People's Homes and the Production of Welfare*. London: Routledge and Kegan Paul, 1981.

Gilbert, Neil. *Capitalism and the Welfare State*. New Haven, Conn.: Yale University Press, 1983.

Gladstone, Francis. *Voluntary Action in a Changing World*. London: National Council for Social Service, 1979.

Greenhut, M. L., C. S. Hung, G. Norman, and C. W. Smithson. "An Anomaly in the Service Industry: The Effect of Entry on Fees." *Economic Journal* 95 (1985): 169–77.

Hansmann, Henry B. "The Role of Nonprofit Enterprise." *Yale Law Journal* 89 (1980): 835–908.

Hanushek, E. A. "Conceptual and Empirical Issues in the Estimation of Educational Production Functions." *Journal of Human Resources* 14 (1979): 352–88.

Hatch, Stephen, and Ian Mocroft. "The Relative Costs of Services Provided by Voluntary and Statutory Organisations." *Public Administration* 57 (1979): 397–405.

House of Commons Social Services Committee. *Children in Care*. HCP 360, session 1983–1984. London: Her Majesty's Stationery Office, 1984.

Judge, Ken, and Martin Knapp. "Efficiency in the Production of Welfare: The Public and Private Sectors Compared." In *The Future of Welfare*, ed. R. Klein and M. O'Higgins. Oxford: Basil Blackwell, 1985.

Judge, Ken, Martin Knapp, and Jillian Smith. "The Comparative Costs of Public and Private Residential Homes for the Elderly." In Ken Judge and Ian Sinclair, eds., *Residential Care for the Elderly People*. London: Her Majesty's Stationery Office, 1986.

Judge, Ken, and Jillian Smith. "Purchase of Service in England." *Social Service Review* 57 (1983): 209–33.

Knapp, Martin. "Private Children's Homes: An Analysis of Fee Variations and a Comparison with Public Sector Costs." *Policy and Politics* 15 (October 1987): 221–34.

———. "The Relative Cost-effectiveness of Public, Voluntary and Private Providers of Residential Child Care." In Anthony Culyer and Bengt Jönsson, eds. *Public and Private Health Care*. Oxford: Basil Blackwell, 1986).

———. "The Turnover of Care Staff in Children's Homes," *Research, Policy and Planning* 3 (1985): 19–25.

———. *The Economics of Social Care*. London: Macmillan, 1984.

Knapp, Martin, and Barry Baines. "Hidden Cost Multipliers for Residential Child Care," *Local Government Studies* 13 (July 1987): 53–73.

Knapp, Martin, Andrew Fenyo, and Barry Baines. "The Demand for Contracted-out Residential Child Care." Personal Social Services Research Unit Discussion Paper 411. Canterbury: University of Kent, 1986.

Knapp, Martin, Andrew Fenyo, and Barry Baines. "The Demand for Contracted-out Residential Child Care." Personal Social Services Research Unit Discussion Paper 411. Canterbury: University of Kent, 1986.

Knapp, Martin, and Spyros Missiakoulis. "Inter-sectoral Cost Comparisons: Day Care for the Elderly." *Journal of Social Policy* 11 (1982): 335–54.

Knapp, Martin, Julia Montserrat Codorniu, and Robin Darton. "Cross-sector, Cross-country Comparisons: Old People's Homes in Catalunya and England." Personal Social Services Research Unit Discussion Paper 513. Canterbury: University of Kent, 1987.

Knapp, Martin, and Jillian Smith. "The Costs of Residential Child Care: Examining Variations in the Public Sector." *Policy and Politics* 13 (1985): 127–54.

Knapp, Martin, Eileen Robertson, and Corinne Thomason. "Public Money, Voluntary Action: Whose Welfare?" Personal Social Services Research Unit Discussion Paper 514. Canterbury: University of Kent, 1987.

Kramer, Ralph. *Voluntary Agencies in the Welfare State.* Berkeley: University of California Press, 1981.

Millward, Robert, and David Parkin. "Public and Private Enterprise: Comparative Behaviour and Relative Efficiency." In R. Millward, David Parkin, Leslie Rosenthal, Michael Sumner, and Neville Tophen, eds. *Public Sector Economics.* London: Longman, 1983.

Sugden, Robert. "Voluntary Organisations and the Welfare State." In Julian Le Grand and Ray Robinson, eds. *Privatisation and the Welfare State.* London: Allen and Unwin, 1984.

Westland, Peter. "The Year of the Voluntary Organisation." *Community Care* (November 19, 1981): 14–15.

Young, Dennis, and Stephen Finch. *Foster Care and Non-Profit Agencies.* Lexington, Mass.: D. C. Heath, 1976.

9

The Use of Government Funds by Voluntary Social Service Agencies in Four Welfare States

RALPH M. KRAMER

The conventional conception of voluntary agencies—free to choose their own clientele and mode of service and financed mainly by philanthropic contributions—has been drastically altered since the 1960s as they have become more dependent on government funds. As nongovernmental providers of public service, voluntary agencies have become subject to the availability of tax funds and to government rules. This raises questions about their independence and accountability.

In this chapter I study these issues, with particular reference to agencies serving the mentally and physically handicapped. The analysis is based on a sample survey of 20 agencies in each of four countries—the Netherlands, England, Israel, and the United States—carried out during the period 1972–1976 and updated in the Appendix. As will be seen, the trends that were apparent 10 years ago have emerged even more sharply now.

The growing reliance on government funding results from the convergence of (1) the acute financial problems of voluntary agencies caused by a decline in real giving and increases in operating costs, both aggravated by an inflational spiral; (2) the continuing expansion of government social service programs with more funds available for purchase of service from nongovernment providers; (3) a lessened confidence, mainly in the United States, in government administration of social programs. Voluntary agencies are caught in a vicious circle in which declining income from contributions leads to increased dependency on government, which leads to the belief of donors that their support is no longer needed. This new cycle

This chapter is a revised and updated version of Chapter 8 of Ralph Kramer's book, *Voluntary Agencies in the Welfare State* (Berkeley: University of California Press, 1981, pp. 144-170). Copyright © 1981 by The Regents of the University of California. Reprinted by permission.

complements an older one in which a downturn in the economy generally increases the demand for voluntary agency services, while at the same time eroding their revenue base.

Voluntary agencies are used because government cannot meet its ever-growing responsibilities, as in England; because voluntary agencies are the providers of first choice, as in the Netherlands; or for more pragmatic reasons in the United States and Israel, where these agencies can provide an economical, flexible service with little red tape and can serve as a means of avoiding bureaucratic and policy constraints. Other advantages to government are the extension of services without a corresponding increase in staff and investment in facilities and the exporting of undesirable, impractical, or low-priority tasks, particularly those involving highly specialized services to a very small clientele. For voluntary agencies, public funds not only compensate for the loss of contributed income but also enable an agency to greatly enlarge the scope of its services.

Both sectors have something to gain as well as to lose in this exchange. My overall conclusion is that both government and voluntary agencies gain, on balance, from this interaction, which is why it has increased so greatly over the past three decades. I first review briefly the four national fiscal policies on the use of public funds by voluntary agencies and some of the consequences for their respective service patterns. This will provide the background for an analysis of three problems for voluntary agencies: vendorism, grantsmanship, and dependency. As a guide, Table 9.1 summarizes government–voluntary agency service patterns and fiscal policies in the four welfare states.

FOUR NATIONAL FISCAL POLICIES AND THEIR CONSEQUENCES

The Netherlands

The situation in the Netherlands must be placed in the context of the dominating principle of subsidiarity, under which voluntary organizations, usually religious in nature, have priority for the provision of education, health, and social services. Most of the costs, however, are covered by government, through an elaborate subsidy system. Consistent with this approach, subsidies to voluntary agencies serving the physically and the mentally handicapped have been included in the budget of the Ministry of Culture, Recreation, and Social Welfare since 1953, when they were introduced as an experiment. Subsidies for all social services increased a thousandfold between 1952 and 1977, from Df. 1.4 million to Df. 1,209 million in addition to another Df. 500 million from social insurance funds for the social services. (Of the total Df. 1,200 million, a little over one-third, or Df. 383.6 million, was for the handicapped.) The growth in subsidies was part of a general trend in the Netherlands from 1955 to 1971, when the ratio of government expenditures to GNP rose more sharply than in Great

Table 9.1. Government–Voluntary Service Patterns and Public Fiscal Policies

	Service Patterns	Fiscal Policy
United States	Mild preference for voluntary agency as an agent and sometimes as a partner, *complementing* a dominant, governmental system that uses a variety of service providers.	A decentralized, grants economy with over one-third of the governmentally financed personal social services provided by non-profit organizations through purchase of service on a contractual or third-party payment basis.
England	Voluntary agency as a partner (junior or silent), *supplementing*, via gap-filling and substitution, for resource deficiencies in a system of primary statutory responsibility for direct administration of comprehensive, universal, personal social services.	Priority for statutory funding and provision. Very limited grant-aids for voluntary agency administration, with local authority payments for service mainly on a deficit-financing basis.
The Netherlands	Voluntary agencies are the primary service delivery system, based on the principle of *subsidiarity*, with government almost exclusively as financier, having only a residual role in service delivery.	Governmental subsidies for administration and social insurance payments provide for almost 100 percent of the staff and program costs of voluntary agencies.
Israel	High degree of interpenetration of institutional sectors, dominated by central government, with voluntary agencies as *complementary* but not necessarily as the preferred provider.	Limited governmental subsidies and deficit financing for a wide range of services.

Source: Reprinted with small revisions, from "Public Fiscal Policy and Voluntary Agencies in Welfare States," by Ralph M. Kramer, *Social Service Review* 53, no. 1 (March 1979): 4, by permission of The University of Chicago Press. Copyright 1979 by The University of Chicago.

Britain or the United States: the proportion of tax revenue to GNP in Holland was twice that in the United Kingdom, six times that in the United States, and twice the average of six other European countries.

As a result of this fiscal policy, almost all of the staff and program costs of voluntary agencies are paid by subsidies and social insurance payments. For example, of the 20 Dutch agencies included in my sample, 12 received 75 percent of their total income from government sources, including 6 agencies supported by social insurance payments that amounted to 90–100 percent of their budget. Another 4 agencies obtained 40–50 percent of their income from the government. None of the 9 agencies that received one-third or more of their income from social insurance obtained any income at all from contributions.

Subsidies in the Netherlands have produced a tremendous expansion of most of the social services and a rising level of quality, at least as reflected in the increased number of professionals on agency staffs. The ability of subsidies to implement government priorities is illustrated in the doubling of the number of day-care centers for the mentally handicapped and the tripling of the number of people served by them between 1969 and 1972. Although subsidies might appear to be an uncertain source of income because they had no legislative sanction, they provided a stable and progressively larger proportion of agency income. They are more effective for the extension of current, conventional programs than for innovative services, which generally require three to five years of operation before they can be accepted for government support.

To the government, however, two other aspects of the subsidy policy were of greater concern: the decline of volunteer participation in the governance of the agencies as their dependency on subsidies increased and, perhaps more seriously, the runaway costs of expenditures for subsidies. One way of coping with the latter was to include coverage for some of the most expensive programs, such as day-care centers for the mentally handicapped, in the scope of "extraordinary medical expenses" covered by social insurance. Of course, this did not contain costs but merely shifted them. In addition, because of the growing number of small agencies eligible for subsidies since the mid-1960s, there have been mounting government pressures for mergers, "scale enlargement," and more efficient management of voluntary agencies. These two developments will be discussed further in the Appendix.

England

In sharp contrast with the Netherlands, public fiscal policy in England has favored the utilization of the government agencies for both financing and service delivery. Since 1970, this policy has been implemented through the reorganized Social Service Departments in each local authority, which are responsible for an extensive array of personal social services. There is, however, official recognition that the demands for service have outstripped a statutory capacity reduced by the inroads of "stagflation." Under these conditions, voluntary agencies continue to fill gaps, often substituting for government and compensating for the inevitable deficiencies of a system aspiring toward universalism.

Grant-aids for the administration of national voluntary agencies are provided by central government and, although these increased from £19,000,000 in 1974–1975 to £35,400,000 in 1976–1977, they have had a negligible impact on agencies serving the physically and mentally handicapped, which rarely receive or even seek such grants. A more realistic assessment of the role of central government in assisting voluntary agencies is evident in the rather modest increase in funds from the Department of Health and Social Security, which grew only from £1,800,000 to £2,800,000 and was divided among 98 organizations during this two-year period. In addition, £4,600,000 was allocated by the Voluntary Service Unit in the Home Office, of which almost half went to the Women's Royal Voluntary Service.[1] For example, only 1 of the 20 agencies in the sample reported as much as 9 percent of its income from central government, and these grants constituted less than 2 percent of the income of the other 5 agencies receiving such funds. A notable exception was the Spastics Society, which reported a tenfold increase in grants in the decade ending 1974–1975, when they went from £20,000 to £211,000.

Similarly, although grants made by the local authorities to nongovernmental organizations for all the personal social services increased from £2,500,000 in 1972–1973 to £7,900,000 in 1975–1976, these, too, have relatively little significance for most voluntary agencies. The grants consist of small sums, rarely exceeding several thousand pounds each. They are allocated to help relieve the deficits of more than 100 organizations, and usually represent less than 1 percent of the total expenditures of a Social Service Department. Because statutory investment in the agencies is so small, there is little interest in any greater control over them or in integrating them into the statutory service system.

Of greater salience are local governmental payments for service, which rose throughout England and Wales from £45,000,000 to £61,500,00 in the year from 1974–1975 to 1975–1976. Twelve out of the 20 agencies studied received payments for service from local authorities; 7 of the 12 relied on these fees for at least one-third of their income; and 4 obtained over 50 percent of their income from this source. Five agencies obtained from 25 to 50 percent and 3, less than 25 percent of their income from these sources.

These statistics should be viewed in the light of the claim by voluntary agencies that governmental payments usually cover only from two-thirds to three-quarters of real costs and that the difference between this and payments made by the local authority must be subsidized from other income. All but two agencies reported increases during the last ten years in all forms of income, mainly in fees for service from local authority. There is evidence that some voluntary agencies have substantially increased their charges to the local authority and that this may have more than compensated for the increase in consumer prices. For example, a survey conducted by the National Council of Social Service of 64 agencies providing personal social services found a 211 percent increase in income from residential care between 1970 and 1975![2]

Almost all the national agencies receiving payments from local authorities provide specialized forms of residential care to persons with particular handicaps. Local authorities usually buy such services from a voluntary agency because their own facilities are inadequate or because the voluntary agency can provide a service more cheaply. For these reasons, and because relatively few physically handicapped persons require residential care, voluntary rather than statutory institutions serve most of these persons. At the same time, there is often an exchange of funds and other resources in the local community between the Social Service Department and voluntary agencies, in which they tend to make up for each other's deficits.

Israel

As in England, practically any social service in Israel is eligible for some governmental support. Similarly, the reach of the welfare state has exceeded its grasp, and voluntary agencies have filled in many gaps in governmental service programs. Within the social services, income maintenance for large families and the aged has had higher priority than services to the mentally and physically handicapped. The administration of the personal social services by 180 different local welfare offices, as well as the reimbursement formulas used by the national government, have further discouraged the development of new or improved services by the municipalities. Since the 1970s, due largely to persistent pressure from one voluntary agency, additional governmental funds have been allocated for the care of the mentally handicapped.

Although all but 1 of the 15 voluntary agencies studied receive government funds, the amounts are relatively small. Only 1 agency obtains 80 percent of its income from governmental payments for service; another gets over half; and most of the rest receive less than 25 percent.

As in the other countries, the policies of the different departments of central government that allocate funds to voluntary agencies are inconsistent. While the conditions under which funds are made available vary greatly, in Israel government funds are rarely used to raise standards among the voluntary agencies; instead, they are given to make up a deficit. Voluntary agencies are, however, expected to be the major source of innovation, and, consequently, there is a minimal governmental investment in research and development and in planning and coordination on both national and local levels.

The ability of voluntary agencies to "create facts" and then to request governmental support has given them a significant, if not a disproportionate, influence on overall service patterns. While it is not difficult for new agencies to emerge in Israel, once they can demonstrate a service, they can usually expect some governmental support or at least to be bailed out if they flounder. This practice is justified on the pragmatic grounds that auspices do not make much difference in Israel and that it is more important that a needed service be provided.

The United States

While governmental agencies are dominant in the United States, as in England, there is very little support in the United States for the British model of a single, comprehensive, "one-door," public social service center in every community. Instead, there is a strong tendency to separate financing from administration by purchasing services from both nonprofit and profit-making organizations. Over the five-year period from 1971 to 1976, the purchase of social services by government grew from 25 percent to approximately two-thirds of the total expenditures under Title XX of the 1974 Amendments to the Social Security Act. At the same time, public funds constituted a growing proportion of voluntary agency income, averaging about 40 percent.[3]

In the U.S. sample, 7 out of the 20 agencies studied received over half of their income from payments for service and grants from governmental organizations. Five of the agencies had budgets of approximately $1 million, mainly from government funds for service payments. One agency received 10 times as much from governmental fees as from all other funds contributed, and three other agencies quadrupled their income from governmental sources within a three-year period.

The 1967 Amendments to the Social Security Act gave impetus to this trend by providing open-ended, matching grants that made possible the tripling of the value of contributed funds.

The rapid expansion of the social services since the 1960s, the loss of confidence in governmental capacity for implementation, and the preference for nongovernmental agencies has attracted new kinds of providers, particularly proprietary ones, so that the service system has become more complex. Such legislation as Title XX amending the Social Security Act in 1974 broadened the boundaries of eligibility and made it possible for government to purchase personal social services for a larger number of middle-class clients, who have traditionally been served by voluntary agencies. In addition to these service payments, a policy of "guided innovation," fueled by a grants economy, has been a source of government funds for agencies operating demonstration projects. These trends have led to governmental demands for greater efficiency, accountability, and service integration. They are reflected in the growing assumption of social planning responsibilities by local governments.[4]

To survive in the turbulent, competitive, and uncertain era of "private federalism," voluntary agencies in the United States have had to become more opportunistic, entrepreneurial, and political than their counterparts in the other countries. Operating in a context of policy direction and financial support by government, many voluntary agencies are experiencing an identity crisis and have expressed grave concern over their dependency and their future role, particularly in an era of cutbacks in public spending.

Table 9.2 summarizes the percentage of voluntary agency income from governmental sources in each country.

THREE ISSUES IN THE USE OF GOVERNMENT FUNDS BY VOLUNTARY AGENCIES

The increased reliance of voluntary agencies on public funds has generated a wide range of stresses on their fiscal resource systems. Three problems resulting from such stresses are most evident in the United States, although

Table 9.2. Percentage of Voluntary Agency Income from Government Funds, 1973–1974

	United States (N = 20)	England (N = 20)	The Netherlands (N = 20)	Israel (N = 15)
None	5	8	2	1
Under 32	5	7	1	9
33–65	5	4	4	3
66–99	4	1	6	2
100	1	0	7	0
Mean	33	22	75	27

they are present in varying degree in the other countries: vendorism, grantsmanship, and dependency.

Vendorism

As vendors, voluntary agencies sell social services to government for an agreed-upon price, usually on a unit-cost basis. Three fiscal dilemmas facing a voluntary agency stem from the gap between actual costs and the price paid by government for the provision of such services as day care, counseling, rehabilitation, and residential or home care. First, if the agency does not receive full reimbursement, then it must make up a deficit. Second, if it does charge the full cost, then the rate of reimbursement may be sufficient to attract competing profit-making organizations. Finally, unless there is some cost advantage, government may decide to operate the program itself.

If voluntary agencies are not reimbursed for their full costs—which is almost always the case in England as well as in the United States—they subsidize government and must seek additional funds to cover the deficit. Often it is not clear who is subsidizing whom because voluntary agencies invariably claim that government does not pay the full cost of care as they compute it.[5] In England, it is expected that, because voluntary agencies are charities, they will charge less than their actual cost and that they will make up the difference by seeking contributions from the public. In the 1960s, local authorities were urged by the central government to reimburse voluntary agencies up to 75 percent of their costs, but this was seldom done. Several Social Service Departments observed that a number of voluntary agencies "acted like a charity" and did not even request specific rates for reimbursement. Instead, they approached the local authority informally with the modest request "pay us what you can." Other agencies expressed their belief in the priority of voluntarism, which they consider to be charity, by describing their function in terms that could be paraphrased as follows: "We make services available to the handicapped, but, unfortunately, they are very expensive and we cannot pay the whole cost. The SSD helps us because we happen to be out-of-pocket."

Some voluntary agencies, such as the Spastics Society, charge only from 60 to 80 percent of their costs in the belief that their independence would be endangered if they were reimbursed in full. In Israel, also, several agencies make a virtue out of necessity and give a concern for autonomy as their reason for not receiving full payment.

In England and the United States and to a lesser extent, in Israel, determination of rates for reimbursement of costs on a per capita or unit basis is usually a matter of bargaining between buyer and seller. Through informal or formal consultation or, in the United States, through lobbying, voluntary agencies can influence the rate schedules. In England, each Social Service Department sets its own rates for payments to voluntary agencies, although there is some standardization in the Greater London area. In the Netherlands, voluntary agencies participate in rate setting through membership in the body that sets the rates for reimbursement under the social insurance system.

In the United States, maximum cost policies for reimbursement are sometimes established on a state or regional basis. These policies result in inequities when an agency cannot provide needed services because allowable costs have been set at an unrealistically low level. The Golden Gate Regional Center in San Francisco, although incorporated as a nonprofit organization, receives all of its funds from the California State Department of Health, whose rigid spending limits on care for the mentally handicapped often make it practically impossible to provide required services. Many problems stemming from the differences between rates allowed by government and the actual costs of voluntary agency services are due to differences in accounting practices and to the administrative complexities of the eight possible payment mechanisms and eleven different variables that enter into rate determination.[6]

A second dilemma occurs if voluntary agencies charge rates that are closer to their actual costs because then competitive, proprietary, or only nominally nonprofit organizations may be attracted to the market. This occurred in the United States and the Netherlands, where social insurance, third-party payments, and vouchers became available when the personal social services were defined as extensions of medical care. The Netherlands' system of third-party payments and social insurance has resulted in what many officials believe is an excess capacity in residential care. In the United States, where proprietary organizations were active mainly in residential care, the availability of government funds has encouraged their entry into the fields of day care, home medical care, vocational rehabilitation, and counseling.[7]

A third dilemma occurs when there is no cost advantage at all to the government in using a voluntary agency. Then, as in England, the local authority can decide to operate a program itself. In addition to pricing themselves out of the market, another threat facing voluntary agencies as vendors is that, as their services became larger in scale, standardized, routine, and organized on a bureaucratic basis, a public agency is more likely to want to take over and administer a program directly, particularly if there is no cost advantage in retaining the voluntary agency. In England, the volunteer meals-on-wheels programs were taken over by some local authorities when the programs became so extensive that they could no longer be run efficiently and reliably by volunteers.

The prospect of such takeovers is, however, not a real one in the Netherlands, where there is little sanction for direct governmental provision. Nor are takeovers likely to occur in Israel, where there are strong budgetary and political constraints on the expansion of any ministry's domain.[8]

Apart from the problems connected with rate determination, some other organizational costs of vendorism that were reported are: long delays in receiving funds from government, which often work to the disadvantage of small agencies that lack sufficient cash reserves to carry them until reimbursed and that are not usually in a position to borrow such funds; uncertainties regarding future funding, as well as the ever-present threat of loss of funding; the red tape involved in complying with recording and reporting requirements; and the diminishing interest of board members and volunteers as government becomes more and more responsible for an agency's income.

Grantsmanship

Grants from governmental agencies or private foundations for specific programs are another source of income for voluntary agencies, in addition to payments for services they provide to designated individuals. Grantsmanship, the know-how required to obtain time-limited funds for a special purpose—research, demonstration, facility construction, or a service program for a particular clientele—has become a fiscal way of life for most public-service organizations in the United States. As a result, governmental and voluntary agencies are becoming more like each other because of their dependency on a grants economy with multiple funding sources in the "banker" state and federal government, as well as in private foundations.[9]

One of the major disadvantages of relying on grants, or "soft money," reported by U.S. agency executives is uncertainty. The vagaries of governmental funding, the frequent policy and regulation changes, legislative shifts, the threat of cutbacks, and the annual struggle over budgets all contribute to recurrent financial crises and a perennial state of insecurity in which program continuity is perpetually in doubt. This is particularly true when governmental spending is under attack and is being reduced.

Another frequently voiced criticism is that the requirements for preparing proposals for funding and for complying with different and changing governmental procedures and regulations consume an excessive amount of staff time and that, by increasing the costs of organizational maintenance, they can deflect resources from the service delivery mission of the agency. The hidden costs of grantsmanship are thus similar to those of vendorism except that there may be an even more disproportionate investment in administrative over program costs.

Finally, reliance on single, categorical, time-limited grants in the United States is also believed to contribute to fragmentation and lack of coordination in the social services. In both the United States and the Netherlands, efforts have been made to involve local government in social planning for the first time as a means of promoting more service coordination.[10] There is little interest in this type of social planning in England, where additional governmental funding is being sought for local councils that would primarily be concerned with strengthening the voluntary sector, rather than with coordinating statutory and voluntary organizations. Similarly, in Israel there is little governmental concern for local social planning, although there have been several demonstration projects over the last decade.

Dependency

In the United States and, to a lesser extent, in England, the rapid acceleration in public funding of voluntary agencies has stirred the fear that their historical, indispensable independence may be lost. A typical expression of this is the following:

Volunteerism is in danger of obliteration . . . the services rendered by voluntary agencies are being displaced, changed, destroyed by the influx of government funds, which in turn demands accountability and adherence to regulations which are unreasonable and unmanageable . . . voluntary agencies, by accepting government funds, participate in a process that will unavoidably lead them to disappear.[11]

The new alliance between voluntarism and vendorism in the United States has raised with new sharpness the old question: What is voluntary about an agency that receives most of its income from tax funds?[12] However, the findings of this study suggest that, posed in this way, the query is somewhat simplistic in its assumption that government funds inherently corrupt, co-opt, or constrain. An African proverb says that "if you have your hand in another man's pocket, you must move when he moves." Little evidence was found in any of the countries to support this belief. The executive leadership of the agencies reported few instances of unacceptable governmental requirements imposed on their service programs, governance, or administration. Nor did governmental funding seem to inhibit advocacy. This is not to say that there were no complaints about red tape or about the burdens of complying with an excessive number of regulations. These were, however, found almost exclusively in the United States, where there is a much greater emphasis on reporting and accountability, as well as more concern with the preservation of independence than in the other countries.

Paradoxically, ideological objections to "control by government" and preference for voluntary funding were expressed in England more often than in the United States. They were rarely expressed in Israel, where the

Israel Cancer Association is the only agency that does not accept directly any government funds for its program on ideological grounds.[13] It was puzzling to find this belief about the corrupting influence of government funds in England, where voluntary agencies receive relatively small amounts of statutory funds and where there are far fewer regulations than in the United States. However, organizations that receive more than 50 percent of their income from central government must conform to governmental salary standards, may not locate their offices in central London, and must submit audited accounts and occasional reports. The perpetuation by voluntary agencies of the spectre of government encroachment by the use of an antibureaucratic, laissez-faire ideology and other "scare" tactics may be a political strategy to strengthen their claim on their respective domains and to win support from those opposed to governmental intervention.

That invoking the threat of governmental control over agency autonomy may be more ideological than real is also suggested by the continuing and unrestrained efforts of voluntary agencies in all four countries to secure more government funds. This was notable in England, where greater statutory funding for the voluntary sector was the principal recommendation of the Wolfenden Committee, which also reported that ". . . in general the amount of influence or control exercised by departments over voluntary organizations to which grants are made is remarkably small."[14]

Evidently, voluntary agencies in other countries have learned that they can have their cake and eat it, too. In the Netherlands, where there is the greatest dependency on governmental financing, voluntary agencies have even fewer constraints on their operations than do their counterparts in England and the United States. While it is not necessary to agree completely with Sidney Hook that "the increasing state control of the economy in democratic countries has not resulted in the progressive diminution of freedoms in political and cultural life,"[15] supporting evidence in the United States and Canada suggests that the impact of government funds in controlling voluntary social service organizations may be much less than is commonly believed.[16]

What might account for this finding in all four countries, which seems so contrary to the conventional wisdom that he who pays the piper calls the tune? Perhaps

he who calls the tune [is] tone-deaf. That is, those who dispense funds may not have complete information, nor are they always rational and consistent. They may hold values that encourage them to react . . . in other than utilitarian terms. In addition and most important, funders are subject to the pressures of conflicting interests and reference groups.[17]

Among the external factors that appear to reduce the constraining effect of government funds on agency autonomy are the following: (1) the payment-for-service form of most transactions, (2) the diversity of income sources, (3) the countervailing power of a service monopoly and a voluntary agency's political influence, (4) low accountability due to the trade-offs in a mutual-dependency relationship.

The most frequent form of financial transaction between government and voluntary agencies is payment or reimbursement for a service provided by a voluntary agency to an individual for whom there is a public responsibility. Such arrangements generally involve fewer measures of control than grants or subsidies and are therefore less likely to weaken autonomy. In England and Israel, government payments are perceived by both parties to be a businesslike way of making up operating deficits. Although governmental payments for services provided by voluntary agencies contain the risks of vendorism cited earlier, the interorganizational relationship is generally perceived by both parties as essentially an exchange, a quid pro quo transaction rather than a threat to agency independence. When, as is most often the case in the United States, arrangements are formalized in a contract or written agreement—itself the product of a bargaining process—the rights and obligations of both parties are made explicit, including that of cancellation.

The agencies that depended on government for more than 40 percent of their income—from 20 to 25 percent of the sample in each country with the exception of the Netherlands—almost invariably received this income from a variety of public as well as voluntary sources. Although the proportion of an agency budget that can be obtained from any single source without adversely affecting the organization is a matter of dispute, there is considerable agreement on the importance of income diversity as a means of avoiding overdependency. This was not the case in the Netherlands, where all but eight of the agencies receiving government funds obtain them from only one government source; yet Dutch agencies have the greatest amount of freedom. In addition, the Dutch agencies receiving funds from several governmental agencies expressed their preference for obtaining them from only one!

There is, however, another side to diversity: while multiple funding sources may contribute to autonomy, some hidden administrative costs reported in the United States are the conflicting requirements of different regulations, standards of reporting and accounting, budget deadlines, standards of evaluation, and recording.

Also aiding independence is the distribution of power between governmental and voluntary organizations, including the strong resources for influence in the voluntary agencies' virtual monopoly of services required by government, as well as their ability to apply political pressure. In all four countries, the voluntary agency typically has a scarce, appropriate resource required by government for clients who have a "right" to the service. Government is often in the position of having authority and responsibility but lacking expertise, staff, facilities, and other necessary resources for service delivery. Having found a voluntary agency willing and able to provide the service, government officials are usually content to leave well enough alone because of their dependency on the agency.

The clearest example of a distribution of political power that favors the voluntary sector is in the Netherlands, where most of the agencies are connected with religious–political blocs. Because they have the support of the denominational political parties that are part of the coalition controlling the central government, voluntary agencies are well-protected against unacceptable bureaucratic demands.

Contrary to the belief that organizations might be afraid to bite the hand that feeds them, the most active advocates in the United States are among the agencies receiving the highest percentage of government funds, although the line between advocacy and self-interest in such instances is very thin. Reliance on tax funds in the United States requires continual monitoring of and involvement in the political process as part of the annual struggle for appropriations and the fight against cutbacks. Where voluntary agencies form an ad hoc coalition or are part of federations that negotiate with the government, as in the Netherlands and the United States, they are a formidable force with which government has to contend, often putting it on the defensive. This is particularly true of organizations serving the blind and the mentally handicapped.

Perhaps the most noteworthy condition mitigating any substantial challenge to the freedom of the voluntary agency is the low level of accountability demanded by government. This is epitomized in the candid statement of one government official who said: "If we knew more, we'd have to pay more."

Two principal forms of accountability are found mainly in the United States: fiscal and service reporting requirements and public policy restrictions on programs. Although extensive record keeping and burdensome reporting requirements were the most frequent complaints among voluntary agencies receiving public funds in the United States—in addition to the perennial objections to inadequate rates of reimbursement—they are not perceived as necessarily or even significantly impairing agencies' freedom. In several instances, United Way requirements in the United States were regarded as more unacceptable. Even in the United States, where there are governmental specifications regarding eligible clientele, staffing, and board representation for certain services,[18] these, too, were not generally viewed as a serious threat to independence, either because they were considered a legitimate and small price to pay for benefits, or because monitoring was insufficient to ensure compliance. Generally, agencies did what they always wanted to do, but for which they previously lacked the means. The use of public funds represented for virtually all of them an opportunity to be seized and enabled them to enlarge the scope of their services as much as tenfold.[19]

A question arises, however. Why was there such a low level of accountability and so little effort to control or regulate these vendors in the four countries? For example, governmental representatives were rarely found on the boards of directors except in Israel; when they were present in other countries, it was clear that they were serving in an unofficial capacity. Reporting requirements were ignored with impunity; one Dutch agency claimed that it had not submitted an annual financial statement for 4 years, yet its subsidy was continued.

Apparently the government bureaucrats in these countries lack the incentive and capacity for requiring stricter forms of accountability.[20] Although government officials complained about their lack of control over costs, the unevenness of voluntary agency services, and the difficulties of coordination, they are nevertheless dependent on what is in most cases a monopoly on service delivery. Also, governmental agencies lack sufficient personnel for close monitoring; in the Netherlands this would be a staggering task because of the almost 3000 agencies that would have to be inspected. The close links between agency sponsors and political parties also discourage a more assertive effort on the part of government supervisors.

In England, the Netherlands, and Israel, one by-product of mutual dependency is a network of informal, "cozy" relationships between the executive leadership of the voluntary agencies and government officials, among persons who share the same professional and administrative subcultures and who believe in live and let live. This condition has been described as "bureaucratic symbiosis"—i.e., a mutual cooptation in which both parties recognize their interdependency and are careful not to disturb it.

From the standpoint of government, the use of voluntary agencies is a pragmatic policy and is rarely justified on ideological grounds. Most voluntary agency services in these countries are, in fact, less expensive than the same services provided by a governmental unit required to conform to civil service regulations. In Israel, it is easier for the Ministry of Social Welfare to obtain funds from the Treasury for service payments than to expand its own staff. Apart from economic advantages, there are organizational benefits to governmental agencies; they can obtain the loyalty of a constituency, extend their domain at a low cost, and, by showing that something is being done about a problem, sustain an impression of governmental responsibility and concern. For the voluntary agency, apart from helping to extend services, government funds constitute a means of access to government and an opportunity to influence public policy. However, once "addicted" to government funds, voluntary agencies are not likely to revert to soliciting contributions. Indeed, it seems reasonably clear that existing levels of services can no longer be sustained without tax funds.

Table 9.3 summarizes the principal advantages and disadvantages of the use of public funds by voluntary agencies.

CONCLUSIONS

These findings illustrate the principle that the degree of governmental constraint may be a function of the method or form of financing.[21] It ob-

Table 9.3. Principal Advantages and Disadvantage of the Use of Public Funds by Voluntary Agencies

Advantages to Voluntary Agencies	Advantages to Governmental Agencies	Disadvantages to Voluntary Agencies	Disadvantages to Governmental Agencies
Enlargement of scope of services; community utilization of specialized resources	More economical service	Inadequate rates of reimbursement Uncertainty of income; delays in cash flow	Lack of sufficient control over costs Unevenness of service delivery
Greater security of income	Extension of service without corresponding visibility or high fixed costs	Red tape; excessive recording; reporting; and compliance with multiple, changing standards	Difficulties in maintaining standards and accountability
Release of other funds for more particularistic purposes	Greater flexibility and responsiveness; easier to serve hard-to-reach groups; easier to initiate and to terminate funding		
Increased community status, prestige, and visibility	Bypass of bureaucratic and political constraints	Undesirable restrictions on service policies and on administration and governance	Fragmentation and less coherent social policy; weakened authority of government and chances of coordination
Access to governmental decision making	Transfer of unwanted tasks	Possible diminution in organizational autonomy, advocacy, and volunteer participation	Possible deterrent to assumption of governmental responsibility
	Gain of a supporting constituency or source of leverage to influence voluntary agency service standards Image of responsibility and cooperation	Becoming more bureaucratic and entrepreneurial; goal-deflection	

viously makes a difference whether government funds are intended as a loan, a grant, a subsidy, or a payment, and whether they are for purposes of building construction, research, and demonstration, or reimbursement for services to persons who are entitled to them. Payments for service generally involve fewer measures of control and are less likely to threaten autonomy. Accordingly, there is a range of potential control by government tied to different modes of funding, with grants at the top of the list, vouchers at the bottom, and service payments in the middle:

Categorical grants
Subsidies
Payments for service
Contracts for purchase of service
Third-party payments for service
Vouchers

While purchase of service requires a voluntary agency to channel its services into what the government defines as reimbursable, there is generally room for negotiation over respective interests. This is why contracts for purchase of service are increasingly regarded as one of the best means for balancing the value of a voluntary agency's independence and the government's need for accountability. Through a bargaining process, mutual expectations can be worked out, and each side has a better idea of what will be expected and required.[22] If a voluntary agency regards the conditions for government funds as unacceptable, it has the choice not to undertake the role of a vendor. As we have seen, the balance of power tends to favor the voluntary agency because of its usual service monopoly.

Another factor affecting the possibility of governmental control is the type of service to be purchased from a voluntary agency and the extent to which performance standards can be specified and monitored. While contracts that specify outcomes can be a major instrument of accountability that can help government stay out of the internal operations of voluntary agencies and avoid infringing on the authority of the management, these service outcomes are often very difficult to define and to measure.[23] For example, it makes a difference whether the service purchased involves meals, medical or nursing care, day treatment, residential care, education or training, community organization, or counseling. These services vary greatly in the degree to which performance criteria and outcomes can be specified. This is why outputs—i.e., activities that easily lend themselves to quantification, such as the number of interviews, meals served, and hospital days— are usually substituted for outcomes. This practice contributes to charges of interference and overregulation stemming from excessive governmental reporting requirements.

Demands for information can be a particular problem for a small voluntary agency because it lacks the administrative resources to comply without seriously cutting into its service capability. A New York City study showed that small voluntary agencies spend proportionately more money to support their governmental programs than do large and medium-size agencies.[24] The fact that purchase of service arrangements may be more disadvantageous to a small agency is ironic because small size, flexibility, and informality are supposed to be the advantages of a voluntary organization

when compared with a government bureaucracy. The virtues that make
the voluntary agency a valuable resource for government are at the same
time the source of conditions that militate against its complying with the
demands of accountability—to compete successfully and to comply with
governmental regulations, the small agency must become more bureaucratic and must lose the very qualities that made it a desirable service
provider.

In addition to the dangers of bureaucratization, which are a particular
concern of small agencies, there is a further fear that the voluntary agency,
as it becomes more preoccupied with efficiency and cost-effectiveness, will
inevitably become more like the profit-making organizations with which it
must compete. The growing entrepreneurism in the social services is regarded with concern by many government officials and social work professionals, who are inherently suspicious of the profit motive and deplore its
growing incursions into a field long dominated by charitable organizations.[25] However, there could be advantages in attracting profit-making
organizations to the social services. These organizations would introduce
choice into an area long characterized by scarcity and voluntary agency
monopoly. Competition might even have the effect of raising standards or
of strengthening the government's resolve to require compliance to higher
standards. The latter, though, could lead to stronger regulatory mechanisms that, if effective, might reduce the independence of voluntary organizations and encourage adversarial relationships between government and
social service providers similar to those found in other fields dependent on
government funds.[26] Another possibility is that because of governmental
deficiencies in monitoring the more subtle and indirect aspects of the social
services, there will be a tendency to simplify and to reduce standards to
quantifiable terms, and that voluntary agencies will be judged by profit-
making criteria.

Finally, there is no agreement on the proportion of an agency's budget
that can come from a single source without dominating the organization.
Although some voluntary agency executives believe that an agency should
not depend on any one source for more than 50 percent of its income, no
evidence proves that this or any other percentage is an effective guideline
for the acceptance of public funds or the preservation of autonomy.[27] There
is, however, consensus on the importance of income diversity as a means
of avoiding overdependency. To put it conversely, although no organization is really "autonomous," the extent of independence is a function of
multiple sources of financing; the lesser the dependency on any single source,
whether voluntary or governmental, the greater the degree of freedom and
choice and the possibility that an agency can influence its own destiny with
a greater degree of discretion. As the Filer Commission observed:

Perhaps the most effective, and most possible, safeguard of autonomy is to have
more than one purse to draw from. The presence of a firm core of private support,
however small, in a private organization that gets major public funding can be of

crucial importance in determining whether the managers of the organization regard themselves and behave as independent operators or as civil servants.[28]

Although income diversity may be good for a voluntary agency, it constitutes a formidable obstacle to efforts to coordinate agencies funded by a multiplicity of governmental agencies, foundations, and other private sources. Reliance by voluntary agencies on time-limited, categorical grants further aggravates the fragmentation, which continues to defy most governmentally sponsored efforts at service integration in the local community. Government grants might appear to be a way in which the voluntary sector could be influenced to develop a more integrated, comprehensive system to counteract that natural fragmentation that results from each agency going its own way. But this assumes a degree of intragovernmental collaboration and planning that does not often occur. Indeed, the lack of consistency and communication among governmental agencies and their conflicting policies and standards constitute one of the most serious administrative problems for voluntary agencies. Perhaps this is part of the price of pluralism and may necessitate lowered expectations about a more coherent service system.

APPENDIX

In the eight years since this chapter first appeared, the utilization of voluntary agencies to implement public policy has not only continued, but each of the four countries saw substantial increases in the income that voluntary agencies received from government in the form of purchases of service, grants, or subsidies.

Although cutbacks in government expenditures for the social services have contributed to the belief that the welfare state was being dismantled, closer inspection of the evidence rather than the rhetoric reveals that, although some growth rates have slowed, the impact on selected programs shows considerable unevenness.[29] There has been an even stronger trend to separate government funding from service delivery and a more extensive use of contracting out and similar procedures as part of the greater utilization of nongovernment organizations.

Regrettably, no new international comparative surveys of the personal social services have been undertaken, but a secondary analysis of extensive data collected in England and the United States, together with more recent information from Israel and the Netherlands can update the trends described during the preceding decade. In the United States, more than in any of the other three countries, voluntary agencies found themselves competing for government funds with other nongovernment agencies, particularly, profit-making organizations.[30] In the process, many nonprofit organizations have become more entrepreneurial in seeking to replace government grants that have been reduced or eliminated.[31] Because nonprofit voluntary organizations and profit-making organizations draw from the same government sources, comply with the same regulations, employ the same type of staff, and utilize similar service technologies, their organizational character has become increasingly similar; that is, more bureaucratic, professional, political, and entrepreneurial. As a result many voluntary agencies have had to confront the goal-deflection tendencies of both vendorism and entrepreneurialism.[32]

As evidence of the mixed economy for providing social services, it is estimated that in the United States the government now delivers about 40 percent of the personal social services, nonprofit organizations another 40 percent and the profit-making sector, the remaining 20 percent.[33] Yet, the use of the concept of "sectors" is somewhat misleading because of the continuing interpenetration of funds and functions, the obscuring of internal diversity, the external convergence of organizational character, and the finding that *intra*sectoral differences in cost effectiveness are greater than intersectoral differences.[34] This evidence reinforces the belief that the auspices of an agency, i.e., the form of legal ownership, may be less significant than organizational variables such a size, age, complexity, degree of bureaucratization and professionalization, type of technology, executive leadership, etc.

In the United States, for the first time, national data on the income sources of the nonprofit sector has been collected by the Urban Institute during the years 1981–1984.[35] Based on a carefully selected sample of over 3400 nonprofit organizations in 16 communities, two-thirds of which were in the social services, government support was found to be the largest single source of revenue for the average nonprofit organization, amounting to more than the total of all other contributed income. Despite federal government cutbacks in certain social services expenditures in the United States beginning in 1981, most voluntary agencies were able to compensate for their losses in government income by increasing fees and obtaining revenue from other state and county agencies, from foundations as well as their own entrepreneurial activities. Indeed, in the San Francisco Bay area, with but a few exceptions, the income of the agencies originally studied continued to rise incrementally year after year. It should be noted, however, that the extent of dependency on government funds by voluntary agencies varies enormously depending on their particular field of service. For example. United Way agency services to the elderly received on average over 70 percent of their income from the government in 1980, whereas agencies serving crippled children and adults averaged 36 percent.[36] Apart from the degree of fiscal dependency on the government, agencies also vary according to their ability to replace lost income and, in general, older, larger, multipurpose organizations in the "right" field of service who had executives with entrepreneurial, political, and managerial skills did much better.

In England, a comprehensive review of research during the last decade on the use of the voluntary sector by government was undertaken by Martin Knapp and his associates at the Personal Social Service Research Unit, University of Kent at Canterbury.[37] Their analysis showed actual growth, not cutbacks, in the voluntary social services. For example, grants from the Department of Health and Social Services to voluntary organizations increased more than 10-fold from 1976–1977 to 1985–1986, an increase from £2.8 million to £32 million. Actual grants during this period from all branches of the central government to all voluntary organizations increased almost 13 percent, and in 1984–1985, total public sector support on all levels to the voluntary sector was over £2 billion.

On a more restricted basis, by 1983–1984 local authority and health authority support of the personal social services had reached a total of almost £161 million and the following year it increased to over £169 million.

Other studies using broader definitions of the voluntary sector, show a 50 percent increase in grants from statutory bodies from 1975–1976 to 1980–1981 and an overall growth of 38 percent in the total revenue of voluntary organizations.[38] This expansion occurred before the election of the Thatcher government, which then proceeded to enlarge further the amount and scope of statutory funds made available to voluntary agencies.

To the extent that it could be determined in any of the four countries, no research found significant evidence that the autonomy or the mission of the voluntary agencies receiving government funds had been seriously impaired by accompanying controls, although regulations may have influenced how they carried out their functions.[39]

Similarly, in Israel the income of the voluntary agencies included in the original study continued to increase year by year, so that by 1982 it was double what it had been a decade earlier in real terms.[40] Increased government revenue accounted for the expansion of two agencies, which had the greatest growth in income and staff; one increased its income 12-fold over a 10-year period ending in 1982 and quadrupled its staff. The revenue of another agency and its staff also increased eightfold. The other organizations, although still dependent on the government for a substantial part of their income, actually increased their revenue proportionately more—from three- to five-fold—by greater productivity in their fund raising in Israel and abroad. This was accomplished during one of the most turbulent decades in the history of Israel, which included two wars, a peace treaty with Egypt, and a change of political regime after 38 years in office. At the same time, there were persistent complaints, typical of agencies depending on government funds, of cash-flow delays that, in an inflation-ridden economy would erode the value of payments by one-third over a three-month period, of deficits incurred because of inadequate payments or delays in the establishment of rates.

In the Netherland, efforts to impose greater government control over the voluntary agencies continued at a slow pace and culminated in the 1981 Framework Law that provided a firmer legal base for the government's social welfare activities, as well as the potential for greater Parliamentary oversight. Scheduled for implementation in 1985, together with the Welfare Law of 1984, additional resources were given to local municipalities to provide social services directly and not rely exclusively on nongovernment organizations.[41] Expenditure cuts in social service budgets by the national government, however, reduced the incentive for municipalities to take a more active role in direct provision of the social services.

Until 1981, some social services were transferred from the subsidy to the social insurance system, but this process was discontinued when it became evident that government had even less control over insurance payments than over subsidies. A trend toward mergers continued as voluntary agencies responded to government pressure for more economies of scale resulting in increasing divisions along functional rather than religious-political lines.

In all four countries the policy of using multiple providers for the distribution of social services had two major consequences. First, from the standpoint of the service delivery system, separation of public financing from delivery meant even greater fragmentation and fewer possibilities for planning and continuity. It also made accountability and access more complex and elusive. To the degree that nongovernment organizations—profit-making or nonprofit—are favored, equity, coverage, and entitlement are even more difficult to promote. Such a policy may encourage "creaming," greater selectivity, and the possibility for a more social class–stratified service delivery system, particularly where there is a large government social service sector.[42]

For the government agency, the greater use of voluntary organizations can result in the gradual transformation of its organizational functions, character, and structure. This has been advocated in England, where the "enabling" role would mean that instead of service delivery, the government would be primarily responsible for licensing, setting standards, determining eligibility, and providing information, referral, and case management, including monitoring and evaluating. Apart from having to overcome the traditional opposition of civil service unions, these roles are usually not perceived favorably by most staff members, who have not been prepared for such responsibilities and who would require extensive retraining.

What is clearly evident is that we have not yet developed the appropriate concepts, models, paradigms and theories to reflect this new reality of the mixed economy of welfare. Assuming that nongovernment organizations will continue to be used to implement public policy, it is essential to learn much more about how this process actually functions and how to make it work better.[43] Future research agendas should therefore give more attention to international comparisons and the analysis of the political economy of purchase of service, as well as the consequences of various strategies of dealing with the interdependency among government agencies and their public service providers.

NOTES

1. Judith Unell, *Voluntary Social Services: Financial Resources* (London: Bedford Square Press of the National Council of Social Service, 1979), p. 9; and Wolfenden Committee, *The Future of Voluntary Organisations* (London: Croom Helm, 1978), pp. 219–230.

2. Judith Unell, ibid., p. 9.

3. Candace P. Mueller, "Purchase of Service Contracting from the Viewpoint of the Provider," in *Proceedings of the National Institute on Purchase of Service Contracting: Child and Family Services,* ed. Kenneth R. Wedel, Arthur J. Katz, and Ann Weick (Lawrence: University of Kansas, School of Social Welfare, 1978), p. 30.

4. Richard S. Bolan, "Social Planning and Policy Development: Local Government," in *Managing Human Services,* ed. Wayne F. Anderson, Bernard J. Frieden, and Michael J. Murphy (Washington, D.C.: International City Management Association, 1977), pp. 85–127.

5. A study of voluntary agency programs in New York City found an average differential of 16 percent between actual agency costs and government reimbursements, resulting in voluntary agencies "subsidizing" the governmentally funded child welfare programs with an additional $48 million. See Greater New York Fund, *Impact of Government Funding on the Management of Voluntary Agencies* (New York: Greater New York Fund/United Way, 1978), p. 10. See also Robert M. Rice, "Impact of Government Contracts on Voluntary Social Agencies," *Social Casework* (1975): 387–95; and William G. Hill, "Voluntary and Governmental Financial Transactions," *Social Casework* (1971): 356–61.

6. Norman V. Lourie, "Purchase of Service Contracting: Issues Confronting Governmental Sponsored Agencies," in *Proceedings of the National Institute,* ed. Kenneth Wedel et al., p. 22. The complexities of rate determination are also discussed in Gordon Manser, "Further Thoughts on Purchase of Service," *Social Casework 55* (1974): 421–34; and Ralph M. Kramer, "Voluntary Agencies and the Use of Public Funds: Some Policy Issues," *Social Service Review* (1966): 15–26.

7. A highly critical view of the role of profit-making organizations is found in Dan Rubenstein, R. E. Mundy, and May L. Rubinstein, "Proprietary Social Services," in *Social Welfare Forum, 1978* (New York: Columbia University Press, 1979), pp. 120–40. An opposing view is H. G. Whittington, "A Case for Private Funding in Mental Health," *Administration in Mental Health* (1975): 23–28. See also Donald Fisk, Herbert Kiesling, and Thomas Mullen, *Private Provision of Public Services: An Overview* (Washington, D.C.: Urban Institute, 1978).

8. Ralph M. Kramer, *The Voluntary Service Agency in Israel* (Berkeley: University of California, Institute of International Studies, 1976), pp. 18–19.

9. Edward K. Hamilton, "On Non-constitutional Management of a Constitutional Problem," *Daedalus* (1978): 111–28.

10. See Robert Agranoff, "Services Integration," in *Managing Human Services,* ed. Wayne F. Anderson, Bernard J. Frieden, and Michael J. Murphy (Washington, D.C.: International City Management Association, 1977), pp. 527–64; and Sheldon P. Gans and G. T. Horton, *Integration of Human Services: The State and Municipal Levels* (New York: Praeger, 1975).

11. Greater New York Fund, *Impact of Government Funding, p. 6.* An eloquent and widely reprinted statement of this view is Alan Pifer, "The Quasi Non-governmental Organization," in *1967 Annual Report of the Carenegie Corporation of New York* (New York: Carnegie Corporation, 1967).

12. Typical of many similar expressions of concern over the impact of government funds on voluntary agency independence are Benjamin A. G. Jenvick, "The Voluntary Agency and the Purchase of Social Services," in *Social Work Practice, 1971* (New York: Columbia University Press, 1971), pp. 152–59; and Elizabeth Wickenden, "Purchase of Care and Services: Effect on Voluntary Agencies," in *Proceedings of the First Milwaukee Institute on a Social Welfare Issue of the Day: Purchase of Care and Services in the Health and Welfare Fields,* ed. Iris Winogrond (Milwaukee: University of Wisconsin, 1970), pp. 40–58. One of the few

dissents from the popular belief is found in a critique of the Filer Report by the Donee Group, which states: "[The commission's] fear of governmental interference is undocumented. It falsely pervades the recommendations and minimizes vouchers and matching grants." (The Donee Group Report and Recommendations, "Private Philanthropy: Vital and Innovative? or Passive and Irrelevant?" in *Research papers Sponsored by the Commission on Private Philanthropy and Public Needs*, Vol. 1 [Washington, D.C.: Department of the Treasury, 1977], pp. 49–88).

13. Vehement ideological objections to the use of governmental subsidies for educational purposes are also found among some of the extreme Orthodox sects in Jerusalem, leading to bitter arguments and even violence between them and their opponents, who minimize the possibility of governmental control or cooptation, see *Jerusalem Post*, International Edition (November 4–10, 1979). p. 14.

14. Wolfenden Committee, *Future of Voluntary Organisations*, p. 68. The absence of constraints is also mentioned by Eda Topliss, *Provision for the Disabled* (London: Martin Robertson, 1975): "There is no evidence that this dependence of voluntary bodies on the financial support of local authorities has seriously limited their activities" (p. 119).

15. "Socialism, Capitalism and Democracy: A Symposium," *Commentary* 65 (April 1978): 48.

16. Representative examples are Novia Carter, *Trends in Voluntary Support for Non-Governmental Social Service Agencies* (Ottawa, Ont.: Canadian Council on Social Development, 1974), pp. 53–55; National Advisory Council on Voluntary Action to the Government of Canada, *People in Action* (Ottawa, Ont.: Author, 1977) pp. 20–21; Felice Perlmutter, "Public Funds and Private Agencies," *Child Welfare* (1971): 264–70; Dennis R. Young and Stephen J. Finch, *Foster Care and Nonprofit Agencies* (Lexington, Mass.: D. C. Heath & Co., 1977); William Burian, "Purchase of Service in Child Welfare: A Problem of Inter-organizational Exchange," Ph.D. diss., University of Chicago, 1970; Louis Levitt, "The Accountability Gap in Foster Care: Discontinuities in Accountability in the Purchase and Provision of Foster Care Service in New York City," Ph.D. diss., New York University, 1972; Maxine L. Harris, "Contracting with Private Agencies for the Delivery of Public Services: Policy Implications of an Emerging Trend," Ph.D. diss., University of Southern California, 1975; and Trudy H. Bers, "Private Welfare Agencies and Their Role in Government-sponsored Welfare Programs," Ph.D. diss., University of Illinois, 1973.

17. George Brager and Stephen Holloway, *Changing Human Service Organizations: Politics and Practice* (New York: Free Press, 1978), p. 43.

18. Illustrations of 16 types of federal and state regulations involved in purchase-of-service agreements are found in Ruth Werner, *Public Financing of Voluntary Agency Foster Care: 1975 Compared with 1957* (New York: Child Welfare League of America, 1976), pp. 11–14, 17–19. Young and Finch, *Foster Care*, pp. 239–41, list 30 different requirements for voluntary agency reporting and notification required in New York City. See also Francine Rabinovitz, Jeffrey Pressman, and Martin Rein, "Guidelines: A Plethora of Forms, Authors, and Functions," *Policy Sciences* (1976): 399–416.

19. This was also one of the conclusions in Greater New York Fund, *Impact of Government Funding*, p. 8 and in Felice Perlmutter, "Public Funds," pp. 264–70.

20. The Greater New York Fund study found that program accountability was not as exacting as fiscal accountability, but that administrative costs had a higher priority than those for programs (p. 17). Other perspectives on these issues are U.S. Department of Health, Education and Welfare, Social and Rehabilitation Service, *Purchase of Social Service; Study of the Experience of Three States in Purchase of Service Contracts under the Provisions of the 1967 Amendments to the Social Security Act* (Washington, D.C.: Author, 1971) and Bertram M. Beck, "Governmental Contracts with Non-profit Social Welfare Corporations," in *The Dilemma of Accountability in Modern Government*, ed. Bruce L. R. Smith and D. C. Hague (New York: St. Martin's Press, 1971), pp. 213–29.

21. Elizabeth Wickenden, "Purchase of Care and Services," p. 42. See also Edmond H. Weiss, "Grant Management: A Systems Approach," *Socio-Economic Planning Sciences* (1973): 457–70.

22. Young and Finch, *Foster Care*, p. 238; Melvin Herman, "Purchase of Service Contracting: Promise or Threat to Social Services?" in *Proceedings of the National Institute on Purchase of Service Contracting*, ed. Anderson et al., pp. 43–49.

23. Young and Finch, ibid., pp. 232–33. See also Lourie, "Purchase of Service Contracting," pp. 17–28; Raymond M. Steinberg et al., *Area Agencies on Aging: A Case Study of a Controversial Contract for Service*, mimeograph (Los Angeles: University of Southern California, Andrus Gerontology Center, 1976); and David Z. Robinson, "Government Contracting for Academic Research: Accountability in the American Experience," in *The Dilemma of Accountability in Modern Government*, ed. Bruce L. R. Smith and D. C. Hague (New York: St. Martin's Press, 1971), p. 110.

24. Greater New York Fund, *Impact of Government Funding*, pp. 15–16, 94–104.

25. See note 7 and Alfred J. Kahn, "A Framework for Public–Voluntary Collaboration in the Social Services," in *Social Welfare Forum, 1976* (New York: Columbia University Press, 1976), pp. 47–62 and the rejoinders by Joseph M. Reid and Merle E. Springer. See also Kurt Reichert, "The Drift toward Entrepreneurialism in Health and Social Welfare: Implications for Social Work Education," *Administration in Social Work* (1977): 123–34.

26. In addition to the long-standing opposition to government regulation by business and industry, increasingly adversarial relations have developed between universities and their federal funding sources in the United States. Paralleling the enormously expanded federal investment in university research and training programs have been widespread complaints of excessive regulation and interference with autonomy and academic freedom. See Don K. Price, "Endless Frontier or Bureaucratic Morass?" *Daedalus* (1978): 75–92; and Derek C. Bok, "The Federal Government and the University," *The Public Interest* (1980): 80–101. Influencing the degree of potential conflict between government and the providers of the personal social services is a high degree of dependency between the public funding agency and a small number of voluntary agencies, some of which practically have service monopolies. On the structural limits of governmental monitoring in this field, see Young and Finch, *Foster Care*, pp. 20–21, 89–93, and 232–34. The general inadequacies of governmental audits are outlined in General Accounting Office, *Grant Auditing: A Maze of Inconsistency, Gaps, and Duplication That Needs Overhauling*, Report to the Congress by the Comptroller General of the U.S. (June 15, 1979) (Washington, D.C.: Author, 1979). See also Ira Sharkansky, *Wither the State? Politics and Public Enterprise in Three Countries* (Chatham, N.J.; Chatham House, 1979), pp. 130–44 on the problem of controlling "organizations on the margin of the State."

27. Kenneth R. Wedel, "Government Contracting for Purchase of Service," *Social Work* 21 (February 1976): 105; Filer Commission on Private Philanthropy and Public Needs, *Giving in America: Toward A Stronger Voluntary Sector* (Washington, D.C.: Department of the Treasury, 1977), p. 17. On six other strategies for coping with dependency, see S. L. Elkin, "Comparative Urban Politics and Interorganizational Behavior," *Comparative Urban Research* (1974): 5–22. In addition to diversity, Alan Pifer, "Quasi Non-governmental organization," pp. 12–13, posits a high degree of technical complexity, high prestige, and size as important factors in minimizing dependency. Also see William Burian, "Purchase of Service in Child Welfare," pp. 173–94.

28. Filer, ibid. p. 98.

29. R. R. Friedmann, N. Gilbert, and M. Sherer, eds., *Modern Welfare States*, (Brighton, England; 1987), particularly Chapter 10. See also A. B. Atkinson et al., "The Welfare State in Britain 1970–1985: Extent and Effectiveness," International Centre for Economics and Related Disciplines (ICERD), London School of Economics, Discussion Paper No. 9 (July 1986).

30. Born, Catherine E., "Proprietary Firms and Child Welfare Services: Patterns and Implications," *Child Welfare* 62, no. 2 (1983): 109–18.

31. Edward Skloot, "Enterprise and Commerce in Nonprofit Organizations," in *The Nonprofit Sector: A Research Handbook*, ed. W. W. Powell (New Haven, Conn.: Yale University Press, 1987), pp. 380–993.

32. Ralph M. Kramer, "The Future of the Voluntary Agency in a Mixed Economy," *Journal of Applied Behavioral Science* 21, no. 4 (1985): 377–91.

33. Lester M. Salamon, "Partners in Public Service: The Scope and Theory of Government–Nonprofit Relations," in Powell, *The Nonprofit Sector,* pp. 99–117.

34. Martin Knapp and Spyros Missiakoulis, "Intersectoral Comparisons: Day Care for the Elderly," *Journal of Social Policy* 11, no. 3 (July 1982): 335–54. See also his "Intersectoral Differences in Cost Effectiveness: Residential Child Care: England and Wales," Chapter 8 in this volume.

35. Salamon, "Partners in Public Service." The major findings in the 16 communities are summarized in this chapter.

36. Ralph M. Kramer, "Voluntary Agencies and the Personal Social Services," in Powell, *The Nonprofit Sector,* p. 246.

37. This data is summarized in Martin Knapp, Eileen Robertson, and Corinne Thomdson, *Public Money, Voluntary Action: An Economic Examination of Public Sector Support of the Voluntary Sector,* A Report to the Voluntary Services Unit of the Home Office. Personal Social Services Research Unit Discussion Paper 500 (Canterbury: University of Kent, 1987), pp. 41, 43, 45–46.

38. Ibid., p. 38.

39. For additional supporting evidence, see Salamon, "Partners in Public Service," pp. 114–116.

40. Ralph M. Kramer, "Voluntary Agencies & Social Change in Israel 1972–1982," *Israel Social Science Research* 2, no. 2 (1984): 55–68.

41. Marie Brenton, "Changing Relations in Dutch Social Services" *Journal of Social Policy* 11 no. 1 (1982): 59–80; and private communication from the Ministry of Welfare, Health and Culture (July 31, 1987).

42. Alfred J. Kahn and Sheila B. Kamerman, *Social Service in International Perspective,* 2d. ed. (New Brunswick, N.J.: Transaction Press, 1980), p. 383.

43. Ralph M. Kramer and Bart Grossman, "Contracting for Social Services: Process Management and Resource Dependencies," *Social Service Review* 61, no. 1 (March 1987): 32–55.

REFERENCES

Agranoff, Robert. "Services Integration." In Wayne F. Anderson, Bernard J. Frieden, and Michael J. Murphy, eds., *Managing Human Services.* Washington, D.C.: International City Management Association, 1977, pp. 527–564.

Beck, Bertram M. "Governmental Contracts with Non-profit Social Welfare Corporations." In Bruce L. R. Smith and D. C. Hague, eds., *The Dilemma of Accountability in Modern Government.* New York: St. Martin's Press, 1971, pp. 213–29.

Bers, Trudy H. "Private Welfare Agencies and Their Role in Government-Sponsored Welfare Programs." Ph.D. diss. University of Illinois. 1973.

Bok, Derek C. "The Federal Government and the University." *The Public Interest* (1980): 80–101.

Bolan, Richard S. "Social Planning and Policy Development: Local Government." In eds. Wayne F. Anderson, Bernard J. Frieden, and Michael J. Murphy, *Managing Human Services.* Washington, D.C.: International City Management Association, 1977, pp. 85–127.

Brager, George, and Stephen Holloway. *Changing Human Service Organizations: Politics and Practice.* New York: Free Press, 1978.

Burian William. "Purchase of Service in Child Welfare: A Problem of Inter-organizational Exchange." Ph.D. diss., University of Chicago, 1970.

Carter, Novia. *Trends in Voluntary Support for Non-governmental Social Service Agencies.*

Ottawa, Ont.: Council on Social Development, 1974.

Donee Group Report and Recommendations, "Private Philanthropy: Vital and Innovative? or Passive and Irrelevant?" In *Research Papers Sponsored by the Commission on Private Philanthropy and Public Needs,* vol. 1. Washington, D.C.: Department of the Treasury, 1977, pp. 49–88.

Elkin, S. L. "Comparative Urban Politics and Interorganizational Behavior." *Comparative Urban Research* (1974): 5–22.

Filer Commission on Private Philanthropy and Public Needs, *Giving in America: Toward A Stronger Voluntary Sector.* Washington, D.C.: Department of the Treasury, 1977.

Fisk, Donald, Herbert Kiesling, and Thomas Mullen. *Private Provision of Public Services: An Overview.* Washington, D.C.: Urban Institute, 1978.

Gans, Sheldon P., and G. T. Horton. *Integration of Human Services: The State and Municipal Levels.* New York: Praeger, 1974.

General Accounting Office. *Grant Auditing: A Maze of Inconsistency, Gaps and Duplication That Needs Overhauling.* Report to the Congress by the Comptroller General of the U.S. (June 15, 1979). Washington, D.C.: General Accounting Office, 1979.

Greater New York Fund/United Way. *Impact of Government Funding on the Management of Voluntary Agencies.* New York: Greater New York Fund/United Way, 1978.

Hamilton, Edward K. "On Non-Constitutional Management of a Constitutional Problem." *Daedalus* 107 (1978): 111–28.

Harris, Maxine L. "Contracting with Private Agencies for the Delivery of Public Services: Policy Implications of an Emerging Trend." Ph.D. diss., University of Southern California, 1975.

Heidenheimer, Arnold J., Hugh Heclo, and Carolyn Adams. *Comparative Public Policy: The Politics of Social Choice in Europe and America.* London: Macmillan, 1976.

Herman, Melvin. "Purchase of Service Contracting: Promise or Threat to Social Services?" *Proceedings of the National Institute on Purchase of Service Contracting.* Lawrence: University of Kansas, 1978.

Hill, William G. "Voluntary and Governmental Financial Transactions." *Social Casework* (1971): 356–61.

Hook, Sidney. "Capitalism, Socialism and Democracy: A Symposium." *Commentary* (1978): 48–50.

Jenvick, Benjamin A. G. "The Voluntary Agency and the Purchase of Social Services." In *Social Work Practice 1971.* New York: Columbia University Press, 1971, pp. 152–59.

Kahn, Alfred J. "A Framework for Public–Voluntary Collaboration in the Social Services." In *Social Welfare Forum, 1976.* New York: Columbia University Press, 1976, pp. 47–62.

Kramer, Ralph M. "Voluntary Agencies and the Use of Public Funds: Some Policy Issues." *Social Service Review* (1966): 15–26.

————. *The Voluntary Service Agency in Israel.* Berkeley: University of California, Institute of International Studies, 1976.

Levitt, Louis. "The Accountability Gap in Foster Care: Discontinuities in Accountability in the Purchase and Provision of Foster Care Service in New York City." Ph.D. diss., New York University, 1972.

Lourie, Norman V. "Purchase of Service Contracting: Issues Confronting the Governmental Sponsored Agency." In Kenneth R. Wedel, Arthur J. Katz, and Ann Weick, eds., *Proceedings of the National Institute on Purchase of Service Contracting: Child and Family Services.* Lawrence: University of Kansas, School of Social Welfare, 1978, pp. 17–28.

Manser, Gordon. "Further Thoughts on Purchase of Service." *Social Casework* 55 (1974): 421–34.

Meiresonne, Jan B. *Care for the Mentally Retarded in the Netherlands.* Utrecht: Dutch National Association for the Care of the Mentally Retarded, 1975.

Mueller, Candace P. "Purchase of Service Contracting From the Viewpoint of the Provider." In Kenneth R. Wedel, Arthur J. Katz, and Ann Weick, eds., *Proceedings of the National Institute on Purchase of Service Contracting: Child and Family Services.* Lawrence: University of Kansas, School of Social Welfare, 1978, pp. 29–36.

National Advisory Council on Voluntary Action to the Government of Canada. *People in Action.* Ottawa, Ontario: National Advisory Council on Voluntary Action to the Government of Canada, 1977.

Perlmutter, Felice. "Public Funds and Private Agencies." *Child Welfare* 1971: 264–70.

Pifer, Alan. "The Quasi Non-governmental Organization." In *1967 Annual Report of the Carnegie Corporation of New York.* New York: Carnegie Corporation, 1967.

Price, Don K. "Endless Frontier or Bureaucratic Morass?" *Daedalus* (1978) 75–92.

Rabinovitz, Francine, Jeffrey Pressman, and Martin Rein. "Guidelines: A Plethora of Forms, Authors, and Functions." *Policy Sciences* (1976): 399–416.

Reichert, Kurt. "The Drift toward Entrepreneurialism in Health and Social Welfare: Implications for Social Work Education." *Administration in Social Welfare* (1977): 123–34.

Rice, Robert M. "Impact of Government Contracts on Voluntary Social Agencies." *Social Casework* (1975): 387–95.

Robinson, David Z. "Government Contracting for Academic Research: Accountability in the American Experience." In Bruce L. R. Smith and D. C. Hague, eds., *The Dilemma of Accountability in Modern Government.* New York: St. Martin's Press, 1971, pp. 103–17.

Rubenstein, Dan, R. E. Mundy, and Mary L. Rubenstein. "Proprietary Social Services." In *Social Welfare Forum 1978.* New York: Columbia University Press, 1979, pp. 120–40.

Sharkansky, Ira. *Wither the State? Politics and Public Enterprise in Three Countries.* Chatham, N.J.: Chatham House, 1979.

Steinberg, Raymond M., et al. "Area Agencies on Aging: A Case Study of a Controversial Contract for Service." Mimeographed, Los Angeles: University of Southern California, Andrus Gerontology Center, 1976.

Topliss, Eda. *Provision for the Disabled.* London: Martin Robertson, 1975.

Unell, Judith. *Voluntary Social Services: Financial Resources.* London: Bedford Square Press of the National Council of Social Service, 1979.

U.S. Department of Health, Education and Welfare, Social and Rehabilitation Service. *Purchase of Social Service: Study of the Experience of Three States in Purchase of Service Contracts under the Provisions of the 1967 Amendments to the Social Security Act.* Washington, D.C.: Department of Health, Education and Welfare, 1971.

Wedel, Kenneth R. "Government Contracting for Purchase of Services." *Social Work* 21 (February 1976).

Weiss, Edmond H. "Grant Management: A Systems Approach." *Socio-Economic Planning Services* (1973): 457–70.

Werner, Ruth. *Public Financing of Voluntary Agency Foster Care: 1975 Compared with 1957.* New York: Child Welfare League of America, 1976.

Whittington, H. G. "A Case for Private Funding in Mental Health." *Administration in Mental Health* (1975): 23–28.

Wickenden, Elizabeth. "Purchase of Care and Services: Effect on Voluntary Agencies." In Ira Winogrond, ed., *Proceedings of the First Milwaukee Institute on a Social Welfare Issue of the Day: Purchase of Care and Services in the Health and Welfare Fields.* Milwaukee: University of Wisconsin, 1970, pp. 40–58.

Wolfenden Committee. *The Future of Voluntary Organisations.* London: Croom Helm, 1978.

Young, Dennis R., and Stephen J. Finch. *Foster Care and Nonprofit Agencies.* Lexington, Mass.: D.C. Heath & Co., 1977.

10

The Voluntary Sector in Housing: The Role of British Housing Associations

JOHN HILLS

Housing associations are one of the largest parts of the nonprofit sector in Britain, now owning and managing nearly 600,000 dwellings, approaching 3 percent of the total housing stock. Although this role is not as large as that played by similar organizations in some other countries (such as West Germany or the Netherlands), the housing association movement is of general interest given its rapid growth (more than doubling in size since 1974) and its emergence as a politically favored alternative to the local authorities that have traditionally dominated British social housing provision.

Housing associations are private, nonprofit organizations mainly providing rental housing at below market rents. They hover between the public and private sectors. On the one hand, they receive their capital finance overwhelmingly from the central government by means of a combination of grants and loans, making their development program very much part of public policy. On the other hand, they are controlled by voluntary management committees, independent of central or local government control, putting them within the private sector for some purposes. The ambiguity of this position has brought the movement distinct political advantages. In the mid-1970s when social housing construction was a priority, associations benefited from the growth in available public capital finance, but they have suffered less heavily than local authorities from the cuts in public spending on housing over the last ten years.

The success of the movement raises questions common to other examples of the nonprofit or voluntary sector. Why has social housing provision been favored over profit-making private landlords in Britain? Given

This chapter is a revised version of a paper presented to the international symposium on "The Non-profit Sector and the Modern Welfare State," June 1987, Bad Honnef, Federal Republic of Germany. The author is very grateful for helpful comments and advice from Estelle James, Anne Power, Euan Ramsay, and students on the LSE Housing Diploma course. The work on which the paper is based was funded by the Suntory–Toyota Foundation.

that it has been, why are associations now growing in importance while the local authority sector declines? Does this growth simply reflect the antagonism between the present British government and the local authorities (which are, especially in the big cities, generally under the control of the opposition Labour Party) and hence the diversion of funds away from the authorities toward the associations? Alternatively, does the organizational form of the associations—resulting partly from their relatively small size—give them advantages in terms of the quality of housing management over the larger, more bureaucratic local authorities? Do the perceived quality advantages of the sector simply reflect a more generous subsidy regime than that available to local authorities? Does a problem of accountability arise when such large sums of public money are chaneled through organizations run by unelected private committees?

This chapter attempts to explore some of these issues.[1] In order to set the recent growth of the sector in context, I start with a general review of the way British housing policy has developed. This explains, in particular, why less than 10 percent of British housing is currently provided by private landlords, a remarkably low figure by international standards and a feature that gives increasing importance to the associations in filling the resultant gap in housing provision. The next section of the paper describes the current characteristics of the sector,[2] and subsequent sections explore issues connected with subsidy and accountability. The conclusion attempts to bring out some general features resulting from the nonprofit character of the associations, which may parallel those of similar organizations elsewhere.

BACKGROUND: HOUSING TENURE AND HOUSING POLICY IN BRITAIN SINCE 1914

Before the First World War housing policy was to a large extent an adjunct of concern about public health. Reports on the shocking housing conditions of many of the inhabitants of rapidly growing nineteenth century cities had stressed the effects on health of overcrowding, lack of amenities, poorly constructed buildings, and infestation by vermin. Local authorities had acquired powers to regulate building standards and to demolish and clear slum areas. The scale of their own construction operations to replace demolished buildings had not been large, however: only about 20,000 houses had been built by the outbreak of war. This was smaller than the size of what was to become the housing association movement. During the nineteenth century various private philanthropic trusts had been established with the aim of providing good quality, well-managed rental housing to the "respectable" working classes. The capital raised by these trusts was given a limited but reasonable return, earning its providers the label of the *5 percent philanthropists*. By 1914 such trusts owned some

Table 10.1.   Housing Tenure in England and Wales, 1939–1985.
(percent of dwellings)

	Owner-occupiers	Rented from Local Authority	Rented from Housing Association	Rented from Private Landlord
1939	33.0	10.3	56.7	
1953	34.5	18.8	46.6	
1961	44.4	24.3	31.3	
1971	52.1	28.2	0.9	18.8
1981	58.6	28.6	2.1	10.7
1985	64.1	24.9	2.6	8.5

Source: Data from Holmans (1987), Table V.1, and Department of the Environment (1986), Table 9.4.

50,000 units, mostly in London. Owner-occupied housing was still very small, whereas 90 percent of housing was rented from private landlords.

The Decline of the Private Landlord

The most striking feature of the history of British housing tenure has been the decline in private renting from nine-tenths of the stock in 1914 to only one-tenth today (see Table 10.1). This has had a number of causes, some of which are connected with the favorable economic treatment given to the other tenures rather than the unfavorable treatment of private landlords. Even before the First World War, enforcement of minimum standards had made the bottom end of the market a less attractive proposition for landlords than it had been. The subsequent decline of the sector cannot, however, be separated from questions of rent restriction, and to a lesser extent, security of tenure legislation, and taxation.

Rent restriction of one kind or another has been part of housing policy since controls were imposed in 1915 in the wake of rent strikes in Glasgow. Unlike other wartime controls, however, they were not lifted after the end of the war. Nor were the levels of rent that could be charged raised to take account of inflation during the war. Between the wars there was some relaxation of the scope of controls and of their levels, but comprehensive restrictions were imposed again on the outbreak of the Second World War. Again they outlasted the war, and their scope was seriously reduced only in 1957. Neither this relaxation nor the establishment of the current "fair rent" system in the mid-1960s was enough to give a return to landlords that would compete with obtaining vacant possession and selling off into owner-occupation. A vicious circle had been firmly established under which controls meant a low return to private landlords, which led to a growing shortage of rented property. This put more pressure on tenancies outside the controls, with higher rents, lower standards, and further pressure for the widening of controls to protect these tenants. The

low returns to landlords also contributed to a low, even nonexistent, standard of repair and maintenance, leading to deterioration of the property
and its eventual loss altogether through slum clearance.[3]

The present government has attempted to introduce new forms of tenancy that would give landlords a higher return, but it has had little effect
on supply. Quite apart from the advantages of the other tenures, the experience of rent restriction has now been so long lasting that prospective
landlords would always perceive a risk that subsequent governments might
impose controls again, whatever the current one did.

Security of tenure legislation has accompanied rent controls throughout
the period; without it, the controls would have been impossible to enforce.
At the same time the tax position of private landlords has not been especially favorable—while taxed on their rental incomes and able to deduct
interest in calculating taxable income, they have not been able to deduct
depreciation as part of their costs. However desirable rent restriction and
security of tenure may have been in terms of protecting those most vulnerable to exploitation, these elements have clearly been against the interests
of potential private landlords and have therefore decreased the supply of
privately rented housing.

When comparing the history of the British rental sector with that in
other countries, one feature that stands out is that private landlords have
never (except for a brief period in the mid-1920s) received any kind of
subsidy to offset the restrictions placed on them for social reasons. This
has been true under Conservative as well as Labour governments. It is not
surprising, ideologically, that Labour governments saw profit-making private landlords as unsuitable either to be reliable conduits for subsidy or
instruments of planned reconstruction. Conservative governments, in contrast, were most interested in promoting owner-occupation and also accepted the terms of the political debate in which the important measure of
achievement was the total number of houses built each year by the public
sector. Numerous dispersed private landlords did not constitute a strong
political lobby and the private rental sector's very poor image, itself in part
a product of the policies affecting it, left it with few political friends.

The Rise of Owner-Occupation

Owner-occupation is now the dominant tenure in Britain. It owes much of
this dominance to its favorable income tax position. Originally this was
much the same as that of private landlords, and with only a minority of
the population subject to direct tax, it was not such a crucial issue anyway.
Owner-occupiers were subject to tax on an "imputed rent" on their property and could deduct their interest payments on housing, as they could
for other forms of borrowing. However, after the mid-1930s the imputed
rents were not adjusted for inflation and in the early 1960s they were
abolished altogether rather than reassessed at a realistic level. Meanwhile

tax relief for mortgage interest survived even as it was abolished for other forms of borrowing. There is now a limit on the amount of a mortgage that can attract relief, but the overwhelming bulk of mortgage interest is still deductible. With most of the population paying direct tax and with high interest rates, the aggregate cost of the relief has become very large. In 1986–1987 its cost, £4.5 billion, was equivalent to 12 percent of total income tax revenue. Its apparent beneficiaries now include such a large proportion of the electorate that withdrawal of it appears a political impossibility.[4] At the same time, although tax was imposed on capital gains on other assets from 1965, gains on owner-occupied housing were exempted, giving home ownership further important advantages compared with other forms of saving.

Combined with a widespread preference for owning one's own home in terms of control over one's life, these tax advantages have fueled the rapid development of owner-occupation as the majority tenure in Britain; indeed the preferences to some extent result from the perception that home ownership has historically represented a very good deal financially. This has been assisted by the success of specialized savings institutions, the building societies, which have become the dominant institution serving the small saver and which have used virtually all of their funds to lend to house purchasers.

These positive advantages of home ownership have been reinforced by problems of the alternatives. The private rental sector has declined and therefore become hard to enter for the reasons given earlier, while access to local authority housing has been rationed and is open only to those with special needs or those who have been on a waiting list for many years. For people establishing a household for the first time or moving from one area to another, owner-occupation has often been the *only* option, regardless of the extent to which it has benefited from implicit subsidy through the tax system.

The Rise and Fall of Local Authority Housing

Local authorities are the major source of subsidized rental housing in the British welfare state. At the high point in the late 1970s nearly 32 percent of all dwellings in Great Britain were rented from local authorities (the figure for England and Wales shown in Table 10.1 is somewhat lower as it excludes Scotland, where over half of the stock was in the local authority sector). This policy choice was not just in preference to the alternative of subsidizing private landlords discussed earlier, but also in preference to means-tested assistance with rent. Just as after the First World War the idea of "homes fit for heroes" (combined with the aim of defusing any kind of revolutionary movement) had led to central government subsidies to local authorities, so in 1945 local authorities were seen as "plannable instruments" (which private landlords were not) through which reconstruction could be accomplished. At the same time means-testing had been thoroughly discredited though the experience of assistance to the unemployed during the Depression of the 1930s. Only in the last few years has means-tested assistance to tenants ("housing benefit") become of major importance. Ironically this has coincided with an increasing residualization of the local authority sector: whereas in the past some of those benefiting from general subsidies to local authority tenants would not have had low incomes, now most do.

A further reason for local authorities being seen as the natural choice for the provision of mass housing lay in their powers of building regulation and demolition and clearance of unfit property. If they cleared the slums, it was natural that they should rehouse those who had lived in them and rebuild on the cleared areas. This, however, has been one of the reasons leading to their current decline. A significant amount of their housing has taken the form of large purpose-built estates. In the mid-1960s a significant proportion of the units built were flats in high-rise buildings, built using "industrialized building" methods, which are now very unpopular. Although most of the stock in fact consists of traditionally built houses, the whole sector has suffered from the image of these unpopular forms and has become stigmatized.

The scale of operation of the authorities has not helped either. Individual bodies have been responsible for the management of tens or even hundreds of thousands of units and adopted a very centralized management style. Tenants have found it difficult to force a remote bureaucracy to carry out repairs. Property has been empty for months while the processes of rerenting are carried out. Once vandalism and disrepair have been allowed to fester, a vicious circle of decline has set in on the worst estates, with only the most desperate—and poorest—tenants prepared to live in them.[5] Further, tenants have not had the power of "exit" because of the lack of any alternative, and their "voice" has been lost amid the other issues entering the local political process.

Since general cutbacks in public spending in 1976, and especially since the current government took office in 1979, the resources going to the sector have been in decline. New building has fallen dramatically (see Figure 10.1) and rents have risen. Meanwhile the lack of proper repair in the past and the unsuitable design of some of the stock have led to a growing backlog of maintenance work. The government's heavy ideological commitment to owner-occupation has given tenants the "right to buy" the properties that they have rented with the benefit of substantial discounts on their market values. The better-off tenants living in the most desirable properties have taken advantage of this on a large scale: 1 million dwellings, over a tenth of the sector's stock (and overwhelmingly the best tenth) has been sold off into owner-occupation since 1979. This in turn has lowered the average quality of the remaining stock, further worsening the public image of the sector.

Figure 10.1. Housing Starts, 1974–1985 (Great Britain). *Source: Data from the Department of the Environment (1986), Table 6.1.*

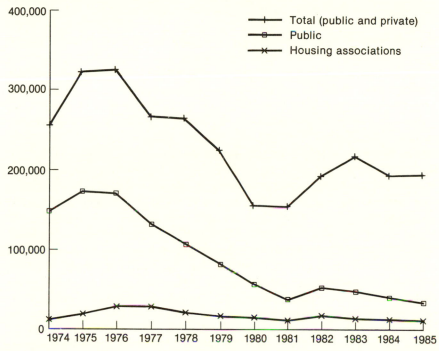

The Current Position

The, hardly surprising, results of these policies can be seen from the trends shown for England and Wales in Table 10.1 (the *trends* have been much the same in Great Britain as a whole). The rate of owner-occupation is now approaching two-thirds, the private rental sector is in danger of extinction, and the local authority sector is in retreat. However, even the current government recognizes that owner-occupation cannot be a sensible route for all households. The young and mobile, the elderly who would not want to carry out their own repairs, and those who simply cannot afford the costs of buying property (even at a discount) are all going to end up as tenants, come what may. The consequences of the decline in building rental units are becoming ever more apparent: the number of families that local authorities have accepted as being homeless (and that they have a statutory responsibility to house) has doubled since 1979. Although the crisis in the availability of rental housing is now recognized, the government is reluctant to loosen its controls over local authority spending, for purely ideological reasons according to its opponents, because of the problems with local authority provision in the past, according to its supporters. There seems little reason to expect that the private landlord could ever be revived on any significant scale.[6] It is against this background that the role of the housing associations has become of increasing importance.

THE HOUSING ASSOCIATION MOVEMENT

There is a great diversity of types of organizations within the nonprofit housing association movement. It encompasses charitable trusts established to run a handful of almshouses 800 years ago as well as more recently established organizations renting out 10,000 or more dwellings, making them landlords on a scale equal to many local authorities. It includes the philanthropic trusts set up in the last century run by enlightened, if paternalistic, managements, as well as more radical organizations established in an attempt to mitigate the inner city housing problems of a century later. Many associations owe their existence to a group (in some cases religious, in others political) of volunteers who wanted to do something to alleviate the housing problems of those in particular need. Others, including some of the largest, started life as agencies run by central government and were later transformed into associations rather than handed over to local authorities or privatized in the conventional manner. Others were established by employers to solve some of the difficulties facing their employees in moving from one area to another, given the attenuated nature of the private rental sector.

The main activity of housing associations is to provide rental housing, with rents controlled at the "fair rent" level set by a local rent officer.[7] They also provide shared housing and hostels for a variety of groups for whom self-contained accommodation might not be suitable. Associations have also been involved in various initiatives to promote low-income owner-occupation. Indeed, a few associations do not provide housing to rent at all; examples are, "coownership societies," established in the 1960s to provide an equivalent subsidy to nontaxpayers to that given by mortgage interest relief to taxpayers (although this form of association is becoming less common as its special advantages have disappeared).

Although more than 2600 associations in Great Britain are currently registered with the Housing Corporation (the public body responsible for channeling central government funds to associations and monitoring their activities), others are not registered. Unregistered associations cannot receive public funds, access to which is dependent on registration with the Housing Corporation. Such associations exist, for instance, as a convenient legal way for several people to own a single building. This chapter is concerned with the registered associations, however. Many associations have official charitable status[8] (62 percent of all those registered with the corporation in 1983[9]), but this is not compulsory, and associations can take other legal forms provided that they do not distribute profits to their members.

In addition to their organizational diversity, associations vary greatly in

Table 10.2 Registered Housing Associations by Size (England and Wales, March 1983)

Number of Units per Association	Number of Associations[a]	Total Number of Units[b] (000s)	Percent of Associations	Percent of Units
over 10000	7	92.4	0.4	20.1
2501–10000	30	122.7	1.9	26.7
1001–2500	60	92.4	3.8	20.1
501–1000	90	66.5	5.7	14.5
101–500	250	58.5	15.9	12.7
26–100	410	19.9	26.0	4.3
1–25	730	7.4	46.3	1.6
Total	1577	459.8	100	100

[a] Associations with fair-rent housing under management.
[b] Units rented or available for renting.
Source: Housing Corporation (1984), Table 3.4.

size, as can be seen from Table 10.2. The table shows the number of associations of different sizes with fair rent units under management in England and Wales in 1983. While 7 associations managed more than 10,000 units, 730 managed 25 or fewer units, including many almshouses and other societies specializing in hostel accommodation for the elderly. As a result there is great concentration of ownership in the largest societies: the biggest 2 percent owned nearly half of the fair-rent units in 1983, and the biggest 6 percent owned two-thirds, whereas at the other end of the spectrum, 72 percent of the associations managed 100 or fewer units each, yet their combined stock was only 6 percent of the total.

By the end of 1985 housing associations owned 554,000 dwellings in Great Britain, representing 2.5 percent of the total stock. Although this figure is small, it represents 6.6 percent of the rented stock and 23.4 percent of non-local authority rentals.[10] It is also growing rapidly, as can be seen from the trends revealed in Table 10.1. Over the decade following the 1974 Housing Act (which established the main features of the current subsidy system) the sector doubled its share of the housing stock and, with the continuing decline of the private landlord, tripled its share of non-local authority rentals.

This rapid growth has resulted from a share of total building activity that has greatly exceeded the sector's share of the existing stock. As Figure 10.1 shows, although the number of new housing starts made by associations has declined since 1976, the proportionate fall has been much smaller than for the public sector as a whole. As a result, over the period 1981–1985 housing associations were responsible for 32 percent of the publicly funded—and 7 percent of all—housing starts in Great Britain.[11] The sector has also grown through purchasing and renovating previously privately owned properties—in 1985 just under 40 percent of the movement's En-

Table 10.3.   Characteristics of Household Heads in Different Tenures
(Great Britain, 1983)

	Housing Association Tenants (%)	Private Unfurnished Tenants (%)	Local Authority Tenants (%)	All Households (%)
Aged 65 or over	49	54	34	28
Economically active				
Nonmanual	15	15	9	27
Manual	25	28	41	36
Economically inactive	60	58	50	36
Usual gross weekly household income				
£80 or less	54	56	50	33
Mean usual gross weekly household income	£95	£92	£92	£144

Source: Data from Office of Population Censuses and Surveys, (1985), Tables 6.9 and 6.14.

gland and Wales fair-rent stock had been acquired by associations rather than newly built by them,[12] and this proportion has been rising. Some associations have also taken a lead in the provision of specialized kinds of accommodation, such as for the elderly, for groups with particular disabilities, or "halfway houses" to help tenants cope with return to the community from institutions. Associations were responsible for 28 percent of starts of dwellings specially designed for the elderly in schemes with a warden between 1981 and 1985, for instance.[13]

Some indication of the characteristics of housing association tenants compared with those in other tenures is provided by Table 10.3. Not surprisingly, tenants in general can be seen to be a much older and poorer group than homeowners. In nearly half of housing association households the head is aged 65 or over, and 60 percent of these heads are economically inactive. Both of these proportions are significantly higher than for local authority tenants, and the proportion of tenants with gross incomes in the bottom third of the national income distribution is, at 54 percent, also somewhat higher.[14] On most of the indicators shown the profile of housing association tenants is similar to that of tenants of private unfurnished accommodation, which has historically contained the poorest households (and which has received no general subsidies). The same is not true, however, of the dwellings provided, as can be seen from Table 10.4. A very high proportion of housing association dwellings are flats or maisonettes—two-thirds, compared with only 18 percent for all tenures taken together. While a greater than average proportion of the buildings were built before 1919, this proportion is much lower than for the private unfurnished sector, and the building program of the last decade has resulted in a very high proportion of post-1964 buildings. As far as quality can be judged by the availability of amenities, the sector is clearly much better

Table 10.4. Characteristics of Dwellings in Different Tenures
(Great Britain, 1983)

	Rented from Housing Association	Rented Privately, Unfurnished	Rented from Local Authority	All Tenures
House	33	72	66	82
Purpose-built flat	53	12	33	14
Converted flat	14	16	1	4
Without private bath or shower	4	13	1	3
Without private inside accommodation	4	16	1	3
Without central heating	34	76	44	36
Built before 1919	32	64	3	24
Built after 1964	55	7	32	26

Source: Data from Office of Population Censuses and Surveys, (1985), Tables 6.17, 6.21, and 6.34.

than the private unfurnished sector and has some advantages over local authority accommodation.

A further feature of association housing that has an important bearing on its role within the national welfare state is the regional concentration of the movement's stock. In Greater London no less than 5 percent of the stock is rented from housing associations; in Wales the proportion is only 1.7 percent. In proportionate terms, the scale of these variations is greater than that for local authorities. The distribution reflects history to some extent: associations were established and have been particularly active in areas of particular housing need, such as the inner cities. The strength of the movement in areas like the north of England also results from the transfer of property from central government regional development agencies.

Finally, Table 10.5 shows how housing association rents have changed in relation to those charged by local authorities and to prices as a whole since 1973. The figures for the first few years are based on a relatively small number of registrations, so it is not clear whether the long-term trend is for rents to be roughly constant in real terms (as they have been over the period as a whole) or to rise at a rate closer to that of earnings (as they have since 1976). The table shows clearly how the differential between housing association rents and those of local authorities narrowed as recurrent central government subsidies were withdrawn from the latter in the early 1980s. Recent proposals by the government for reforming the system for controlling association rent levels[15] would imply a higher level of rents, but at the time of writing (October 1987), it is not yet clear how much higher.

In summary, although housing associations only house 1 household in 40 at present, that proportion is rising rapidly. Already nearly a quarter

Table 10.5. Housing Association Registered Rents, 1973–1985
(England and Wales; all registrations)

	Mean Registered Rent (£/year)	Index of Real Rent Level[a]	Housing Association Rents as Percent of Local Authority Rents
1973	257	100	144
1974	323	108	166
1975	373	101	172
1976	399	92	161
1977	469	94	163
1978	524	97	172
1979	556	91	167
1980	651	90	162
1981	726	90	122
1982	812	92	116
1983	892	97	123
1984	970	100	127
1985	1024	100	126

[a] Adjusted by Retail Price Index.
Source: Department of the Environment (1986), Tables 11.5 and 11.1 (and equivalent tables in earlier volumes).

of non-local authority tenancies are managed by associations. The tenants of associations come from groups that are targetted for housing provision. Parts of the sector have pioneered the provision of sheltered housing for the elderly as well as the renovation of run-down inner city properties. The quality of housing provided compares well with other rented housing. Because of their great diversity and, in general, much smaller size than the average local authority, associations are often seen as able to provide much more flexible, innovative, and sensitive management than council housing departments. Although some of the larger associations compare in size with local authorities, their adoption of a more decentralized management has protected them from some of the criticisms that generally go with large overall scale.

As their own federation has put it, "Housing associations have proved themselves adept at this particular job, which involves painstaking work with local communities and with the existing—often elderly—tenants in neglected older property."[16] Given all of this, and given that associations are neither profit-making private landlords nor arms of local government, it is not surprising that the movement has enjoyed a considerable degree of bipartisan support. One of the central recommendations of the recent *Inquiry into British Housing* chaired by the Duke of Edinburgh was for a wider range of "approved landlords" to offer rented accommodation along lines not dissimilar to housing associations.[17] As far as central government spending is concerned, the movement has steadily increased its share of the overall housing program, sharing in the growth in spending up to

1976, but suffering much less severely from the subsequent cuts. By 1985–86 net loans and grants to housing associations represented 42 percent of the central government's *net* capital expenditure in England[18] (although this figure also reflects the high proportion of gross local authority expenditure that is now funded by the proceeds of sales under the right to buy).

Housing associations are not, however, without their critics. Part of the criticism concerns the scale of support associations have received and how this compares with that going to local authorities. A further focus of criticism has been the extent to which the committees that run them (and that receive very large amounts of public money) are accountable. These two issues are now discussed in turn.

CENTRAL GOVERNMENT HOUSING SUBSIDIES

Subsidies to Housing Associations

The basis of the current system of housing association funding—a large capital grant from central government payable on completion of a new development, known as a Housing Association Grant (HAG)—was established in 1974, laying the basis for the rapid expansion of the sector since then. Once a project is completed, "fair rents" are set by the local rent officer, and a calculation is made of the net income that the association will be left with after deducting allowances for management and maintenance costs (set by the central government on the basis of property type, location, etc.). This net income is assumed to be available to service debt and the maximum size of loan which it can service (on a conventional annuity basis) is worked out. The loan is generally much less than the capital cost. The balance, typically 80 percent or more, is paid by HAG. Both the grant and loan come from the public sector and count toward public spending on housing.

This system allows associations to balance their books in the first year of a project's life. As time goes by rents rise with inflation (as do management and maintenance costs) but loan servicing costs do not. A gap therefore opens up between the association's income and costs. Originally associations were able to retain such a surplus to fund other new building or recurrent spending. In 1980, however, legislation was passed introducing Grant Redemption Funds, which are designed to cream off the surpluses. The proceeds are remitted centrally.

The introduction of Grant Redemption Funds means that the true grant element is much lower than the proportion of capital cost covered by HAG. Precisely how much lower depends on the way in which rents and costs grow in the future. The more rapidly rent rises, the greater the value of the Grant Redemption Fund payments and the lower the true grant element in the system. Even when one takes a narrow range of estimates (based on market expectations) of the key variables, the true grant element could be anything from 20 to 70 percent of a project's cost. This variation in and uncertainty about the true value of current arrangements is in itself something of a problem for policy evaluation.

The system has other inherent problems. In particular it has several features that mean that at the margin additional spending is subsidized at a rate of 100 percent or additional income "taxed" at a rate of 100 percent. For instance, HAG is calculated on the basis of the size of loan that can be serviced from the project's net income. An extra pound of capital cost does not affect the size of loan; it just means an extra pound of HAG, and makes no difference to the associations's financial position. Similarly, the size of the Grant Redemption Fund payment that an association has to make depends on the difference between its actual income and allowances for spending. Higher rents simply mean higher Grant Redemption Fund payments, again with no effect on the association's net financial position.

Such features mean that incentives for cost control are eroded and, in the case of rents, the associations have no reason to press for rent review (the "fair rents" are to some extent supposed to represent the results of arbitration between landlord and tenant). Although housing associations are reputed to be responsible and, as nonprofit housing bodies, do not exploit the system to pay out dividends to any owners, the system necessitates relatively tight central control and scrutiny. New projects are, for instance, scrutinized by the Housing Corporation to make sure that they come within standard cost guidelines. If the proposed cost of a project falls far outside these guidelines, it will not be approved for grant; similarly overruns of approved costs will not be covered by grant. The need for these kinds of controls is entirely at odds with what are supposed to be the main advantages of the housing association movement: its decentralized structure and flexibility.

Virtually all of the finance used by the associations for capital development comes from the public sector and counts toward public spending and public borrowing, the limitation of which is the main instrument of macroeconomic control being used by the current government. Even though some of the finance passed to associations is in the explicit form of a loan and some of the rest is an implicit loan (generating future flows of Grant Redemption Fund), the spending constraints are applied as if all of the spending represented grant.

It is not surprising therefore that the current discussion of possible reform to the subsidy system involves the extent to which nonconcessionary private finance could be used to supplement government grants. This would allow public spending to be concentrated on the grant element and would permit a larger program to be funded within the same public spending limits without any necessary change in rent levels. The potential increase in the program would be greater if *indexed* borrowing (with the nominal cost of interest and repayments rising each year with the general price level) was used to fund the balance. Indexed finance has a lower initial servicing cost than conventional finance, so the level of grant necessary to allow associations to break even initially would be lower than at present, perhaps two-thirds of capital cost on average. The same amount of public spending could therefore fund up to 50 percent more units every year. At the same time, switching to indexed finance would allow the removal of Grant Redemption Funds, with their unfortunate side effects.[19] The government has suggested a change in this direction, but coupled with a reduction in the grant element; this would mean higher rents.[20] It remains to be seen what system will emerge from the negotiations now underway.

Subsidies to Local Authorities

Local authorities vary greatly in the levels of cost carried on their housing accounts. Those that did most of their building in the 1940s and 1950s now have very low debt servicing costs on their housing stocks. Those building more recently have higher debt servicing costs—not only because interest rates have been higher but also because inflation has had less time to eat away at the real value of the debt. As the former may well have more desirable, traditionally built properties and the latter more unpopular, system-built estates, the resulting rent pattern can be perverse: good property having a lower rent than bad.

In an attempt to cope with this problem, the system of housing subsidy to local authorities takes account of the rents and management and maintenance costs that might be expected on existing property as well as on their new developments. Authorities that the government thinks should be able to generate a surplus from their existing units do not receive subsidy on their new developments. Given the level of rents that the government thinks desirable (50 percent higher in real terms than when it came into office), most local authorities are no longer eligible for housing subsidy.

For the minority of authorities that still receive subsidy, the system reacts to new developments as follows. Initially the authority's subsidy receipts from the central government increase by the equivalent of 75 percent of the debt service on the new development plus an allowance (based on the authority's past level of spending per unit) for management and maintenance. In future years the subsidy declines, however, as the margin between rents and management and maintenance costs is assumed to grow.

Although based on ostensibly different principles, this system has much in common with that for housing associations described earlier. Developments are financed by a long-term conventional loan (from the central government) and a subsidy is given in a way that is highest at the start of the process, when real loan servicing costs are highest, but that falls over time as rents rise with (or beyond) inflation. That the two different systems should end up with such a similar result is not coincidence: a key problem of housing finance is the "front loading" of debt charges when there is inflation. With such a long-lived asset as housing this creates serious imbalances in the financial costs facing its owner over its lifetime.[21] The subsidy systems have evolved in a way that corrects for this.

ISSUES OF ACCOUNTABILITY

Local Authorities

On the face of it, the question of accountability is clear in the case of local authorities; indeed, this is the classic argument in favor of local government rather than nonprofit provision of services. The full-time officials running local authority services are answerable to the elected councilors, who in turn are answerable to their electorate. If public funds are being used inefficiently by an authority or if it is providing a poor quality service, then the councilors will be replaced at the next election. However, two different lines of criticism have been made of this traditional model. The first is that made by the current government, that in practice this mechanism of accountability to *ratepayers* (those paying the local property taxes) does not work very well. A rather different line of criticism questions whether it is only the ratepayers to whom local authority housing departments should be accountable, but whether the *tenants* should also have a role.

Despite large increases in rate bills (property taxes) in high spending areas (many under the control of radical opposition councilors) as a result of the combination of high spending and consequent withdrawal of central government grants as a penalty, voters have continued to elect many of the councilors. The councilors argue that the electors value the services they are providing and recognize that most of the increase in local taxes has resulted from central government action, in terms of rigging the grant system against urban (mostly Labour) authorities. The government argues that most of those voting in the elections do not pay the resultant taxes and so are indifferent to the cost of the services provided. This happens for three reasons. First, the tax is formally levied only on the householder; other members of the household do not have to pay the bill directly. Second, the social security system means that people with very low incomes are completely insulated from any change in their local tax bills: higher rates are matched by higher benefit entitlements. In some of the inner city areas this includes the majority of households. Finally, part of the local tax bill is paid by local businesses, which do not have a vote.

In an attempt to deal with the problem it perceives, the government has proposed the abolition of rates and replacement with a poll tax (which it describes as a "community charge") payable by all adults resident in an area. Furthermore, the rules of the social security system will be changed so that everyone, no matter how poor, will have to pay 20 percent of the poll tax and so will be affected by council spending decisions. The rates levied on businesses will be at a flat national rate, so that councils will not be able to gain extra revenue from businesses in their area. The government hopes that these reforms will lead to greater accountability of councils to their voters. In the meantime it has limited the spending of certain councils directly (under a process known as "ratecapping"). However, as yet this has had comparatively little effect, as the councils subject to spending limits have found ingenious ways round the financial controls through what has become known as "creative accountancy."

Regardless of what one thinks of the government's actions and proposals—and given their regressive nature they are highly controversial—it is clear that there is a crisis in the system of local government accountability, which can no longer be considered to be self-evident. The systems of Rate Support Grants and (to a lesser extent) housing subsidies have become so complicated and so politicized that few people understand the trade-offs between spending decisions and local tax levels. The rate level emerges as a random variable, depending on political favoritism, luck, or skill in beating the system rather than having a clear relationship to spending. The imposition of ratecapping has meant the diversion of management efforts into finding ways round the restrictions in order to defend existing service levels; inevitably less attention is given to normal management responsibilities. The limits are therefore having a perverse effect on improving value for money.

These arguments are all in terms of the traditional model of responsibility of an authority to local voters. In the case of a service such as housing, however, the group most affected by spending decisions and efficiency of service provision is more restricted than voters as a whole (who will take many other issues into account when they vote). The questions arise of whether local authority housing departments are responsive enough to their tenants (and prospective tenants) and, if not, how this could be remedied. A first problem is that of the scale of management. As the size of the stock controlled by authorities grew, they tended to adopt highly centralized management structures. As a consequence, tenants have found themselves without accessible people to whom they can, for instance, report repairs required or complain that previously reported repairs have not been carried out. Getting a response from distant and anonymous officials in the town hall has proved frustrating and ineffective.[22]

Responses to these problems have come in three forms, rather limited in impact as yet. First, there is a move (promoted by the central government department responsible for housing) toward decentralization of certain housing services onto estates and out of the town halls. This approach has had notable successes with some of the most run-down estates in the country.[23] Second there have been calls for greater tenant control and participation in management. The government's main response to this issue has been to point to its sales program under the right to buy program; those who have bought exercise all the control that goes with ownership. Nevertheless, despite the very large sales program, nine-tenths of tenants have not bought their homes. For them increased rights to take action if the authority fails to carry out repairs have been of more importance. A further new proposal would allow local authority tenants to opt to change their landlord (for instance, to a housing association) in certain circumstances, the intention being to give tenants a further opportunity to exercise their power of exit and "vote with their rentbooks" against inefficient and unresponsive Housing Departments.[24]

Housing Associations

Housing associations are under the control of voluntary unpaid management committees (constituted under rules that must conform to a model
laid down by the Housing Corporation). Where day-to-day management
is in the hands of a full-time professional staff (which it is for all associations of significant size), they report to the management committee. The
committees are elected by the association's members. In some cases, housing cooperatives, this membership may include all the association's tenants. In others it is a much more limited group of people, perhaps those
who set up the association in the first place. In general committee membership is very stable, with the committee itself making recommendations
for new members on the basis of some particular skill or expertise. Some
30,000 people are involved in the housing association movement in this
way, and their voluntary time and dedication must be regarded as one of
the major assets of the sector, one that results directly from its nonprofit
nature.

In qualification of these advantages, it has been suggested that the membership of committees is frequently dominated by middle class professionals, particularly those involved in housing-related activities, such as archi-
tects, estate agents, accountants, and so on.[25] Such committee members
may be more interested in the development side of the associations' work,
with the visible results coming from increasing the number of units receiving more attention than the management of existing tenancies. More generally there is a danger that committees become "self-perpetuating oligar-
chies." At the same time, with the larger associations, voluntary committees
may simply become rubber stamps for the full-time management staff and
exercise little useful role.

Associations are also subject to detailed financial scrutiny and monitoring by the Housing Corporation. The corporation, as a public body, is in
turn responsible to the central government and the national electorate. The
level of monitoring and control exercised by the corporation is fairly intense. Roughly, once every two years the corporation examines the association's papers and accounts and can make detailed recommendations about
procedures and efficiency. In the case of problems that are not remedied
or instances of corruption, the corporation has the power to remove people from the management committee and make its own appointments. This
power is rarely exercised, however. With its general knowledge of costs
for other associations with comparable stock, the corporation is in a good
position to tell whether an association is managed efficiently or whether
there are impending financial problems. The corporation also has a role in
promoting good management practice—for instance, in respect to rental
policies or making proper provision for long-term repairs and maintenance—although its advice is not binding.

These scrutiny arrangements are likely to be very effective in exposing
corruption, incompetence, and clear examples of bad practice. They are

less likely to respond to the needs of tenants. Here, the associations claim significant advantages over local authorities in terms of more decentralized management, greater contact between tenants and management staff, and larger numbers of staff members "on the grounds," such as caretakers and so on. If a problem goes unremedied, tenants should be able to contact the management committee, which should itself have tenant representation of some kind. Ultimately, tenants can appeal to the Housing Corporation and the National Federation of Housing Associations if this route fails them. In recent years there have been attempts to secure greater tenant representation on management committees. Although some of the older philanthropic trusts retain their somewhat paternalistic attitude toward tenants,[26] in general it appears that associations have made more progress in terms of this kind of accountability than the authorities.

Comparison is more difficult regarding the allocation policies of associations toward new tenants. Many associations rely on the local authorities in the areas in which they operate to make nominations when vacancies arise. The local authority's criteria for giving different groups priority—established by a democratically elected council—are then what determines who gets access. Other associations have their own waiting lists and allocation systems that may be ad hoc to say the least. Given that housing is a publicly subsidized commodity, its allocation is a matter of public concern. In recognition of this problem, associations are now monitoring the characteristics of their tenants in order to check that they match those of the local populations from which they draw their client groups.

CONCLUSIONS

Housing associations have been successful in establishing themselves as an increasingly important part of the rental housing sector in Britain. In their origins, associations owe much to the energy of those motivated by philanthropic, charitable, or political concern about the housing problems of those in need. Their growth, on the other hand, has been largely due to the support given to them by central and (to a lesser extent) local government. To understand the level of support they have received one has to take account of the political reasons why social housing has been supported over the years and why local authorities are now seeing a reduction in their role.

The reasons for public intervention in the British housing market are similar to those that actuated intervention in other countries. These include a concern with minimum standards, the use of housing as a way of redistributing income, and a fear that private landlords will exploit the local monopoly power they may enjoy over their tenants. It would be possible (and indeed occurs in other countries) for these concerns to be met with a combination of public *regulation* of private activity, subsidies to private landlords, and means-tested assistance to tenants. This has not been the route followed in Britain. The public sector has been seen as the appropriate instrument for tasks such as slum clearance and redevelopment, and the profit-making private landlord has been rejected as a trustworthy recipient of public subsidy. There has been increasing use of means-tested assistance with rent, but this has brought its own problems in terms of distorting the housing and labor markets, so the general practice of below-market rents in the social sector remains.

To this history one can add the reasons why associations have increased their share of housing provision in recent years. Their variety and organizational style have given them a good reputation both for innovation and good management. They harness the enthusiasm and expertise of large numbers of voluntary management committee members while using professional staff to run their day-to-day operations. They have also been seen in recent years by central government as an alternative to the use of local government, with parts of which it is locked in a deep ideological battle. This has resulted in an increasing share of the public capital budget for new building going to associations and now to proposals that local authority tenants should have the right to choose associations to take over the management and other landlord functions from the authorities.

The questions arising from this situation are those that arise with other nonprofit interventions in the traditional welfare state. In recent years the capital programs of associations have been almost wholly funded by the public sector. One issue arising from this is the scope for injecting private finance to supplement the public input. Another issue is that within a sharply reduced public housing budget, associations have increased their share. In contrast, general government policy toward the authorities has left many of them in a position where they suffer significant penalties on additional spending. In this respect the associations have been in a more favorable position. The very fact that two kinds of institutions providing much the same service are treated in completely different ways financially is in itself a problem in evaluating their relative effectiveness.

A final issue is that of accountability. The issue is not as clear-cut as might have been expected, however. The British local authority sector is currently a political battleground, with major conflicts between central and local government overshadowing all other policy considerations. Some central government initiatives to produce "more accountability" may actually have had perverse effects. Housing associations are responsive to their tenants but not necessarily to the wider electorate. As far as their financial accountability is concerned, the relevant public body, the Housing Corporation, has successfully evolved a system for close monitoring of association operations. When it comes to the further issue of accountability to tenants, the local authorities and associations face exactly the same problems. In some ways, such as responsiveness to the needs of existing tenants, the associations have been more successful than the local authorities. In others, such as procedures used in choosing new tenants, the question of democratic control in allocating publicly subsidized commodities is more problematic for the nonprofit organizations.

It would be a mistake to think that Britain's housing problems could be solved by dropping them on the shoulders of the housing association movement. The movement is not equipped or designed to provide comprehensive coverage for all those needing rental accommodation. What it has done is to develop expertise in providing housing for particular groups and in particular areas. Its experiences have given useful lessons to the more traditional sectors of the welfare state. It is hard, however, to see it as a substitute for those sectors.

NOTES

1. An empirical analysis of the relative efficiency of the sector compared with local authority housing will have to await the results of a study currently underway at the University of Glasgow.

2. This section draws heavily on A. E. Holmans, *Housing Policy in Britain* (London: Croom Helm, 1987).

3. A similar cycle has been observed elsewhere, for instance, in New York City.

4. Again, a similar phenomenon has been seen elsewhere, for instance, with the tax advantages of owner-occupiers emerging unscathed from the recent U.S. tax reform.

5. See A. Power, *Property before People* (Hemel Hempstead: George Allen and Unwin, 1987), for a detailed account of this phenomenon.

6. This is, however, one of the Government's main objectives, as spelled out in its recent white paper, Department of the Environment, *Housing: The Government's Proposals* (London: Her Majesty's Stationery Office, 1987).

7. Under the government's proposals there would be a change in the system of rent control, but they would remain below market levels.

8. In Britain charitable status can be granted to organizations whose purposes are the advancement of education, religion, the relief of poverty, or otherwise beneficial to the community. Charitable housing associations qualify under the last two of these categories. The positions of the tenants of charitable and noncharitable associations differ, most importantly in that the latter have the right to buy the property they rent.

9. J. Posnett and J. Chase, "Housing Associations in England and Wales," *Charity Statistics 1984–85* (Tonbridge: Charities Aid Foundation, 1985).

10. Department of the Environment, *Housing and Construction Statistics 1975–1985*, (London: Her Majesty's Stationery Office, 1986), Table 9.4.

11. Ibid., Table 6.1.

12. Housing Corporation, *Analysis of the 1985 Statistical Returns from Registered Housing Associations in England and Wales*, (London: Author, 1986).

13. Department of the Environment, *Housing and Construction Statistics*, Table 6.7.

14. This reflects not only a housing association rental policy, but also the fact that a greater proportion of their rentals have been made in recent years than those of local authorities; and during that time increasingly desperate groups have had to be housed by both organizations.

15. Department of the Environment, *Finance for Housing Associations*.

16. Inquiry into British Housing, *The Evidence* (London: National Federation of Housing Associations, 1985), p. 131.

17. Inquiry into British Housing, *Report*, (London: National Federation of Housing Associations, 1985), pp. 28–29.

18. Her Majesty's Treasury, *The Government's Expenditure Plans 1986–1987 to 1988–1989*, Cmnd 9702–II (London: Her Majesty's Stationery Office, 1987).

19. See J. Hills, *When is a Grant not a Grant? The Current System of Housing Association Finance,* Welfare State Programme Discussion Paper No. 24 (London: London School of Economics, 1987) for a detailed discussion of the issues.

20. The proposals in Department of the Environment, *Finance for Housing Associations,* are not specific about the level of grant that would be allowed, but it appears that the government would like to see the average level cut to 50 percent, which would mean rent increases of 50 percent or more in most cases.

21. This similarity is explored in more detail in J. Hills, *Subsidies to Social Housing in England: Their Behavioural Implications,* Welfare State Programme Discussion Paper No. 24, (London: London School of Economics, 1987), which also takes into account the way in which the general system of central government grants to local authorities (Block Grants) greatly complicates their position, a complication that there is no space to go into here.

22. See A. Power, *Property before People.*

23. See A. Power, ibid., and A. Power, *The PEP Experience* (London: Department of the Environment Priority Estates Project, 1987).

24. Department of the Environment, *Housing: The Government's Proposals.*

25. D. Noble, "Committee System," *Roof* (January 1980).

26. R. Cowan, "A Conflict of Interests," *Roof* (May–June 1985).

REFERENCES

Baker, C. V. *Housing Associations.* London: The Estates Gazette Ltd., 1976.

Cowan, R. "A Conflict of Interests," *Roof* (May–June 1985).

Department of the Environment. *Housing: The Government's Proposals,* Cm 214 London: Her Majesty's Stationery Office, 1987.

————. *Finance for Housing Associations: The Government's Proposals.* London: Her Majesty's Stationery Office, 1987.

————. *Housing and Construction Statistics 1975–1985.* London: Her Majesty's Stationery Office, 1986.

Hills, J. *When is a Grant Not a Grant? The Current System of Housing Association Finance.* Welfare State Programme Discussion Paper No . 13. London: London School of Economics, 1987.

————. *Subsidies to Social Housing in England: Their Behavioural Implications,* Welfare State Programme Discussion Paper No. 24. London: London School of Economics, 1987.

HM Treasury, *The Government's Expenditure Plans 1986–87 to 1988–89,* Cmnd 9702-II. London: HMSO, 1986.

Holmans, A. E. *Housing Policy in Britain.* London: Croom Helm, 1987.

Housing Corporation, *Analysis of the 1985 Statistical Returns from Registered Housing Associations in England and Wales.* London: The Housing Corporation, 1986.

————. *Analysis of the 1983 Statistical Returns from Registered Housing Associations in England and Wales.* London: Housing Corporation, 1984.

Inquiry into British Housing. *The Evidence.* London: National Federation of Housing Associations, 1985.

Inquiry into British Housing, *Report.* London: National Federation of Housing Associations, 1985.

Noble, D. "Committee System", *Roof* (January 1980).

Office of Population Censuses and Surveys. *General Household Survey 1983.* London: HMSO, 1985.

Posnett, J., and J. Chase. "Housing Associations in England and Wales," in *Charity Statistics 1984–85.* Tonbridge: Charities Aid Foundation, 1985.

Power, A. *Property before People.* Hemel Hempstead: George Allen and Unwin, 1987.

————. *The PEP Experience.* London: Department of the Environment Priority Estates Project, 1987.

11

The British Deed of Covenant as a Tax Incentive for Charitable Donations: Vestige or Viable Alternative?

J. MARK DAVIDSON SCHUSTER

Most Western governments have provisions in their tax law to provide incentives for contributions to charitable organizations. Often it is unclear from the legislative record whether these provisions were originally intended to provide fiscal incentives for charitable donations or to simply help define the boundaries of taxable income. Nevertheless, the incentive effects of these provisions are now widely acknowledged, and recognition of these incentives has played an important role in debating and understanding the effects of recent changes in tax law on the flow of charitable contributions.

Fiscal incentives for charitable contributions are currently of two types: the charitable contribution deduction, well known in American tax law and implemented in a number of other countries, and the so-called "deed of covenant," a lesser known and poorly understood system in force in Great Britain, Ireland, and Denmark.[1] Though the deed of covenant is more the exception than the rule for tax-induced donations, its structure and implementation provide a fascinating and instructive counterpoint to the charitable contribution deduction. A comparison of the two systems from a public policy perspective highlights the advantages and disadvantages of each and offers a clearer understanding of the types of incentives

This article is an abridged and revised version of "Tax Incentives for Charitable Donations: Deeds of Covenant and Charitable Contribution Deductions," an article that originally appeared in the *University of San Francisco Law Review*, 19, no. 3–4 (Spring–Summer 1985). The research was supported with funds from a general purpose grant to the Program on Non-Profit Organizations at Yale University from the Rockefeller Brothers Fund. I am grateful to Paul DiMaggio, John Simon, and Michael Montias of PONPO, to Norman Donaldson of the Charities Aid Foundation, and to David Denton of Inland Revenue for their comments on earlier drafts. Copyright © 1985 by the *University of San Francisco Law Review*. Reprinted by permission.

present in each system and their effects on donors, charitable organizations, and the tax collecting authorities.

This chapter describes the structure and administration of deeds of covenant in Great Britain, identifies the incentives this system offers for charitable donations in comparison to those offered by the charitable deduction, and speculates about the effects of the system on charitable organizations.

THE DEED OF CONVENANT

The Situation before 1980

The British deed of covenant, unlike the charitable contribution deduction in American law, was not originally created as an incentive to charitable giving.[2] The principle underlying the covenant can be traced back to the origin of the British income tax in Addington's Act of 1803,[3] in which it was established that transfers of income from one taxpayer to another would, for income tax purposes, be treated as the income of the recipient and not as the income of the transferror, though it was not until the 1920s that the principle was first applied to transfers to charitable organizations.[4] Such transfers were subjected to a number of requirements to guarantee that they not be used to dodge income taxation. Thus, for example, such transfers were required to be made under a written agreement (the "covenant") on an annual basis for a period capable of exceeding six years.

The applicability of this provision to charities is clear when it is coupled with the fact that charities themselves are exempt from income tax. Thus, a transfer of income from a taxpayer (either an individual or a corporation) to a charity made under a deed of covenant is not treated as the taxable income of the taxpayer-donor, but as the nontaxable income of the tax-exempt charity.[5]

For example, consider an individual taxpayer who has entered into a deed of covenant with a charity. Because the British tax collection procedure is based primarily upon the PAYE system (Pay-as-You-Earn), most income tax is withheld at the source, and the taxpayer has only after-tax income with which to pay his or her deed of covenant obligations. Typically, this means that the donor who enters into a "net covenant" agrees to donate a fixed annual amount of after-tax income to the charity for the duration of the covenant agreement. In theory, the charity can recoup all of the taxes already paid by the taxpayer on that income by reclaiming them from the Inland Revenue. Thus, unlike the charitable deduction by which the donor channels the entire donation to the charity in one payment—including the taxes that would otherwise be due and the donor's private (net of tax) contribution—the deed of covenant system separates the flow of money into two streams. The donor's private contribution flows directly from the donor to the charity, and the foregone taxes flow first to the government and then to the charity upon reclamation.

A simple example will help make this clear. An individual taxpayer whose income is taxed at the "basic" British income tax rate pays 30 percent. That taxpayer signs a net deed of covenant with a charity promising to make an annual payment of £100 after taxes to the charity. Each year the taxpayer sends a check for £100 to the charity, and the charity then reclaims the taxes the taxpayer paid on his or her gross income leaving him or her with the £100 available for a charitable donation. In this case the taxes paid by the taxpayer would be £43 (£43 = 30 percent of £143, £100 in donation + £43 in taxes paid), and it is this amount the charity is entitled to reclaim from Inland Revenue.

Throughout much of its history, the application of deeds of covenant to charitable donations has, in one important aspect, violated this general principle: charities have only been allowed to reclaim taxes at the basic rate of tax, the lowest income tax rate applicable at a particular point in time. As a result, until the passage of the Finance Act of 1980 the taxpayer-donor who paid higher income tax rates paid more in taxes on the income involved in this transfer than the charity was able to reclaim, and the difference was retained by the government as part of its general income tax revenue.

By contrast, a charitable deduction allows for continuous adjustment to the donor's actual marginal tax rate. No explicit calculation of the actual private after-tax contribution need be made by the donor. Once he or she decides the amount of the total (gross) contribution, the tax foregone is automatically included in the donor's check, and it is deducted from the donor's tax liability as part of his or her annual tax reckoning. (The total contribution is deducted from the donor's gross income as part of the process of determining net taxable income.) In this sense, the charitable deduction system ensures that the charity receives the full benefit of the taxes foregone, while the deed of covenant, in its pure form, does not.

Despite a number of technical changes, the deed of covenant remained basically unchanged until the Finance Act of 1980 made several changes in the rules governing deeds of covenant for donations to charity, changes that represent a rather rapid transformation of the covenant system into one that more closely resembles the charitable contribution deduction.

The Finance Act of 1980

In 1979 the Conservative Party came back into power in Great Britain. Its fiscal policies were designed to deemphasize the income tax and to further exploit other sources of taxation, particularly the broad-based Value Added Tax. The Finance Act of 1980 has been considered something of a watershed for charities because in translating these Tory policies into law, it included major provisions that have had a direct financial impact on charities.

The major reform in the income tax took the form of reduced tax rates; the standard rate was lowered from 33 to 30 percent (after having been lowered from 35 to 33 percent between 1976–1977 and 1977–1978 by

Labour governments), and the higher rates were correspondingly decreased (the highest from 83 to 60 percent but retaining an additional surcharge of 15 percent on unearned investment income). The change in the basic rate lowered the incentive for charitable giving. It also caused a transition problem for charities with outstanding deeds of covenant, because the net contributions of individual donors would be supplemented by taxes reclaimed at a lower rate than those in effect when the covenants were first written.[6]

Such changes in the tax law and their attendant consequences clearly illustrate the effect that seemingly unrelated changes can have on charitable activities as the behavior of taxpayer-donors responds to the financial incentives as they spread throughout the system. This sort of change is particularly difficult to highlight in a system of charitable income tax deductions, where responses to changes in marginal tax rates cannot be easily identified by any of the interested parties. Of course, changes in tax rates affect the incentives for giving in a similar way in a system that uses the charitable deduction: a change in the tax rate changes the price of giving, which changes the amount given by a donor. The important point is that under the charitable contribution deduction the amount to be contributed is not set by any advance agreement; the donor adjusts his or her giving freely in response to any changes in financial incentives including changes in the tax rates.

On the positive side, the most important provision of the Finance Act of 1980 for charities is the relief it offers from higher rates on charitable deeds of covenant. Up to a specified ceiling on gross gifts,[7] covenanted giving by individuals to charity is no longer regarded as the income of the donor for higher rate tax purposes; thus, the individual donor can subtract the gross value of the covenanted donation from his or her income and thereby avoid paying higher rate taxes on the donation.[8] The donor still pays the basic rate to the government because that portion is reclaimed by the charity.

An example of a taxpayer in the 50 percent marginal tax bracket who has entered into a £100 net covenant with a charity will help illustrate. The donor pays the £100 net covenant to the charity. The charity can then reclaim £43 from Inland Revenue as before, leaving the charity with a net increase in its income of £143. With higher rate relief, however, the donor can get a rebate of the higher rate taxes paid on the gross donation by reclaiming the difference between his or her marginal tax rate and the basic tax rate (50 percent − 30 percent = 20 percent), as applied to the gross donation (20 percent × £143 = £29). Thus, higher rate relief effectively reduces the net cost of a donation for donors in the higher marginal tax brackets. Notice that, in the first instance, the higher rate relief works directly to the financial advantage of the donor not to the charity.

One by-product of higher rate relief, which can be clearly seen in this example, is that donations made under deed of covenant by higher rate taxpayers are no longer cleanly separated into the two financial flows of taxes foregone and private contribution. Under higher rate relief the net covenant payment that such a donor makes actually includes two pieces, the donor's real net cost plus the taxes foregone through higher rate relief. In this example, the donor's net cost for the donation is £71, but the check the donor sends to the charity as payment of his or her net covenant is for £100 as it includes the £29 in taxes foregone as higher rate relief. This gives the donor a degree of control over the final disposition of this portion of the foregone taxes that is not available under the pure deed of covenant.

Another change in the Finance Act of 1980 affects the mandatory length of deeds of covenant for charitable donations. Previously, charitable covenants had to be capable of exceeding six years which, practically speaking, meant that most covenants were written for seven years. Now they only have to be capable of exceeding three years which, in turn, may lead to most covenants being written for a duration of four years.

This outline of the deed of covenant can now be used as the base for a more detailed discussion of the incentives and impediments present in the system and how they are perceived by each of the actors in it: the individual donor, the corporate donor, the charity, and the Inland Revenue.

INCENTIVES AND IMPEDIMENTS

The Individual Donor's Perspective

In asking how the donor perceives and understands the deed of covenant, I turn first to a theoretical consideration of various ways in which the donor might perceive the financial incentives. In this discussion I begin by assuming that the donor is making decisions with perfect knowledge of the tax implications of either the deed of covenant or the charitable deduction.

In studying the American system of charitable income tax deductions, economists have found the marginal price of a contribution to be a particularly important predictor of the amount an individual finally gives.[9] The marginal price of giving is the net cost to the donor of getting an *additional* dollar (or pound) to flow to a charity. When this price is lowered, an additional contribution to charity becomes a more attractive use of the donor's money.

Under a charitable contribution deduction the marginal price of giving is one minus the donor's *marginal* tax rate. A donor in a 20 percent marginal tax bracket, for example, would have to pay $.80 to get an additional $1.00 to flow to charity; the marginal price of giving is $.80. Under the charitable contribution deduction the price of giving is, therefore, expressly linked to the donor's marginal tax rate. This result has been criticized as being inequitable because it provides a greater financial incentive for the charitable contributions of the high-income donor than for the lower-income donor.[10]

Prior to the implementation of higher rate relief, the marginal price of

Table 11.1. The Marginal Price of Giving under Various Assumptions

Donor's Marginal Tax Rate	Donor's Marginal Price of Giving			
	Charitable Deduction	Deed of Covenant (within limit)	Deed of Covenant (outside limit)	No Tax Incentive
30 percent	0.70	0.70	0.70	1.00
50 percent	0.50	0.50	0.70	1.00
60 percent	0.40	0.40	0.70	1.00
75 percent	0.25	0.25	0.70	1.00

giving under the deed of covenant system was identical for all taxpayers: one minus the *basic* tax rate. Thus, in its simplest form the deed of covenant system is the financial equivalent of a tax credit system in which the rate of tax credit is determined by the basic tax rate in force at that time.[11] Perhaps more accurately, because the flow of money is separated with the taxes foregone flowing first to the government and then to the charity and the private after-tax contribution flowing directly from the donor to the charity, the deed of covenant is, in essence, a flat matching grant for charitable contributions in which tax incentives are offered at a flat matching rate.[12]

Higher rate relief has dramatically changed the marginal price of giving by deed of covenant for the donor, and it is no longer equal for all taxpaying donors. Instead, the price is linked to the donor's income as it is under a charitable deduction. For donors with the same marginal tax rates, the price of giving, up to the limit on higher rate relief, is now identical in both systems.[13] This represents a large change in the marginal price of giving and a dramatic movement of the deed of covenant system toward the charitable deduction. Up to the limit on higher rate relief, donors with identical marginal tax rates face identical marginal prices for their charitable donations in both the deed of covenant and the charitable deduction systems. The marginal price of giving is compared for each type of incentive in various marginal tax brackets in Table 11.1.

Prior to higher rate relief any taxpayer-donor in a higher tax bracket was unable to get the full value of his or her donation to the charity because the government retained the difference between taxes paid at the basic rate of tax and taxes paid at the higher rate. This "leakage" is still true for any donations above the limit on higher rate relief. This difference among the various incentive systems can be embodied in a second financial indicator, the donor's "effort." This indicator asks, How many dollars (or pounds) must a donor earn in order to get one dollar (pound) to charity?[14] The donor's marginal effort is compared for various systems in Table 11.2.

Admittedly, it is difficult to visualize the donor who would explicitly ask how much money has to be earned in order to give a certain amount to a

Table 11.2. The Marginal Effort for Giving under Various Assumptions

Donor's Marginal Tax Rate	Donor's Marginal Effort			
	Charitable Deduction	Deed of Covenant (within limit)	Deed of Covenant (outside limit)	No Tax Incentive
30 percent	1.00	1.00	1.00	1.43
50 percent	1.00	1.00	1.40	2.00
60 percent	1.00	1.00	1.75	2.50
75 percent	1.00	1.00	2.80	4.00

charity. But, arguably, the realization that a deed of covenant system does not necessarily allow a charity to reclaim all of the taxes paid prior to an individual's donation may inhibit the donor. Nearly without exception, British debates on the structure of the deed of covenant have marshaled evidence against the covenant by presenting data on the system in a way that emphasizes the donor's effort while neglecting the marginal price.[15]

The choice of cost indicator, price or effort, to evaluate the deed of covenant is a subtle one with important consequences. The mathematical relationship between the two leads to an interesting paradox. Focusing on the marginal price and considering only those donations made within the limit on higher rate relief, one would conclude that the system is overly advantageous to the rich. Focusing on the donor's effort and looking at donations beyond the limit on higher rate relief, on the other hand, one would conclude that the system is overly punitive to the rich.

The importance of price and effort as indicators to help explain donor behavior ultimately lies less in an economic or psychological theory of how donors ought to react than it does in empirical observation of actual donor behavior. Unfortunately, the data are not available to make such an analysis, and any guess about the net effects proceeds necessarily from fragmented, anecdotal information.

Though the financial incentives and disincentives built into both systems are doubtless important in affecting donor behavior, the structural and administrative complexities of the covenant may be more important in dissuading donors. This view is certainly often expressed, though it is very difficult to substantiate. A number of such hurdles, both real and imagined, are frequently discussed:

- Donors may be unwilling to make a multiyear commitment. Perhaps even the new four year minimum is too long for the donor to feel confident about his or her ability to continue to pay.
- Donors may be unwilling to make a continuing commitment to the same charity for several years in a row.
- The system does not offer any financial incentive for onetime, spur of the moment donations.

- The amount of paperwork necessary to initiate a deed of covenant, ensure annual payment, inform the government of amounts paid to allow the reclamation of tax, and claim higher rate relief may be unnecessarily complex and burdensome.[16]
- The system is too complex to be easily explained to potential donors.

As it happens, the first three of these problems can be easily circumvented by someone with a good knowledge of the covenant system. The fourth continues to be a nuisance in the system, but one that the Inland Revenue would argue helps to adequately monitor and police it. The fifth may or may not be true; its seems that the burden lies on the charities to clearly describe the system and to explain the financial incentives it offers to potential donors. The evidence suggests that British charities have had rather unequal success in exploiting the covenant system, particularly with respect to the explanations they offer in their fund-raising literature.[17]

The Corporate Donor's Perspective

Corporations may also make donations to charities, and as with individual donors, they also can take advantage of the financial incentives embodied in the deed of covenant. But because the deed of covenant works through the income tax and not through the corporation tax, several interesting twists are introduced.

Corporations typically make charitable donations through "gross covenants" by which they guarantee the total amount the charity will receive. This includes the net payment from the company, foregone corporation taxes, and the taxes that will be reclaimed from the government. Consider a gross covenant for £100. The company sends £70 directly to the charity (as would an individual donor). However, because the company is not subject to income tax, it has to forward to the government the £30 that the charity will be entitled to reclaim. The company's own tax bill is calculated under corporation tax, and for purposes of computing the company's liability to corporation tax, the gross amount of the covenant is deductible from its pretax profits. The typical company is liable for corporation tax at a rate of 52 percent. The deduction of a £100 covenant from pretax profits lowers the company's tax bill by £52, the taxes it otherwise would have had to pay. The marginal price of giving for this company is £0.48; it has to spend 48 pence in after-tax income to channel a pound to a charity via a deed of covenant. (There are no taxes retained by the government from the income used to generate the donation.)

The Charity's Perspective

Perhaps the most interesting aspect of the deed of covenant system from the charity's perspective is the separation of flows of money to the recipient charity. For each charitable donation under covenant the charity re-

ceives two payments instead of the one found under a charitable contribution deduction. This separation was especially clear prior to the passage
of higher rate relief. At that time the payment the individual donor made
directly to the charity, the net covenant, was paid entirely out of the donor's after-tax income. Thus, it was purely the donor's "private" contribution and did not include any of the taxes foregone as a result of the
covenant. The taxes foregone by the government formed the second payment to the charity, a payment made when the charity reclaimed the taxes
owed to it on its deeds of covenant.

As a result of this separation, the flow of charitable donations was structured so that it was absolutely clear to the charity what the various origins
of its funds were: private contributions from private donors and taxes
foregone as a result of government legislation. Under a charitable contribution deduction this distinction is lost as there is only one payment to the
charity including both the donor's private contribution and the taxes foregone. The charity perceives the entire contribution as coming from the
donor. It may be easy for the charity to lose sight of the fact that part of
most donations is the direct result of governments adopting policies to
forego taxes in favor of certain activities and that the bill for these foregone taxes is borne by all taxpayers who are contributing to the general
government budget.

At first glance this distinction may seem to be without any practical
significance, but it becomes absolutely critical when considering the degree
to which public policy deems it appropriate for donors to restrict and constrain their donations. With respect to the private contribution portion of
a donation, it is eminently reasonable to allow the donor to have entire
control over its expenditure. However, to the extent that public policy has
encouraged and helped support donations through taxes foregone it might
be argued that the public in general ought to have a voice in its dispersal.
Under the charitable contribution deduction the donor is freely able to
place whatever conditions he or she desires (within rather broad legal limits) on the entire donation, private contribution, and taxes foregone. The
donor decides not only which charity will receive the donation but perhaps
also the way in which the donation is to be spent by the charity.[18] At the
other extreme would be direct government aid to charity, in which the
government would directly subsidize charitable activity out of tax revenues, deciding itself which charities would receive the benefit of this tax-
supported aid and perhaps even specifying how the charities should spend
it.

In the pure deed of covenant system (before higher rate relief), this degree of donor influence is limited to the donor's private contribution. The
taxes foregone will, of course, flow to the same charity, and to that extent
the donor has placed a restriction on its expenditure. The charity, though,
no longer has to think of those taxes foregone as the result of a decision
by a particular donor with particular (or peculiar) wishes. They are simply
included in the sum total of all foregone taxes being reclaimed by the

charity. Thus, the deed of covenant stakes out a middle ground between direct government aid to charities and aid in the form of taxes foregone under a charitable contribution deduction. This middle ground seems justifiable from the standpoint of a public policy that aims to strike a balance between private decision making and public expenditure.

In this view, one of the unfortunate effects of the Finance Act of 1980 is the erosion of this distinction between the sources of the payments charities receive from individual donors. The process of reclaiming taxes foregone at the basic rate of tax is unchanged, and the check the charity receives directly from the individual donor is the donor's net covenant payment. But, this now includes both the donor's private net of tax contribution and the additional taxes foregone by the government in higher rate relief. It is no longer simply the donor's private contribution. (This is also true for the annual net payments made by corporations under covenant, which include the corporation's after-tax contribution plus part of the corporation taxes foregone.)

Even though higher rate relief was presented by the government as an increase in the financial incentives for charitable donations, the Finance Act of 1980 provided that higher rate relief would accrue directly to the donor as a rebate on the net covenant rather than to the charity by increasing the amount the charity could reclaim. This is primarily because of Inland Revenue's policy not to disclose the affairs of individual taxpayers. Repaying higher rate relief to the charity would also be an administrative nightmare since, under the current system in which the government assesses each taxpayer's tax liability, the donor's marginal tax rate may not be finally established for years.[19]

A particularly puzzling element in the debate pitting the deed of covenant against the charitable contribution deduction is the contention that they differ substantially in that under the (pure) covenant system the charity receives the benefit of the tax incentive, whereas under the charitable deduction the donor receives the benefit. This view rests on a basic misunderstanding of the net effects of the charitable deduction. While it is true that the donor receives the benefit of the tax incentive through a lower tax bill at the end of the year, he or she has already passed those foregone taxes on to the charity in the original payment. The charity is the final recipient. To its credit, the Goodman Committee recognized that "giving could be so arranged under either system to achieve a similar result" and went on to explore other differences between the two systems.[20] The real issue, which applies equally to both systems, is the extent to which the donor uses the existence of the tax incentive to reduce what he or she would have given in the absence of such an incentive, an entirely private contribution. Only if the donor reduces his or her private net contribution in this way can the benefit truly be said to be going to the donor.

From the charities' perspective the ultimate question is: How have donors adjusted their charitable donations in response to the 1980 and 1983 changes in tax law? The National Council for Voluntary Organisations has estimated that "if every higher rate taxpayer with a covenant passed on their refund, charities could benefit by up to £20 million a year."[21] Have charities convinced their donors to translate higher rate relief into correspondingly larger deeds of covenant, or will donors keep the new benefits to themselves? Some scattered evidence indicates that the number and size of covenants have both gone up, but data that would allow definitive conclusions are not available (nor are they ever likely to be because of Inland Revenue's policies.)[22] And it is nearly impossible to tell yet to what extent any change represents a real increase rather than a rewriting of covenants to take advantage of the new shorter minimum time period.

One interesting result of higher rate relief is that certain charities have realized that higher rate relief is unlikely to help them very much because their donors are not in the higher marginal tax brackets. This interaction between the tax incentive and the type of recipient has long been recognized and sometimes lamented as a side effect of the charitable contribution deduction. Donor tastes for certain types of charitable activities interact with their marginal tax rates to distribute the tax benefit proportionally more toward those charities favored by the wealthy; that is, the arts and education.[23] In this important respect, the effect of higher rate relief is not neutral across all charities. Indeed, prior to the Finance Act of 1980 those charities represented by the National Council for Voluntary Organisations (NCVO) had argued for further tax incentives for individual donations to charity but in such a way that "the net amount received by a charity under a deed of covenant should be deemed to have suffered income tax at an average rate of 45 percent."[24] The 1982 Report of the NCVO Fiscal Working Party argued once again in favor of this recommendation, supporting it as a composite system that would incorporate the administrative advantages of the deed of covenant and increase the financial incentives for all donors equally without offering undue advantages to the charities favored by the rich.[25] But there is no unanimity on this point within the charitable community.

Charities have long argued that one of the most desirable characteristics of the deed of covenant is the requirement that it be written for a certain number of years. The perceived advantage is that it introduces an important element of security into the charity's income flow, making it easier to budget from year to year and minimizing the cost of fund raising. This characteristic of the deed of covenant system led Bouuaert, in his major report to the European commission on the tax provisions for charity in the member states, to conclude that the continuity inherent in covenant giving provides considerable advantages over a charitable deduction.[26] Whether this is actually true is difficult to ascertain; no data yet exist that would show how the British taxpayer would respond to the elimination of the four-year minimum on covenants. If such data had been available, it would have been interesting to study the change in donor behavior in response to changing the minimum period from seven to four years. It is not known whether the eventual result of shortening the period will be a net increase in contributions via donors who were not previously willing to enter into a longer commitment or a net decrease as donors respond by simply making shorter covenants for the same, or only slightly increased, annual amounts.[27] One possibility is that charities may like the reduction to four years because it may allow them to renegotiate covenants sooner and to adjust them upwards to account for inflation.

Inland Revenue's Perspective

Inland Revenue's primary role vis-á-vis charities is through the process of reclamation of income tax on deeds of covenant, though it does play a limited role in checking and challenging the charitable status of charities. (The Charity Commission, founded in 1960, is directly responsible for granting charitable status.) The structure of the deed of covenant offers an easy way for Inland Revenue to monitor and affect the distribution of funds by charities. Through its inspectors, Inland Revenue spot checks charities to make sure that they are spending their income on charitable purposes. If it is found that income is being spent on noncharitable purposes, Inland Revenue simply denies reclamation of taxes on deeds of covenant.[28] Inland Revenue has resisted changes in the tax incentive that would allow all monies to flow to the charity directly and eliminate this control on the system.[29]

A related argument has to do with taxpayer fraud under a charitable contribution deduction. It is certainly true that there are taxpayers who take deductions for charitable contributions that were never made, thereby simply reducing their tax bill. The deed of covenant system would seem to nearly eliminate this type of fraud.[30]

CIRCUMVENTING THE SYSTEM

One stream of criticism that runs throughout the discussion of the deed of covenant has been its supposed lack of flexibility in responding to the various needs and desires of donors. In fact, though it is not obvious to the casual observer, the basic structure of the deed of covenant allows for a multitude of administrative arrangements that legally circumvent the system, thereby greatly increasing its flexibility.[31] Apparent problems in the structure of the system may actually be problems in the provision of information to the public concerning options that are already available to the donor. Several of the more important options are discussed in this section.

Discretionary Giving

Some donors may not wish to commit themselves to one particular charity even though they are willing to commit to making charitable donations over a number of years. Such donors can use a "halfway house charity" as the conduit for their contributions. Donors make their net covenant contribution to the halfway house charity, which reclaims the foregone taxes due at the standard rate. The halfway house charity then redistributes the total to other charitable recipients according to the wishes of the original donor. Donors can create their own grant-making charitable trusts to serve as such a conduit or use the services of the Charities Aid Foundation (CAF), which has had considerable experience in administering this type of arrangement. CAF issues its donors checks that they can use to make their charitable contributions in whatever amount to whatever charitable recipients they choose up to the amount of the credits they have accrued in their CAF account.[32]

This scheme reintroduces one of the issues that the pure deed of covenant system avoids, donor control over the reclaimed taxes. Use of a halfway house charity allows the donor to exert control over the expenditure of the taxes reclaimed at the standard rate by placing conditions on the charity to which he or she contributes.

Length of Time Commitment

How binding is the statutory limit of four years on a deed of covenant? The legal wording states that a deed of covenant must be able to exceed three years and cannot be revoked by the donor within three years of the first payment. This wording allows a donor to write into a covenant a variety of clauses that are able to exceed three years, but in certain events might not. For example, the donor may consider the following alternatives: "annually as long as the donor shall live," "annually as long as the Conservative government remains in power," "annually as long as the donor's income exceeds a certain amount," and so on. Through such clauses the donor can specify certain events that would terminate the charitable giving agreement. Inland Revenue seems to take a very relaxed attitude toward escape clauses, being more concerned with the actual frequency with which people exercise such clauses than with the theoretical ease of doing so.

Even without an escape clause the donor can shorten the period considerably. For example, on April 5, 1984, the donor could sign a covenant for four years from April 6, 1983 and pay the first installment on April 5, 1984; the second on April 6, 1984; the third on April 6, 1985; and the fourth on April 6, 1986. Thus, the payments fall into four separate deed years but actually span only two years and two days.[33]

A related question is what would happen if a donor simply terminated his or her payments early. The covenant is an agreement between the donor and the charity, and in theory the charity could sue to claim the donation it is due under the covenant. In practice charities are very reticent to pursue this course of action and in all likelihood will stop after sending the donor a couple of reminders. Furthermore, a donor can ask a charity to release him from the covenant agreement, which is voided if the charity agrees.

Single Donations

It is even possible to extend the tax advantages of the deed of covenant to a single donation through the use of a loan-covenant. A donor who wishes to make one large donation to a charity can make it in the form of an interest-free loan. At the same time, the donor writes a four-year covenant with the charity with a net annual payment equal to one-fourth of the loan. Each year the charity repays one-fourth of the loan to the donor, and the donor makes the covenanted payment. (This can simply be a bookkeeping transaction.) The net result is that the charity receives the total private contribution at one time but reclaims the taxes due in four equal payments from the government. It is able to get most, though not all, of the gross benefit of the donation up front. The loan-covenant should be particularly useful in securing large donations for capital projects.

Trading Income

For charities in both Great Britain and the United States there are often questions concerning the income tax status of unrelated business income. Theoretically, such income is taxable in both cases, though there is often quite a bit of leeway in determining just which income is "unrelated." In Great Britain charities have avoided this problem through the use of covenants. A charity that has considerable trading income can create a subsidiary for trading purposes (e.g., the Oxfam shops), and because there is no limit on the amount a corporation may covenant to charity, these subsidiaries can covenant all of their pretax profits to their parent charity and thus avoid all taxes on the transfer. From Inland Revenue's perspective, this procedure must be balanced with avoiding unfair competition for profit-making companies. So far Inland Revenue has allowed it to be used relatively freely.

These, and other, administrative schemes go a long way to improving the flexibility of the deed of covenant system, but they are sufficiently complex to suggest that donors do not use them as often as they might with better information. No matter how much information is available, it is still considerably more burdensome, for example, to enter into a loan-covenant agreement to make a one-time donation than it is to send one check under a charitable contribution deduction.

CONCLUSION

The pure deed of covenant differs from a charitable deduction in three fundamental ways: it is a long-term commitment to charitable giving; tax relief is at the basic rate of tax, making it the functional equivalent of a tax credit; and the portion of the contribution that represents foregone taxes cannot be earmarked by the donor. A number of the public policy issues that surround the use of tax policies to provide incentives for charitable contributions can be highlighted by recognizing these differences and speculating as to their effects.

Changes since 1980 have removed many of these differences. The reforms of the deed of covenant in the Finance Acts of 1980 and 1983, particularly higher rate relief, moved the deed of covenant closer to the charitable contribution deduction in two ways. First, with higher rate relief the financial incentives for taxpayers with the same marginal tax rates are now identical in both systems; and second, donors have been given the opportunity to stipulate and restrict the expenditure of a portion of the taxes foregone via the deed of covenant. The first change represents a significant change in the financial incentives for giving, particularly for higher rate taxpayers, but whether that will ultimately be turned into increased revenues for charities depends upon how successful charities will be in convincing donors to increase their covenants and pass along the new tax savings. The second change is a bit harder to pin down in that it depends on how donors tend to interact with different charitable sectors and with different charities. More recent changes have explicitly allowed limited charitable deductions for the first time.[34]

While increasing the financial incentives for charitable giving, all of these changes have also abandoned two aspects of the covenant system that, I have argued, might have been appropriate to retain in a public policy vis-à-vis charity: the principle of weighing each donor's gift equally for the purposes of tax incentives and the principle of dividing the charitable contribution into two financial streams, separating all the taxes foregone under the tax incentive from the donor's private net of tax contribution. From a public policy viewpoint both of these principles have desirable characteristics.

Another important factor that has been discussed is the relationship between flexibility in the system and the ability of the revenue authority to monitor charities' expenditure of their income. The deed of covenant is a system designed to give the Inland Revenue some teeth in carrying out that monitoring.

Predictability of income is also touted as a virtue of the deed of covenant. Though there is little evidence to argue for or against this view, it is widely believed to be true. British charities are concerned about the instability in their incomes, the increased costs of fund raising, and the changes in their relationships to their other sources of funding that a change to a charitable contribution deduction might entail.

One system is not clearly preferable to the other. A number of very subtle public policy issues are involved, issues whose resolution is likely to differ from one society to another depending upon the structure of its charitable sector, the structure of its tax law, and the relationship between charity and government. Reform of the deed of covenant and the recent implementation of limited charitable deductions may not be entirely in line with good public policy vis-à-vis charities, donors, or taxpayers. At the same time, the British experience with the deed of covenant suggests some factors that ought to be considered in the design of any tax incentives for charitable contributions. Whether the principles embodied in the deed of covenant will continue to be seen as sufficiently important to continue its use as a viable alternative to the charitable deduction or whether it will increasingly be seen as an anachronistic vestige of the views on tax incentives of an earlier political era remains to be seen.

NOTES

1. J. D. Livingston Booth, "Covenanted Giving—A New Era?" in Charities Aid Foundation, *Charity Conference Report: Charity Finance—Prospects, Opportunities and Management* (Tonbridge, England: Charities Aid Foundation, 1981), p. 18. For an excellent set of papers outlining possible alternative forms of tax incentives see Volume IV, Part V, "Alternatives to Tax Incentives," in the Commission on Private Philanthropy and Public Needs, *Research Papers* (Washington, D.C.: Department of the Treasury, 1977).

2. The origins of the charitable contribution of deduction and the deed of covenant are discussed in James Douglas and Peter Wright, "English Charities: Part I—Legal Definition, Taxation, and Regulation," Program on Non-Profit Organizations Working Paper 15 (New Haven: Institution for Social and Policy Studies, Yale University, 1980), pp. 69–70.

3. J. D. Livingston Booth, "Address Given to a Meeting of Charity Representatives at the Middlesex Hospital" (July 23, 1980), available from Charities Aid Foundation; and Donald R. Spuehler, "The System for Regulation and Assistance of Charity in England and Wales, With Recommendations on the Establishment of a National Commission on Philanthropy in the United States," in the Commission on Private Philanthropy and Public Needs, *Research Papers*, vol. V, pp. 3073–75.

4. Michael Chesterman, *Charities, Trusts, and Social Welfare* (London: Weidenfeld and Nicholson Ltd., 1979), p. 234.

5. Thus, whereas in American law it is appropriate to think of and analyze the charitable deduction as a tax expenditure, in a system with a deed of covenant that perspective may be less helpful. Ironically, the deed of covenant system separates the taxes foregone into a separate financial stream that would greatly facilitate the identification and estimation of a tax expenditure.

The careful reader will note that I have not insisted on using the term *tax expenditure* in this chapter even though the analysis is clearly within this school of thought. It is less important to reach agreement on whether a particular provision of tax law is a tax expenditure than it is to understand the effects that changes in tax law have on charitable donations. In this regard, Francis Gladstone, head of policy planning for the National Council for Voluntary Organisations, has concluded, "it is quite clear that tax concessions for charities are not a right but a privilege granted by Parliament—a privilege that has to be justified like any other public policy" (Francis Gladstone, *Charity, Law and Social Justice* [London: Bedford Square Press, 1982], p. 143).

The government, itself, seems to be of two minds on this question. It feels that higher rate relief, for example, "is not a tax expenditure, it's letting people have more of their own money," but it grants the relief to individuals who make a particular type of expenditure, which can only be made to charities (interview with Anthony Gray, Policy Division, Inland Revenue, July 8, 1983). And the government now publishes an estimate of tax expenditures in which taxes foregone via covenants are estimated. "Britain's Tax Expenditure," *The Economist* (January 27, 1979): 60–61.

Nevertheless, among researchers who have addressed the question of tax incentives for charitable contributions there is no unanimity as to whether it is appropriate to use the expenditure concept to study charitable contributions. The tax expenditure concept is most comprehensively discussed in Stanley Surrey, *Pathways to Tax Reform* (Cambridge, Mass.: Harvard University Press, 1973).

6. An earlier example of transitional relief is discussed in Hubert Picarda, *The Law and Practice Relating to Charities* (London: Butterworths, 1977), pp. 543–44.

7. The limit on higher rate relief was set at £3000 in 1980, raised to £5000 in 1983, and is currently £10,000. The limits have been raised to keep pace with inflation.

8. An admirably clear description of higher rate relief can be found in Chapter 5 of Michael Norton, *Covenants: A Practical Guide to the Tax Advantages of Giving* (London: Directory of Social Change, 1983), pp. 34–46.

9. An excellent summary of the research on the economic effects of the charitable deduction is contained in Charles T. Clotfelter, *Federal Tax Policy and Charitable Giving* (Chicago: University of Chicago Press, 1985), pp. 16–99.

10. Paul R. McDaniel, "Study of Federal Matching Grants for Charitable Contributions," in the Commission on Private Philanthropy and Public Needs, *Research Papers*, vol. IV, pp. 2420–30; and Alan L. Feld, Michael O'Hare, and J. Mark Davidson Schuster, *Patrons Despite Themselves: Taxpayers and Arts Policy* (New York: New York University Press, 1983), pp. 29–30.

11. For a description of a tax credit system (in addition to some other possible tax incentive schemes) see David A. Good and Aaron Wildavsky, "A Tax by Any Other Name: The Donor Directed Automatic Percentage Contribution Bonus, A Budget Alternative for Financing Governmental Support of Charity," in The Commission of Private Philanthropy and Public Needs, *Research Papers*, vol. IV, pp. 2399–2400.

12. McDaniel, "Study of Federal Matching Grants," pp. 2417–82.

13. This comparison is limited in the sense that donors in each of the two systems may have identical marginal tax rates but because of different definitions of taxable income and different tax brackets may be in rather different economic positions.

14. For a detailed discussion of the concept of effort see J. Mark Davidson Schuster, "Tax Incentives for Charitable Donations: Deeds of Covenant and Charitable Contributions Deductions," *University of San Francisco Law Review* 19 (Spring–Summer 1985): 342–46.

15. An excellent example of this type of argument is contained in the report of the National Council of Social Service's Committee of Inquiry into the Effect of Charity Law and Practice on Voluntary Organisations (commonly referred to as the Goodman Committee after its chairman, Lord Goodman), *Charity Law and Voluntary Organisations: Report of the Goodman Committee* (London: Bedford Square Press, 1976), paragraph 116. In discussing the covenant at a point in time when the highest marginal tax rate was 98 percent and there was no higher rate relief on covenants, the Goodman Committee dwelled on the fact that a donor in the highest tax bracket had to have £3250 in income in order to get £100 to flow to charity via a covenant, an effort of 32.5! That was still less than the effort a donor would have had to exert without the benefit of a covenant: 50.0. At that time the marginal price of giving for all taxpaying donors was 0.65, a point unexplored by the committee.

16. Descriptions of the paperwork involved in a deed of covenant can be found in Norton, *Covenants*, pp. 91–118 and in Charities Aid Foundation, *Charitable Deeds of Covenant* (Tonbridge, England: Author, 1981), pp. 26–36.

17. Norton, ibid., pp. 91–104.

18. For a general discussion of the impact of donor-placed restrictions see Gerard M. Brannon and James Strnad, "Alternative Approaches to Encouraging Philanthropic Activities," in The Commission on Private Philanthropy and Public Needs, *Research Papers*, vol. IV, pp. 2368–72. A more detailed discussion of these restrictions on the arts can be found in Feld, O'Hare, and Schuster, *Patrons Despite Themselves*, Chapter 6, particularly pp. 156–69.

19. Correspondence with G. Norman Donaldson, deputy director, Charities Aid Foundation (August 17, 1983).

20. Goodman Committee, *Charity Law and Voluntary Organisations*, paragraph 116; and Booth, "Covenanted Giving—A New Era?" p. 18.

21. National Council for Voluntary Organisations, "Charities Say: 20 Million Pound

Tax Concession Isn't Working," Press release (August 13, 1983), p. 2. This estimate is based on government figures for the taxes foregone as a result of the tax concessions to charities in the Finance Act of 1980. If every taxpayer actually passed on this refund to charities, the benefit to charity would actually be greater because the charity could also reclaim taxes on it at the standard rate. Raising the ceiling on higher rate relief from £3000 to £5000 was estimated to have a full-year cost of £3 million (Inland Revenue press release [March 15, 1983]).

22. Schuster, "Tax Incentives for Charitable Donations," pp. 356–58.

23. See, for example, Feld, O'Hare and Schuster, *Patrons Despite Themselves*, pp. 24–50 and 216–20. The Royal Commission on the Taxation of Profits and Income in the United Kingdom in its 1954 report rejected replacing the covenant system with a charitable contribution deduction stating, in part, that, "there would be some redistribution of income over the range of charitable recipients, and the redistribution might bear heavily on some which do excellent work without much public notice." The report did not say why it was that the covenant system had happened to have achieved a distribution among charitable recipients that was in line with public policy. Gwyneth McGregor, *Personal Exemptions and Deductions under the Income Tax with Special Reference to Canada, the U.S., and the U.K.*, Canadian Tax Papers No. 31 (Toronto: Canadian Tax Foundation, October 1962), p. 39.

24. National Council for Voluntary Organisations (NCVO), *Report of the NCVO Working Party—1982* (London: Author, 1982), p. 3.

25. National Council for Voluntary Organisations, *Report of the NCVO Working Party—1982;* and interview with Francis Gladstone, head of policy and planning, National Council for Voluntary Organisations (July 12, 1983).

26. Ignatius Claeys Bouuaert, *Taxation of Cultural Foundations and of Patronage of the Arts in the Member States of the European Economic Community*, Commission of the European Economic Community Report XII/670/75-E (September 1975), p. 104.

27. Irrespective of the limits specified in the Finance Acts, it seems that fund raisers tend to favor and believe they can get donors to agree to longer periods, such as ten years. Charities Aid Foundation, *Charitable Deeds of Covenant*, p. 10.

28. Spuehler, "The System for Regulation and Assistance of Charity," pp. 3069–70.

29. Interviews with Anthony Gray, policy division, Inland Revenue (July 8, 1983) and G. Norman Donaldson, deputy director, Charities Aid Foundation, (July 11, 1983); and Charities Aid Foundation, *Charity Conference Report*, p. 25.

30. Douglas and Wright, "English Charities," p. 70.

31. All of these schemes for circumventing the deed of covenant system are detailed in Norton, *Covenants*, Chapters 3–9; most are discussed in Charities Aid Foundation, *Charitable Deeds of Covenant.*

32. For a fuller discussion of the many services provided by the Charities Aid Foundation see Norton, ibid., Chapter 6; Spuehler, "The System for Regulation and Assistance of Charity," pp. 3076–79; and Douglas and Wright, "English Charities," pp. 75–81.

33. Correspondence with G. Norman Donaldson, deputy director, Charities Aid Foundation (August 17, 1983).

34. Since April 1, 1986, corporations have been allowed to deduct one-time charitable contributions from their income up to a limit of 3 percent of dividends paid. As of April 1, 1987, individuals will be allowed to make deductible contributions through payroll deduction plans up to a limit of £100 per employee per year. These contributions can be designated to any charities in any amount. Employers will turn over the aggregate of the collected deduction to a designated "agency charity" that, in turn, will redistribute the contributions to the intended recipients. Agency charities are currently being designated. They may keep the donations for up to one year before redistribution (the interest realized being a form of payment for their services), and they may also charge employers a fee for redistributing the charitable donations. Both individual and corporate donors are still able to take advantage of the deed of covenant provisions.

REFERENCES

Bouuaert, Ignatius Claeys. *Taxation of Cultural Foundations and of Patronage of the Arts in the Member States of the European Economic Community.* Commission of the European Economic Community Report XII/670/75-E, 1975.

Charities Aid Foundation. (CAF) *Charitable Deeds of Covenant.* Tonbridge, England: Author, 1981.

Chesterman, Michael. *Charities, Trusts, and Social Welfare.* London: Weidenfeld and Nicolson Ltd., 1979.

Clotfelter, Charles T. *Federal Tax Policy and Charitable Giving.* Chicago: University of Chicago Press, 1985.

Commission on Private Philanthropy and Public Needs. "Alternatives to Tax Incentives." In *Research Papers.* Washington, D.C.: Department of the Treasury, 1977, vol. IV, Part V.

Douglas, James, and Peter Wright. "English Charities: Part I—Legal Definition, Taxation, and Regulation." Program on Non-Profit Organizations Working Paper 15. New Haven, Conn.: Institution for Social and Policy Studies, Yale University, 1980.

Feld, Alan L., Michael O'Hare, and J. Mark Davidson Schuster. *Patrons Despite Themselves: Taxpayers and Arts Policy.* New York: New York University Press, 1983.

Gladstone, Francis. *Charity, Law and Social Justice.* London: Bedford Square Press, 1982.

House of Commons, Eighth Report from the Education, Science and Arts Committee, Session 1981–82, *Public and Private Funding of the Arts,* vol. I. London: Her Majesty's Stationery Office.

McGregor, Gwyneth. *Personal Exemptions and Deductions under the Income Tax with Special Reference to Canada, the U.S., and the U.K.,* Canadian Tax Papers No. 31. Toronto: Canadian Tax Foundation, 1962.

National Council of Social Service, Committee of Inquiry into the Effect of Charity Law and Practice on Voluntary Organisations. *Charity Law and Voluntary Organisations: Report of the Goodman Committee.* London: Bedford Square Press, 1976.

Norton, Michael. *Covenants: A Practical Guide to the Tax Advantages of Giving.* London: Directory of Social Change, 1983.

Picarda, Hubert. *The Law and Practice Relating to Charities.* London: Butterworths, 1977.

Schuster, J. Mark Davidson. "Tax Incentives for Charitable Donations: Deeds of Covenant and Charitable Contribution Deductions." *University of San Francisco Law Review* 19 (Spring–Summer 1985).

Spuehler, Donald R. "The System for Regulation and Assistance of Charity in England and Wales, With Recommendations on the Establishment of a National Commission on Philanthropy in the United States." Commission on Private Philanthropy and Public Needs, *Research Papers,* vol. V. Washington, D.C.: Department of the Treasury, 1977.

Surrey, Stanley. *Pathways to Tax Reform.* Cambridge, Mass.: Harvard University Press, 1973.

III
ECONOMIC DEVELOPMENT AND HUMAN RIGHTS

12

The Nonprofit Sector in Developing Countries: The Case of Sri Lanka

ESTELLE JAMES

This study should be viewed as a pilot project in a broader exploration of the role of the nonprofit sector in Third World countries. My object was to discover whether a nonprofit (NPO) sector exists in Sri Lanka and, if so, how it contrasts with the nonprofit sector in the United States. Does it do things that are or could be done by private enterprise or government and, if so, which arrangement is more efficient and equitable?

This chapter is based on field work carried out in Sri Lanka in 1979–1980. Since then the political situation has changed dramatically from tranquility to violence. This has undoubtedly altered the operations of the nonprofit sector in ways that are now impossible to study. However, I believe the generalizations made in 1980 still apply to many developing countries.

I especially want to thank A. P. Jinadassa, my senior research assistant, who collected most of the data with assistance from A. G. De Silvan and M. Rajendraseelan. I particularly appreciate the help provided by Bogoda Premaratne and Hema Goonatilake, in various stages of this project. I also thank the many people who allowed me to interview them and share their ideas, including: A. T. Ariyaratne, Sarvodaya; S. Rajasuriya, Sarvodaya; Anoja Fernado, Mahila Samiti, E. C. Fernando, Family Planning Association; Alice Shimamura, AID; Ron Rote, NOVIB; Paul Bishoff, FNS; Malsiri Dias, Ministry of Plan Implementation; E. Kuruppu, Ministry of External Resources; Leel Gunasekera, Department of Social Service; Mr. C. Basnayake, Department of Social Service; Swarma Jayaweera, Colombo University; Susantha Goonatilake, Peoples' Bank; Dudley Dissanayake, Sri Lanka School of Social Work; Vinitha Jayasinghe, Women's Bureau.

I also gratefully acknowledge the support for this project that was provided by the Program on Non-Profit Organizations, Institution for Social and Policy Studies, Yale University. An earlier version of this paper was presented at the American Economic Association/Grants Economics meetings in September 1980. Comments on the earlier version by J. M. Montias, Egon Neuberger, John Simon, and Martin Spechler were helpful in the revision process. This is a slightly revised version of a paper that was originally published in the *Journal of Comparative Economics* 6 (1982): 99–129. Copyright © 1982 by Academic Press, Inc. Reprinted by permission.

in Sri Lanka and, if so, how it contrasts with the nonprofit sector in the United States. Does it do things that are or could be done by private enterprise or government and, if so, which arrangement is more efficient and equitable?

My basic answer is: Sri Lanka has an active nonprofit sector, indeed a dual nonprofit sector, which is there called the "nongovernmental" (NGO) sector. The semantics perhaps arise from the NGO's functional similarity to, and therefore need to differentiate itself from, the government.

One part of this dual structure is made up of large multipurpose organizations that combine monetary donations from abroad with domestic donations of volunteer labor, in order to undertake a variety of public-sector—income-redistribution-type activities. The other part is made up of smaller (health and welfare) organizations that depend primarily on government grants for financial support. Unlike the situation in the United States, private domestic contributions and income from sales play only a minor role. Since foreign donations greatly exceed government grants to NGOs, the organizations that can make the leap into the first group are the ones that seem destined to flourish and grow. I would hypothesize that this pattern is typical of many less developed countries.

Why do foreign donors contribute, and to a much greater extent than domestic? Why do domestic contributions primarily take the form of volunteer labor? Why are direct government grants an important source of support for this sector which calls itself nongovernmental?

Sri Lankan NGOs can get monetary donations from abroad because they belong to an international NPO/NGO network; many foreign donors are willing to contribute to the nongovernmental sector but not to the government directly. In fact, one rationale for the existence of NGOs in the Third World is to enable and encourage this flow of funds to take place. NPOs in Western countries have played a key role in founding Sri Lankan NGOs, shaping their tastes, choices and decision-making procedures. This, then, constitutes a major example of the international transmission of socioeconomic institutions.

Sri Lankan NGOs also receive domestic donations in the form of volunteer labor—partially because they are able to generate a sense of sharing, participation, and cooperative action and partially because of more direct benefits received by volunteers. Implicit in these contributions is an element of trust which donors of time and money have toward the NGO that they do not have toward the government; this factor, which has been said to play an important role in the theory of American NPOs, may be similarly important in examining the international network of NPO/NGOs.

From the viewpoint of international comparisons, I would formulate the following hypotheses and questions that relate the nature of the "third sector" to the stage of development of a country:

1. The elements of donations and volunteerism are common to NPOs everywhere. However, foreign donations will be more important the less developed is the economy, the less restrictive its foreign-exchange markets, and the more open

it is to international trade. Volunteer labor will be more important in an economy in which a large segment of the population is unemployed or not in the labor force. Domestic donations of money will be more important if the income distribution is unequal and a wealthy subgroup exists. If the economy is poor, egalitarian, and discourages inflows of foreign funds, its NPO sector is likely to be small.

2. One can trace the spread of NPOs from the West to Sri Lanka, especially through the actions of Christian missionaries and as a defensive reaction thereto. This historical observation suggests that a similar institutional form may not exist in economies that do not have a colonial missionary background and have been insulated from other Western influences.

3. I would expect formalized NPOs to predominate in the cities, as providers of "collective" services, which in rural areas are more likely to be supplied by the extended family or informal community groups. The benefits of "formalization" are tied to scale of operations and fund-raising whereas most costs are lump-sum and once-over. Therefore, the former will exceed the latter where concentrations of people and resources are high, as in cities.

4. Many Sri Lankan NPOs are engaged in social services and income-transfer activities, like their American counterparts. However, unlike the situation in the United States, some of them engage in the production of social-overhead capital—the building of roads, irrigation canals, wells, and sanitation facilities—which we would think of as a governmental responsibility. Also, they engage in activities specifically designed to raise the earning capacity of their beneficiaries—including training programs and the granting of small loans. I would hypothesize that this growing emphasis on social-overhead capital, human capital, and other income-generating ventures is a function of the stage of development, and would expect to find similar activities in other developing countries.

5. In Third World countries, as in the United States many managers of nonprofit organizations attempt to maximize their utility by engaging in a combination of profitable and loss-making activities that cross-subsidize each other. Since volunteer labor is usually tied to a specific product by the donor, the opportunities for managerial discretion through cross-subsidization will increase as monetary donations replace donations of time in the course of economic development.

Most of these hypotheses are explored below with respect to Sri Lanka. The special characteristics of Sri Lanka that appear to be relevant to these issues are: its colonial history, its lack of economic development (1978 GNP=$24 billion, per capita income=$170), scarcity of capital, surplus of labor, predominantly rural character, openness of foreign trade, and recent shift from a planned to a more laissez-faire political economy.

The plan of this chapter is as follows: The first section summarizes my model of the NPO (presented more fully in another paper), describes my methodology, and defines the scope of the present study, including a brief characterization of the size and activities of the NGO sector in Sri Lanka. I then proceed to examine the behavior of each of the main actors in the model. Thus the following sections consider in detail the role of foreign donors and volunteer labor (including NPO managers) and relations with the government (including tax privileges, direct grants and regulations).

Finally, the conclusion reviews my findings, comments on the impact of NGOs on economic development and social welfare, and raises some questions about the future of the "third sector" in Sri Lanka. (The terms NPO and NGO are used interchangeably although NPOs often refer to Western organizations, and NGOs to their Sri Lankan counterparts.)

METHODOLOGY AND SCOPE OF STUDY

The NPO/NGO as an Institutional Form

The "third sector" in Sri Lanka and elsewhere includes a wide variety of institutions: producer and consumer cooperatives; labor unions; trade associations; and educational, health-related, and social-service organizations. Broadly speaking, these situations fall into two main categories: the first (type I) consists of organizations providing some shared facility or service where the people who pay (through membership or usage fees) are also the direct and principal beneficiaries and exclusion is possible (e.g., schools, hospitals, churches, and opera). For-profit private enterprise can also carry out these functions although their provision may not be optimal if information is asymmetric.[1]

The second main category (type II) consists of organizations where many beneficiaries pay little or nothing and many people who pay do not receive direct benefits. These organizations are supported by voluntary contributions of time and money, usually supplemented by government support through grants or tax privileges. This is the subset with which I am primarily concerned. The questions that naturally arise here are: Why do people make voluntary contributions, why is the government willing to render support without control, and does the NPO use its resources and power in a socially efficient way?

In this paper I argue that voluntary NPO/NGOs serve as interest-based communities (rather than regionally based communities) for providing impure public goods in cases where the externalities are not geographically limited, and, in fact, may cut across national borders. These "communities of interest" may play a particularly important role where product variety is possible and economies of scale are small enough to permit differentiated tastes to be satisfied.[2] While donors may benefit from the goods and services of the NPO directly (as in type I), they often benefit indirectly as well (as in type II), e.g., from the consumption or goodwill of others and the income redistribution achieved when the organization sells its services at a zero or below-cost price. Exclusion is not possible from these "external"- or "redistribution"-type benefits, nor can the impact of marginal revenues be readily monitored by potential donors; hence, they will ordinarily be undersupplied by the private market.

The NPO/NGO is viewed as an alternative institutional form to which donors contribute their time and money in an "implicit social contract" with others having similar preferences; the element of mutual trust among donors and between donors and NPO is obviously important. The voluntary donations may then be considered an index of relative externalities received from each product variant while the government subsidy helps to overcome the free-rider problem which all face in common.[3]

The government is willing to delegate decision-making power to an organization that it subsidizes (rather than demanding direct control) as an incentive and reward for the supplemental resources collected on a voluntary basis. As will be shown, this enables the government to provide impure public goods at a lower (money and real) cost and, sometimes, at higher quality as well, thereby helping government officials to get re-elected.

In another paper I present a model of NPO decision making, in which the manager maximizes his utility through his choice of input and output mix, subject to a zero-profit constraint. Since, overall, revenues must equal costs, the NPO manager is constrained by the (public and private) donation function. Nevertheless, space often exists for NPO managerial discretion, and the manager can thereby benefit from utility-yielding organizational consumption.[4] In the following pages I examine, in turn, the motivation of individual and institutional donors, labor volunteers, NGO managers, and government subsidizers/regulators, and, finally, evaluate the welfare implications of their actions.

Activities of the NGO Sector

In this study I concentrate on an important part of the NPO/NGO sector—"voluntary organizations" which are supported by contributions of time and money as well as by government grants. Within this category, most of my analysis focuses on a further subset: approved charities. These are voluntary organizations that have met the discretionary criteria established by the Minister of Finance for tax-exempt status, i.e., organizations set up and formally registered to provide a socially desirable service for the benefit of others.[5] Informal grass-roots organizations, churches, schools and hospitals are not included in this subset, although they are part of the broader nonprofit sector.

Although information was not available about these organizations on a central computerized basis, I was able to obtain a complete list of the 431 approved charities, of which 18 were intensively studied. (See Table 12.1 for names of the 18 organizations included.) Since I attempted to choose the largest and most important organizations, my sample was neither random nor representative. In particular, it is biased toward the "international" urban-based multipurpose organizations. While the smaller "indigenous" organizations are underrepresented numerically, they are probably overrepresented relative to their share of total voluntary resources.

Annual reports, financial statements and other materials were obtained from the organizations selected for my sample. In addition, numerous for-

Table 12.1.   Organizations in the Sample

Name	Year of Origin	Religious Connection	International Affiliation
All Ceylon Buddhist Congress	1919	—	
All Ceylon Young Men's Muslim Assoc.	1958	—	
Bhikku Training Center	1958	—	
Ceylon Boy Scouts Assoc.	1912		—
Ceylon Cancer Society	1948		
Ceylon National Assoc. for the Prevention of TB	1948		—
Ceylon Red Cross	1936		—
Ceylon School for the Deaf and Blind	1912	—	
Colombo Buddhist Theosophical Society	1880	—	
Family Planning Assoc.	1953		—
Girl Guides Assoc. of Ceylon	1917		—
Lanka Jatika Sarvodaya Shramadana Sanamaya	1958	—	
Lanka Mahila Samiti	1930		—
Mahabodhi Society of Ceylon	1891	—	
Prisoners Welfare Assoc.	1927		
Ramakrishna Mission of Ceylon	1924	—	—
Saukiyadana Volunteer Medical Aid Mvt.	1959		
Sri Lanka Assoc. for the Advancement of Science	1945		

eign donors and government officials were interviewed. The results presented in this paper, then, are based partly on impressions garnered from these interviews as well as on the "hard data" in the financial reports.

Tables 12.2 and 12.3 present breakdowns of the major activities of the

Table 12.2.   Major Activities of All Approved Charities

	No.	%[a]
Social service—general (incl. day-care centers, aid to needy, emergency relief)	148	34
Education and vocational training	129	30
Health care and family planning	59	14
Homes for destitute children and elderly	58	14
Religion	147	34
Rural development and social overhead capital	8	2
Sports and recreation	40	9
Art and culture	20	5
Environment and wildlife	3	1
Other	18	4
Total	630	147

[a]That is, the proportion of total organizations (431) that engage in each activity. This adds up to more than 100 percent because many organizations had secondary as well as primary activities.

Source: Judgement of an informed consultant in Sri Lanka.

Table 12.3. Major Activities of Sample Organizations[a]

	No.	%[b]
Social service—general (incl. day-care centers, aid to needy, emergency relief)	13	70
Education and vocational training	13	70
Health care and family planning	7	39
Homes for destitute children and elderly	5	28
Religion	8	45
Rural development and social overhead capital	3	17
Sports and recreation	2	11
Art and culture	1	5
Environment and wildlife	1	5
Total	53	290

[a]The average number of activities per organization in the sample was almost 3, while the average number for the population as a whole, given in Table 12.2, was 1.5. The difference stems from two sources: (1) Large multipurpose organizations are over-represented in the sample; and (2) The careful perusal of annual reports for the sample enabled us to identify more functions than my informed consultant was aware of, for the population as a whole.

[b]This gives the proportion of the 18 organizations in my sample that engage in each activity to a significant extent. It totals more than 100 percent because most organizations had two or more activities.

Source: Derived from annual reports of each organization.

431 approved charities and the 18 organizations in the sample. Of the total group, one-third have a religious affiliation and purpose. These are primarily Christian and Buddhist, but a few important Hindu and Moslem organizations are also found. The predominance of religious voluntary organizations is hardly surprising in view of their origin plus the fact that religion has, for centuries, been the basis for community and collective action. While the church does not now, in most Western countries, possess the power of compulsory taxation, it does have a tradition of taxation through the tithe. Christianity, in particular, holds out the prospect of eternal salvation in return for faith and good works—surely a powerful private reward for seemingly altruistic behavior.

Most NGOs were involved in social-service activities (running day-care centers, providing aid to the needy, operating homes for destitute children and the elderly) and human capital formation (education, vocational training, and health care). While some of these activities (e.g., immunization campaigns and education for citizenship) provide social benefits to the country as a whole, and hence are typically carried out by public or quasi-public bodies, others (e.g., nursery schools, training programs), have a large private component and, in many other countries, are produced in the for-profit market. Capital-market imperfections combined with the low income of the Sri Lankan clientele, however, make it unlikely that they would be willing or able to pay for such services, some of which constitute an investment in the future rather than the satisfaction of more immediate needs. Income redistribution—tied to the consumption of "merit goods" chosen by the donor rather than the recipient—is clearly an important element here and constitutes a raison d'être for provision through the public or voluntary rather than the private sector. The possible reasons for NGO rather than governmental production will be discussed in Section 5.

As expected, art, culture, and environmental concerns ranked low on the list of NGO activities—probably because these are income-elastic activities, found primarily where the general standard of living or the wealth of a significant subgroup is high enough to make such organizations viable.

More surprisingly, several organizations—including the largest—participate in the provision of social overhead capital (building roads, water tanks, irrigation canals, wells, and sanitation facilities) which we tend to think of as a governmental responsibility. They also engage in activities specifically designed to raise the incomes of their beneficiaries—including the provision of working capital and market outlets. I would hypothesize that this participation in social overhead capital formation and income generation is a function of the stage of development, and would expect to find similar activities among NGOs in other developing countries.[6]

NGO Revenues and Assets

Tables 12.4 and 12.5 present data on sources of revenue and total assets for the 18 organizations in my sample. The following conclusions emerge:

1. The total revenues and wealth of "approved charities" in Sri Lanka is small by American standards, both in absolute terms and relative to GNP. While we do not have data for the entire sector, I believe I have captured more than one-third of the total resources in my sample.[7] This would imply that total voluntary monetary resources were about $12 million, only 0.5 percent of GNP.[8] Inclusion of imputations for volunteer labor ($4.7 million), tax privileges ($1 million), rental value of buildings owned and occupied by NGOs ($2 million), and other in-kind support ($1 million) would increase these estimates of total resources by about 75 percent. These figures have been growing rapidly in recent years, a trend that will probably continue.
2. By American standards, most Sri Lankan NGOs are very small. Indeed in 1978 only one organization—Sarvodaya—had total revenues and total assets in excess of 1 million dollars.[9]
3. The NGO sector is also highly concentrated: the single largest organization controlled 64 percent of the total resources in my sample and the top three controlled 90 percent. Given the bias in my sample toward large organizations, the distribution of resources for the total population of NGOs would be even more skewed; i.e., I have omitted a large number of very small organizations. This skewness comes mainly from the concentration of foreign funds; government and local contributions are much more equally distributed.
4. Foreign contributions, primarily from NPOs abroad, are by far the largest single source of income, providing 87 percent of total revenues. Moreover, we find a strong positive correlation between rank order by total revenue and rank order by size of foreign contributions. (Spearman's rank-order correlation coef-

Table 12.4. Sources of Income (in 000s Dollars), 1977 or 1978[a]
(in Rank Order of Total Revenue)

Organization	Total Revenue	Contributions from Abroad[b]	Percentage Contributions from Abroad	Contributions from Government	Member Dues & Domestic Contributions[c]	Sales[d]	Rent and Interest
1	2573	2405	94	0	5	138	24
2	830	737	89	3	7	85	0
3	277	256	92	2	15	0	5
4	70	69	99	0	1	0	0
5[e]	70	27	39	2	33	0	7
6	50	37	74	0	3	0	9
7	36	0[f]	0	7	23	1	5
8	34	11	34	4	1	14	3
9	30	1	4	26	3	0	0
10	29	7	25	4	9	0	8
11	22	8	38	4	1	8	1
12	13	0[f]	0	7	3	0	3
13	10	0[f]	0	7	2	0	2
14	9	0[f]	0	1	8	0	0
15	8	0	0	0	3	4	1
16	5	0	0	5	0	0	1
17	2	0	0	0	0	0	2
18	2	0	0	2	0	0	0
	$4070	$3556		$72	$120	$251	$71
Percentage of total	100%	87%		2%	3%	6%	2%

[a]Rupees are converted into dollars at a 15/1 exchange rate. Since many goods and services not traded in international markets are cheaper in Sri Lanka than in the United States, this understates the relative purchasing power of Sri Lankan NGOs substantially. While most data reported are from 1978, in some cases the latest information available is from 1977; this, however, did not appear to affect the major conclusions cited in the text.

[b]Most of these funds come from NGOs abroad. However, in the case of one large organization virtually all of its funds came from foreign (Middle Eastern) governments. Although an attempt was made to include in-kind contributions from abroad (e.g., equipment and food), often such information was not available.

[c]Dues and contributions are included in the same category since they are both very small and the distinction between the two is often arbitrary. This category includes special fund-raising efforts such as "flagdays," raffles, and benefit performances, which are, more accurately, a joint contribution/sales category.

[d]Gross sales revenues are reported here. Net revenues (i.e., profits from production units) are much smaller and, in some cases, negative, a total of only $28,000.

[e]Only total contributions were given in the income statement. The breakdown between foreign and domestic donations is my approximation, based on information given in the annual report.

[f]Although these organizations did not obtain any contributions from abroad in 1978, their balance sheets showed that earlier contributions were received and some of these remained to be spent. In the calculation of rank-order correlation these were assigned a higher rank than organization 15, 16, 17, and 18.

Source: Annual reports and income and expenditure statements of each organization. Organizations are not identified by name, since the funding picture of specific organizations is not important to the study.

ficient = 0.95.) This sharply contrasts with the American situation, where sales, e.g., by hospitals and universities, constitute the major revenue source, domestic dues and contributions an important secondary source.

5. The NGOs are divided into two groups: those with substantial foreign funding (which we shall call the "international" subgroup) and those with little or no foreign funding (which we shall call the "indigenous" subgroup). The nine organizations in the former group received 97 percent of total revenues, with foreign sources accounting for 90 percent of that; within this group the rank-

Table 12.5.   Assets and Liabilities (in 000s Dollars), 1977 or 1978[a]
(in Rank Order of Total Revenue)

Org.	Fixed Assets	Investments and Fixed Deposits	Current Assets	Total Assets	Liabilities	Net Worth
1	729	243	1052	2024	NA	NA
2	69	0	232	301	20	281
3	NA	NA	NA	NA	NA	NA
4	NA	NA	NA	NA	NA	NA
5	191	53	17	261	11	250
6	25	0	28	53	0	53
7	82	21	34	137	0	137
8	17	22	7	46	1	45
9	64	0	31	95	2	93
10	11	43	15	69	6	63
11	16	27	14	57	3	54
12	52	9	6	67	45	22
13	14	16	9	39	6	33
14	1	2	7	10	1	9
15	135	15	26	176	7	169
16	63	8	9	80	1	79
17	NA	NA	NA	NA	NA	NA
18	0	0	6	6	0	6
	$1469[b]	$459	$1493	$3421[b]		

[a]See footnote a to Table 12.4.
[b]Actual market value is much greater than book value, due to rapid inflation in land and building prices in recent years, especially in Colombo.
Source: Annual reports and balance sheets of each organization.

order correlation between these two variables is 0.97. The nine organizations in the latter group received only 3 percent of total revenues, but 22 percent of all domestic revenues, and 75 percent of all government grants. Within this group, government was the single largest source (48 percent) and we find a positive correlation between rank order by total revenues and by size of government grants (Spearman's rank-order correlation coefficient $= 0.79$).[10]

There is a significant scale difference, but no significant difference in activity mix between these two groups at the gross level of aggregation used for "activities" in this study.

6. Total assets are also heavily concentrated, albeit not as much so as current income. By comparing the income and asset statements, we learn that some organizations that flourished in the past still have, as a legacy, substantial assets, largely embodied in land and buildings, although very little current revenues with which to finance current activities.

THE ROLE OF FOREIGN DONORS

This section examines the role of foreign donors. We postulate the development of an international network of NPO/NGOs, starting in the West and spreading through much of the world. This then constitutes a major example of the international transmission of legal socioeconomic institutions.

We would expect this institutional form to be most prevalent where:

1. colonial and/or missionary influence was strongest in the past;
2. capital is scarce;
3. the economic system is sufficiently decentralized and foreign exchange controls sufficiently few to allow the continuation and expansion of an internationally funded "third sector."

The presence of large numbers of voluntary foreign donors suggest the presence of international externalities and the (at least partial) absence of free-riderism. We find that Western NPOs serve an intermediary role between the originating sources of foreign funds—whether individual or governmental—and the Sri Lankan NGO recipients. The key qualities supplied by the NPOs to the donors are information, trust and selectivity. The existence of the NPO-NGO network enables a flow of funds to occur that otherwise would not and hence, allows these international externalities to be taken into account.

Under these circumstances, a Darwinian process operates: those Sri Lankan NGOs that are able to attract sufficient foreign resources survive and flourish, while those that do not remain small and, in a relative sense, wither away. The discretionary control exercised by the Western NPOs regarding resource allocation means that their managerial objective functions are particularly important in this Darwinian process. In the following pages, each of these propositions is developed further and illustrated.

The Historical Spread of the NPO-NGO Institution

Historically, much of the education and social-service activities in Sri Lanka were provided informally through the extended family and the Buddhist temple. With the advent of colonialism and the concomitant movement of labor to plantations and cities, these traditional structures began to break down. At the same time, Christian missionaries appeared on the scene, setting up schools and hospitals and taking on a variety of charitable functions. Many of these organizations still exist today as some of the largest and most prestigious in the country.

The revival of nationalism in the twentieth century stimulated the establishment of Buddhist educational and social-service organizations, to counter the power of the Christian missionaries. In addition, branches of secular international organizations were established. Hence, the NPO/NGO institution-type took root and spread, providing educational, health, and social services as a joint- or by-product of a religious or political proselytizing effort.

Currently, then, we find the following typology of NGOs in Sri Lanka:

1. Groups that are Christian Church—related, directly or indirectly, many of them receiving assistance from their parent or sister organizations abroad (examples

are Catholic and Methodist social-service organizations, the Salvation Army, the YMCA and YWCA).
2. Branches or affiliates of secular international organizations (examples are Girl Guides, Boy Scouts, Mahila Samiti, Family Planning Association, Red Cross, and Lions Club).
3. Local organizations, often Buddhist in nature, that are independent but receive funding from abroad (examples are the All Ceylon Buddhist Congress and Sarvodaya).
4. Local organizations that have virtually no international connections or resources (examples are the Prisoners' Welfare Association, Bikkhu Training Center, Sri Lanka Maha Bodhi Society, Buddhist Theosophical Society).

As we saw in the previous section, the latter constitute the small-scale purely indigenous part of the dual NGO sector in Sri Lanka. The first three groups comprise the internationally oriented part of the NGO sector; they are relatively large, wealthy, multipurpose, and increasingly run by a paid professional staff. With the advent in 1977 of a new government that has encouraged free enterprise and removed foreign-exchange controls, the Sri Lankan NGO sector has been expanding, and that part with connections abroad has been expanding fastest of all.

The International Donor

Where do these international funds come from? Some of them come directly from foreign governments (such as Sweden, Denmark, Saudi Arabia, and the United States) or from U. N. agencies (such as UNESCO or UNICEF). However, by far the largest share comes from Western NPOs. These Western NPOs, in turn, get their money from individuals or governments abroad. Therefore, we need to explain, first, why such individuals and governments wish to contribute to Sri Lanka and second, why their contributions are funnelled through Western NPOs to Sri Lankan NGOs, rather than directly to the private or public sectors there.

The Individual Donor
Consider first an individual donor, i, whose utility depends partially on the consumption or goodwill of a specified subgroup of people (e.g., children or Christians or potential Christians) in various parts of the world. Assume further that for very poor subgroups, j, the marginal utility i receives from an incremental $1 of j's consumption exceeds his marginal utility from his own consumption. Then, he will be willing to contribute $1 voluntarily, despite the free-rider problem.

Going beyond that point, he may consider himself involved in an implicit social contract with n others having similar preferences, both the preferences and the implicit contract reinforced, possibly, by common membership in a local church, secular group, or social group. If the reinforcement is sufficient, each will then be willing to contribute $1 voluntarily, so long as the benefits received from the n of additional consumption by j exceeds the marginal utility from $1 of own-consumption.[11]

However, such potential donors may not have the information or expertise to make productive donations to foreign individuals directly. Nor, given its multipurpose nature and the consequent difficulties in monitoring the impact of marginal revenues, do they trust the foreign government enough to use it as a conduit for the specific purpose desired. Instead, a network of NPO middlemen has evolved, serving as intermediaries between the individual Western donor on the one hand and the Sri Lankan recipient on the other, supplying the vital elements of information and selectivity. The individual donates to a domestic NPO with international ties, often with a specific clientele or purpose, which in turn seeks out worthwhile projects in Sri Lanka and elsewhere, and funnels the donation to them.[12]

Tax laws in the West further reinforce this process: by following this routing contributions are often tax-deductible, whereas they would not be if the NPO-NGO connection were bypassed. Western NPOs and NGOs abroad may in fact tailor their structure and activities to be eligible for this special tax treatment. Tax laws in one country, then, can affect the viability of socioeconomic institutions in another.

Since there are probably economies of scale and spillovers in expertise, we would expect the same set of NPO intermediaries to operate in many developing countries; they constitute a truly international "third sector."

The Governmental Donor
Consider now the Western government that donates through this NPO-NGO network. These contributions may take a number of forms:

1. A Western government may be the sole or partial support of the Western NPO.[13]
2. A Western government may provide matching funds directly to a Sri Lankan NGO, because this NPO is also supported by an NPO of its own nationality.[14]
3. A Western government may implicitly provide matching funds to a Sri Lankan NGO, by permitting tax deductibility of contributions to domestic NPOs, which in turn send these contributions abroad.[15]
4. A Western government may give money to an NPO of its own nationality implicitly or explicitly earmarked for a corresponding NGO in Sri Lanka.
5. A Western government may influence the flow of NPO funds by intercession and persuasion (and vice versa).

Why does the foreign government sometimes operate through the NPO-NGO network, rather than dealing exclusively with its own counterpart—the government of Sri Lanka? Suppose that the objective function of governmental decision makers includes the desire to win friends at home (by responding to domestic preferences) in order to get reelected, and to win influence abroad in order to enhance their national (and hence their personal) prestige. It follows from the latter that such governments may wish to support those NGOs abroad which they view as being sympathetic in goals and orientation.[16] The government may, moreover, choose to support these NGOs indirectly, through intermediating Western NPOs because:

1. in doing so the government is killing two birds with one stone, gaining domestic and foreign friends at the same time;
2. foreigners may "trust" donations coming from NPOs as having fewer political strings attached, while direct government donations may be regarded as tainted and therefore less effective at winning friends;
3. this procedure enables foreign governments to avoid the red tape and bureaucracy often encountered in direct governmental transactions, as well as the outright restrictions in dealing with politically sensitive areas;[17]
4. the NPO may have greater expertise in selecting productive NGO recipients or may permit the Western government unofficially to pinpoint the desired project—whereas recipient governments might jealously guard their prerogative to control this allocation decision;
5. The NPO may serve as a "project caretaker" at lower cost and arousing less political antagonism than would the foreign government in a direct operation.

Once again, information and selectivity play a major role in explaining the use of Western NPOs as intermediaries in the international flow of funds. Since these qualities enhance the productivity of a contribution, as perceived by the donor, they may also increase the total amount of contributions donors are willing to make, and enable the market for externalities to function more smoothly than it otherwise would.

The Western NPO

How, then, do the Western NPOs operate? What are their objectives and how do they implement these goals through the selection of foreign projects and project managers?

I postulate, first of all, that the NPO managers care about control and impact, i.e., discretionary power which they can use to maximize their utility. It follows that they prefer to work with nongovernmental bodies, which they can select and influence, rather than the government, whose size, power, and monopoly status make it relatively immune to pressures from an NPO. As noted above, tax laws in the West (which often allow deductions for donations that remain in the NPO/NGO sector) also encourage them to deal with NGOs. Hence, the development of NGOs in Sri Lanka and elsewhere in the Third World can partially be seen as an institutional response to this potential supply of funds from the West.[18]

The desire for impact and control also means that the NPO is likely to focus on some target group. Often this is defined along religious lines; as we have seen, many foreign donors have (explicit or implicit) religious objectives. Other target groups include managers, youth, women, and the urban and rural poor.

Most NPOs claim to seek out projects and target groups that other donors have not taken in, thereby having greater influence than if they were simply part of a bandwagon effect. Running counter to this is the observation that a record of successful past projects is considered by many to be the best indicator of future success and, as we have seen, foreign resources are heavily concentrated in a small number of NGOs.

I infer further, from interviews, that the NPO managers derive utility from good personal relations with their NGO recipients—a form of nonpecuniary compensation in which those who allocate donations are able to indulge. Moreover, they do not have perfect information about all potential projects in Sri Lanka. As is often the case when set-up costs are involved and a change of partners requires additional (transactional and informational) expenses, long-term associations are formed between donor and recipient, with personal contacts playing an important role both in the initial and subsequent grants. This means that NPOs that have the greatest ability to communicate with foreign donors will flourish and their fundraising task will become easier through time—leading to the dominance of organizations that are based in urban rather than in remote rural areas, those with international affiliations, and those with English-speaking university-educated managers who are culturally and linguistically "at home" with their NPO counterparts. Thus, the foreign funding of Sri Lankan NGOs increases the resources at their disposal but also determines the product mix for which these resources will be utilized and exerts more subtle influences on the social and cultural climate of the country.

THE ROLE OF VOLUNTEER LABOR

This section considers the use of donated labor by voluntary organizations in Sri Lanka. Four major questions are asked: How much labor is volunteered and how does this alter the real income and expenditures of NGOs? Why do people volunteer? Is this a socially efficient arrangement? And finally, can we expect it to continue?

Quantity of Volunteerism

Data on volunteerism are difficult to secure and particularly unreliable. Nevertheless, I have attempted to estimate the amount of volunteer labor employed by the 18 organizations in my sample, on the basis of information supplied in annual reports and interviews. I obtained a total of 2525 full-time-equivalent people years, approximately the same as the number of full-time paid employees. Most of these volunteers are part-time unskilled workers engaged in "shramadama" (work camp) construction or clerical activities. Others, however, were providing part-time managerial and medical services. If we price their services at $1.50 per day (using a 3/1 weighting of unskilled and professional wages) for 160 work days per year, we obtain a total value of $985,000 annually.

Volunteer labor appears to be a positive function of an organization's monetary revenue, but more closely tied to domestic contributions and grants than to foreign resources and sales. That is, complementarity in supply appears to strongly dominate for the former, while, as discussed below, we find a mixture of complementarity and substitutability for foreign contributions (and workers producing goods for sale are often paid). Thus, the "indigenous" subset of my sample, which has only 3 percent of all financial revenues but 44 percent of domestic revenues less sales $(DR + S)$ has 14 percent ($135,000) of volunteer labor (VL), while the "international" subset has almost 100 percent of foreign resources plus sales $(FR + S)$, 56 percent of $DR - S$ and 86 percent ($850,000) of volunteer labor. Because of its size, the international sector has more volunteer labor than the indigenous sector, but the imbalance is much less than that for foreign contributions or for all financial resources.

The nature of my data did not permit me to perform a multiple regression analysis with VL as the dependent variable. However, to get an approximation of the possible relationship between VL and the various sources of monetary revenues, I utilized the information we have about total VL, DR, FR, and S in the indigenous and international subsets and solved for a and b in the following equation, assuming these derivatives are the same in both sectors:

$$VL_i = a(DR - S)_i + b(FR + S)_i.$$

I obtained a "domestic resources" coefficient of 1.15, a "foreign resources" coefficient of 0.18. That is, each $1.00 of domestic contributions plus grants implies $1.15 in volunteer labor; each $1.00 of domestic contributions plus grants implies $0.18 in volunteer labor, and these two effects are additive. Based on our earlier estimates of FR, DR, and S in the entire NGO sector, we may impute a total VL value of $4.7 million. This is four times our estimate of domestic private monetary contributions and 50 percent greater than monetary resources from all domestic sources. Consistent with my hypothesis, this is a much larger role, relative to monetary contributions, than we find for volunteer labor in a more highly developed economy, the United States.[19]

In addition, some degree of "volunteerism" is probably involved for many paid workers, whose NGO wages are lower than they would be elsewhere. Clearly, volunteer labor is the major means of local support for the NGO sector.

Should we, then, add this imputation as part of the real value of services provided by NGOs, i.e., the amount these services would have cost if produced in the market place? A closer examination of the reasons why people volunteer reveals that to do so would be only partially justified and would, in fact, involve an (indeterminate) amount of double-counting. For, in addition to the "altruistic" and private nonpecuniary reasons for donating time, some of which will be discussed below, volunteers also receive private material benefits that have already been counted as organizational resources and costs.

First of all, shramadana volunteers are typically remunerated with a subsistence allowance, usually in kind. In some cases this may simply be a disguised way of paying a competitive wage that would otherwise be considered to fall below the legally or socially acceptable minimum. In other cases, the value of the goods in kind may be so great that they exceed the going market-wage rate. This occurs, for example, when foreign donations to a particular project have been made in the form of imported food items with a high resale value. The volunteer may then trade these goods for money in the market place, in effect receiving a high pecuniary wage.

Volunteers are also rewarded by opportunities to travel—at lower levels within Sri Lanka and at higher levels, to international conferences and workshops. The shadow price on the latter was particularly great under the preceding government, when opportunities for purely private travel were limited due to severe foreign-exchange controls. One NGO attempted to recruit volunteers with the slogan, "Join—and see the world."

To the extent that "volunteers" are indeed remunerated, either by travel opportunities or by payment in kind, their inputs have already been accounted for in the books of the organization and by adding an imputation for their services we would, in fact, be double-counting. This also means that the apparent factor mix of the organization differs from the real factor mix, with labor costs understated and nonlabor costs overstated. Unfortunately, the available data did not allow me to quantify these effects.

Finally, people may view volunteering as a means of acquiring on-the-job training and access to labor-market information, which will help them to find wage-paying jobs later on. Consistent with this interpretation, several NGOs have a policy of hiring their best volunteers subsequently. Moreover, several organizations reported that former volunteers had eventually acquired closely related jobs in other NGOs or government agencies (e.g., as creche or hospital workers, administrators, or military personnel). If such investment in human capital is carried on, we should include current foregone earnings as a real cost (probably small) borne by the volunteer, but the general training as a jointly supplied benefit of the NGO.

NGO Managers

NGO managers constitute a particularly important class of volunteers, albeit one which, in the future, will become increasingly professionalized. As discussed above, most large Sri Lankan NGOs are based in Colombo and managed by the upper-class English-speaking elite, a situation that is likely to continue. This is the group that, in the past, has been willing to donate its time and, in the future, will be best able to establish good working relationships with the foreign financial donors and justify paid positions. Since the benefits from acquiring formal status as an "approved charity" are a positive function of fund-raising ambitions and scale of operations, and since Sri Lanka lacks a widespread transportation and communications network, we would expect to find a concentration of registered NGOs and their leadership in the country's capital city. Nevertheless, this is a narrow base on which to draw in a country in which 85 percent of the population is rural.

Branches of many organizations do exist in the smaller towns. However, their independent funds are meager; access to the foreign donor as well as to government grants usually remains in the hands of the Colombo office. Nor, in most cases, is there any systematic attempt to move branch "managers" into positions of leadership in the central organization. Instead, the leadership of NGOs often remains in the same hands from year to year and "interlocking directorates" in which the same people sit on executive committees or boards of several different organizations, are not uncommon.

Little direct evidence is available on the objective functions of these NGO managers. However, a recent study of women's organizations suggests that many of their leaders are motivated by a desire to "do good" (sometimes with a strong patronizing element built in), to acquire social prestige and approbation among their peers, and to travel.[20] Both interviews and written statements indicate a preference for active participation in the organization's decision-making process. In a few cases, a desire to win political influence is probably also involved. Some material rewards for volunteers were mentioned above and, as the management group becomes professionalized, pecuniary incentives will play an increasing role. The question arises, then, whether the NGO sector will reflect the preferences of the broader population or is primarily another mechanism for providing utility to the already wealthy and influential few. The Conclusion will comment further on this point.

Volunteerism and Social Efficiency

I would argue that true volunteer labor serves a potentially useful function in a labor-surplus economy that has, simultaneously, unemployed labor and unmet needs. Its dilemma is how to mobilize the former, which has low opportunity cost, to solve the latter. This is a generalization of a familiar question in the development literature: How can underemployed rural labor be used to create productive capital, in economies with too much of the former, too little of the latter?

Where the unmet needs involve public goods or significant positive externalities, the classical solution is for the government to raise funds through taxation to hire the necessary production factors, so long as the summation of marginal social benefits exceeds real marginal costs. However, government may be required, by law, to pay a wage in excess of labor's opportunity cost. In addition, the process of compulsory taxation itself introduces distortionary economic effects that add to the real cost. Moreover, there are practical political limits to taxation for politicians who wish to be reelected; these may, for example, cause an underinvestment in public goods that are strongly desired by a few while the tax burden is spread over many. Thus, both real social costs and apparent money costs may exceed the factor's opportunity cost. Perceived political costs may be greater yet—leading to a kind of "planning failure" when the government is operating in a democratic political, market economic system.[21] While this "planning failure" applies to all resources it is particularly striking with respect to labor when unemployment is high and opportunity costs are correspondingly low.

These failures may be avoided in a centralized command economy, where the government may simply draft and allocate unemployed labor. But this is not considered an acceptable device in most peacetime democracies.

In this context, the voluntary sector may be seen as an alternative mechanism for allocating resources to public goods, a mechanism that shapes peoples' tastes, exerts social pressure and offers nonpecuniary rewards to induce them to contribute their time for the common good. The disadvantages of volunteerism, of course, are its undependability, instability, and the likelihood of its inadequacy; i.e., the free-rider problem will not be completely avoided. It also may lead to an inequitable distribution of the voluntary tax burden upon those with the greatest social conscience, rather than those with the greatest benefit or the greatest ability to pay.[22] The offsetting advantage is that it avoids the artificial wage floors, the distortionary effects of compulsory taxation, and the political limits to spending and has the potential to draw most heavily on those with the lowest opportunity cost, the unemployed, or those not even in the labor force. Indeed, in economies with high underemployment the real costs of volunteerism may be negative; it may reduce frustration and social unrest among the country's underutilized youth. As an added bonus, in situations where different types of public goods are possible (e.g., a choice between roads in different locations, wells versus reservoirs, etc.), this system of voluntary taxation reveals people's preferences—which may otherwise be unknown to the government planner—and also implements these preferences in a very direct way.

Professionalization of the Voluntary Sector

I would predict that, as opportunities in the market for the labor force increase, and unemployment falls, the supply of volunteer labor will correspondingly decline. Domestic donations will then take the form of money rather than time, enabling (some) NGOs to hire a paid staff, and those which survive will appeal to people with high incomes, i.e., a high opportunity cost of labor, rather than those with a low opportunity cost.

The professionalization of the "volunteer" has already been observed in the United States and knowledgeable people claim that it is beginning to happen also in Sri Lanka. While more and more young unskilled people, particularly in rural areas, are participating in shramadana-type activities, the opposite is occurring in the cities, at the managerial and white-collar levels. Educated young women who in the past would have volunteered their time to "worthwhile causes" are now seeking remunerative employment instead. This is partly because more jobs are open to them and partly because the changing social climate makes market employment more acceptable and prestigious.

The process of professionalization has also been accelerated by the increased availability of foreign funds in recent years. As foreign donations flow in, people who previously served on a volunteer basis tend to become paid staff, an effect that has been bemoaned by many of the "old-timers." To the extent that this substitution occurs, the foreign contributions do not produce additional services but, instead, represent a transfer payment to these workers.

The numbers cited earlier in this section, comparing volunteerism in the indigenous and international subsets, are evidence that the use of volunteer labor is indeed more positively linked to domestic donations. However, the derivative of foreign donations remains positive, albeit small. Several counteracting forces seem to be at work, concerning the impact of foreign donations on the supply and productivity of volunteers. On the one hand is the simple transfer effect, just described. On the other hand, many of these volunteers might eventually have sought paid employment in any event, as opportunities increase and the wealthy leisure class declines; in their case, the wage represents a true factor cost, not a transfer. Moreover, the possibility of fundable jobs later on may induce new volunteers to serve temporarily as unpaid apprentices. Also, most importantly, foreign funds enable the NGO to purchase materials and equipment that are complementary with volunteer labor, enhancing the attractiveness and productivity of their work. On balance, it appears likely that although some transfer payments occur, the latter three effects far outweigh it in their positive impact on NGO output.

I would hypothesize that the move toward professionalization is an inevitable accompaniment of the move toward a more highly developed market-oriented economy. The foreign funds (plus domestic monetary donations, if these emerge) will enable the growth of those organizations which can attract them and use them to shift from a volunteer to a paid managerial staff.

THE GOVERNMENT VERSUS THE VOLUNTARY SECTOR

As described above, the NGO sector in Sri Lanka produces public goods or goods with a strong income-redistribution component and to that extent encroaches upon governmental territory. By doing so, it provides competition and reduces the monopolistic power of governmental officials but it also increases peoples' satisfaction with the level of public services and, hence, their chances of getting reelected (or, in countries without free elections, reduces the probability that they will be overthrown). Therefore, we would expect an ambivalent attitude on the part of the government toward the NGOs: approval and support for their existence, combined with an attempt to regulate and control. Indeed, this is exactly what we find in Sri Lanka.

Government Support for NGOs

Repeatedly, government officials interviewed affirmed their support for the NGO sector as enabling the provision of social services that the country could not otherwise afford—because it operates at lower cost and draws upon resources that would not be available to the government. To encourage these organizations, the government provides the following tangible support:

1. Direct Grants
For many smaller NGOs, as we have seen, government grants are the most important source of funds. While government supplied only 2 percent of all monetary resources in my sample, the proportion was much higher, 48 percent, for the small-scale indigenous subgroup. For the entire population of NGOs, government grants probably total close to $1 million, primarily from the Departments of Rural Development, Social Services, Child Care, and Health. The government grants are typically modest, by international standards, and are designed to sustain ongoing inframarginal activities, rather than being tied to expansion, innovation, and the development of specific new projects, as are the foreign grants. This behavior, thus, is consistent with our hypothesis that government wishes to support the NGO sector but is not eager for it to grow and compete.

NGO recipients of government funds are expected to mobilize other resources as well (e.g., volunteer labor, cash donations, gifts of food in kind). In return for doing so, the NGO gets day-to-day managerial control over the total amount, subject to meeting specified standards and filing annual reports. Of course, the larger the share of revenues that comes from the government, the more the preferences of government officials must be taken into account.

2. Material Assistance and Expertise
In addition to financial support, the government often provides the raw materials which are then combined with volunteer labor to produce public or quasi-public goods—e.g., gravel for roads or latrines installed by shramadana volunteers. Likewise, government health officials and technicians may make their expertise available to the NGO.

3. Tax Privileges
As in the United States, "approved charities" receive certain tax advantages. In effect, this represents an additional subsidy from the "potential" public budget to the NGOs, a subsidy that depends upon and "matches" relative donor preferences for each organization, (partially) compensating for their tendency to free-ride. The tax subsidy, then, delegates the alloca-

tive decision to donors and makes public contributions a positive function of private donations while the direct-grant subsidy implies greater allocative decision-making power and corresponding control over NGOs for the government planner. The more decentralized the economic system, the larger the relative role I would therefore predict for tax subsidies.

However, poor countries, where relatively few people pay income tax, cannot rely heavily on tax deductibility as a method of public subsidy. For example, in Sri Lanka, only 2 percent of the population, clustered in the urban areas, pay any income tax.[23] More generally, when donations come primarily from abroad and from a small group of domestic donors, the government may not wish their preferences to dictate the allocation of public support. These forces would tend to increase their reliance on direct grants.

What then are the types and quantities of tax privileges enjoyed by NGOs in Sri Lanka?

The Inland Revenue Act of 1979 contains the following provisions regarding "approved charities":

1. Their profits are exempt from income tax if used solely for a charitable purpose, provided (a) the work is performed mainly for beneficiaries of that organization or (b) the organization receives grants from the government of Sri Lanka and the business activity is of a casual nature.
2. Other income (e.g., rental on buildings, interest on deposits) is taxable if it exceeds 12,000 rupees ($800) yearly.
3. While income-tax rates for individuals vary from 7½ to 70 percent and profit-tax rates on companies vary from 20 percent to 50 percent, charitable institutions pay a flat 20 percent.
4. An individual may deduct donations made to an approved charity, providing this does not exceed one-third of his assessable income.
5. Property that is owned and occupied solely by a charitable organization is exempt from the wealth tax.
6. Regarding other property (e.g., which the charity owns but rents to others): a flat ½ percent rate applies to charitable organizations while the ordinary wealth tax varies from ½ to 2 percent. (the first 200,000 rupees ($13,333) of wealth is always tax-deductible.)

In addition to the above, when contributions in kind are made from abroad, import duties are often, but not always, waived, at the discretion of the Minister of Finance.

What is the monetary value of these tax privileges? If we assume that the net profit from sales of the charitable organizations in my sample were completely exempt, whereas an (average) 40 percent rate would otherwise have applied, this would constitute an implicit subsidy of 0.4 ($28,000) or $11,200. By similar reasoning, the implicit subsidy on rent and interest was 0.2 ($71,000) = $14,200; on domestic contributions 0.4 ($120,000) = $48,000 and on wealth $28,350.[24] The total estimated tax subsidy for my sample, then (aside from import duties foregone, on which we have no data), was $102,000, or approximately $1 million for the entire population of approved charities—roughly the same as direct government grants.[25] For the reasons given above the relative role of tax subsidies is much higher in the United States.[26]

Government Control of NGOs

While the government provides this assistance, it also tries to control the resultant NGO sector and its revenue sources. For example, government-sponsored NGO "Rural Development Societies" have been established, to make use of the huge potential supply of volunteer labor, but these have had only mixed success. Along similar lines, in 1973 the government created a "governmental" NGO, the Freedom from Hunger Fund, designed to capture some of the foreign funds and channel them to selected voluntary organizations. More generally, all foreign donations to NGOs require prior government approval, to assure that they are in the national interest; however, this has been readily granted, in most cases, under the present government.

Thus, when the government recently proposed sweeping regulations of the NGOs, it came as a surprise to many of those involved in the third sector. The proposed bill would require every voluntary social-service organization to register and would give the government the power to: enter its premises; inspect and take custody of its books at any time; attend all general and executive committee meetings; summon such meetings and give directions to the executive committee; dissolve the organization and dispose of its assets in cases where fraud or mismanagement were believed to have occurred.[27] The stated purpose of this measure was to reduce fraud and misappropriation. The real motivation, many people believe, is the fear that foreign monies flowing in, ostensibly for charities, were in fact being used to create social unrest. A more general explanation would focus on the government's suspicion of a sector which has been growing in size and providing increased competition in both the economic and political spheres. Viewed in this light, a proposal for stronger regulation was not surprising and is consistent with the expected ambivalence of the government toward the NGOs.

An important question for further study is: Under what circumstances is a country's "third sector" financed by the government? This is true, for example, of the "independent" school systems in many countries. Is it in society's best interest for the government to delegate decision-making power over public funds to independent NGO managers? Conversely, what are the accompanying regulations? Since control over funds inevitably means some control over actions, how do we then distinguish between the governmental and nongovernmental sectors?

CONCLUSIONS: NGOs, WELFARE, AND ECONOMIC DEVELOPMENT

In this paper I conceive of voluntary organizations as "communities of interest" for providing impure public goods, often with a redistributive

objective, in cases where recipients of positive externalities are not geographically based and may, in fact, cut across national borders. Donors
contribute their time and money voluntarily, in an "implicit social contract" with others having similar preferences. These communities of interest may have a comparative advantage when product variety is possible
and economies of scale are sufficiently small to permit differentiated tastes
to be satisfied.

I explore the role of the "third (NGO) sector" in Sri Lanka, a labor-
surplus, low-income, developing country, and contrast it with that of the
"third (NPO) sector" in the United States of America. A dual nonprofit
sector was found, consisting of large internationally oriented organizations
and smaller indigenous organizations. We also observed a growing emphasis on social overhead capital, human capital, and other income-generating
(rather than income-transferring and consumption-oriented) activities.

The NPO-NGO institutional form was exported from the West to other
countries, including Sri Lanka, through missionary action and use of foreign capital. Today, financial donations from abroad continue to play a
major role. We have modeled individual foreign donors as having arguments in their utility functions regarding the welfare or friendship of particular subgroups or the consumption of particular goods in developing
countries, such as Sri Lanka; hence they will voluntarily contribute part of
their income for these purposes. They do so through an international network of NPOs, which provide them with information, selectivity, and trust.
The foreign NPOs, in turn, donate to Sri Lankan NGOs rather than government or private enterprises, in order best to control and monitor the
use of their funds. This has become the primary monetary resource for Sri
Lankan NGOs, a resource that would not be available to government or
private enterprise, and the preferences of foreign donors dictate, to a large
extent, which NGOs will dominate the scene. This influence from abroad
is not found in the U. S. or most other developed countries.

Sri Lankans contribute, too, mainly in the form of volunteer labor. They
are motivated by certain private benefits received in return, and by a variety of social pressures designed to overcome the free-rider problem, by
instilling satisfaction from participatory decision making and working for
the common good. This enables the mobilization of resources with a low
opportunity cost, which would otherwise be unemployed or underemployed. It avoids the political limitations on and distortionary effects of
compulsory taxation, as a mechanism for allocating these resources for the
production of public goods. The NPO arrangement substitutes instead a
system of voluntary taxation that simultaneously reveals and implements
people's relative intensity of preferences for different types of public goods,
when product variety exists. People vote directly with their voluntary contributions of time and money. While volunteer labor is also used in the
United States, its role is particularly important and efficient in a labor-
surplus country.

We model government officials as having the twin objectives of getting

reelected and increasing their power. The government's attitude toward
the "third sector" consequently will be ambivalent—welcoming it as a
mechanism for low-cost production of public goods, and a provider of
additional resources for developmental projects, all of which increase voter
satisfaction—but fearing it as a source of economic and political competition. Therefore, we would expect, and do indeed find, efforts to support,
contain, and control the "third sector" at the same time.

The NGO managers, then, are constrained by the willingness of foreign
donors to donate money and of individual Sri Lankans to donate time,
and, to a lesser extent, by government grants and regulations. This sets
limits on the quantities they can produce, on their product mix, on quality
choices, and on ability to save for future activities. However, it does leave
them some discretionary power, except in polar cases.

In another paper, I investigated whether this discretionary power will be
used to achieve Pareto-optimality, and found no inexorable force pressing
in that direction. Thus, while the existence of the NGOs constitutes a move
toward efficiency because it creates a market in which preferences about
externalities can be directly revealed and implemented, this arrangement
does not necessarily bring us to the Pareto-optimal frontier. Instead, there
may be underproduction of some goods and overproduction of others, depending on the preferences of the NGO managers, as well as their ability
and willingness to undertake careful benefit–cost analyses.[28] This generalization regarding efficiency holds for the United States as well as Sri Lanka.

The Sri Lankan situation, however, raises two basic questions about the
appropriate criterion for social efficiency. First, we have seen that most
(financial) donors to Sri Lankan NGOs live abroad and do not benefit
directly, while most direct beneficiaries live in Sri Lanka and are not able
(or willing) to pay. We have postulated that the foreign donors are willing
to contribute because into their objective function enters the consumption
of specific goods by specific groups in Sri Lanka; income redistribution via
these "merit goods" is a source of utility to people abroad. In defining
Pareto-optimality from the worldwide point of view, then, we must add
these foreign benefits to the domestic benefits. Because of the huge income
disparities, the subjective valuation of the former is much greater than the
latter, hence the different proclivities to donate. It follows that: (1) although Sri Lanka benefits from the actions of the NGOs, it would probably prefer to spend the equivalent resources in other ways, if given completely free choice; (2) foreign preferences not only determine the resources
and actual behavior of Sri Lankan NGOs, they also determine the efficient
product mix, from the worldwide perspective; (3) by enabling a flow of
funds that reflects these foreign preferences, the existence of NPOs may
facilitate a movement toward worldwide efficiency; and (4) an allocation
that is Pareto-optimal from the international point of view may not be
Pareto-optimal from the national point of view, where only domestic benefits and costs are considered, and normatively, a choice must be made
between the two.

Secondly, evaluation of efficiency is complicated by the fact that many NGOs have taste change as an explicit objective. For example, the Family Planning Association works actively to alter peoples' preferences about optimum family size. Sarvodaya stresses "personality development" and "village awakening," altering peoples' attitudes toward socioeconomic change and inculcating "community improvement" through "shared labor" as an argument in their utility functions. In general, religious organizations attempt to change peoples' values and tastes. When they succeed, the ex ante and ex post evaluation of benefits may differ, and economists have difficulty making welfare comparisons in such cases.

What are the prospects for the future? We have seen that, as economic development takes place, the supply of volunteer labor will probably decline. I would expect foreign donations to increase in the short run but to level off and, relative to real GNP, decrease in the longer run, as international income disparities (hopefully) contract. This is also in accordance with the nationalistic aspirations of Sri Lanka and the state intentions of many donors.[29]

The continuation of the NGOs when volunteer labor and foreign donations decline will depend on whether domestic monetary donations replace them, implying that the Western NPO concept has fully taken root. If this does not happen the NGOs must either concentrate on income-generating products that can cover their cost in the market place (thereby behaving more like private profit-maximizing firms), or they must, increasingly, depend on the government for support (which is likely to be accompanied by control). Thus, unless domestic monetary donations grow, we will eventually see a diminution in the role of the "third sector" and a reversion to a "two-sector" economy in Sri Lanka.

NOTES

1. H. Hansmann, "The Role of Nonprofit Enterprise," *Yale Law Journal* 89 (1980): 835–901.

2. This interpretation is consistent with Weisbrod's view that a primary function of NPOs is to produce public goods that are undersupplied by the government, possibly because of heterogeneous tastes. See Burton Weisbrod, "Toward A Theory of the Voluntary Nonprofit Sector in a Three-Sector Economy," in *Altruism, Morality and Economic Theory* ed. E. Phelps (New York: Russell Sage Foundation, 1975), pp. 171–191; *The Voluntary Non-profit Sector* (Lexington, Mass.: Lexington Books, 1977).

3. Ibid.

4. See Estelle James, "How Nonprofits Grow: A Model," *Journal of Policy Analysis and Management* (Spring 1983): 350–65; Estelle James and Egon Neuberger, "The University Department as a Non-profit Labor Cooperative," *Public Choice* 36 (1981): 585–612.

5. Churches per se are excluded from this definition, although many church-related charitable organizations are included. Schools are not considered "approved charities," although special adjunct organizations such as scholarship funds and PTAs may qualify. Although health-related institutions are included, hospitals are either government or private proprietary in Sri Lanka; they do not fall into the "voluntary" category. Thus, the tax-exempt "charitable

sector" in Sri Lanka is only a small subset of the activities usually associated with the tax-exempt "philanthropic sector" in the United States, which are heavily dominated by education and health.

6. Provision of social-overhead capital was a function of voluntary organizations in other countries as well during the early stages of their development, for example, in Palestine during the interwar period (see N. Gross, "The 1923 Recession and Public Sector Finance in Palestine," Falk Institute Discussion Paper 794, 1979) and in sixteenth century Great Britain (see Weisbrod, *Voluntary Non-profit Sector*).

7. This is based on the assumption that my sample includes 40 percent of all foreign resources and income from sales, but only 10 percent of all other domestic monetary resources.

8. Weisbrod, *Voluntary Non-profit Sector*, pp. 21–23, estimates that "philanthropic" organizations in the United States have total revenues equal to 10 percent of our GNP. However, these figures are not comparable because of the large amount of intrasector transfers, which involve double counting, in his numbers. Eli Ginzberg, Dale L. Hiestand, and B. J. Reubens, *The Pluralistic Economy* (New York: McGraw-Hill, 1965), p. 86, estimate that expenditures of U.S. NPOs are about 5 percent of GNP; however, I only consider "approved charities," a subset of all NPOs, in my analysis of Sri Lanka. The most comparable figure may be Dickinson's estimates for philanthropic donations by private individuals and corporations, plus income from endowments, which totaled 2.4 percent of U.S. GNP in 1959. See F. D. Dickinson, *The Changing Position of Philanthropy in the American Economy* (New York: National Bureau of Economic Research, 1970), p. 9.

9. Sarvodaya Shramadana Sanamaya means "village awakening through shared labor." The organization stresses rural income-generating activities and construction of social-overhead capital with volunteer labor, all carried out with a strong Buddhist philosophical emphasis. With the resources at its disposal greater than the total budget of the government's Rural Development Department and with a multiplicity of activities and subunits, it almost constitutes a minigovernment in itself.

10. All my rank-order correlation coefficients were significant at the 0.01 level. Perusal of balance sheets shows that the larger organizations in the "indigenous" group did receive foreign contributions in the past and some of these funds remained to be spent in 1978. In my calculations of rank-order correlation between total and foreign revenues, these organizations were assigned a higher rank. When looked at over a longer time period, more organizations would undoubtedly be found in the "international" group, with foreign resources playing an even more important role.

11. Additionally, many NPOs try to mitigate the free-rider problem by personalizing and concretizing the impact of the contributions. Examples are organizations that permit you to "adopt" a child abroad for a monthly payment or tell you how many bottles of milk or immunizations each dollar's contribution will purchase.

12. Dickinson, *Changing Position of Philanthropy*, pp. 77–90 has provided data on private philanthropy from the United States to other countries for 1929–1959. This shows that there are, indeed, personal remittances, but most of this goes to European relatives of immigrants to the United States. The institutional remittances, on the other hand, go mainly to countries outside of Europe or the Western Hemisphere. Interestingly, 80 percent of the institutional transfers were from religious organizations, with Protestant and Jewish groups leading in alternating years and both exceeding Roman Catholic remittances. If we exclude personal (mostly intrafamily) transfers, we find that private foreign philanthropy was only 2 percent of all private philanthropy in the United States in 1959. However, these donations constitute a much higher proportion of the monetary resources of voluntary organizations in the non-Western recipient countries, as we have seen for the case of Sri Lanka.

13. For example, in Germany each political party has its own government-supported foundation, which operates both domestically and abroad. Interestingly, although the political parties they represent are rivals in Germany, they have made a pact to divide the market and avoid competition abroad. The Dutch government contributes to NOVIB, an NPO that is

also supported by private individuals in the Netherlands and that has been the major sup-
porter of Sarvodaya in Sri Lanka.

14. For example, NORAD and SIDA operate in this manner, matching some contributions
to Sri Lanka NGOs made by church groups in Norway and Sweden.

15. The United States, whose tax laws are among the most liberal with respect to tax
deductibility of NPO contributions, is a major example.

16. For example, the U.S. AID supports the YMCA, and SIDA (Sweden) supports the Sri
Lankan cooperative movement, probably for this reason.

17. For example, CEY-NOR, a Norwegian-supported NGO, is operating in the politically
tense Tamil-dominated north, while the Norwegian government might have been asked to
"keep out."

18. This preference for dealing with NGOs was highlighted in a controversy regarding
legislation recently proposed that would have imposed sweeping regulations over the Sri Lankan voluntary sector. In strongly opposing this legislation, Sjet Theunis, the secretary-general
of NOVIB, a major Dutch NPO donor, publicly declared (via the Sri Lanka Broadcasting
Corp., December 12, 1979): "We would be very disappointed with such a piece of legislation,
as it is the NOVIB principle to cooperate exclusively with private nongovernmental organizations. Under the new law such NGOs would be considered government-ruled bodies. Under
these circumstances we would feel compelled to withdraw NOVIB aid and consequently to
accept the fact that many developmental projects would face severe setbacks."

19. For example, Dickinson, *Changing Position of Philanthropy*, p. 10, cites a study in
which volunteer labor in the United States was estimated to be 2 percent of our GNP, approximately the same as private monetary contributions to philanthropic organizations and
much less than their monetary resources from all domestic sources. See also Weisbrod, *Voluntary Non-profit Sector*, p. 17.

20. See H. Goonatilake, "A Study of National Women's Organizations in Sri Lanka,"
mimeograph, Colombo, Sri Lanka, 1979.

21. See Burton Weisbrod, *Voluntary Non-profit Sector*, for a further discussion of "government failure."

22. By *social conscience* I mean those who act as they would like others in society to act,
in accordance with an implicit social contract, even though they have no guarantee that
others will do so. An additional disadvantage faced by voluntary organizations is the need to
incur fund-raising costs to elicit donations of time and money. This transactions cost is the
voluntary sector's counterpart to the distortionary costs of government taxation.

23. This situation arises because the first 12,000 rupees ($800) of income, well above the
national average, is deductible; and furthermore much of Sri Lankan output is agricultural
production for household consumption or informal exchange, which therefore does not pass
through the formal market.

24. Obtained for 15 of the organizations in my sample assuming that the first $13,333 of
net wealth would in any event be tax free, that of the remainder an average 1 percent tax
rate would otherwise apply, and that the organizations use 90 percent of their assets for
charitable purposes. Then, $[0.1(0.005) + 0.9(0.01)]$ [$3,421,000 (gross assets) − $250,000 (estimated liabilities) − $188,000 (estimated deductions) = $28,350.

25. The extrapolation to the entire population of approved charities in Sri Lanka is based
on the assumption that my sample includes 10 percent of all domestic monetary resources
and wealth, as in note 7.

26. It is difficult to secure data on direct government grants and tax subsidies to the nonprofit sector in the United States. However, Weisbrod, *Voluntary Non-profit Sector*, p. 24,
estimates government grants to educational NPOs plus federal grants to health NPOs to be
$1,229 million, as compared with private contributions of $13,771 million in 1973. If these
contributions were tax deductible, on average, at a marginal rate of 33 percent (which is
probably a conservative estimate), the income-tax deduction alone would total $4,590 mil-
lion. Property- and income-tax exemptions for these organizations would probably bring the
total tax subsidy to over $6 billion, or five times the value of government grants to these two

activities, which constitute a major part of the voluntary sector in the United States. The ratio of tax subsidy to direct grants for religious organizations (the other major component), and therefore to the sector as a whole, would be even higher.

27. Bill 98 for Registration and Control of Voluntary Social Services Agencies, presented to Parliament by the Sri Lankan Minister of Social Services (October 18, 1970).

28. See Estelle James, "How Nonprofits Grow: A Model," *Journal of Policy Analysis and Management* (Spring 1983): 350–65. In fact, few organizations have carried out benefit–cost studies before initiating a project and, ex post, it appears that at least some NGO resources have been misallocated as a result. For example, vocational training has become an increasingly popular NGO activity in the last few years, with numerous organizations simultaneously initiating projects of this sort. The implicit expectation is that jobs will be available or that self-employment is a viable alternative. But jobs have not been found by all trainees and they often lack the working capital, marketing outlets, or managerial skills to start their own businesses. It is not always clear ex post that the "right" set of skills has been imparted. Some NGOs (e.g., Mahila Samiti and Sarvodaya) are now trying to remedy this by providing training in basic managerial skills, and starting marketing outlets or revolving funds for small business loans. However, these activities are still in the nascent stage. It is also worth noting that most training programs for women stress traditional handicrafts by very low-productivity labor-intensive methods, which will scarcely raise their incomes much or give them access to the modern sector of the economy.

29. Several donors interviewed expressed concern about the catch-22 situation they are in. Although their stated aim is to make the developing country more self-reliant, their actual effect, as least in the short run, is greater foreign dependency. How do they resolve their contradictory position? One foreign donor claims that it will stay in a given country for only 10 years; after that, the recipient must, somehow, become self-supporting. Another donor prefers projects that have some income-generating dimension, so that it is more likely to continue after foreign aid stops. Some donors try to avoid the installation of high technology, which cannot be maintained without outside help; instead, local technology and materials, as well as locally repairable equipment, are used whenever possible to relieve dependence on foreign aid.

REFERENCES

Dickinson, F. D., *The Changing Position of Philanthropy in the American Economy.* New York: National Bureau of Economic Research, 1970.

Dissanayake, D. "A Country Case Study on 'Involvement of Women's Organizations as Non-governmental Agencies, in Relating Social Welfare to Family Planning Objectives and Programmes.'" Paper prepared for the ESCAP, Colombo, Sri Lanka, 1977.

Ginzberg, Eli, Dale L. Hiestand, and B. J. Reubens. *The Pluralistic Economy.* New York: McGraw-Hill, 1965.

Goonatilake, H. "A Study of National Women's Organizations in Sri Lanka." (Mimeograph,) Colombo, Sri Lanka, 1979.

Gross, N. "The 1923 Recession and Public Sector Finance in Palestine." Falk Institute Discussion Paper 794, 1979.

Hansmann, H. "The Role of Nonprofit Enterprise." *Yale Law Journal* 89 (1980): pp. 835–901.

James, Estelle. "How Nonprofits Grow: A Model." *Journal of Policy Analysis and Management* (Spring 1983): 350–65.

James, Estelle, and Egon Neuberger. "The University Department as a Non-profit Labor Cooperative." *Public Choice* 36 (1981): 585–612.

Marga Institute. "National Non-governmental Organizations in Sri Lanka and Their Rele-

vance to Potential for Involvement in the Development Programmes of the Government." (Mimeograph), Colombo, Sri Lanka, 1979.

Weisbrod, Burton. "Toward a Theory of the Voluntary Nonprofit Sector in a Three-Sector
Economy." In E. Phelps, Ed., *Altruism, Morality and Economic Theory*. New York:
Russell Sage Foundation, 1975, pp. 171–91.

Weisbrod, Burton. *The Voluntary Non-profit Sector*. Lexington, Mass.: Lexington Books,
1977.

Numerous annual reports, financial statements and other material supplied by Sri Lankan
NGOs.

13

More than Altruism: The Politics of European International Charities

BRIAN H. SMITH

In addition to the important role charitable agencies have played in the historical evolution of social services inside Western nations, they have also been conduits of humanitarian assistance sent abroad. For nearly 400 years, in fact, nonprofit groups (beginning with missionary societies in Europe in the sixteenth century) have been sending aid overseas that now assists the needy in Asia, Africa, Latin America, and the Middle East.

During the height of the colonial era (from the mid-nineteenth to mid-twentieth centuries) a variety of religious and secular nonprofit organizations served important home-country interests by bringing educational, cultural, and social services to the territories in Africa and Asia controlled by Great Britain, France, Belgium, Portugal, Germany, and the Netherlands. In fact, many were subsidized by their respective home governments since they were seen as important instruments to spread European values and control in the colonies.[1]

During and immediately after the two World Wars in this century new European nonprofit organizations (NPOs) emerged to carry out relief work in war-torn countries. Given their humanitarian focus they could accomplish what was impossible for nation-states to do directly. For example, they were often licensed by warring governments to reach groups that the contenders in the conflict could not (or would not) aid.[2]

In the post-World War II era another generation of European NPOs emerged as colonialism was coming to an end. In order to maintain some influence in the societies of newly emerging nations (whose leaders wanted to lessen their heavy dependence on European governments), European citizens established private organizations (forerunners of the U.S. Peace

This essay draws heavily on material in Chapter 7, Brian H. Smith, *The Politics of International Charities* (Princeton, N.J.: Princeton University Press, forthcoming). A shorter version of this chapter also appears as a paper in the United Nations University Euro-South project under the title, "The Politics of European Development-oriented Non-governmental Organizations."

Corps) to send volunteers and technical assistance to new nations in Africa and Asia. Again, European governments found such agencies very useful for enhancing goodwill in these societies and countering feelings of distrust toward Europe after 100 years of colonial domination. In several instances, in fact, public officials provided subsidies to these new NPOs (especially the volunteer-sending groups), or even gave them semiofficial status.[3]

Historically, therefore, there was often a close symbiotic relationship between European governments and charitable organizations that went abroad with humanitarian aid. At the very least, such organizations were considered by European foreign (or colonial) ministries as complements to their own official policies. In some cases, moreover, NPOs served as conduits for public aid, since they were able to present a more "human face" for European interests abroad than government agencies themselves.

In more recent years, however, many of these European international charitable agencies (totaling over 1000 by the mid-1980s) have begun openly to oppose their respective governments' official aid and trade policies toward developing countries, arguing that these are harmful to, and even exploitative of, the poor in such societies. They are also officially espousing substantial structural changes inside developing countries and attempting to support private development organizations in the Third World (now totaling between 6000 and 8000) that are committed to mobilizing the poor to pressure their own government and economic elites for a more equitable distribution of resources and services.[4]

This new direction for many of the larger European charitable organizations has resulted from a growing disillusionment among students, intellectuals, and left-of-center labor and political leaders with traditional aid programs for developing countries. Since the early 1970s there has been widespread feeling among these groups (who form a major part of the support base of nonprofit aid agencies) that major political changes in the North Atlantic countries as well as in the Third World are needed to alleviate global poverty. They have emphasized the need for alterations in tariffs, commodity pricing agreements, and multinational corporation investment patterns for developed countries. For developing countries they have stressed the need for land and tax reform, credit and training for the hard-core poor, and greater input into public policy formation by low-income sectors. These policies form what is now termed the agenda for a *New International Economic Order* (NIEO).[5]

Ironically, at the same time that many European nonprofit aid agencies have begun to act as political pressure groups often opposing their own governments on foreign policy issues, their reliance on home-government subsidies has substantially increased. In 1973 all of these agencies received a combined total of less than $100 million (in 1986 dollar values) from their respective home governments, but by 1985 the amount had jumped to about $500 million (a real increase of over 500 percent). In fact, in 1985 approximately one-third of the resources of European international

NPOs came from public assistance—despite the fact that they now espouse a contestatory, as opposed to a complementary, role for themselves vis-à-vis government agencies regarding Third World issues.[6]

How can we explain this paradox? Why do European governments continue to support, in increasing amounts, organizations that are hostile to official policies? Does the aid come with political strings attached that deter the organizations from pursuing some of their goals? And, what strategies do they use to generate the two-thirds of their resources that come from private sources? This chapter addresses these closely related problems.

I argue that, despite their contestatory positions, nonprofit aid agencies in Europe still continue to perform useful functions for governments in North Atlantic societies, as they have in the past. They serve as cost-effective conduits of aid to the poor overseas, act as surrogates for sensitive foreign policy objectives of the home governments, and also provide important support for domestic agendas of political elites in their own societies. Moreover, when necessary, public policymakers can and do employ a series of legal, economic, and political sanctions to restrict the political impact of these transnational nonprofits, and thus far have been successful in preventing them from becoming serious obstacles to official foreign policy formation or implementation.

ADVANTAGES TO GOVERNMENTS IN COFINANCING INTERNATIONAL CHARITIES

Clearly one major advantage for European governments in cofinancing the overseas activities of charitable organizations based in their own societies is to assure that some of their own aid reaches the poor abroad and does so cost effectively. The alternative to using NPOs as a conduit is government-to-government aid. But most governments in Third World countries generally cannot be counted on to channel aid to the bottom 40 percent in their societies, who constitute the hard core (and hard-to-reach) poor. Moreover, overhead costs inside government bureaucracies sometimes reach 30 to 40 percent of total expenditures. Nonprofit organizations through their private counterparts overseas (who administer their charitable income) consistently reach this target population and do so with overhead costs of only 20 percent due to low salaries and a considerable degree of voluntary time and talent.

In addition, even European charitable organizations who oppose official foreign policy agendas of their own countries are useful alternate channels of communication and influence abroad, when it is impossible or undesirable for European foreign ministries to take direct action on certain fronts themselves. In situations of authoritarian regimes (Left or Right), for example, European governments sometimes prefer not to give direct aid. By channeling public revenues through charitable organizations—especially those that espouse greater popular participation in their overseas programs—European officials can avoid assisting such governments and also sometimes aid indirectly those groups opposing authoritarian policies.

After the military coup in Chile in 1973, the Social Democratic (SPD) government of Willy Brandt in West Germany aided both the poor and the former leftist supporters of the Allende government bearing the brunt of military repression. SPD officials did so by sending economic aid through German Catholic (MISEREOR) and Protestant (EZE) charitable organizations who were supporting Chilean church-sponsored humanitarian projects in the post-coup period. In 1978, the subsequent SPD government of Helmut Schmidt (under strong pressure from the young militant JUSOS in the party) made a symbolic gesture of solidarity with black liberation movements in the southern Africa region. They did so by sending small amounts of medical and sanitation supplies to the Patriotic Front in Rhodesia through the Friedrich Ebert Foundation, a German nonprofit organization controlled by the SPD but separate from the government.[7]

The Conservative government of Margaret Thatcher in Great Britain finds nonprofit aid agencies an attractive means whereby to exercise some influence inside Nicaragua without assisting either the Sandinistas or the Contras. Although the Thatcher administration has terminated all official bilateral aid to Nicaragua, it has continued to cofinance certain projects inside Nicaragua supported by the two leading church-sponsored foreign charitable organizations in the United Kingdom: Christian Aid (CA), and the Catholic Fund for Overseas Development (CAFOD). The British government provides grants through these London-based NPOs to private groups in Nicaragua engaged in small-scale agriculture and community health so as to strengthen the autonomy of civil society against the state in that country.[8] Direct British government assistance to private organizations inside Nicaragua could endanger such organizations or not be permitted at all. Since many of them are church-related, however, they are permitted to import resources for relief and development from abroad from private agencies. International charities, in turn, can then act as conduits for larger public institutions to assist the private sector in Nicaragua.

In addition to serving as surrogates for the sensitive foreign policy agendas of their home governments, European charities are also relied upon by policymakers for domestic political purposes. The very fact that these organizations keep the needs of foreign countries before the public eye and generate considerable private contributions for overseas activities ($1 billion in 1985)[9] makes them attractive partners to public policymakers in the overall foreign aid process. Citizen support for official foreign aid has declined in much of Europe in recent years due to the recession of the late 1970s and early 1980s and a growing focus on domestic social concerns. Amidst this decline in public enthusiasm for government assistance to developing countries and the corresponding growth of a "home-country first" attitude, legislators have looked for allies who support the continuance of aid commitments abroad. In fact, this was one of the primary reasons European governments escalated subsidies to these NPOs in the late 1970s.

Charitable agencies, through their public advocacy efforts, encourage citizen support for greater resource flows to Third World nations—both private and public.

Since few interest groups act as pressure groups on behalf of foreign aid, these nonprofit groups are valuable allies to parliamentarians and policymakers alike concerned with maintaining a domestic base of support for foreign commitments. They come forward to testify on behalf of foreign aid appropriations in parliamentary committees when such legislation is being considered—and can also count, on the average, on 3 to 4 percent of overall government aid allocations being channeled through their own private networks.[10]

In some instances, charitable agencies have provided European political parties (particularly on the Left) with important ideas and strategies for a new approach to overseas aid. The small Green Party in Germany, which focuses most of its efforts on disarmament and environmental issues, has relied heavily on both secular and religious charitable agencies for information, analysis, and suggestions in its formulation of an alternate policy that would include more equitable trade arrangements and commodity pricing for developing countries.[11]

Both the Greens and the largest opposition Social Democratic Party (SPD) saw international charities as a useful tool to challenge official aid policies after the Christian Democrats (CDU) came to power in 1982. The CDU has tried to achieve greater trade and investment concessions from developing countries by conditioning German bilateral aid accordingly. The Greens and the SPD, as a way of embarrassing the CDU, have together argued in the *Bundestag* for a major privatization of German bilateral aid that would channel more government resources through charitable organizations working primarily with the poor, thus guaranteeing a more humanitarian and selfless image of German aid abroad.[12]

After the Socialists were victorious in France in 1981, Jean-Pierre Côt, the new Minister of Economic Cooperation who represented the sector of the party identified with progressive Catholics, set up a regular consultation process for several French religious and secular NPOs with officials in his ministry. In so doing, he hoped that they could inject new ideas into the French aid bureaucracy (long dominated by political conservatives primarily interested in aiding only French overseas territories and former colonies) along the lines of a basic human needs approach that identified the hard core poor throughout the Third World as main targets for French overseas aid.[13] Between 1980 and 1985, in fact, government subsidies to French international charities—especially those with sympathies for the Left and a commitment to this new agenda in French foreign aid—increased from $4 million to $43 million (in 1986 dollar values).[14] Moreover, some of these charities dedicated to New International Economic Order (NIEO) objectives regularly were given free time on French government-owned television to explain Third World needs and to argue for significant changes in French trade and domestic consumption patterns so as to meet these needs more effectively.

Conservative political leaders in Europe also occasionally find international charitable agencies (even those with a left-of-center ideology) useful in their own political battles at home. When Margaret Thatcher is criticized on the floor of Parliament by Labourites for her refusal to give any direct British aid to the government of Nicaragua, she points out that public subsidies to British charitable agencies continue and that such channels are the best way to guarantee that aid reaches the Nicaraguan poor cost effectively and does not go to the Marxist, and purportedly inept, Sandinista regime. Many British charitable agencies who send money to Nicaragua, such as CA, CAFOD, and Oxfam UK, are generally supportive of the goals and accomplishments of the Sandinistas but work only with private organizations in that country. What the Thatcher government sends to Nicaraguan private groups through some of these NPOs at home is miniscule (a few hundred thousand dollars) compared to the millions in official government-to-government aid to Nicaragua that has been terminated for several years. The Conservative government can thus accomplish several goals at once—counter some of the objections of the Left at home by continuing symbolic assistance to the poor in Nicaragua, reduce overall foreign aid expenditures, and also (as described earlier) strengthen the private sector in that socialist-oriented Central American country.[15]

STRATEGIES USED BY EUROPEAN GOVERNMENTS TO RESTRICT POLITICAL ACTION BY INTERNATIONAL CHARITIES

If international charities can offer European governments several positive benefits, they also face boundary lines imposed by policymakers when their political opposition is deemed too great. Possible penalties include invocation of legal sanctions, provision of more public subsidies for some types of projects than others, diversion of public aid away from politically troublesome organizations toward those that policymakers consider more acceptable, and ultimately, a cut-off of grants to charitable groups who fail to change their behavior after these other signals have been sent.

For example, by mutual agreement between governments and NPOs throughout Europe, public subsidies may not be used abroad to support military activities by indigenous groups committed to the armed overthrow of their respective governments. The government of the Netherlands, which allows considerable discretion to Dutch NPOs in the use of its grants overseas, has written into its formal cofinancing agreement with four large charitable agencies prohibitions forbidding support for activities abroad "aimed at undermining the political independence of any state or at bringing down a legal government by unlawful means." Dutch NPOs who sign such an agreement are also required to consult with the Minister for Development Cooperation "should there be any doubt surrounding the interpretation or appreciation" of this above restriction, "or concerning any adverse consequences that the financing of particular projects could have" for the Dutch government. Thus far, this prior consultation requirement has not been used by Dutch charitable agencies. Nor has there been any case where they have violated the written agreement or caused serious diplomatic problems for the Dutch government in their dispersal of funds to private groups abroad.[16]

In Great Britain since the seventeenth century, charities laws have regulated the behavior of nonprofit institutions. These forbid charitable groups from allocating funds or engaging in activities wholly or substantially devoted to political persuasion. Although the language is vague, no change in the wording of the law has been made for three centuries to give a precise definition of what constitutes "substantial" commitments to "political persuasion." The charity commissioners have thus been able to interpret this clause with flexibility over the years. From time to time in fact (depending on the political character of the government and the number of complaints received from private citizens), the commission will initiate investigations, issue warnings, and in some cases actually revoke the charitable status of agencies it judges to have engaged in too much "political persuasion."[17]

After repeated complaints to the charity commission in the late 1970s about the overtly partisan political nature of the education programs being carried out at home by War on Want (a British foreign charitable agency with long close ties to the Labour party), during Margaret Thatcher's first year in office the commission revoked its privileges as a nonprofit organization. War on Want was forced to establish a new organization, War on Want Campaign, separate from its overseas aid–sending operations in order to continue its domestic advocacy work. The new, second agency must pay taxes as any other partisan political organization in Great Britain and contributions to it are not tax deductible by donors.[18]

In addition to legal sanctions, a series of other political tactics is available to governments to keep the activities of charitable agencies from becoming a political embarrassment. All European governments (except the Dutch) still operate for the most part on a prior project-by-project approval for cofinancing with charitable agencies. NPOs must normally submit individual project descriptions to government aid ministries before receiving any subsidies. If projects are located in politically sensitive regions of the world (e.g., the western Sahara, the Middle East, Central America) policymakers scrutinize them more carefully, demand more specifics about their scope and purpose, and sometimes delay the approval process so as to dissuade charitable agencies from controversial undertakings.

Organizations that persist with politically sensitive activities can find their overall public subsidies begin to decline. Oxfam Belgium, for example, which has provided aid (with some Belgian government grants at first) for health and refugee projects run by the Palestinian Red Crescent in the Middle East (with close ties to the PLO) and to the Sahraoue Red Crescent in western Sahara (sympathetic to the Polisario movement), has experienced a decline of overall public assistance in recent years. Conversely,

Belgian charitable agencies that deliver humanitarian or technical aid to less controversial organizations in the Middle East, Africa, and elsewhere have experienced a steady increase in Belgian government aid.[19]

Of the $76.7 million given to 103 international charities by the Belgian government between 1976 and 1981 (in 1986 dollar values), in fact, only 21.9 percent went to those including among their overseas socioeconomic activities political consciousness raising and social mobilization among the poor. Moreover, these political-empowerment type NPOs had only 47 percent of their proposed projects approved for Belgian government cofinancing during this five-year period, whereas the approval rate for Belgian NPOs emphasizing the immediate relief of human suffering was 56 percent, and 58 percent for charities targeting technical training or building up of the physical infrastructure abroad.[20]

On the home front, governments can use both a "carrot and stick" approach with charitable agencies. The Thatcher government has substantially reduced public aid to development education projects by NPOs (from $4 million in 1978 to $250,000 in 1983), arguing that in a time of overall revenue cutbacks scarce foreign aid resources should be spent overseas in helping the poor not at home for political action work. The administration also gives 90 percent of this $250,000 to the Center for World Development Education (CWDE), a new British NPO that assiduously avoids attacks on government policies and focuses its general informational campaigns about developing countries on conservative business organizations and schoolchildren. Other organizations that engage in controversial advocacy work, such as Oxfam UK, CA, and CAFOD (all of whom criticize British investments in South Africa, pre-1985 Brazil, and other rightist authoritarian regimes), have been refused any public subsidies for their home front activities—in addition to being scrutinized more carefully by the charity commission in recent years for possible violations of the "political persuasion" clause with the donations they receive from private sources.[21]

INBUILT RESTRAINTS ON POLITICAL ACTION: VARIEGATED BASES OF PRIVATE SUPPORT

In addition to the external restraints on European charities imposed by home governments, the diversity in their private bases of support also places restrictions on their pursuit of political objectives at home or abroad. A variety of perspectives and motivations among private donors requires that NPOs pursue multiple objectives, not only political empowerment of the poor abroad or agitation for structural changes in international trade and investment policies. It also motivates them to target their most explicit political messages at home to some (and these a minority) of their overall private donor base. These factors also reduce further the potentially negative political fallout of charitable activities for European public policymakers.

Private donations to European international charities have for the past several years hovered at the $1 billion level (in 1986 dollar values).[22] One reason for their continuing popularity is that such charities almost invariably include support for humanitarian as well as technically oriented development projects. The most dramatic short-term increases in private donations to European foreign charities, in fact, still occur during times of disasters abroad—for example, the Ethiopian famine crisis in late 1984 and 1985—since all types of NPOs focus on such well-publicized calamities.[23]

Most of the politically oriented foreign charities have thus developed multiple private support bases, as well as different styles of information dissemination and reporting, depending on the set of donors with which they are communicating. Target groups are divided into three sectors: (1) well-informed regular contributors sharing the political commitments of these charities; (2) less politically motivated donors interested primarily in good, technically executed projects; and (3) humanitarian crisis supporters who give sporadically to alleviate immediate suffering abroad during well-publicized natural or humanmade disasters.

As indicated earlier, many European international charities have elements in their support bases that espouse political positions both domestically and internationally: trade unions, left-of-center parties, ethnic minorities, intellectual or religious elites. These often are the most consistent and individually generous contributors to such nonprofit groups. They are also the ones who receive the most complete information on the types of projects being supported overseas and the most politically explicit literature distributed by the organizations.

There is normally, however, a wider circle of contributors, who are less aware of the political orientation of the organizations. They are larger in number than the hard-core, politically committed supporters but receive less explicit details both about overseas projects and the domestic agendas of the charities. They are reached through broad-based fund-raising appeals that tend to downplay political messages but emphasize instead the comparative advantages these charities have in reaching the poorest people overseas and finding cost-effective, long-term solutions to their socioeconomic problems.

Finally, a third group of donors gives primarily during moments of well-publicized natural and humanmade disasters overseas. These are usually the largest in number but shortest in the duration of their giving. More and more European NPOs in recent years—including those with explicit political agendas—are becoming active during emergency situations (such as the Ethiopian famine) precisely to tap such crisis donors. They use the resources collected from these contributors to support relief activities in the affected regions abroad during the emergency, always hoping to keep at least some as ongoing supporters for other projects once the crisis has passed. As in the case of group 2, these crisis donors receive very little information about the political agenda of the charities who are appealing for their support primarily on humanitarian grounds.[24]

Christian AID (CA), for example, the major Protestant foreign charity in Great Britain, in 1985 had 12,600 people who made formal commitments, or covenants, to contribute a fixed amount of money annually to the organization. These donations accounted for 6.5 percent of the agency's 1985 income. They received the most complete information about overseas projects and are well aware of the social justice emphasis of CA in the selection of its overseas projects and in its denunciations of human rights abuses by repressive regimes.

The total number of donors to CA, however, amounts to several million. Many are reached by door-to-door appeals made by the organization every May throughout the country. These people are much less aware of the political nature of the projects CA supports overseas (e.g., in Central America), or of its campaign at home in support of economic sanctions against South Africa, since these aspects of its work are played down during door-to-door appeals. In 1985, however, such donors accounted for one-third of CA's income.

In addition appeals were made in 1984 and 1985 by CA, jointly with CAFOD, Oxfam UK, and Save the Children Fund, in media campaigns for contributions to alleviate famine in Ethiopia. These ads emphasized humanitarian issues, avoided politics completely, and brought in over half of CA's resources for 1985.

Fundraising efforts by CA (door-to-door requests for general contributions and media appeals for African famine relief) thus accounted for 83.5 percent of its resources in 1985. Aside from the 6.5 percent from the covenanters, the final 10 percent was obtained from government subsidies. Hence, although donors reached by these wider appeals may give less individually than those who have made formal covenants with CA, as a group they are far more crucial for the organization's financial maintenance and growth than the covenanters and the government combined. Through these techniques of multiple targeting, in fact, CA has more than doubled its annual budget in the early 1980s, from $11.6 million in 1982 to $25.5 million in 1985 (in 1986 dollar values)—the largest increase coming from the windfall of support during the Ethiopian famine crisis.[25]

Other European international charities that espouse political change abroad and at home also have pluralistic private support bases and similarly tailor their financial appeal and information dissemination according to donor target preferences and tastes. In the early 1980s Oxfam Belgium, for example, had 20,000 donors, 2000 of whom committed themselves to giving 1 percent of their annual income to the organization. This smaller group, constituting 10 percent of private contributors, receives all Oxfam materials, including specific information about overseas projects, and knows very well that the organization is supporting groups sympathetic to the

PLO in the Middle East and the Polisario movement in the western Sahara. The other 90 percent receive only general reports that do not give much detail. They are told of the basic socioeconomic nature of the organization's work in different parts of the globe but not about the controversial political aspects of some of the specific projects. Their prime motive in contributing is to further self-help socioeconomic development among the Third World poor, not to promote radical political change abroad, and their impression is that Oxfam Belgium is doing the first but not the second. Moreover, after special appeals in 1984 and 1985 on behalf of the starving in Ethiopia, Oxfam Belgium picked up 10,000 new donors primarily interested in helping to alleviate famine. As a result of such multiple appeals, Oxfam Belgium almost doubled its resources from $2.2 million in 1982 to $4.1 million in 1985 (in 1986 dollar values), precisely at the time when Belgian government subsidies to the organization were gradually declining because of its controversial activities overseas and at home (as described earlier).[26]

The Catholic Committee Against Hunger and for Development (CCFD) in France also has a small committed core of supporters reached through its local development education committees around the country. These are well aware of CCFD's commitment to liberation of the poor from oppression through development work and its espousal of the NIEO agenda. The vast majority of its supporters, however (who account for 60 percent of its resources) are reached through special collections taken up at Sunday Mass during Lent. Since practicing Catholics in France as a group tend to be on the Right politically, they are not given much detailed information about CCFD's overseas work and ideology. Their reasons for giving are frequently based on humanitarian motives, and they gave most generously during the Ethiopian famine crisis. As a result of this two-track fundraising strategy, CCFD's income expanded from $8.9 million in 1982 to $12.7 million in 1984 (in 1986 dollar values)—a jump of over 40 percent in just two years.[27]

The Catholic-sponsored international charity in Germany, Campaign Against Hunger and Disease in the World (MISEREOR), uses a similar strategy among its different sets of donors. During its major Lenten fundraising campaign in Catholic churches (whence comes most of its resources), it downplays controversy so as to maximize income and stresses the socioeconomic aspects of its overseas work among the poor. During periodic disasters when it makes appeals to the general public it emphasizes the need to alleviate immediate suffering. Throughout the year during its development education work in parishes, in universities, and among labor groups, it includes information on human rights violations in countries such as Brazil and South Africa and stresses the need for policy changes abroad and at home to change such structural inequities.

By separating temporally development education efforts from fund raising appeals in local churches, MISEREOR finds that politically conservative donors are less likely to penalize the organization by reducing their contributions. Moreover, specialized groups who are more open to social justice appeals (e.g., university students and union members) are targeted specifically for some of MISEREOR's more political messages. Its total income (in 1986 dollar values) has also risen dramatically in recent years, growing almost 40 percent between 1980 ($80.2 million) and 1985 ($112.1 million).[28]

These multiple appeals of European foreign charities thus satisfy various private support groups who feel their own particular interests are being met: political change benefiting the oppressed, socioeconomic development assisting low-income sectors, emergency aid alleviating the suffering of disaster victims. Various groups within the charities are also satisfied. Project officers and executives interested in promoting policy changes abroad and at home feel at least some donors are aware of, and committed to, these causes. Fund-raising personnel are happy with steadily growing revenues, and board members are pleased with expanding institutional growth in recent years as well as with the flexibility of options a diversified funding base provides (including greater autonomy from government).

PERIODIC EXPOSÉS OF INTERNATIONAL CHARITIES

Satisfying the multiple clusters of donors requires keeping many uninformed about some of the work of international charities at home and abroad and about the political preferences of staff and executives that shape the decisions about such activities. Periodically, however, individual donors who give to these agencies for development or humanitarian reasons become aware of political agendas and withdraw their support.

When some contributors to CA read its advertisement printed in three major London newspapers in November 1985 calling for British citizens to boycott South African goods and to write to their MPs in support of economic sanctions against that regime, they wrote angry letters terminating their donations to CA. MISEREOR in Germany has also lost a number of contributors in the pews when they have subsequently been exposed to some of its materials denouncing oppressive policies of governments in Latin America or Africa. Oxfam Belgium prior to the Ethiopian hunger crisis of 1984–1985 was finding it hard to expand its number of private contributors due to criticism by some politically conservative Belgians that it was sympathetic to communism.[29]

Usually these withdrawals or criticisms are among a few individuals and do not significantly hurt a charity because their disaffection or anger receives little publicity. Moreover, in some cases new contributors are gained by development education campaigns critical of home government policies toward developing countries or repressive regimes in the Third World. MISEREOR, for example, has generated new contributors in recent years among politically committed university students.[30]

There are, however, exposés in the media about politically sensitive projects supported by international charities. In such circumstances, the credibility of an organization is challenged publicly and large numbers of citizens, including actual and potential donors, are forced to question whether they are getting their money's worth from their contributions. At such times, moreover, the international charities community can experience serious internal splits along political lines.

The attempt by the Socialist government in France in the early 1980s to use charitable agencies sympathetic to the Left for some of its new foreign policy objectives precipitated a strong reaction by the political opposition that attempted to discredit these charities, and in so doing pitted one charitable agency against another. A charitable agency, Doctors Without Frontiers (MSF) whose leaders were personally identified with the political Right, denounced publicly another nonprofit organization, Brothers of Humanity (FDH), that had been using free time on national television to denounce traditional French aid and trade policies. MSF had impeccable humanitarian credentials due to its excellent record in assisting the starving and sick abroad (e.g., in the Sahel and Ethiopia). It was also larger and better known throughout France than FDH. The argument of MSF was that FDH was propagating a campaign of false guilt on television and offering simplistic solutions to Third World problems that were due largely to dynamics inside such nations and not to French consumption tastes or policies.[31]

At the same time, some prominent newspapers and journals with rightist political sympathies (such as *Le Figaro, Figaro-Magazine,* and *Le Quotidien de Paris)* published a series of articles identifying several of the overseas projects supported by the Catholic Committee Against Hunger and for Development (CCFD), highlighting those that were politically controversial and mostly unknown to the average church-going Catholics contributing to the charity. The exposés in these newspapers and journals (well read by practicing Catholics who generally are politically conservative) revealed that CCFD gave support to government-controlled television programs in Vietnam (at the request of the Archbishop of Hanoi), refugee camps administered by the South West Africa People's Organization (SWAPO), and to a newspaper and labor group in New Caledonia linked with FLNKS, the major indigenous political movement agitating for independence from France. The series also identified some Chilean organizations with leftist political sympathies that had recently received CCFD assistance. The articles claimed that only 5 of the 23 projects in Chile that CCFD supported in 1985 were administered by organizations under direct local church supervision, concluding that approximately $173,000 of the $219,000 sent to Chile in 1985 (in 1986 dollar values) by the CCFD went to political projects run by secular groups opposing the Chilean government.[32]

The themes of this exposé—repeated several times in the series—were that CCFD executives and staff have a leftist political agenda not representative of the majority of their French Catholic supporters and that the agency deceives most donors by not giving them an accurate account of what it is actually doing with their funds. The articles also claimed to be based on evidence provided by an on-site inspection of the projects CCFD supports in Chile done by an independent group of interested French observers.

CCFD strongly denounced such attacks as defamatory and fraught with distortions. At a press conference it produced several letters of support from prominent clerics and others in Chile denying any linkage of CCFD-supported projects with Marxism. The Chilean groups that had received CCFD aid also indicated that they had never been visited by any French delegation purporting to be carrying out an inspection of CCFD-aided projects. CCFD spokespersons, however, did not deny having supported the TV project in Vietnam, nor the journals and research center in Chile that are run by political opponents of the regime.[33]

It is not yet clear how such an exposé will affect future private donations to CCFD. The image of CCFD among French conservative Catholics (the main source of its private resources) has certainly been damaged. The French bishops subsequently received expressions of concern and outrage from lay persons abut the type of work CCFD is supporting abroad, including a letter from 200 Catholics in New Caledonia denouncing CCFD's contributions to organizations closely associated with political independence movements in their territory.

The hierarchy in France since 1986 has taken steps to establish greater ecclesiastical control over CCFD activities, setting up a joint committee with episcopal and CCFD representation to revise the statutes of the organization. The changes include more direct hierarchical involvement in the choice of CCFD's leadership and the requirement that host-country bishops be consulted by CCFD before providing support for any project located in their respective dioceses.[34]

Hence, the strategy of double or triple reporting styles by European international charities to their multiple support bases in the private sector makes them vulnerable to exposés—especially if they are, in fact, supporting projects abroad or carrying out advocacy campaigns at home whose political orientation some donors do not share. Even if criticism articulated in such exposés is not completely accurate and orchestrated for partisan political objectives, as the media attacks on CCFD have been in France, they are not totally prefabricated. The half-truths contained in them are sufficient to tarnish a charity's credibility—precisely when so little detail is given to the majority of donors about its politically controversial activities.

CONCLUSIONS

The relationship among many international charities, subsidizing governments, and private donors in Europe involve a series of political trade-offs. The delicate game that is thus being played out requires a very careful balancing act within and across partner groups, and a certain amount of secrecy is an essential ingredient in maintaining the nonprofit aid system.

Despite the clear left-of-center political priorities of executives and staffs in many international charities committed to the NIEO agenda, there is sufficient pluralism (and shrewdness) within these organizations to support multiple activities, including relief work during times of overseas disasters. This legitimates them in the eyes of many private donors (actual and potential) who do not share (and are not cognizant of) the political objectives of these organizations abroad or their partisan work at home. Such multiple targeting of resources not only maximizes the opportunity for private income from diverse sources in society but also provides the charities with credibility as humanitarian agents and a reputation for technical competence, both of which are essential to the wider framework of legitimacy in which other more controversial agendas can be pursued.

So long as these humanitarian and development functions of European international charities are maintained, government policymakers who are aware of other latent political agendas can use these groups to achieve some of their own purposes. Were the political objectives the only objectives of such charities, their partisan nature would be clear to all, many host-country leaders would perceive them as direct threats to national sovereignty, and the activities of charities abroad would be forbidden or tightly controlled. Home-government policymakers would, therefore, no longer find such agencies attractive alternate conduits for sensitive foreign policy objectives and subsidies would be cut back or very restricted. Moreover, many private donors in Europe interested in the other-than-political work of nonprofits would cease supporting them if a partisan agenda were dominant and patent. The entire system, therefore, is dependent on having a multiplicity of activities as well as a "creative packaging" of them in reporting procedures to diverse groups.

Both the Left and the Right in Europe have discovered the usefulness of international charities in contacting and assisting groups in Third World countries that the limits of national sovereignty and diplomatic protocol prevent them from dealing with directly. The flexibility that governments in Europe allow NPOs in administering public revenues abroad are, in fact, essential to prevent this delicate political work from being traced back directly to themselves. Both sides of the political spectrum in Europe have also found international charities very helpful as surrogates and allies in appeasing dissidents within their own ranks or in fending off the opposition. Moreover, a whole series of direct and indirect restrictions can be used by government officials to limit the potential political damage that may rebound from the more controversial work of NPOs. Charities are also restrained by the narrow targets of some of their most aggressive fundraising messages at home and the necessity to include in their overseas activities many noncontroversial projects so as to court more conservative private donors.

Certain difficulties, however, make the status of these current relationships unstable and, if not handled very delicately, can cause the private aid system to break down. One of the original objectives of government policymakers in subsidizing international charities in the 1970s was to bolster a sagging consensus in European society for continued foreign aid commitments. There is little evidence to date that charities have helped to achieve this goal, since much of their development education is narrowly targeted and politically partisan in nature.

Public policymakers in Europe, hence, are faced with a dilemma. The political attractiveness of some charities to government officials requires their preserving a partisan dimension in ways that we have already described. However, in order to convince a broad spectrum of the populace as to the overall importance of foreign aid, NPOs will have to shed their partisan character and expand development education to a wider spectrum of citizens. Government officials must decide which objective is more important to them, whether both can be achieved simultaneously, and what are the trade-offs between the two. NPO leaders, too, must make this choice. Evidence from Great Britain indicates that policymakers are willing to pressure charities to be nonpartisan on the domestic education front, but that most charities committed to a leftist political agenda are unwilling to alter the nature, focus, or intensity of their advocacy work.

Another source of instability arises from the growing tension between rightist European governments and leftist international charities. The subtle strategies of the British government under Thatcher has been to find ingenious ways of using even those charities with leftist political agendas to serve its own conservative interests. In France, however, the Right has responded less subtly by encouraging partisan battles between charities with rightist and leftist political sympathies. Thus, serious divisions among NPOs are being played out before a large public audience, and the unity, credibility, and humanitarian character of the entire nonprofit community is being damaged. Moreover, as this occurs the cover is being blown off the partisan political orientation of some charities, which is likely to precipitate disillusionment and anger on the part of many private donors who heretofore believed they were contributing to nonpartisan causes. If this process continues many citizens who prefer the nonprofit community to be nonpartisan are likely to curtail drastically their own monetary support and also to demand that governments do the same.

According to some theorists,[35] the very attractiveness of the nonprofit sector in Western democracies is the degree of public trust it enjoys in carrying out certain tasks with more honesty and credibility than governments or profit-making enterprises. What is occurring through some European international charitable organizations, although useful to many elite groups in the private and public sectors, may eventually undermine such trust in large sectors of the domestic population. A certain amount of secrecy and duplicity is necessary for the present system to continue, and this is a direct threat to the public trust emphasized in some of the theory about the rationale for the very existence of the nonprofit sector itself.

It is not clear, therefore, whether the current trajectory is viable or whether the entire system of private foreign aid in Europe is headed for a breakdown due to a crisis of public trust. This will depend upon the willingness of both the charities and the political leaders to exercise self-restraint and to do something abut informing the public more adequately about the other-than-altruistic objectives being pursued by all parties through the transnational nonprofit network.

NOTES

1. Kenneth Scott Latourette, *Christianity in a Revolutionary Age: A History of Christianity in the Nineteenth and Twentieth Centuries,* 5 vols. (New York: Harper and Brothers, 1958–1962); see especially Volume 3, *The Nineteenth Century Outside Europe* (1961), and Volume 5, *The Twentieth Century Outside Europe* (1962); Jorgen Lissner, *The Politics of Altruism: A Study of the Political Behaviour of Voluntary Development Agencies* (Geneva: Lutheran World Federation, 1977), pp. 58, 60; Edward B. Berman, "Educational Colonialism in Africa: The Role of American Foundations, 1910–1945" *Philanthropy and Cultural Imperialism: The Foundations at Home and Abroad,* ed, Robert F. Arnove (Boston: G. K. Hall and Co., 1980), pp. 179–201.

2. David P. Forsythe, *Humanitarian Politics: The International Committee of the Red Cross* (Baltimore: Johns Hopkins University Press, 1977); Ben Whitaker, *Bridge of People: A Personal View of Oxfam's First Forty Years* (London: Heinemann, 1983); Brian H. Smith, *The Politics of International Charities* (Princeton, N.J.: Princeton University Press, forthcoming), Chapter 2.

3. Smith, ibid., Chapter 4; Robert C. Morris, *Overseas Volunteer Programs: Their Evolution and the Role of Government in Their Support* (Lexington, Mass.: D. C. Heath, 1973), pp. 2–5; Ernst Michanek, *The Role of Swedish NGOs in International Development Cooperation* (Stockholm: Swedish International Development Authority [SIDA], 1977); *Not by Government Alone: Non-governmental Organizations in the Development Decade* (London: Overseas Development Institute [ODI], 1964); Organization for Economic Cooperation and Development [OECD], *Development Assistance Efforts and Policies of the Members of the Development Assistance Committee, 1967 Review* (Paris: OECD, 1967), pp. 47–52.

4. Smith, ibid., Chapter 5; Lissner, *Politics of Altruism,* pp. 255–70, 290–98; OECD, *Directory of Non-governmental Organizations in OECD Member Countries Active in Development,* 2 vols. (Paris: OECD Development Centre, 1983); *International Council of Voluntary Agencies (ICVA) News* No. 110 (Geneva, March 1985), pp. 1–2.

5. International Labour Organization (ILO), *Employment, Growth and Basic Needs: A One-world Problem* (New York: Praeger, 1977); Jan Tinbergen, *Reshaping the International Order (RIO): A Report to the Club of Rome* (New York: E. P. Dutton, 1976); Independent Commission on International Development Issues (Brandt Commission), *North–South: A Programme for Survival* (Cambridge, Mass.: MIT Press, 1980).

6. Hendrik van der Heijden, "The Reconciliation of NGO Autonomy, Program Integrity and Operational Effectiveness with Accountability to Donors," *World Development* 15, Supplement (Autumn 1987): 103–112. Canadian international charitable agencies have followed the same trajectory as their European counterparts—namely, a movement toward a greater contestatory role vis-à-vis large public development agencies while coming to rely on the home government for a greater percentage of their operating expenses in recent years. The case in the United States, however, is somewhat different from both Europe and Canada. American international charities are, by and large, just as dependent on government subsidies as their counterparts in Europe and Canada, but very few openly criticize any official foreign policy positions of the U.S. government. There is no significant political Left in the United

States (as there is both in Europe and Canada) and persons who work for U.S. international charities tend to avoid public identification with any partisan political movements. The U.S. government itself also places stringent conditions on its subsidies to American charitable agencies that restrict overt political activities.

7. Brian H. Smith, *The Church and Politics in Chile: Challenges to Modern Catholicism* (Princeton, N.J.: Princeton University Press, 1982), pp. 325–27; Gerard Braunthal, *The West German Social Democrats, 1969–1982: Profile of a Party in Power* (Boulder, Colo.: Westview Press, 1983), p. 284.

8. Telephone interview with Claire Dixon, project officer for Latin America, Catholic Fund for Overseas Development (CAFOD), London (April 22, 1986).

9. Van der Heijden, "Reconciliation of NGO Autonomy," Table 2, p. 105.

10. Smith, *Politics of International Charities,* Chapter 4; OECD, *Collaboration between Official Development Cooperation Agencies and Nongovernmental Organizations* (Paris, 1981), pp. 18–71.

11. Telephone interview with Jan Reinders, assistant executive director, Protestant Association for Cooperation in Development (EZE), Bonn (March 26, 1986).

12. Ibid.

13. Jean-Pierre Côt, *À l'épreuve du pouvoir: Le tiers-mondisme, pourquoi faire?* (Paris: Éditions du Seuil, 1984), pp. 93–102, 192–210; Stephane Hessel, "France and the Third World," paper presented at the conference, Continuity and Change in Mitterrand's France, Center for European Studies (Cambridge, Mass.: Harvard University, December 5–7, 1985); Stephanie Baile, *Survey of European Nongovernmental Aid Organizations: A Guide to NGOs and Their Perception of the World Bank* (Washington, D.C.: International Bank for Reconstruction and Development [IBRD], 1986), p. 55.

14. Van der Heijden, "Reconciliation of NGO Autonomy," Table 2, p. 105.

15. Ibid., Vincent Cable, *British Interests and Third World Development* (London: Overseas Development Institute [ODI], 1980), pp. 23–25; telephone interview with Claire Dixon, CAFOD.

16. Official translation of the letter of November 21, 1983, by which the Netherlands Minister for Development Cooperation formalized the renewed program subsidy model to the four cofinancing organizations (CFOs), pp. 1, 4; Interview with Rev. S. S. van Dijk, head, Latin American department, Protestant Interchurch Coordination Committee for Development Projects (ICCO), Zeist (September 30, 1983).

17. Baile, *Survey of European Nongovernmental Aid Organizations,* p. 7; Benedict Nightingale, *Charities* (London: Allen Lane, 1973), pp. 45–67, 221; interviews with Alonso Roberts, project officer for Latin America and the Caribbean, Christian Aid (CA), and Claire Dixon, CAFOD, London (September 9, 1983).

18. Baile, ibid., p. 38.

19. Telephone interview with Pierre Galand, director, Oxfam Belgium, Brussels (September 27, 1983 and May 5, 1986).

20. Baudoin Piret and Pierre Galand, *L'aide de la Belgique aux pays en développement* (Brussels: Contradictions et Vie Ouvrière, 1983), pp. 214–16, 221.

21. Baile, *Survey of European Nongovernmental Aid Organizations,* pp. 8, 18; interviews with Alonso Roberts, CA, and Claire Dixon, CAFOD.

22. Van der Heijden, "Reconciliation of NGO Autonomy," Table 2, p. 105.

23. Baile, *Survey of European Nongovernmental Aid Organizations,* passim.

24. Smith, *Politics of International Charities,* Chapter 7.

25. Telephone interview with Alonso Roberts, CA, (April 29, 1986).

26. Telephone interview with Pierre Galand, Oxfam Belgium (May 5, 1986).

27. Telephone interview with Colette Dugua, assistant to the director, Latin American department, Catholic Committee Against Hunger for Development (CCFD), Paris (April 21, 1986); Baile, *Survey of European Nongovernmental Aid Organizations,* p. 56.

28. Telephone interview with Heinzberndt Krauskopf, head, Latin American department, Campaign Against Hunger and Disease in the World (MISEREOR), Aachen (April 21, 1986).

29. Telephone interviews with Alonso Roberts, CA, and Heinzberndt Krauskopf, MIS-EREOR; interview with Pierre Galand, Oxfam Belgium.

30. Telephone interview with Heinzberndt Krauskopf, MISEREOR.

31. Christian Rudel, "Frères des Hommes: Contre le mal-développement," *La Croix* (Paris, December 20, 1983); Gérard Viratelle, "Au Colloquie de 'Liberté Sans Frontières': Le débat sur le tiers-mondisme reste ouvert," *Le Monde* (Paris, January 26, 1985), p. 4; Pierre Castel, "Débat: Le tiers-mondisme au rancart?" *Croissance des Jeunes Nations,* no. 270 (Paris, March 1985): 10–13; "Débat: Les tiers-mondistes contre-attaquent," *Croissance des jeunes Nations,* no. 271 (April 1985): 9–11.

32. Guillaume Maury, "Charité chrétienne ou subversion marxiste?" *Figaro-Magazine* (October 26, 1985): 25–34; Jean Bourdarias, "Chili: L'engagement politique du CCFD," *Le Figaro* (March 25, 1986): 2; Gérard Leclerc, "L'argent des chrétiens au service de la revolution," *Quotidien de Paris* (March 25, 1986): 23; Bourdarias, "Une épine dans la chair de l'Église," *Le Figaro* (March 25, 1986): 2; Maury, "CCFD: C'est de plus en plus inquiétant!" *Figaro-Magazine* (April 19, 1986): 21–24.

33. "Intervention de Bernard Holzer (President of CCFD) à la conference de presse du 5 Mai 1986: le CCFD répond et dénonce," mimeograph; Le Comité Catholique Contre La Faim et pour le Developpement (CCFD), Paris, 1986.; Michel Cool, "Le CCFD contre-attaque,"*La Vie,* no. 2124 (May 15–21, 1986): 27–28; Henri Tincq, "Le Comité catholique contre la faim riposte devant les tribunaux," *Le Monde* (May 8, 1986), p. 14.

34. Bourdarias, "Une épine dans la chair de l'Église"; Leclerc, "L'argent des chrétiens au service de la révolution."

35. The strongest proponent of the public trust rationale for the nonprofit sector vis-à-vis profit-making enterprises is Henry Hansmann, an economist. See his article "The Role of Nonprofit Enterprise," *Yale Law Journal* 89, no. 5 (April 1980): 835–901. See also James Douglas, *Why Charity? The Case for a Third Sector* (Beverly Hills, Calif.: Sage Publications, 1983). The latter, a political theorist, argues for the unique contribution NPOs make vis-à-vis governments, especially when they allow minorities in a democracy to carry out tasks for which there is no majoritarian mandate for government to perform. Here Douglas also underscores the public trust rationale for NPOs by arguing that the majority must be satisfied that the minority objective being pursued by NPOs (with tax exemption) is reasonable and not something repugnant to the majority consensus or forbidden by law (pp. 130–32).

REFERENCES

Arnove, Robert F. *Philanthropy and Cultural Imperialism: The Foundations at Home and Abroad.* Boston: G. K. Hall and Co., 1980.

Baile, Stephanie. *Survey of European Nongovernmental Aid Organizations: A Guide to NGOs and Their Perception of the World Bank.* Washington, D.C.: International Bank for Reconstruction and Development (IBRD), 1986.

Berman, Edward B. "Educational Cononialism in Africa: The Role of American Foundations, 1910–1945." In Robert F. Arnove, ed., *Philanthropy and Cultural Imperialism: The Foundations at Home and Abroad.* Boston: G. K. Hall and Co., 1980, pp. 179–201.

Forsythe, David P. *Humanitarian Politics: The International Committee of the Red Cross.* Baltimore: Johns Hopkins University Press, 1977.

Latourette, Kenneth Scott. *Christianity in a Revolutionary Age: A History of Christianity in the Nineteenth and Twentieth Centuries.* New York: Harper and Brothers, 1958–1962.

Lissner, Jorgen. *The Politics of Altruism: A Study of the Political Behaviour of Voluntary Development Agencies.* Geneva: Lutheran World Federation, 1977.

Michanek, Ernst. *The Role of Swedish NGOs in International Development Cooperation.* Stockholm: Swedish International Development Authority (SIDA), 1977.

Morris, Robert C. *Overseas Volunteer Programs: Their Evolution and the Role of Government in Their Support*. Lexington, Mass.: D. C. Heath, 1973.

Nightingale, Benedict. *Charities*. London: Allen Lane, 1973.

Organization for Economic Cooperation and Development (OECD). *Directory of Nongovernmental Organizations in OECD Member Countries Active in Development*, 2 vols. Paris: OECD Development Centre, 1983.

———. *Collaboration between Official Development Cooperation Agencies and Nongovernmental Organizations*. Paris: Author, 1981.

Smith, Brian H. *The Politics of International Charities*. Princeton, N.J.: Princeton University Press, forthcoming.

———. *The Church and Politics in Chile: Challenges to Modern Catholicism*. Princeton, N.J.: Princeton University Press, 1982.

Whitaker, Ben. *Bridge of People: A Personal View of Oxfam's First Forty Years*. London: Heinemann, 1983.

World Development 15, special issue devoted to NPOs Supplement (Autumn 1987), international development cooperation.

14

Private Voluntary Organizations and Development in West Africa: Comparative Perspectives

HELMUT K. ANHEIER

Comparative research on nonprofit organizations (NPOs) has long noted the differential size, composition, and importance of nonprofit sectors within and between countries.[1] Focusing primarily on African nonprofit organizations active in development (private voluntary organizations or PVOs for convenience), this chapter first analyzes the political and economic role of PVOs in three West African countries: Nigeria, Togo, and Senegal. The PVO sectors in these countries appear as a product of the interplay among religious, political, and economic forces. To a large extent, their developmental impact depends on the role of other major organizational actors, in particular the state. Nor will the developmental contribution of PVOs necessarily be the same cross-nationally. As will be shown throughout, PVOs face radically different dilemmas in different countries.

The African state is generally weak in political and economic terms. With a few exceptions such as Nigeria and possibly the Ivory Coast and Cameroon, the West African state faces the dilemma between greater reliance on PVO inputs and increased political control of PVO operations by the government. The tension between "more resources" and "more control" points to an underlying question: to what extent is it desirable to have PVOs determine, or at least strongly influence, the development agenda? In this, the African state faces a problem similar to that of Western societies of the late nineteenth and early twentieth centuries: can *imperio in imperium,* "private governments," be tolerated politically or constitutionally for economic reasons, and how can such "private governments" be controlled in political terms?[2]

In Togo, economic co-optation by the state appears as the constituting factor for the PVO-sector in general and government–PVO relations in particular. In Senegal, political co-optation by the government presents a

340 Economic Development and Human Rights

dilemma for PVOs, whereas in Nigeria secular–religious frictions and interreligious rivalries play a decisive role in shaping the country's PVO sector. This chapter analyzes the reasons why the present role and developmental potential of PVOs vary across and sometimes even within countries. To provide further evidence for within-country variations, I analyze a different subset of NPOs, organizations for the rehabilitation of the handicapped in Nigeria. Finally, I discuss a number of implications concerning the formulation of comparative theories of nonprofit organizations.

The countries selected for this study are interesting for our purposes for several reasons. Togo represents a country where political stability and far-reaching political control of society by a one-party regime has been achieved at the expense of economic and social development. Togo's nonprofit sector forms a liberal enclave in society and has become an important relay in development financing. Senegal is characterized by Islamic hegemony and growing friction between rural and urban areas. The importance of Senegal's nonprofit sector derives from its political role in helping the government to bypass traditional rural power structures. Nigeria differs in all major aspects from both Senegal and Togo. As a country, it is characterized by continuous political and economic instability. While the economy in Senegal and Togo has been stagnating and even declining for the past decade, Nigeria experienced several years of rapid economic growth between 1975–1982, followed by an equally rapid decline since then. Of the three countries selected, Nigeria is the most complex in social, political, and economic terms. Nigeria's PVO sector is of little relevance to the overall economy but has become a highly politicized organizational arena that mirrors fundamental political, religious, and regional cleavages. Nigeria's basic value conflicts take place in the country's PVO sector.

A PROFILE OF THE PVO SECTOR IN NIGERIA, SENEGAL, AND TOGO

There is no prototypical African PVO. They range from modern to traditional, from genuinely African to imported, from more or less governmentally controlled to grass-roots organizations, from organizations created in the course of development projects with excellent ties to international donors to organizations existing in the backwaters of African societies. There are large-scale community development organizations in Senegal with operating budgets close to those of some Senegalese provinces and social welfare organizations like the YMCA of Nigeria. The Progressive Young Farmers Association from Ijebu-Ode in Yoruba land is as much part of the PVO-sector as is the Society for the Victory of Islam or the Church of Christ in Nigeria. There is a large international agricultural research institute, with several hundred scientists devoted to crop and soil improvement, located next to a small Nigerian PVO advocating popular participation and appropriate farming technology at the village level.

For the purposes of this chapter (and unless otherwise indicated), PVO

Table 14.1. Project Domains of Member Organizations of PVO Consortia in Nigeria, Senegal, and Togo[a] and Project Domains for U.S. PVOs Active in Africa

Domain	Nigeria %	Senegal %	Togo %	U.S.[b] %
Economic Development	22.4	28.4	32.6	29.0
Cooperatives, businesses	6.7	8.4	6.5	6.0
Rural development	15.7	20.0	26.1	23.0
Social Development	71.8	68.4	56.5	70.0
Community development	7.8	21.1	17.4	23.0
Education	22.2	13.7	6.5	7.0
Health services	13.8	6.3	6.5	12.0
Nutrition	2.1	2.1	4.3	3.0
Welfare, relief	18.0	12.6	10.9	17.0
Family, children	7.9	12.6	10.9	8.0
Evangelism	5.8	3.2	10.9	—
Total	100.0	100.0	100.0	99.0
Number of Projects	478	308	101	2,736

[a]Although no complete data base exists for PVOs in the three countries, it can be assumed that in the case of Senegal and Togo, consortia include the vast majority of development-oriented PVOs. The Nigerian consortium, although including the larger PVOs, does not contain many smaller organizations operating in eastern and northern Nigeria. In the absence of reliable data, it is difficult to estimate the representativeness of consortium membership.
[b]Based on data from *Interaction* (1985): 31–34; error due to rounding.

refers to private nonprofit organizations including local, independent chapters and counterparts of American or European PVOs active in development project planning, financing, and implementation. As basically intermediary organizations, PVOs are structurally located between the grass roots of African societies and the donor community. They provide and channel funds, services, expertise, and information to target groups (farmers, medical doctors) and organizations (schools, hospitals, cooperatives). Self-help groups and cooperative societies are not covered in this paper[3] nor are hospitals and schools, two other important types of nonprofit organizations.

Range of PVO Activities

Although the organizational composition of African PVO-sectors is very heterogeneous, their activities tend to be concentrated in areas of social rather than economic development. As Table 14.1 demonstrates, the members of the Nigerian PVO consortium are predominantly engaged in education and welfare-relief. In Nigeria, PVOs occupy more traditional nonprofit grounds, whereas in Togo and Senegal PVO project choices in rural and community development reflect the more problematic economic situation of these countries. Consequently, with the help of international donors, PVOs in Togo and Senegal concentrate on food production, irrigation, agrobusinesses, and farming projects. Due to the greater influence of

Table 14.2. Religious–Secular Composition of PVO
Consortia and Religious Composition of Population in
Nigeria, Senegal and Togo

	Nigeria %	Senegal %	Togo %
Religious	64	19	61
Secular	36	81	39
Total	(100%)	(100%)	(100%)
Number	59	42	23
Population:[a]			
Catholic	15–25	5–10	20–22
Protestant	10–20	?	7–10
Muslim	40–44	75–85	12
Other	15–30	5–10	50–55

[a]Percentages for Nigeria and Senegal in particular are most unreliable and
should be interpreted as rough approximations only.

foreign donors, the distribution for Senegal and Togo is closer to that of
U.S. PVOs than it is to Nigerian ones. The largest differences exist in the
two categories of education and community development.

Religious Affiliations of PVOs

Differences in the religious–secular composition of PVO sectors (Table 14.2)
are more pronounced. In both Nigeria and Togo, (Christian) religious and
church-related PVOs account for the majority of consortia members. In
Senegal, due to the predominance of Islam, Christian PVOs represent a
minority. Moreover, Senegal's PVO sector shows very little involvement
by organizations linked to Islam. As will be seen shortly, Islam in Senegal,
in contrast to other parts of the Islamic world, provides little ground for
PVO development.[4]

The Christian churches have universally acted as the major founders of
nonprofit institutions. James shows that religious PVOs are concentrated
in social service and, as in our case, social development because their objective is not to maximize profits but to maximize believers and faith.[5]
Churches and missionary societies have been actively involved in the fields
of education and health services in Africa since the colonial period. The
maximization of believers, the claim to bring the gospel to as many non-
believers as possible, introduces a competitive element into interdomina-
tional affairs and implies a built-in conflict for church-related or religious
PVOs. Ultimately, worldly objectives like education and development assistance are subject to religious objectives. In Nigeria in particular, the
dual goal structure of religious PVOs continues to constrain their developmental impact. The goal structure of religious PVOs represents a mixture of religious objectives, advocacy, and development, which together
provide fertile ground for interreligious and religious–secular conflicts.

Table 14.2 shows that in all three countries the percentage of Christian

and church-related consortia members is higher than the proportion of
Christians in the population. In Togo government regulation of religious
affairs and a large reservoir of traditional believers (50 to 55 percent) account for a relatively conflict-free interreligious and religious—secular environment. Nigeria, in contrast, is characterized by a high degree of interreligious competition—a factor to which we will return further later. In
Senegal, Islamic hegemony and the acceptance of a minority status by the
Christian churches have created a relatively conflict-free interreligious environment.

Financial Importance of PVO Sectors

Nigeria is one of the very few African countries in which official development aid plays an insignificant role. Based on the preponderance of flows
from the private for-profit sector to Nigeria, it can be assumed that contributions by international PVOs are negligible in comparison to the total
foreign exchange coming into the country. In Nigeria, the PVO sector plays
virtually no role in the overall economy.

The importance of the PVO sector in Togo is radically different from
Nigeria. Faced with diminishing private investment flows and increasingly
restricted access to concessional development aid from both bilateral and
multilateral sources in the form of soft credits, Togo sees its PVO sector
as a vitally important source of finance. This is clearly indicated in the
1981–1985 National Development Plan, which calls upon international
and Togolese PVOs to contribute to the plan within the policy boundaries
set by the government by combining their resources with those of state
agencies.[6] The PVO sector in Togo offers a necessary and most welcome
opportunity for resource expansion in an otherwise severely limited international arena for concessional finances. In contrast, the Nigerian Development Plan does not mention the role of PVOs in developing Nigeria.

In Senegal, the financial necessity for greater utilization of PVO inputs
from Organization for Economic Cooperation and Development (OECD)
countries is less urgent than in Togo, but nevertheless more pronounced
than in Nigeria. The preponderance of concessional finances and a renewed influx of private export credits reduce the financial necessity of PVO
inputs. The role of indigenous and international PVOs is strongly influenced by the Senegalese political situation. The Senegalese government,
more or less overtly, regards international and indigenous PVOs as instruments to reduce the influence of Islamic leaders in the country's backward
rural areas.

PVOs, SOCIETY, AND THE STATE: MAJORITARIAN CONTROL, RESOURCE SCARCITY, AND RELIGIOUS CONFLICT

This section looks at the relationship between PVOs and the state in the
three West African countries and examines government responses to the

tension between broadening the country's resource and revenue base with the help of PVOs and the problem of political control. If, as is the case in Togo and Senegal, PVOs bring in substantial resources from abroad, they potentially form a "private government" that could threaten the "public government" and majoritarian control. Yet the "public government," especially in cases such as Togo, may not exemplify majoritarian control either. In Togo and similarly in Burkina Faso, Mali, Benin, and Niger, where the government opted for "more" resources rather than for increased control, we find that in authoritarian regimes PVOs enjoy considerable influence and may increase political freedom within a country. In Senegal, a democratically elected government attempts the dual, and often conflicting, strategy of encouraging and controlling PVO operations at the same time; whereas the Nigerian government, independent and not reliant on PVO resources, opted for control and partial take-over of PVO operations.

Togo

In Togo the importance of the nonprofit sector derives from its economic and financial significance. The political consolidation of the military regime in the 1970s resulted in relative political tranquility.[7] However, the Togolese version of development, *planification*, a bureaucratic approach to economic development within a politically controlled society, has been costly. *Planification* resulted in a low degree of decision-making capacity at lower party and administrative levels. Lack of efficiency and information, and insufficient feedback mechanisms, led to high administrative costs as well as low plan fulfillment rates. Political stability has been achieved without and possibly at the expense of economic performance and development. With Togo's economy experiencing serious difficulties, the nonprofit sector has become an important source of additional financing. For example, the 1980–1981 budget of Togo's PVO consortium, CONGAT, amounted to 52.1 percent of the annual administrative investment budget of the Ministry of Plan and Administrative Reform, as allocated in the then current development plan.[8] Moreover, in one of Africa's most authoritarian countries, Togo, PVOs were almost equal partners alongside the government during recent negotiations regarding World Bank–sponsored projects.

The PVO sector represents a liberal enclave in Togolese society that projects an independent image to overseas financing agencies. Although CONGAT operates under the Ministry of Plan in legal terms, the PVO sector is not directly controlled by the government. However, the great financial importance of the nonprofit sector has mobilized greater government interest. PVOs in general, and their consortium, CONGAT, in particular, feel that because "many governmental bureaus are without substantial resources" the "government is pushing non-profits to take on more and more projects, and to accept new responsibilities."[9]

The government expresses its financial reliance on PVOs in less overt terms. When a cooperation agreement between the government and CON-GAT was signed on November 22, 1983, it made the front page of the state-owned newspaper *La Nouvelle Marche,* Togo's single daily: the Minister of Plan advised PVOs to adhere to the government development targets and to remain within the policy framework of *planification*.[10]

CONGAT potentially forms a "private government," which the "public government" tolerates for economic reasons. The government must acknowledge the financial clout of the nonprofit sector and, at the same time, stress state supremacy in developmental efforts. Not surprisingly, the relationship between government and PVOs is a most delicate one—which may change rapidly through either a substantial improvement in government revenue or a change of regime.

Senegal

The key to understanding Senegal's political and economic system lies in the compatibility of traditional social structures and Islam. Characteristic of Senegalese society is the importance of patron–client arrangements in the form of religious brotherhoods.[11] The brotherhoods are divided into religious leaders (marabouts) and followers (taalibe). The approximately 5000 marabouts, who have great economic power, are patrons to their numerous clients, the taalibes.[12] More than 50 percent of the total peanut production, Senegal's most important cash crop and largest export item, is produced on marabout land by the free labor of the taalibes. The power of the marabout has always existed at the local level, predominantly in the rural areas, and only the Mouride order has succeeded in building up a national organization.[13]

Two successive historical developments helped the marabouts translate their growing economic importance into political power. First, the French colonial administration incorporated the marabouts into the administration of rural Senegal.[14] The marabouts became middlemen between the colonial administration and the rural population. Second, since the Second World War, the marabouts have emerged as the key to greater access to rural votes for political parties. Because party organizations were still underdeveloped, weak, and basically urban-based, recourse to the Moslem leaders provided a welcome multiplication of political followers via the clientele system of the brotherhoods.[15]

The marabouts, representing an indispensable relay between the state and the rural population, brought considerable advantages for the government in Dakar.[16] The marabouts collaborated with the legal authorities in matters of administration; for example, tax collection and, more important, securing the legitimacy of the government in the rural areas via the loyalty of the taalibes. The marabouts profited handsomely in return. Moreover, the marabouts provided the necessary political stability by remaining politically neutral in the process of redemocratization during the

1970s, which ultimately increased the political power of the marabouts who continue to function as providers of political legitimacy and as a financial relay between the rural population and cosmopolitan Dakar.[17] The political fate of the present Diouf government depends on the traditional religious hierarchy.

At one time the former government attempted to bypass the marabouts to gain direct access to rural areas through the large-scale establishment of rural cooperatives. This attempt proved to be a costly political and economic failure that threatened Senegal's entire state budget. Equally unsuccessful were attempts to reduce the influence of Islamic law (Sharia). The government learned through its various attempts to gain greater access to the rural population that direct confrontation between the government and the Islamic brotherhoods can be avoided if government agencies neither represent nor appear as prime actors.

As a relatively homogeneous country characterized by Islamic hegemony, Senegal shows little indigenous development of PVOs and other nonprofit organizations. Instead, the large majority of Senegalese PVOs are either extensions or independent local chapters of foreign PVOs. Therefore, in terms of organizational structure and finance, Senegal's PVO sector is removed from both government and Islam. International and indigenous PVOs, which are not formally part of the government and are independent of the Islamic brotherhoods, are seen as alternative organizational instruments for achieving political and developmental objectives in rural areas.

A community and enterprise development project, financed by US-AID and jointly run with the Senegalese government, illustrates the government use and cooptation of PVOs. According to US-AID, previous government development projects in the region of Sine Saloum have left "an aversion to government structures and government intervention. An approach to the local producer groups through PVOs, a non-governmental channel, is therefore a more appropriate means at present."[18] For the government, PVOs appear as a less direct and less expensive means in a continuing struggle for sovereignty in the rural areas.

In other instances, the government attitude to PVOs is less favorable. In the Région du Fleuve of Eastern Senegal, PVOs appear as a threat to the government "monopoly of intervention."[19] The conflict between one of Senegal's largest PVOs and the Ministry of Social Development offers a good example in this respect. In 1983–1984, government finances were severely strained and the Ministry of Social Development had to announce its inability to allocate the total scheduled program and project budget. At this time this PVO received a substantial grant from a Canadian foundation, amounting to about half the size of the budget of the Ministry of Social Development. Many of the PVO's activities are concentrated in selected rural areas. The PVO's generous endowment relative to the government's financial strain implied a de facto PVO monopoly in a region traditionally a stronghold of the ruling Socialist Party.

This situation occupied the attention of the First Session of the National Assembly on June 1, 1983. The National Assembly demanded an inquiry into the financial affairs of PVOs and requested a coordination of PVO and state activities. In particular, the assembly demanded that PVOs should "obey the policy of rural development as defined by the government," and refrain from following their own particular explicit or implicit political causes.[20] In other words, PVO activities are welcome in Senegal if they are in accordance with government policies and if they do not pose a challenge to the state monopoly in the politics of social and economic development.

Nigeria

In Nigeria's system of development financing, PVOs play virtually no significant role. In recent years PVOs have not become an item on the agendas of the Federal Ministries in Lagos as far as development policy is concerned.[21] The oil boom and the huge sums of government revenues did not result in PVO sector expansion. On the contrary, the government employed its enlarged finances to take over hospitals and related institutions previously run by churches and missionary societies. The take-over, carried out in an erratic and uncoordinated manner, however, remained ultimately incomplete. As soon as the federal government's financial position became strained, state subsidies dried up. This caused decline in both the quality and the quantity of health services and education.[22] The ultimately counterproductive government take-over of church-related PVO operations can only be understood within the context of the relation between the state and organized religion and the tension between increased control of PVOs and more resources provided by PVOs.

Nigeria is a prime example of religious heterogeneity and the use of PVOs as a competitive device by religious organizations. Relations among religions and between religion and the state are of utmost complexity in Nigeria. No religion dominates the federation. Islam, the Roman Catholic Church, several Protestant denominations, and a growing number of African churches have been engaged in an on-going struggle for religious and political influence at local, state, and federal levels for almost one century.[23]

Islam in Nigeria

Islam has been the dominant religion in northern Nigeria for several centuries. British indirect rule brought considerable advantages to Islam. Protected by the British, Muslim leaders, traders, and missionaries penetrated into new areas of western Nigeria. Overall, in northern Nigeria and other places in West Africa during the colonial period, "Islam made considerable headway."[24] Yet Islam was not the only religion expanding. Christian missionaries and the introduction of a modern educational system presented a challenge to Islam. The missionaries offered access to modern education (at nonprofit schools). Because modern education and conversion to Christianity were almost synonymous and understood as such by Christian missionaries, Islamic leaders feared an exclusion of Moslems from the political and economic life in the new urban centers. The Islamic sensitivity that modern education could prove to be a Trojan Horse in the end stimulated a number of responses to face the challenge of Christian education. One important aspect of the Islamic response to Christian education was the founding of several voluntary associations "to prevent the conversion of Muslims from backwardness," as written in the constitution of the Ijebu-Ode Muslin Friendship Society in 1927.[25] The voluntary associations did not run formal schools but did offer informal education and instruction.

Islam has lost the educational battle in Nigeria, but it provided Islam with an opportunity to build new, additional organizational bases, and above all, two national organizations: the Muslim Youth Organization, and the Muslim Association of Nigeria. At the end of the colonial period, Islam had almost national character and had already built up the organizational structures necessary to maintain and further its influence.

The two Muslim associations, which were designed parallel to the existing Muslim hierarchy to combat Christian dominance in education, were succeeded by the Islamic Council of Nigeria (ICN), established in 1973, and the Jama'atu Nasril Islam (JNI), the Society for the Victory of Islam, founded in 1961. Whereas the ICN remains in the background of political affairs unless challenged by government policies, the JNI plays a more active role in the expansion of Islam and development. The development aid component of the JNI further contributes to its dominant status. The JNI represents the Nigerian Muslim community in foreign affairs with the Arab world and acts as a financial intermediary for aid flows from (Arabic) OPEC countries. For grant applications from Islamic Nigerian PVOs, JNI examines eligibility criteria and assists (Arabic) OPEC agencies in the screening and monitoring process. If smaller Muslim organizations like the Ansar-Ud Deen Society or the Madrassa-al-Azhariyya School in Ilorin apply for financial aid, Saudi or Kuwaiti agencies request JNI to approve and confirm the applicant's authenticity and eligibility. Although no data are available on the amount of funding involved, it can be assumed that funding levels are below and more irregular than those supplied by Christian donors to Nigerian PVOs. As a direct competitor of Christian missionary societies the political importance of JNI in particular has grown substantially since the mid-1970s. Its increased influence has paralleled the decline of the locally based power of the emirs and mallams.[26]

However, the true challenge to Islam in Nigeria, and perhaps in other countries with a large Muslim population, is not so much Christianity but secularism that reduces the influence of religious organizations, Islamic and Christian, on society. This dilemma found its clearest expression in the heated Sharia debate of the late 1970s. In 1975 the constitutional drafting committee began designing a new Nigerian constitution as an essential step toward the scheduled return to civilian rule by 1979. The committee stated in a chapter on "The State and Its Fundamental Objectives" that "Nigeria is an indivisible, sovereign Republic, secular, democratic, and social."[27] The notion of Nigeria as a secular state caused the strongest reaction and opposition of Muslim leaders, JNI, and ICN. Secularism was rejected on the ground that it implied a separation of religion, justice, and the state—a separation that challenged the very fundamentals of Islam.

Since the Sharia, or sacred Islamic law, does not differentiate between religion and law, JNI and ICN argued for a separate legal system for Muslims. Politicians, however, feared that allowing a special constitutional status for the Muslim religion would ultimately threaten the fragile unity for Nigeria. But Sharia also challenged the Christian churches. Many Christian leaders interpreted the Muslim claim for Sharia as a subtle form of the holy Islamic war with the ultimate goal of achieving hegemony in Nigeria. The Sharia debate was finally solved when the committee decided not to endorse Sharia law and courts. However, the controversy was revived in 1986 when the military government, in an unprecedented and surprising move, decided to join the Organization of Islamic Conference.[28] Similarly, the 1987 religious riots and often violent conflicts in northern Nigeria were fueled by claims at hegemony by both Christian and Islamic leaders, which together continue to present a threat to the secular nature of the Nigerian state.

The Christian Churches in Nigeria

Since the Portuguese Mission of 1472–1621 first visited the kingdom of Benin, missionary activities have experienced profound and far-reaching changes in policy orientation, organizational set-up, evangelical method, fund-raising, and recruitment arenas and church–state relationships.[29] Between 1790 and 1850 a multiplicity of Catholic and Protestant missionary societies were founded in America, Britain, Germany, and Switzerland. The reshuffling of religious and secular power in Europe during the Napoleonic period opened the way for new patterns of cooperation and conflict between the colonial administration and the missions.[30] By the beginning of the First World War, a large number of Protestant churches and missions had entered Nigeria as congregational or nondenominational societies.

Two diametrically opposed forces have affected the nature of interdenominational cooperation and conflict among the Protestant churches and missions. The first one is the principle of comity, born by commonly shared problems and based on the theological notion of church unity. The other is the principle of expansion based on the evangelical claim of bringing the gospel to as many people as possible. The principle of comity was soon tested when an increasing number of missionary societies and churches began operating in Nigeria. At first, the different missions were scattered across the country, making the density of missionary personnel overall low and disputes over missionary boundaries nonexistent. However, once the density of different missions increased, thereby decreasing unclaimed "pagan" areas, conflict began to emerge.

With five missionary societies working in eastern Nigeria, and the Roman Catholic church moving in on an increased scale, the missionary societies agreed to divide eastern Nigeria into "spheres of influence." Like the Lutheran Church of America (Missouri Synod), the Catholics refused to accept boundary agreements and rejected the principle of comity. The advance of Catholicism in eastern Nigeria was interpreted by Protestant missions as an intrusion.[31] The Catholic church was "viewed with mixed feelings at first, and with open antagonism later on."[32] Because the Catholic Church did not adhere to the principle of comity that helped to prevent competition and duplication of missionary efforts, all Protestant churches faced a common challenge. This challenge, and the need to avoid and regulate conflict necessitated the creation of intermission and interchurch councils. The Evangelical Union of Eastern Nigeria, together with similar organizations emerging in other parts of the colony, were the nuclei of the Christian Council of Nigeria (CCN), founded in 1930, which emerged as the major relay for external development finances to Protestant PVOs in Nigeria.

Many attempts at institution building resulted in still-born organizations. On a theological level the belief in the unity of Christianity, the biblical prescription of the oneness of the church, acts as a driving force for church unification and institutionalized cooperation or ecumenism. Yet the integration of churches threatens their integrity and autonomy. But without such institutions, Islam, secularism, and interchurch competition might cause the disintegration of organized Christianity in Nigeria. This dilemma also explains why institution building among Nigerian churches and church-related PVOs "seemed like the ecclesiastical version of the scramble for pieces of the national cake—as the politicking by various tribes and regions over power and resources in Nigeria was called."[33] As a result, the developmental impact of PVOs is extremely impaired. Thus religious competition may increase the number and activities of PVOs but may also decrease their effectiveness in achieving the economic development they ostensibly seek.

Organizations for the Handicapped in Nigeria

This section looks at a particular subset of NPOs on which data is available, organizations for the handicapped. It investigates the extent to which regional differences in religious and ethnic heterogeneity and homogeneity are reflected in the distribution of organizations for the handicapped according to founder (Christian organization, secular organization, individual, and government) and owner status (private nonprofit, government institution). Although only fragmentary information is available on the demand for services provided by such institutions,[34] it can be assumed that excess demand exists that could be met by either religious or secular NPOs.

Table 14.3 shows that only 6 percent of all organizations for the handicapped in northern Nigeria have private nonprofit status. The government is principal founder of such institutions. Northern Nigeria is characterized

Table 14.3. Nigerian Organizations for the Handicapped by Region, Owner, and Founder

Region	Owner (%)			Founder (%)					Number
	Priv.	Gov.	Total	Church	Sec.	Indiv.	Gov.	Total	
North	6	94	100	13	0	13	74	10	48
West	72	28	100	34	0	34	32	100	36
Lagos	63	37	100	26	32	16	32	100	19
East	80	20	100	57	0	31	12	100	35
Middle	45	55	100	55	0	5	40	100	20
Total	49	51	100	35	4	20	41	100	158

Note: Based and compiled on information in Federal Ministry of Social Development 1981. For purposes of this analysis, individual states were put into regional categories that, with the exception of Lagos, are identical to pre-1976 administrative and political units.
Priv. = private nonprofit organization.
Gov. = government institution.
Sec. = secular organization.
Indiv. = individual founder.

by both ethnic (Hausa-Fulani) and religious (Islam) hegemony. For historical (Christian missionaries were barred from operating in most parts of northern Nigeria) and political reasons, Christian churches found it difficult to establish nonprofit organizations for the handicapped in this region.

The situation in western Nigeria is different. In this region, ethnic homogeneity coexists with religious (Christian, Islamic, traditional) heterogeneity. The large majority of organizations for the handicapped are private, and the Christian churches together with individual philanthropists (mostly expatriates and wealthy Nigerians) founded two-thirds of all organizations for the handicapped in this region.

Lagos, the Nigerian capital, is most heterogeneous in ethnic and religious terms. Moreover, it is strongly influenced by Western culture. Table 14.3 shows that Lagos is the only region in Nigeria where secular organizations (which originate from the colonial period and are usually run by expatriates) founded institutions for the handicapped.

Eastern Nigeria comes closest to presenting the Christian mirror image of northern Nigeria. As a region, it is largely Christian and ethnically dominated by the Igbo. Four out of five organizations for the handicapped are private and mostly church related. Together with western Nigeria, this region appears to have the strongest tradition of individual philanthropy.

Finally, the middle belt, ethnically as well as religiously heterogeneous and geographically located between the ethnic and religious power centers, shows an almost equal involvement by both the government and private, exclusively Christian, NPOs. Christian nonprofits are basically located in Christian areas, whereas government organizations for the handicapped are found in Islamic and, to a lesser extent, in Christian areas of the region.

In summary, although for Nigeria as a whole private nonprofit and government institutions for the handicapped are about equally distributed in terms of owner and founder status, there are nevertheless substantial regional differences. Under the condition of excess demand, such differences can be attributed largely to the degree of religious heterogeneity combined with the politicized nature of the religious and ethnic factors in Nigeria. Establishing a Christian organization for the handicapped in northern Nigeria, or creating an Islamic asylum or leprosy center in eastern Nigeria, is not only an act of charity but ultimately also a political act.

THEORIES OF NONPROFIT ORGANIZATIONS AND THE WEST AFRICAN CASE

The previous pages have demonstrated that the PVO sector is part of an interplay among religious, political, and economic forces. Which of the three forces is dominant varies from country to country. In Senegal, it was the political factor whereby PVOs are used to bypass existing rural power structures and criticized for challenging the legitimacy of the state by building up de facto PVO monopolies. In Togo, the economic and financial component acts as a major force in shaping the PVO sector. Togo's authoritarian regime, which allows the PVOs to operate in a liberal enclave, uses PVOs to attract and allocate badly needed development funds and delegates functions to them, while stressing party supremacy. In Nigeria, the complex interaction among religious PVOs and between PVOs and the state, expression of a continuing struggle between secularism and attempts at religious hegemony, impaired the emergence of a PVO sector and its contribution to the country's development. In each of the three countries, PVOs are faced with dilemmas: a political dilemma of co-optation in Senegal, an economic dilemma of cooptation in Togo, and the dilemma of secularism and interreligious rivalry in Nigeria.

Within this context two related theories of nonprofit organizations, which bear special reference in a comparative perspective, will be discussed, Douglas' categorical constraint theory, and James' heterogeneity theory.[35] Douglas' basic thesis is that because the state has to serve all of its constituencies, it is categorically constrained in its spending pattern and flexibility. PVOs, not facing the state's categorical constraint, combine the flexibility of markets with the production of public and semipublic goods.

Applied to West Africa, the categorical constraint thesis implies that the state has to provide "development" (as a public good) to all of its citizens. This is precisely the function that the West African state performed badly. First, spending patterns and development plans favored urban areas and, by neglecting rural development, governments in this region contributed to the present malaise. Second, official donors and governments overestimated the developmental capacity of the public sector. However, one response, the creation of public development corporations, proved ineffective because of the dual goal structure of public corporations; they were expected to pursue "both commercial and social goals and to answer to many different constituencies,"[36] This led to constant conflict between managers, politicians, clients, and donors. Third, some West African governments, such as Senegal, have limited access to the total population and, therefore, the state has yet to reach the categorical constraint situation. Others, like Nigeria, are characterized by multiple, often competing, regional power centers. In this case, even if the state were not subject to categorical constraints (which indeed to some extent happened in the mid-1970s when finances were no longer a constraining factor for the Gowon regime due to the influx of oil money) political constraints, introduced by fragmented elites, would still be in effect.

Applied to the West African situation, the categorical constraint thesis needs to be modified in several respects. The most important modification concerns the general weakness of the West African state, combined with an overextension of the public sector. It could be argued that the categorical constraint thesis best fits countries with a relatively stable and established state apparatus.

James' theory, an extension of the categorical constraint thesis, hypothesizes a strong and positive relationship between a society's religious heterogeneity and the size and importance of its PVO sector. Heterogeneous countries such as the Netherlands develop a large PVO sector, while homogeneous countries like Sweden are characterized by a small PVO sector. Although differentiated demand for services such as education explains the differential size of nonprofit sectors in developed countries, excess demand for services combined with donor preferences and religious competition among suppliers explains differences in the Third World.[37] Basically, the excess demand and foreign donor thesis are applicable to Senegal and Togo. It appears, however, that political factors, in particular the degree of state "weakness" combined with financial considerations, played an intervening role and acted as a "distorter variable" in the relationship between heterogeneity, excess demand, and donor preferences, on the one hand, and PVO sector size, on the other. The Senegalese case seems to indicate that religious hegemony and government weakness increase the importance of secular PVOs. In this case, PVOs can exist in the presence of religious homogeneity if government weakness encourages the growth of secular PVOs. In Togo, we found that authoritarianism and economic austerity resulted in a PVO sector in which both secular and religious PVOs gain in importance. In Togo, the preference of foreign donors to work through nongovernment channels rather than the state apparatus and the willingness of the state to accept this, given its strong resource needs, play a decisive role. Finally, the Nigerian case demonstrated that extreme degrees of competition among religious groups combined with political issues may have the paradoxical effect of reducing the size and importance of a country's PVO sector.

NOTES

1. Estelle James, "The Nonprofit Sector in Comparative Perspective," in *The Nonprofit Sector: A Research Handbook,* ed. W. Powell (New Haven: Yale University Press, 1987), pp. 397–415; "Differences in the Role of the Private Educational Sector in Modern and Developing Countries," Program on Non-Profit Organizations Working Paper 112 (New Haven; Conn.: Yale University, 1986); J. Douglas, *Why Charity? The Case for a Third Sector* (Beverly Hills, Calif.: Sage, 1983); R. Kramer, *Voluntary Agencies in the Welfare State* (Berkeley: University of California Press, 1981).

2. This dilemma represents the nonprofit analogue to the controversial debate of the role of the transnational corporations in Third World development.

3. See H. K. Anheier, "Indigenous Voluntary Associations, Non-profits, and Development in Africa," in Powell, *The Nonprofit Sector,* pp. 416–33.

4. P. B. Clarke, *West Africa and Islam: A Study of Religious Development from the 8th to the 20th Century* (London: Arnold Ltd., 1982).

5. Estelle James, "Nonprofit Sector."

6. Republique Togolaise, Ministere du Plan et de la Reforme Administrative, *Plan de Developpement Economique et Social 1981–1985* (Lome: Ministere du plan, 1980), p. 29.

7. K. Ziemer, *Demokratisierung in Westafrika?* (Paderborn: Schoningh, 1984).

8. Republique Togolaise, *Plan de Developpement,* p. 217.

9. Personal interview with CONGAT staff in Lome (October 1983).

10. *La Nouvelle Marche* (Lome, November 22, 1983).

11. D. P. Gamble, *The Wolof of Senegambia* (London International African Institute, 1975). W. W. Foltz, "Social Structure and Political Behavior of Senegalese Elites," in *Friends, Followers and Factions: A Reader in Political Clientelism,* ed., S. W. Schmidt et al. (Berkeley: University of California Press, 1977), p. 242–50.

12. L. Behrman, "Muslim Politics and Development in Senegal," *Journal of Modern African Studies* 15 (1977): 272. The marabout's gift of grace constitutes the basis of his relationship with the taalibes. In contrast to traditional patron–client arrangements, the marabout can distribute grace in unlimited quantity to a taalibe, which implies that the marabout is absolved from the "normal requirements of dispensing monetary gifts to his client" (Foltz, "Social Structure and Political Behavior," p. 244). Thus, gifts of labor and material resources flow unidirectional from the follower to the marbout; the wealthier and the more prestigious a marabout is, the greater his potential to confer grace and salvation.

13. O. D. Cruise O'Brian, "A Versatile Charisma: The Mouride Brotherhoods 1968–1975," in *Archives Enropeenes de Sociologie* 18 (1977): 84–106.

14. C. Cournot, "Developpement, administration territoriale et participation de la population. L'example du Senegal (1960–1977)," *Revue Francaise d'Administration Publique* 7 (1978): 503–523.

15. For the last preindependence elections, the Khalifa-General of the Mouride order, for example, could potentially have mobilized 400,000 votes, a substantial share of votes in a population of then 3.2 million.

16. C. Coulon, "Les Marabouts senegalais et l'etat," *Revue Francaise d'Etudes Politiques Africaines* 158 (1979): 15–42.

17. I. Fall, *Sous-developpement et democratie. L'experience senegalaise* (Dakar: Abidjan, 1977); B. Ndiaye, "La participation a la gestion des affaires publiques: les communautes rurales senegalais," *Revue Francaise d'Administration Publique* 11 (1979): 79–112.

18. US-AID, Senegal, *PVO Community and Enterprise Development (Project document),* No. 685–0260, Dakar: 1983, p. 4.

19. *Le Soleil* (Dakar) (June 2, 1983).

20. Ibid.

21. See W. I. Zartman, ed., *The Political Economy of Nigeria* (New York: Praeger, 1983) on Nigeria's political economy.

22. See E. O. Akeredolu-Ade, *Social Development in Nigeria: A Survey of Policy and Research* (Niser: Ibadan University Press, 1982).

23. See J. F. A. Ajayi, *Christian Missions in Nigeria, 1881–1891* (London: Longmans, 1965); J. H. Boer, *Missionary Messengers of Liberation in a Colonial Context: A Case Study of the Sudan United Mission* (Amsterdam: Editions Rodopi, 1981); O. Kalu, ed., *Christianity in West Africa: The Nigerian Story* (Ibadan: Daystar Press, 1978); *The History of Christianity in West Africa* (Harlow: Longman, 1980); E. P. T. Crampton, "Christianity in Northern Nigeria," in *Christianity in West Africa: The Nigerian Story,* ed. O. Kalu (Ibadan: Daystar Press, 1978).

24. P. B. Clarke, *West Africa and Islam.*

25. Cited in ibid., p. 225.

26. In contrast to Senegal, where the influence and power of the marabouts even increased during the post-colonial period, the 1968 local government reform in Nigeria resulted in a loss of formal judicial powers held by emirs and mallams.

27. Federal Republic of Nigeria, *Report of the Constitution Drafting Committee* (Lagos: Federal Ministry of Information, 1976).

28. The Organization of Islamic Conference was founded in 1969. Its 46 member-nations seek to promote Islamic solidarity and cooperation in political, economic, and cultural areas. At the international level, the Organization of Islamic Conference is perhaps the major international Islamic organization.

29. R. Gray, "The Origins and Organisation of the Nineteenth-Century Missionary Movement," in Kalu, *History of Christianity,* p. 15.

30. E. A. Ayandele, "The Missionary Factor in Northern Nigeria 1870–1918," in Kalu, *History of Christianity,* pp. 133–58. Indirect rule in northern Nigeria is a good example of how colonial and missionary interests did not coincide. The most controversial by-product of indirect rule in northern Nigeria was the barring of Christian missionaries from evangelical activities in the emirates to avoid any challenge to the Muslim monopoly. The colonial powers employed the Muslim monopoly as a strategy to maintain control.

31. F. K. Ekechi, *Missionary Enterprise and Rivalry in Igboland, 1885–1914* (London: Frank Cass, 1972), p. 72.

32. Catholic Church of Nigeria, *The History of the Catholic Church in Nigeria* (Lagos: Academic Press-Macmillan, 1982), p. 39.

33. O. Kalu, *Christianity in West Africa,* p. 75.

34. E. O. Akeredolu-Ade, *Social Development;* Federal Ministry of Social Development, Youth, Sports and Culture, *Directory of Institutions for the Rehabilitation of the Handicapped in Nigeria* (Lagos: Author, 1981).

35. Douglas, *Why Charity?* p. 116; James, "Nonprofit Sector."

36. M. M. Shirley, *Managing State-owned Enterprises,* World Bank Staff Working Paper, No. 577, Management and Development Series No. 4 (Geneva: World Banks 1983) p. 13.

37. Estelle James, "The Non-profit Sector in International Perspective: The Case of Sri Lanka," *Journal of Comparative Economics* 6 (1982): 99–129, Chapter 12 in this volume; "Differences in the Role of the Private Educational Sector."

REFERENCES

Ajayi, J. F. A. *Christian Missions in Nigeria, 1881–1891.* London: Longmans, 1965.

Akeredolu-Ade, E. O., ed. *Social Development in Nigeria: A Survey of Policy and Research.* Nigeria: Ibadan University Press, 1982.

Anheier, H. K. "Indigenous Voluntary Associations, Non-Profits, and Development in Africa." In W. Powell, ed., *The Non-profit Sector: A Research Handbook.* New Haven, Conn.: Yale University Press, 1987, pp. 416–33.

Ayandele, E. A., "The Missionary Factor in Northern Nigeria 1870–1918." In O. U. Kalu, ed., *The history of Christianity in West Africa*. London: Longman, 1980, p. 133–158.

Behrman, L. "Muslim Politics and Development in Senegal." *Journal of Modern African Studies* 15 (1977): 261–77.

Boer, J. H. *Missionary Messengers of Liberation in a Colonial Context: A Case Study of the Sudan United Mission*. Amsterdam: Editions Rodopi, 1981.

Catholic Church of Nigeria. *The History of the Catholic Church in Nigeria*. Lagos: Academic Press-Macmillan, 1982.

Clarke, P. B. *West Africa and Islam: A Study of Religious Development from the 8th to the 20th Century*. London: Arnold Ltd., 1982.

Conseil des Organisations Non Gouvernementaux au Togo (CONGAT). "Proposal for the Position of (a) Program Coordinator, CONGAT/Service Grant Proposal." Lome: CONGAT, Author, 1983.

Coulon, C. "Les Marabouts senegalais et l'etat." *Revue Francaise d'Etudes Politiques Africaines* 158 (1979): 15–42.

Cournot, C. "Developpement, administration territoriale et participation de la population. L'example du Senegal (1960–1977)." *Revue Francaise d'Administration Publique* 7 (1978): 503–23.

Crampton, E. P. T. "Christianity in Northern Nigeria." In O. Kalu, ed., *Christianity in West Africa: The Nigerian Story*. Ibadan: Daystar Press, 1978.

Cruise O'Brian, O. D. "A Versatile Charisma: The Mouride Brotherhoods 1968–1975," *Archives Europeenes de Sociologie* 18 (1977): 84–106.

Douglas, J., *Why Charity? The Case for a Third Sector*. Beverly Hills, Calif.: Sage, 1983.

Ekechi, F. K. *Missionary Enterprise and Rivalry in Igboland, 1885–1914*. London: Frank Cass, 1972.

Fall, I. *Sous-developpement et democratie. L'experience senegalaise*. Dakar, Abidjan, 1977.

Federal Ministry of Social Development, Youth, Sports and Culture. *Directory of Institutions for the Rehabilitation of the Handicapped in Nigeria*. Lagos: Author, 1981.

Federal Republic of Nigeria. *Report of the Constitution Drafting Committee*. Lagos: Federal Ministry of Information, 1976.

Foltz, W. J. "Social Structure and Political Behavior of Senegalese Elites." In S. W. Schmidt et al., eds., *Friends, Followers and Factions: A Reader in Political Clientelism*. Berkeley: University of California Press, 1977, pp. 242–50.

Gamble, D. P. *The Wolof of Senegambia*. London: International African Institute, 1975.

Gray, R. "The Origins and Organisation of the Nineteenth-Century Missionary Movement." In O. U. Kalu, ed., *The History of Christanity in West Africa*. Harlow: Longman, 1980, pp. 14–21.

Interaction, "Diversity in Development: U.S. Voluntary Assistance to Africa. Summary of Findings." New York: Author, 1985.

James, Estelle. "The Non-profit Sector in Comparative Perspective." In W. Powell, ed., *The Non-Profit Sector: A Research Handbook*. New Haven; Conn.: Yale University Press, 1987, pp. 397–415.

———. "Differences in the Role of the Private Educational Sector in Modern and Developing Countries." Program on Non-Profit Organizations Working Paper 11. New Haven, Conn.: Yale University, 1986.

———"The Non-profit Sector in International Perspective: The Case of Sri Lanka." *Journal of Comparative Economics* 6 (1982): 99–129; Chapter 12 in this volume.

Kalu, O., ed. *The History of Christianity in West Africa*. Harlow: Longman, 1980.

———. ed. *Christianity in West Africa: The Nigerian Story*. Ibadan: Daystar Press, 1978

———. *The Divided People of God. Church Union Movement in Nigeria: 1875–1966*. New York: NOK Publishers, 1978.

Kramer, R. *Voluntary Agencies in the Welfare State*. Berkeley: University of California Press, 1981.

Ndiaye, B. "La participation a la gestion des affaires publiques: les communautes rurales senegalais." *Revue Francaise d'Administration Publique* 11 (1979): 79–112.

La Nouvelle Marche (Lome, November 22, 1983).

Republique Togolaise, Ministere du Plan et de la Reforme Administrative, *Plan de Developpement Economique et Social 1981–1985.* Lome: Author, Ministere du Plan, 1980.

Shirley, M. M. *Managing State-owned Enterprises.* World Bank Staff Working Paper, No. 577, Management and Development Series No. 4. Washington: World Bank, 1983.

Le Soleil (Dakar, June 2, 1983).

US-AID, Senegal. PVO *Community and Enterprise Development.* Project Document No. 685–0260, 1983.

Zartman, W. I. ed. *The Political Economy of Nigeria.* New York: Praeger, 1983.

Ziemer, K. *Demokratisierung in Westafrika?* Paderborn: Schoningh, 1984.

15

Nonprofit Organizations as Opposition to Authoritarian Rule: The Case of Human Rights Organizations in Chile

HUGO FRUHLING

This chapter examines the experience of Chilean nonprofit organizations (NPOs) as promoters of human rights in an authoritarian situation, as experienced in Chile since 1973. The particular case of Chile between 1973 and 1984 is analyzed, drawing comparisons with that of Argentina.

In spite of their differences, which will be referred to later, the experiences of these two countries show some similarities. First, the establishment of the authoritarian regimes was preceded by political and social polarization. The cases of Argentina and Chile illustrate especially well the failure of moderates to prevent a collapse of the political system and intervention by the military.[1] Second, this situation offered the armed forces and the conservative technocrats who collaborated with them the necessary conditions for attempting to completely reshape the state and the existing economic and social relations. Third, with this aim in mind, these regimes have sought to exclude the lower classes from any exercise of power. This exclusion has meant intense repression of political dissidents and control of the press and labor unions. Fourth, the state in the two cases has attempted to forge new and different links with the international market. Fifth, in Argentina and in Chile, a network of horizontal links among human rights organizations, church institutions, and private research centers developed to denounce human rights violations, deliver social services to the poor, and to conduct research on prevailing social conditions. NPOs have provided political dissidents with one of the very few organizational settings where they could unify to face a hostile environment. In this sense, the experience of Chilean NPOs, viewed in a comparative perspective, deserves the attention of all those who are interested in the process of redemocratization and the role NPOs could play in such situations.

This chapter argues that the development of Chilean NPOs was made possible in the first place by the international support that they were able to attract in the form of diplomatic backing, foreign assistance, and consolidation of collaborative links with human rights NPOs of international standing. Second, the engagement of the Catholic Church in human rights has provided the NPOs with a protective umbrella.[2] Third, despite the prolonged period of widespread terror that Chile experienced under its new rulers, the government was unable or unwilling to completely destroy an image of adherence to Western values. This made impossible the institutionalization of authoritarian rule along the lines of a one party corporate state and has prevented an agreement between the military hierarchy and its civilian backers on conducting an all out attack against NPOs. NPOs, therefore, continued to serve as a haven for human rights advocates in an otherwise prohibitory setting.

THE CHILEAN AUTHORITARIAN REGIME: EMERGENCE, CONSOLIDATION AND NPO OPPOSITION

The Chilean military coup that occurred in September 1973 attracted considerable attention both for its initial brutality and because it put an end to one of the most stable democracies of the Western hemisphere. The negative international reaction to the Chilean coup and its aftermath restrained some of the worst excesses that the military could have committed. Nevertheless, during the first years after the downfall of President Allende, the regime conducted an intensive repressive campaign against supporters and sympathizers of the Allende government. The methods of repression most widely used were executions without trial, detentions for undefined periods, and court-martials to judge and punish people who had been in positions of responsibility in the previous Allende government.[3] After 1974, detentions became more selective as the repressive apparatus became more centralized and established priorities among target groups.

By 1976 the regime began to take some steps in the direction of institutionalizing a historical break with the democratic past and creating symbols and institutions capable of consolidating the social and political changes that had taken place. These steps aimed at shaping all economic relations in accordance with free market principles and at the elaboration of a political plan to ensure the stability of this new social reality. The 1980 Constitution, approved in a carefully controlled plebiscite, embodied both goals. The Constitution established a "period of transition" that would last until 1989 and that ensured the continuity of the same structure of power. In 1988 the military junta would select a presidential candidate to be elected by plebiscite. There were no restrictions on the commander in chief of the army, General Pinochet, remaining for another term of office.

The phase of consolidation of the authoritarian regime that began in 1978 included some changes in repressive policies. The policy of destroying opposition forces was replaced by one of containment. This meant that there was great fluctuation in the intensity of repression, depending on the threat posed by the opposition.[4]

By the end of 1981 the Chilean economy experienced a crisis that culminated in 1982 in the severest recession since 1930. The economic crisis deprived the government of the image of success that it had enjoyed among conservative circles up until then. It also extended public discontent against authoritarianism and it accelerated divisions among government supporters. To respond to increasing mobilization of the opposition, the government drastically increased the level of repression at first. Then, in August 1983, it decided to implement a second track policy by calling the centrist opposition to a dialogue, and by allowing some exiled politicians to return to the country. The dialogue failed once the government reaffirmed that the presidential term would not be shortened and refused to consider significant changes in the 1980 Constitution.

The emergence, consolidation, and present decline of the Chilean authoritarian regime shapes the historical and social context within which Chilean NPOs have grown and evolved. Despite changes in the modes of repression and fluctuations in its intensity, violations of human rights continued to occur during this entire period. Also during this period we have a striking example of the important role that NPOs can play in the promotion of human rights, in developing assistance programs for the disadvantaged, and in creating a frame for intense intellectual creativity within an authoritarian political system. Objective international and political circumstances in Chile created favorable conditions for the expansion of the NPOs' programs and influence whereas in Argentina these conditions were less favorable.

To begin with, human rights violations in Chile attracted considerable international concern. As the deputy assistant Secretary of State for Human Rights during the Carter administration has stated, "Chile became a catalyst for the human rights movement forces."[5] In contrast, international pressures were less effective in the case of Argentina, for two reasons. First, with the exception of the Communist party, Argentinian political parties have not been members of the international organizations that group parties of the same ideology in the industrialized world, and therefore their international connections were relatively weak. Second, Argentina was able to diversify its commercial and diplomatic links under authoritarian rule, and the Soviet Union became its most important commercial partner.[6] Therefore, the Western governments were left with relatively weak instruments of power with which to pressure the military to respect human rights.

The work of NPOs in Chile was also favored by the nature of the repressive policies implemented by the regime. Although repression was continuous, from 1978 on it became a flexible instrument to maintain the regime in power rather than a weapon utilized to eliminate all opposition. An attempt was made to give a semblance of legality to repressive methods and to limit disappearances and killings.

In contrast, repression in Argentina was more extensive, as shown by the fact that dozens of lawyers and journalists and hundreds of workers and student leaders not connected with the guerilla organization were made to disappear; altogether approximately 9000 people were said to have disappeared.[7] Nor did the Argentine military make any conscious effort to legalize their repressive actions. For the most part, detentions were not acknowledged or were attributed to paramilitary forces over which the government had no control. The characteristics of repression in Argentina make most noteworthy the organization and growth, even there, of a network of NPOs opposed to authoritarian rule. It also illustrates the enormous obstacles that these NPOs faced under the military regime.

The Chilean political context created more favorable circumstances for the expansion of NPOs' influence. Moreover, Chilean NPOs were able actively to use these circumstances to their advantage. For example, many bishops welcomed the onset of the 1973 coup d'etat, and many other members of the hierarchy felt at times that their support for human rights was dangerous for the unity of the church.[8] Nevertheless, human rights and church activists succeeded in convincing church leaders that accepting the pressures coming from conservative Christians could have tragic consequences for the Chilean people. Unfortunately, this attitude was not adopted by the church in Argentina.

The following analysis focuses on four aspects that represented major organizational challenges for the NPOs analyzed. I discuss the emergence and institutionalization of human rights NPOs, the extent and limits of their effectiveness, the relationship between NPOs and the political opposition, and the tensions derived from NPOs' reliance on foreign funding and external pressure.

THE EMERGENCE AND INSTITUTIONALIZATION OF HUMAN RIGHTS NPOs

Church Groups

In early October 1973 leaders from the Catholic, Methodist, Baptist, Greek Orthodox, and Jewish religions inaugurated the Committee of Cooperation for Peace (COPACHI) in Santiago. The copresidency was held by Lutheran Bishop Helmut Frenz and the Catholic auxiliary bishop of Santiago, Fernando Ariztia. The founding act of COPACHI mentioned three objectives: (1) to give material aid to the people affected by the present situation; (2) to provide legal aid to defend personal rights; and (3) to collect information on irregular situations "which gravely affect personal dignity and which surely are not desired by the Supreme Government."[9] This act clearly did not define either the scope or the extent of the programs to be carried out, and it was phrased in terms that did not antagonize the government.

Over the next several months three interrelated steps took place. The first was to establish international contacts in order to receive financial aid and other kinds of support as well as to disseminate information abroad on human rights violations. The second was to expand the original scope of COPACHI's mission by carrying out a whole array of programs that required devising a complex administrative structure. The third step was to reach out to those who needed COPACHI's help.

International financial help was arranged by Bishop Frenz through the World Council of Churches, which also helped disseminate COPACHI's reports abroad. The initial support from the World Council of Churches was complemented by grants from other Protestant and Catholic organizations in Western Europe and by the Inter-American Foundation, which began to support some of COPACHI's projects in 1974.

From October 1973 through December 1975 COPACHI experienced spectacular growth, with representatives in 25 different cities. In Santiago alone its employees grew from 5 in November 1973 to 108 in August 1974. By that time, through its various programs, COPACHI had assisted 18,438 people and, in many cases, their families as well.[10]

By 1974 COPACHI had established a complex administrative structure. At its apex stood a directory comprised of representatives from various religious groups. Day-to-day activities were supervised and controlled by an executive secretary who was a Catholic priest. The executive secretary presided over a financial and administrative staff (which administered foreign donations and presented projects to financial agencies) as well as a research and public relations staff. The different programs were organized in three main areas: the assistance area; the development projects area; and the area of coordination with provinces.

The assistance area comprised several departments. The legal department provided legal assistance at court martial proceedings, presented writs of habeas corpus in favor of people detained under the state of siege authority and presented legal actions of various kinds in favor of people who had disappeared. By December 1975, when COPACHI was disbanded, the legal department had attended more than 7000 persons in Santiago alone.[11] The labor department defended workers dismissed from their jobs for political reasons, seeking either their reinstatement or just compensation. By August 1974 it had either defended before the special labor courts or given legal counsel to 4240 workers.[12] The university department gave legal assistance to hundreds of university students expelled from the university because of their political beliefs and prepared reports on the situation of the universities. The department of material assistance and health dispensed food, clothing, and medical attention and also coordinated 400 soup kitchens that provided hot meals to more than 30,000 undernourished children.[13]

The development projects area gave technical and financial support to unemployed workers so that they could establish small self-help enterprises managed by the workers themselves. Peasants' unions were also given legal counsel.

The expansion of COPACHI's programs and the number of people assisted shows quite clearly that its aim of reaching out to the community was quite successful. This success was precisely what the government did not want to accept. Several of these programs and activities created tensions between the church and the government. COPACHI's constant reporting on human rights conditions to the bishops encouraged church activism in social and political matters. Objective collection of information on human rights violations contradicted the government's assertions before international forums. COPACHI's legal actions constantly presented the government as violating its own legality. Finally, COPACHI's grassroots projects were helping to reconstitute social groups fragmented and demoralized by the present sociopolitical situation.

The combination of these factors provoked a series of retaliatory measures by the government. These included revoking the residence permit of the German-born Bishop Frenz, copresident of COPACHI, periodic arrests of COPACHI's members, and forcing the director of the legal department, J. Zalaquett, to leave the country. The government put strong pressures upon church leaders to close down COPACHI.

In December 1975, Cardinal Silva Henriquez announced that the organization would be dissolved and suggested that the Catholic Church would continue to support the poor within its own structures. One month later he created the vicariate of solidarity, directly under the control of the Catholic Church, to carry out many of the same programs that had been developed by COPACHI.

In the beginning, some members of COPACHI who continued working for the vicariate feared that the vicariate would reduce its programs in order to avoid clashes with the government. However, the contrary happened. The reasons are twofold: (1) by this time, the church hierarchy, especially in the capital, was very sensitive to the repressive character of the military regime and was conscious that any curtailment of its human rights programs would have tremendous social consequences; and (2) a significant human rights community already existed, which played a role in shaping the vicariate's work. These included former members of CO-PACHI and relatives of persons who had suffered political repression. As examples of the vicariate's activism: between 1976 and 1978 several petitions were filed by church authorities before the Supreme Court to request an objective investigation into the fate of the disappeared. Between 1978 and 1980 the legal aid department of the vicariate assisted nearly 50,000 Chileans with counsel or legal action.[14] Public denunciations increased as the vicariate began to publish a monthly report on the human rights situation in Chile that was sent to a list of national and international persons.

The role of denunciation of human rights violations that the vicariate preserved for itself created constant tensions with the government, as shown by the fact that in 1984 the government revoked the residence permit of the Spanish-born vicar of solidarity, Ignacio Gutierrez, who was in Europe at the time. Furthermore, members of the vicariate are presently being tried by the military courts under "arms control" legislation, and one of them was assassinated in March 1985. Nevertheless, the vicariate has continued to carry on its defense of human rights.

The Birth and Growth of Other Human Rights NPOs

Once a human rights organization is established and gains legitimacy and space for its activity, it opens the road for the creation of new institutions. This has been the case in most authoritarian regimes and makes for the diversity of organizations in the human rights field. Some NPOs emerged to take care of programs that were not carried out by the church, thereby complementing its work. Other NPOs were created to carry out similar programs, such as human rights education, but to reach other segments of the population or, alternatively, stressing an ideological approach absent in the church's programs. Many members of the opposition believed that the struggle for human rights should not belong solely to the church, that secular institutions representing the entire political spectrum were needed in this area. Finally, new groups have been created to increase the involvement of all segments of the population, based on the belief that human rights have become the most important ideological symbol for the opposition. Most of these organizations have followed steps similar to those taken by COPACHI, (e.g., establishing their objectives, forging links with other similar foreign institutions, and gaining internal legitimacy by reaching out to the community).

The first of the NPOs created outside the umbrella of the Catholic Church was the Social Help Foundation of the Christian Churches (FASIC in Spanish). It emerged at the end of 1974 as a working group that would assist political prisoners condemned by court martials to exchange their prison sentences for external exile. Since 1974 FASIC's programs have expanded. To begin with, the assistance given to political prisoners leaving the country was complemented by a program of family reunification that allowed their families to join them abroad. Later on, a second program was created to assist political prisoners in their grievances inside the jails and to give financial assistance and scholarships to former detainees who desired to continue their education. It also gives social assistance, including occupational scholarships, to exiled people allowed to return to Chile. Finally, FASIC has developed a mental health area that provides psychological treatment to people affected by torture and to relatives of people who have disappeared or who were executed. Mental health treatment has been complemented by research studies that analyze different aspects of this unique medical experience.[15]

While FASIC's directory comprises members of five different churches, its executive secretary is not a priest or minister.[16] It has been supported by its links with Christian churches as well as by secular international organizations such as the Intergubernamental Committee for European Migrations and the U.N. High Commissioner for Refugees.

Among the human rights institutions linked with opposition political parties, the Chilean Commission of Human Rights is certainly the most important. It was created at the end of 1978 by many social and political leaders who believed that the defense of human rights should not be an exclusive task for religious groups, especially since internal political tensions within the churches might at some point endanger their commitment to carry out human rights programs. During its first year the commission affiliated itself with a series of international human rights organizations that would protect its development.[17] Simultaneously, it convoked all other domestic organizations and activists to a seminar on future strategies toward human rights violations. That more than 200 activists responded to this invitation legitimized the newly created institution as well as laid the foundation for taking subsequent steps. At the beginning of 1980 the commission had obtained sufficient resources to establish its headquarters in downtown Santiago, where the Commission for the Rights of the Youth (CODEJU in Spanish) and the Committee in Favor of the Return of Politically Exiled People (Comité Pro Retorno) were also allowed to function.

The opening of more political space for the opposition since the economic crisis of 1981 has helped to expand the commission's work. Numerous grass-roots human rights committees have been established in Santiago and the provinces. The commission provides legal aid to political dissidents and issues monthly reports on human rights violations, including a specially prepared international report. Although its paid staff is small, it claims to mobilize about 1000 persons on a volunteer basis, as it covers the ample spectrum of opposition political parties.[18] According to the commission's officials, the close links established with international human rights organizations have given the commission a protective umbrella that has enabled it to survive, despite its links with the political opposition in Chile.

In sum, in this authoritarian situation, even under conditions of extreme duress, human rights NPOs have emerged as defenders of human rights. Most of these organizations have been institutionalized following three clearly differentiated steps: they define the mission of the organization and establish its organizational structure; they establish international links with similar organizations in other parts of the world to seek moral, political, and financial support; and they reach the community through concrete programs and public actions. Although these steps are quite universal within Chile and other authoritarian regimes such as Argentina, the internal characteristics of the human rights movement as well as its capabilities of expanding its programs depend to an important extent on broader conditions within the country. Among these, international links and dependencies, the role played by the Catholic Church, and the intensiveness and extension of repression within each country are particularly noteworthy and, as shall be seen, bring about different outcomes in the cases of Chile and Argentina.

INFLUENCE AND LIMITS OF HUMAN RIGHTS NPOs

Chile

Chilean human rights NPOs today operate a whole variety of programs and most of them have been able to expand their functions protected by the Church or other international links. How effective have they been in achieving their objectives and what are the sources of their influence and limitations?

Most human rights activists interviewed in Chile asserted that they did not maintain regular contacts with government officials or with supporters of the government regarding human rights questions. The church as such has kept formal relations with the government, but silent diplomacy has showed disappointing results. Therefore, whatever influence NPOs have had in changing the course of events has been the result of their own programs and denunciation; rather than the consequence of amiable agreements with the ruling elite.

It is very difficult to discern the extent to which changes in repressive or socioeconomic policies respond to the NPOs' work. Our conclusions here are based upon personal observations and upon the beliefs of people we interviewed. Three major sources of influence have emerged.

First, human rights NPOs have played a role in establishing organizations where political dissidents have been able to interact with each other and to devise strategies to confront the hostile environment, in a situation in which open political activities were prohibited. In the case of Chile, this side effect of the establishment of NPOs has been of more importance to the Left than to the Christian Democratic Party, which has enjoyed greater tolerance on the part of the government. Activities organized by NPOs have increased contacts among opposition politicians who bitterly fought each other during the Allende government (1970–1973).

Thus, an important role played by NPOs is one of helping to reconstitute the social and political landscape. For example, legal defense gave dissidents moral support and contact with the outside world. Psychological assistance to people who had been tortured enabled them to cope with this traumatic experience and eventually to return to their activities in church, human rights, and political groups. Assistance to industrial and peasants' unions has helped to maintain these organizations and has enabled their leaders to show their members they are capable of functioning despite being marginalized by the government. Human rights education at the local level has been instrumental in maintaining democratic ideals and in creating conditions for the emergence of new social and political leaders.

This reconstitution of social and political forces has had an influence upon government's repressive policies. Once the initial justification for state terror fades away and the authoritarian regime faces new economic and political problems, repression shows its limits. The cost of increasing state violence is that it helps to delegitimatize a regime that is anxious to maintain its legitimacy, especially to international eyes. The Chilean regime has felt compelled to show that it is targetting repression at isolated groups who lack social support and importance. By breaking down isolation, NPOs discourage this repression and keep the opposition movement alive.

Second, human rights NPOs have mobilized both external and internal sources of opposition to authoritarian acts. During the mid- and late 1970s, the Ministry of External Affairs' most relevant task was to respond to external pressures concerning the prevailing human rights situation, arising in part from the objective documentation of human rights violations by NPOs. This also created frequent clashes between career diplomats and domestic political authorities and led some influential groups within the regime to advocate that internal security policies should take into consideration the effects their actions would have abroad.

Church-sponsored human rights NPOs and their influence within the church's hierarchy have generated permanent tensions between the church and the government, a second source of central concern for the Chilean regime. In a few instances the church has been able to put pressure upon the regime to show restraint in its repressive policies.

Legal defense of human rights in Chile has met with some success. Legal defense activities have enjoyed press coverage and major cases have acquired public notoriety. Slight advances have been achieved in areas such as freedom of expression through favorable decisions of the civil courts.[19] In a few cases, ministers of the higher courts have been able to visit secret prisons to verify the conditions under which a detainee is being held. The courts have become a public forum where repressive policies are debated.

As a third source of influence, NPOs have raised the level of consciousness concerning the importance of human rights in political sectors that are very close to the Chilean authoritarian regime. The conservative newspaper *El Mercurio* has advocated in various instances that the security apparatus should be restrained and has indicated that repressive policies implemented during 1973–1977 still stand as major obstacles for the institutionalization of the regime.[20] The progovernment magazine *Qué Pasa* has protested against torture.[21] Nevertheless, how deep or lasting the influence of the NPOs' ethical discourse has been is not at all clear. In fact, the maintenance of the authoritarian regime in Chile to this day shows that repressive policies are still considered to be justifiable by the ruling elite.

Comparison with Argentina

It may be useful to contrast at this point the effectiveness of Chilean human rights NPOs with those in Argentina. Although some human rights NPOs were created in Argentina before the 1976 coup d'etat, their development and work were severely hampered by a lack of protection from the church, by the relative autonomy of the state from outside pressures as discussed earlier, and by the intensive and unpredictable character of repression. As a result of these inhibiting factors, the most vigorous international denunciation of human rights violations were carried on by organizations formed by relatives of victims of repression. At least until 1979 "the Mothers of Plaza de Mayo" and the "Relatives of the disappeared and detainees for political reasons" played a major role in agitating the human rights question abroad. Relatives of people who had disappeared felt they should run the risk of speaking out. Although these organizations facilitated interaction among those who had suffered most under the dictatorship, by their very nature they could not have a general membership. Since they formed around family relationships with the disappeared, they could not provide a source of integration for members of the opposition as effective as the one Chilean NPOs have created. This role was played to some extent by the Permanent Assembly for Human Rights, which conducted seminars for young members of political parties; but until the military regime experienced significant deterioration, those activities could not be expanded.[22]

The intensity of state terror in Argentina also prevented the development of human rights programs to the same degree as had been achieved in Chile. Legal aid for people repressed was not institutionally centralized until the Center for Legal and Social Studies (CELS) was officially created in March 1980, a rather late date. CELS was created precisely because up to then most legal actions and judicial petitions had been carried out by relatives of the disappeared persons themselves, given that lawyers risked their lives by taking on human rights cases. These circumstances hampered collection of precise information on repressive practices, limited the ability of human rights NPOs to reach the broader community, and therefore prevented the effective denunciation of state terror.

Although Chilean NPOs therefore have been more effective than those in Argentina in protecting human rights, it must be recognized that the limits on their capabilities are severe. NPOs, including the church, are not power alternatives within authoritarian regimes, nor should they be. Whereas NPOs have provided a forum where different strategies for the opposition are discussed, they do not devise concrete political alternatives to the authoritarian situation.

Along similar lines, the ability of NPOs to affect the social structure are severely limited. Small development projects assisted by the church have helped thousands of poor people to satisfy some basic needs. However, NPOs' capabilities in this type of program cannot be compared with those of the government or the profit-making sector. At the most, these projects succeed in being schools of participatory democracy. The same is true for human rights educational programs, which still reach only limited sectors of the population, in contrast to the broader coverage of government-controlled media. For all these reasons, NPOs should not be expected to achieve major changes in social, economic, or political structures in a society.

RELATIONSHIPS BETWEEN HUMAN RIGHTS NPOs AND OPPOSITION PARTIES

Chile

This section deals in greater detail with the relationship between human rights NPOs and opposition political parties. Most human rights activists interviewed in Chile pointed out that their work had a clear political dimension because the struggle for human rights was part of the struggle against the authoritarian regime. They generally maintained that all opposition political groups should be included in their work.

Nevertheless, human rights activists are in general associated with the center and leftist sectors of the Chilean political spectrum. When asked whether effective protection of human rights required a transformation of prevalent social and economic structures, most activists gave a positive response. The executive secretary of SERPAJ pointed out that state violence in Chile was closely linked to the preservation of a highly unfair capitalistic system. The first people who offered their skills to assist victims of repression were leftist sympathizers. Moreover, since open political activities by the Left have not been permitted, human rights–oriented NPOs have offered them the possibility of work that is open, public, and permits them to reach significant sectors of the population. Christian Democrats who actively participate within NPOs are usually, but not always, members of the Left of that party. They are more willing than conservative militants to engage in common work with Marxists.

It is clear in the Chilean case that human rights NPOs have grown partly because party politics per se have been prohibited. Some party members discovered during these years that human rights activities permitted them to reach more people and to be in closer contact with reality than clandestine political activity. Human rights NPOs have been valued by party organizations as important organizational settings for building up the public image of party members, especially lawyers or doctors who have gained importance through their human rights work. Most of them were relatively unknown figures before the coup d'etat.

The proscription of party politics by the Chilean regime has diffused the borders between NPOs and political parties. The Chilean regime has maintained that NPOs are not legitimate human rights groups but rather political fronts utilized by the Left to carry on subversive activities against the government. This interpretation is certainly false, but it raises the issue of the identity of human rights NPOs as such. To the outside observer it is clear that NPOs take on specific missions that, although they crosscut the goals of opposition parties, are nevertheless more central to the NPOs.

Legal aid for dissidents, denunciation of human rights violations, and human rights education are programs that are supported by the parties but that do not define their main role in society. NPOs, unlike parties, do not devise overall policy alternatives to those implemented by the regime nor do they aspire to exercise government power once a transition to democracy takes place. In fact, among many human rights activists there is the perception that those NPOs that advocate a concrete political program are weakening the legitimacy that human rights organizations have gained throughout the years.

The diffusion of the boundary lines between parties and NPOs in Chile does not mean that party activists are the only or the most important components of human rights organizations. Many independent figures are involved in human rights work. Some of them became involved from the very beginning, gaining increasing public recognition for their work. Their lack of formal ties with political parties proscribed by the regime allowed them to play an important public role during the years that followed the military coup. To gain the allegiance or trust of these independent figures, party activists have to play by the "rules of the game" of human rights NPOs. In other words, they need to show that they respect the general principles upon which the organization's work rests. This usually prevents them from manipulating the organization's activities to their own parties' benefit. Thus, there is another side to the influence that NPOs have received from the party opposition: the influence that the human rights style of work imprints upon party members.

In sum, in an authoritarian situation like the Chilean one, in which formal politics are suppressed, party politics will be partially replaced by human rights work. This means that NPOs face an important political power dilemma. On the one hand they have become conduits of the opposition, on the other they have to prevent their organizations from becoming partisan in order to gain legitimacy within the country and abroad. Solving this political power dilemma is not easy. Tension among human rights activists usually reflects the need to draw a line between the organization and the party opposition. If the organization moves too close to becoming a party organization, it loses credibility as a human rights organization. However, if it tries too hard to avoid being "political," it risks curtailing its own legitimate activities and coming under attack by its own constituency.

Argentina

It is useful once again to contrast the Chilean with the Argentinian situation. In the case of Argentina, political activity by the opposition parties was prohibited as it was in Chile. However, relationships between NPOs and the most important parties (the Radical and the Peronist parties) were much more tense than in Chile. Before the regime experienced a significant deterioration, relationships between NPOs and party organizations were either formal or weak. The most aggressive human rights organizations were those composed of relatives of disappeared persons, and they did not provide the parties with an adequate conduit to reach the population. They were too isolated from the rest of the society. The Permanent Assembly for Human Rights incorporated some distinguished political leaders in its board of directors.[23] However, they were not the most important leaders of their parties at that time, nor was the assembly an organization that had the freedom to expand its programs, helping the parties to reproduce their network of militants within the society.

Argentine political leaders were also self-conscious of the traditional weakness of the Argentine party system in a society where the military had constantly intervened in politics. Therefore, they believed that a transition to democracy would be accelerated by disassociating themselves from the NPOs that were viewed by the military as institutions supportive of terrorist organizations. Thus, the relative isolation of NPOs from the rest of the society as well as the historical nature of the relationship between major parties and the military prevented a closer relationship between the opposition parties and NPOs.

Once the legitimacy of the authoritarian regime eroded, that of human rights NPOs expanded. They were able to evoke the support of hundreds of younger members of the parties. Their platform, which demanded justice for the crimes perpetrated by the military, played an important role in defining the position of the parties toward the military. However, relationships between NPOs and the parties became conflictive once again as elections drew closer, and especially once a democratic government took office. The parties maintained that the stability of the democratic system depended upon developing pragmatic relations with the armed forces. This position contradicted the ethical claim of most NPOs that all crimes committed under the military regime should be punished.

Thus, in the two cases examined, NPOs have faced the need to show that they are legitimate human rights groups in a political context within which they are part of the opposition. This "political power dilemma" is not easy to solve and the outcome was very different in Chile and Argentina. The existence of stable parties that had no expectations about the liberalization of the regime and in which the political opposition was suppressed encouraged Chilean party activists to become involved in human rights institutions. In contrast, Argentine parties believed that in order to encourage a transition to democracy they had to dissassociate themselves from the human rights organizations that were narrowly based and strengthen the role of broadly based parties per se.

THE INFLUENCE OF FOREIGN FUNDING UPON NPO ACTIVITIES

At one point or another all human rights NPOs have received foreign funding for their activities. In some cases funding came at the beginning, whereas in other cases it came after the organizations were already developing their work. This funding was significantly supplemented by moral support as well.

NPOs have almost no alternative to seeking foreign support. The wealthy sectors of society are generally supportive of authoritarian regimes. As reported to me, most efforts by Chilean activists to raise money within the country have failed. Given the scarcity of monetary resources, many human rights NPOs develop their programs with the help of volunteers. Although this furthers their possibilities for reaching different sectors of society, it has the drawback of preventing the professionalization of their work. Volunteers usually work only sporadically for these organizations. They often treat their work as a secondary rather than primary commitment. A side effect of this phenomenon is that they do not remain permanent members of the institution as they must face the need to make a living or confront new requirements in their professional lives.

Thus, foreign funding has been of the utmost importance for the development of human rights NPOs. This has created some problems for them because it has created a relation of dependence by NPOs on their donors. Many human rights activists feel that the stability of their organizational work is always at stake since funding for their projects is usually approved for short periods and their renewal depends upon many factors over which NPOs have little control. There have been some attempts by the Chilean government to limit the flow of foreign funding for NPOs.[24] NPOs compete among themselves to get their projects approved. Furthermore, the regional priorities of foreign donors might change as they channel their resources around the world. Domestic political changes might compel some agencies to limit their donations to a particular country.

Within the Catholic Church, the issue of foreign dependency creates peculiar problems. As Smith has pointed out, a significant percentage of bishops, priests, and lay leaders feel that foreign church aid has prevented the Chilean church from developing its own internal resources.[25] This criticism is probably unfair because the activism of the church in human rights issues has alienated the support of wealthy Chileans. However, it illustrates the complex considerations involved in the solving of this financial dilemma.

Dependency on foreign funding has not meant, however, the undue influence of foreign donors on the content and style of the work carried out by each organization. Such influence was emphatically denied by the people I interviewed. Some of them asserted that foreign donors usually understood the peculiar nature of each organization and the programs they implemented. Others pointed out that they had rejected funding that required them to carry out programs in accordance with the wishes of foreign agencies rather than their own priorities. The autonomy that Chilean NPOs have in this respect has a clear explanation. Within the Third World, South American human rights NPOs are among the most developed. The vicariate of solidarity in Chile has provided a model followed by many human rights NPOs from other parts of the world. The experience accumulated by these NPOs has shaped their programs as well as the style of their work. Therefore, it becomes difficult for foreign donors to impose changes upon well-established institutions with an international reputation that have developed their work through years of experimentation. At the same time, it must be recognized that these institutions are the "survivors." Institutions unable to obtain foreign support because their objectives diverged from those of potential donors are no longer alive to be questioned on this issue, and perhaps they were never born.

CONCLUSIONS

The phenomena of political repression and socioeconomic inequality are not new or unique to Latin America. What is certainly original is the institutionalization and growth of human rights NPOs that have played a significant role in checking the state's violence. In authoritarian situations such as those in Chile and Argentina, NPOs have emerged as important actors that respond to human rights violations and to the deterioration of living conditions for the poor.

All these NPOs face similar dilemmas in the process of institutionalizing themselves, in devising adequate strategies to mobilize their resources, in gaining a nonpartisan image, and in forging international links. However, it would be a mistake to analyze NPOs in the abstract without taking into consideration the peculiar characteristics of each authoritarian situation. Human rights NPOs, in particular, present different characteristics in Chile and Argentina. The nature of each country's international links and dependencies determines the extent to which each regime is sensitive to external pressures to restrain its repressive policies and tolerate human rights NPOs. Also, the existence of an institution that is relatively immune from government pressures and that is willing to provide a protective umbrella to NPOs (e.g., the Catholic Church in Chile) is essential for the expansion of NPO programs. And, the relationships developed in each case between NPOs and major opposition parties have an impact upon the internal characteristics of these NPOs and can either stimulate their growth or limit their development. Conflictual relations between human rights NPOs and the two major parties in Argentina worked against the former until the regime experienced a significant deterioration, for completely other reasons.

Chile is perhaps the country where these objective circumstances combined in the best possible manner to help the expansion of NPOs. This explains why Chilean human rights NPOs provide other Third World countries with a model of imaginative implementation of human rights strategies. Chile is also an example of the limited influence and capability that NPOs have vis-à-vis the government or the profit-making sector to produce fundamental political and social changes. Authoritarian rule still persists in Chile. Throughout this paper this paradoxical situation has been stressed. NPOs accomplish major successes in checking government repression, in helping to reconstitute the social and political landscape, and in offering a consistent criticism of authoritarian policies. Yet, their effectiveness in terms of transforming prevalent political, social, and economic structures is limited.

Although there seems to be no way in which NPOs could overcome this fundamental weakness, this consideration in no way diminishes the important role they have played under authoritarian regimes. They have helped to integrate opposition forces atomized by the authoritarian regime's policies; they have deprived the regime of some of its moral and political legitimacy; and most important, they have given a new relevance to human rights ideals to be taken into account by parties and social organizations. These are their most important contributions to processes of transition to democracy.

NOTES

1. On the political processes that led to the establishment of these authoritarian regimes, see Arturo Valenzuela, *The Breakdown of Democratic Regimes: Chile* (Baltimore: Johns Hopkins University Press, 1978); Liliana de Riz, *Retorno y Derrumbe: El Ultimo Gobierno Peronista* (Mexico City: Folios, 1981); Manuel A. Garreton and Tomas Moulian, *La Unidad Popular y el Conflicto Politico en Chile* (Santiago: Ediciones La Minga, 1983).

2. Brian H. Smith, *The Church and Politics in Chile: Challenges to Modern Catholicism* (Princeton, N.J.: Princeton University Press, 1982). See also his "Churches as Development Institutions: The Case of Chile, 1973–1980," Program on Non-Profit Organizations Working Paper 50, Institution for Social and Policy Studies (New Haven, Conn.: Yale University, April 1982). L. José Aldunate, Fernando Castillo, and Joaquin Silva, *Los Derechos Humanos y la Iglesia Chilena* (Santiago: ECO Educacion y Communicaciones, 1984).

3. On repressive policies in Chile see Hugo Fruhling, "Stages of Repression and Legal Strategy for the Defense of Human Rights in Chile: 1973–1980," *Human Rights Quarterly* 5 (November 1983): 510–33.

4. Ibid., pp. 519–22.

5. Mark Schneider mentioned, among others, the following facts that support his conclusion that Chile acted as a catalyst of human rights movements: (1) the U.N. Human Rights Commission established a working group for the first time (1976) and later a special rapporteur to report to the General Assembly on human rights violations in Chile; (2) the Inter-American Commission on Human Rights issued four reports on the human rights situation in Chile at the request of successive OAS General Assemblies in 1974, 1976, 1977, and 1985. Mark Schneider, "Human Rights on the Agenda: Chile as Catalyst," *Chile: Ten Years and Beyond* (Washington, D.C.: Office on Latin America, 1984), p. 19.

6. Mario Rapoport, "Entre los Estados Unidos y la URSS: las Relaciones Argentino-Sovieticas y el Esquema Triangular," *Ideas en Ciencias Sociales* no. 2 (April–June 1984): 50–54.

7. See *Nunca Mas. Informe de la Comision Nacional Sobre Desaparicion de Personas* (Buenos Aires: Eudeba, 1984).

8. See Brian Smith, *Church and Politics in Chile*, Chapter 7, Table 7.2; and "Churches as Development Institutions," pp. 50–51.

9. Minutes of the Organizational Meeting of the Committee of Cooperation for Peace in "El Comité para la Paz en Chile. Cronica de sus Dos Anos de Labor Solidaria," mimeograph (Santiago, 1975).

10. "El Comité para la Paz en Chile: Una Tarea que Debe Continuar," mimeograph (Santiago, 1974), pp. 1, 4.

11. See note 9.

12. Ibid.

13. Ibid. See also U.S. Congress, House Subcommittee on International Organizations of the Committee on International Relations, "Prepared Statement of José Zalaquett Daher, Chief Legal Counsel, Committee of Cooperation for Peace in Chile," *Chile: The Status of Human Rights and its Relationship to U.S. Economic Assistance Program* (Washington, D.C.: 94th Congress, 2d. session, 1976), pp. 57–65.

14. *Vicaria de la Solidaridad: Quinto Ano de Labor, 1980* (Santiago: Arzobispado de Santiago, 1981), p. 15.

15. The work done by FASIC in this area has been recognized as of outstanding importance by international as well as national mental health specialists. Members of the mental health program received a prize from the Chilean Association of Psychologists in 1983. See "Premio Colegio de Psicologos 1983. Psicologia y Derechos Humanos," FASIC, Colegio de Psicologos de Chile, 1983. See also Lira K. Elizabeth "Psicologia y Derechos Humanos en una Situacion Represiva: La Experiencia de la FASIC," in *Represion Politica y Defensa de los Derechos Humanos,* ed. Hugo Fruhling (Santiago: Programa de Derechos Humanos Academia de Humanismo Cristiano—CESOC/Ediciones Chile y America, 1987), pp. 269–91.

16. The board of directors comprises members of the Methodist, Catholic, Orthodox, Pentecostal Methodist, and Evangelical Lutheran churches.

17. The Chilean commission is affiliated with the International Commission of Jurists, the International League for Human Rights, the International Federation of the Rights of Men, and the International Movement of Catholic Jurists.

18. Interview with German Molina (May 15, 1984).

19. Of particular importance in this respect is a sentence of the Supreme Court that asserted that censorship of the press was not authorized by the powers granted to the government by the state of emergency. See "Recurso de Proteccion en Contra de la Division Nacional de Comunicacion Social," *Fallos del Mes* no. 307 (June 1984): 238–42.

20. See "Condenas a Muerte" in "La Semana Politica," *El Mercurio* (May 23, 1982): 3; "Malos Dias" in "La Semana Politica," *El Mercurio* (March 28, 1982): 3; "La Semana Politica," *El Mercurio* (May 8, 1983): 3.

21. "Tortura y Opinion Publica," *Qué Pasa* no. 708 (November 1–7, 1984): 7.

22. Before 1980 the following human rights groups were acting in Argentina: the Permanent Assembly for Human Rights, which made general pronouncements addressed to the government or the judiciary and which recorded and documented the cases of disappeared persons; the Argentine League for the Rights of Men connected to the Communist party, which provided legal counsel in some cases; the Ecumenical Movement for Human Rights, which gave social and economic assistance to relatives of the disappeared; SERPAJ, which worked in close contact with relatives of the disappeared; "The Mothers of Plaza de Mayo"; and "Relatives of disappeared and detainees for political reasons."

23. For example, the President of Argentina, Raul Alfonsin, was at one time copresident of the assembly when he was the leader of a minoritarian faction within the Radical Party.

24. In many instances the vicariate of solidarity has been criticized by government spokesmen for receiving money from abroad to support dissident activities. Brian Smith has also reported attempts by the government to restrict the amount of funds granted to Chilean organizations by the Inter-American Foundation. Smith, "Churches as Development Institutions," p. 43.

25. Ibid.

REFERENCES

José, Aldunate L., Fernando Castillo, and Joaquín Silva, *Los Derechos Humanos y la Iglesia Chilena.* Santiago: ECO Educación y Comunicaciones, 1984.

"Condenas a Muerte," in "La Semana Politica." *El Mercurio* (May 23, 1982): 3.

de Riz, Liliana. *Retorno y Derrumbe: El Ultimo Gobierno Peronista*. Mexico City: Folios, 1981.

Elizabeth, Lira K. "Psicología y Derechos Humanos en una situación Represiva: La Experiencia de la FASIC." In Hugo Fruhling, ed., *Represión Política y Defensa de los Derechos Humanos*. Santiago: Programa de Derechos Humanos de la Academia de Humanismo Cristiano—CESOC/Ediciones Chile y America, 1987, pp. 269–91.

Fruhling, Hugo. "Stages of Repression and Legal Strategy for the Defense of Human Rights in Chile: 1973–1980." *Human Rights Quarterly* 5 (November 1983): 510–33.

Garretón, Manuel A., and Tomas Moulian. *La Unidad Popular y el Conflicto Político en Chile*. Santiago: Ediciones La Minga, 1983.

"La Semana Política," *El Mercurio* (May 8, 1983): 3.

"Malos Días," in "La Semana Politica." *El Mercurio* (March 28, 1982): 3.

Nunca Más. Informe de la Comisión Nacional sobre Desaparición de Personas. Buenos Aires: Eudeba, 1984.

Organizational Meeting of the Committee of Cooperation for Peace. "El Comité para la Paz en Chile. Crónica de sus Dos Años de Labor Solidaria." Mimeograph. Santiago, 1975.

———. "El Comité para la Paz en Chile: Una Tarea que Debe Continuar." Mimeograph. Santiago, 1974.

"Premio Colegio de Psicólogos 1983. Psicología y Derechos Humanos." Social Help Foundation of the Christian Churches (FASIC). Santiago: Colegio de Psicologos de Chile, 1983.

Rapoport, Mario. "Entre los Estados Unidos y la URSS: las Relaciones Argentino–Soviéticas y el Esquema Triangular." *Ideas en Ciencias Sociales* no. 2 (April–June 1984): 50–54.

"Recurso de Protección en Contra de la División Nacional de Comunicación Social." *Fallos del Mes* no. 307 (June 1984): 238–42.

Schneider, Mark. "Human Rights on the Agenda: Chile as Catalyst." In *Chile: Ten Years and Beyond*. Washington, D.C.: Office on Latin America, 1984.

Smith, Brian H. *The Church and Politics in Chile: Challenges to Modern Catholicism*. Princeton, N.J.: Princeton University Press, 1982.

———. "Churches as Development Institutions: The Case of Chile, 1973–1980". Program on Non-Profit Organizations Working Paper 50, Institution for Social and Policy Studies. New Haven, Conn.: Yale University, April 1982.

"Tortura y Opinión Pública." *Qué Pasa* no. 708 (November 1–7, 1984): 7.

U.S. Congress, House Subcommittee on International Organizations of the Committee on International Relations. "Prepared Statement of José Zalaquett Daher, Chief Legal Counsel, Committee of Cooperation for Peace in Chile". *Chile: The Status of Human Rights and its Relationship to U.S. Economic Assistance Program*. 94th Congress, 2d session, Washington, D.C.: Author, 1976, pp. 57–65.

Valenzuela, Arturo. *The Breakdown of Democratic Regimes: Chile*. Baltimore: Johns Hopkins University Press, 1978.

Vicaría de la Solidaridad: Quinto Año de Labor, 1980. Santiago: Arzobispado de Santiago, 1981.

Index